TUTTLE
DICTIONARY
—— OF ——
ANTIQUES &
COLLECTIBLES
TERMS

TUTTLE DICTIONARY

OF

ANTIQUES &

COLLECTIBLES

TERMS

DON & JOAN BINGHAM

CHARLES E. TUTTLE COMPANY
Boston • Rutland, Vermont • Tokyo

To Sally, Gary, Heather, and Jason Batchelder;
Ardeth, Jim, and Evan Bolin; Juanita Butcher (a
super aunt); Susan Finlay; Stephanie, Wendy, and
Peter Gorman . . . with love.

Published by the Charles E. Tuttle Company, Inc. of
Rutland, Vermont & Tokyo, Japan with editorial offices at
77 Central Street, Boston, Massachusetts 02109.

Cover design by Linda Koegel.

Library of Congress Cataloging-in-Publication Data
Bingham, Don 1930-
    Tuttle dictionary of antiques & collectibles terms / Don &
Joan Bingham.
    p.   cm.
    Includes bibliographical references.
    ISBN 0-8048-1756-1 (pbk. : alk. paper) :
    1. Decorative arts—Dictionaries. 2. Collectibles—Dictionar-
ies.
I. Bingham, Joan. II. Title. III Title: Tuttle dictionary of
antiques & collectibles terms.
NK30.B54 1992
745' .03—dc20   91-67337
                                                 CIP

First printing 1992
PRINTED IN THE UNITED STATES

CONTENTS

ACKNOWLEDGMENTS

Every book, like every play, has a cast of people who work behind the scenes to create the finished product. Without these experts, few plays would be produced and few books would ever go to press.

We'd like to thank those who worked behind the scenes to make this book a reality instead of just a dream. First, our wonderful agent, Blanche Schlessinger for her expertise in marketing our idea. Then to Peter Ackroyd, president and C.E.O., and Linda L. Smith, managing editor, of Charles E. Tuttle Company for seeing the merit in it. Our gratitude also goes to Irene Somishka for her assistance. We are especially indebted to Claudia Mahoney for her professional, expert, caring job of editing. Working with her was a joy.

And, of course, there are the many dealers, collectors, auctioneers, and friends who shared with us the knowledge they'd garnered over the years.

Thanks to all of you—we couldn't have done it without you!

INTRODUCTION

Antiques and Collectibles

What Are They?

Defining *antiques* isn't a cut-and-dried task. According to United States Customs, an object must be at least 100 years old to be called "antique." But *Webster's Dictionary* defines *antique* as "a relic or object of ancient times or of an earlier period than the present." Does this mean depression glass and art deco furniture are antiques? We think so; these are, after all, "objects of an earlier period." Although the purists in this field who abide by the 100-year rule would not agree with us, the 100-year rule doesn't always apply. Automobiles are a good example. Collectors' antique cars are primarily from the 1920s and 1930s — "of an earlier period."

The term *antique* is obviously a slippery one to define. We tend to use it to refer to articles from before World War II. However, the definition varies from one expert to another and one category of antiques to another, so you must be wary when something is presented to you as "antique." If you're buying the object, question the seller closely about its true age, then decide if the seller's definition of *antique* coincides with yours.

Collectible is easier to define. According to *Webster's Dictionary*, it's "an object that is collected by fanciers." Almost everything, from barbed wire to poker chips to hat pins, is fancied by and collected by someone. There are antique collectibles, those that are just a few years old, and collectibles that are brand new. With a few exceptions, such as automobiles, collectibles are small items, appropriate for storage and display in the collector's home.

We were asked how many of the definitions in this book apply to antiques and how many to collectibles. That's a hard call to make. Of the more than 4,000 definitions we've included, many of them apply to both categories. For instance, some clocks are collectible and also antique, so the terms we use are describing both antique and collectible clocks. The same applies to jewelry, glass, toys, and most decorative accessories.

Who Collects?

Interest in antiques and collectibles has enjoyed enormous growth during the past decade. Children and adults from all walks of life have been bitten by the collecting bug. A parent or grandparent may start a child collecting dolls, bells, music boxes, trains, baseball cards, marbles, or perfume bottles, with the hopes that these things will appreciate in value or at least spark an interest in collecting as a hobby. Often a vocation or avocation inspires a passion for a particular collectible. Buttons and thimbles are often sought by people who have an interest in sewing; a firefighter may collect fire memorabilia, a police officer may look for badges and other articles from yesterday's police forces; and a banker may seek out old iron banks.

People who have the financial resources often collect expensive items like guns, Lalique glass, or gold watches. But collecting isn't confined to the wealthy; inexpensive items like salt and pepper shakers, post cards and greeting cards, and simple figurines of dogs, cats, or other animals are highly prized collectibles.

While some collectors think of their acquisitions as investments, it's wiser to view collecting as a personally fulfilling, rather than a financially rewarding, hobby. The field is ever-changing, and collecting as an investment can prove to be a losing proposition if your collectibles fall from grace.

Where and How to Begin the Search

If you want to become a collector, you can probably start the search in your own community. You might even want to take a look in your own, your parents', or your grandparents' attic. One generation's castoffs often become the next generation's treasures. On any given day, there are thousands of auctions taking place in this country. Every city and many small towns boast antiques shops with a variety of merchandise ranging from elegant, formal furnishings with impeccable pedigrees, to the primitive furniture and utensils used by our forefathers, to pieces that are of questionable origin. Large and small antiques shows also abound. Flea markets offer some of the best buys in antiques and collectibles to discerning buyers. It's here that you can often find treasures that have values and even identities that are a mystery to their sellers.

If you decide to collect something that hasn't caught on with other collectors, then you'll be in uncharted waters as you figure out what's desirable and what's not. But, for any well-known collectible, there's plenty of information. Visit a museum that has an exhibit of your specialty. Read all the articles and books you can about your chosen treasures. Talk with dealers and other collectors; find out where they find examples, how much they pay, and what they look for. If you don't have the time to comb the markets, tell reputable dealers what you want. They'll be pleased to look for you.

If you've chosen a popular collectible, chances are there's at least one club that specializes in it. There are button clubs, marble clubs, salt-and-pepper clubs, ephemera clubs, clubs for people who collect depression glass or carnival glass, tip tray clubs, clubs for match cover lovers, and advertising memorabilia clubs — the list is almost endless. Members of these clubs exchange information and are often on the lookout for particular examples of their specialty. Many of the clubs have newsletters that report the latest gossip and finds, keep members abreast of who is looking for what, and have a classified section advertising items for sale. Almost any public library can provide you with the names and addresses of specific collectors' clubs.

There are specialty shows for most of the better-known collectibles such as trains, toys, buttons, and guns. These are mines of information — the dealers and collectors who set up there love to talk about their hobbies.

Knowing the Language

In the years we've spent admiring, collecting, and dealing in collectibles and antiques, we've become convinced of the need for a book of this type. Almost without exception, every person who frequents auctions, shops, shows, and flea markets encounters unfamiliar terms used in reference to the merchandise that's being sold. Dealers often label pieces with information aimed at helping the customers to identify them. But honest dealers sometimes make honest mistakes when labeling, and an occasional dishonest dealer will intentionally mislabel pieces in an attempt to bilk the public. In either case, if the descriptive jargon is foreign to the dealer or to the consumer, it's of little value in communicating important information. By knowing and using the terminology accurately, the honest dealer protects his reputation, and the customer is armed with the language necessary to ask the right questions and make informed decisions. This book is for both knowledgeable and neophyte collectors and dealers, because no one ever knows all there is to know about this absorbing subject.

Using This Book

We've designed this book for easy use. It's set up in strict alphabetical order with most entries followed in parentheses by the categories to which the word most commonly applies. For example, the term *bezanted* is followed by its category *(armor).* Some items are known by several different names. The variation may be regional, or it may be that somewhere along the line an object was dubbed with several nicknames. Whatever the reason, we've given each individual name or term a listing of its own. For instance, *hair pencils,* defined as "brushes of many sizes called, according to size, crow, pigeon, duck, goose, extra small swan, and (the largest) big swan," are also called *quill pencils* and are listed and defined under that name, too. *Perambulator,* "a baby carriage or buggy," is also called *pram* and is defined again under that listing. Cross references for synonymous terms are marked with "also called . . ." References to related terms that provide additional information about a subject are marked with "see also . . ." at the end of a definition.

We have included over 4,000 entries in this book, phrases and terms that we feel are most useful to everyone buying and selling. We hope those of you who share our interest in this vast field will find the book useful, particularly at auctions, where fast, on-the-spot research can save you from making an unwise purchase or from letting a great treasure get away.

Auctions

Once you've got auction fever, chances are you'll never recover. Everyone who's hooked on these sales has a favorite auctioneer and a favorite type of auction. There are low-key outdoor auctions where people bring along glorious picnic lunches and enjoy the sun and the social occasion as much as they enjoy the auction itself. There are on-site estate auctions that take place at houses, yards, or country barns where you either stand or provide your own chairs. There are auctions in small regional auction houses owned by the presiding auctioneers and those which take place in rented halls or other facilities. Exalted international auction houses, such as Sotheby's and Christie's, grace major cities and offer the finest and rarest merchandise available from all over the world.

Some auctions are legitimately called junk auctions. At these, you'll find everything from old suitcases to broken china to secondhand (but not antique) furniture to an occasional overlooked treasure. On a very lucky day, a canny person may get something for a few dollars that is actually worth a few hundred dollars or maybe more. An estate auction might include both fine antiques and everyday household goods and gadgets. You can pick up some wonderful bargains at general estate auctions — dealers and serious collectors in the audience aren't interested in secondhand overstuffed chairs, electric frying pans, and television sets, but those may be the very items for which you are looking.

An auction house might decide to consign part of an estate to a general auction but save the best examples of any given type of antique or collectible for a specialty auction, which features like items — all antique and collectible toys, for example — from many consignors. This type of auction will usually attract motivated special-interest collectors.

Presale Exhibits

When you plan to attend an auction, find out when the auctioneer or auction house will be holding the presale exhibit of goods to be auctioned. Usually this preview is held the day of the auction or a day or two before, and larger houses often run exhibits for several days prior to an auction. Attend the preview and carefully examine anything in which you are interested. Don't be afraid to ask auction house representatives questions about a piece you like. Bring along a tape to measure furniture; a magnifying glass to examine markings on small accessories like glass, pottery, and silver; and a magnet to test brass and other metals. Check for cracks, chips, missing hardware, and other flaws. An old soft-paste plate or bowl with some damage may be a fine example of its period and command a high price despite the damage, because soft paste is so perishable that not much of it has survived intact. But with rare exceptions, a damaged piece is worth a small fraction of what that same piece would bring in mint condition.

Many auction houses and auctioneers provide catalogs that list all of the items to be put up for bid. Usually you will pay a nominal fee for a catalog. It's a good idea to purchase one at the presale exhibit and take it with you to the auction. Items will be numbered in the catalog, displayed at the presale exhibit with corresponding numbers, and auctioned off in numerical order. The simplest catalogs are numbered lists reproduced on copy machines. Although they contain brief descriptions of the items, in many cases, these descriptions fall far short. For instance, you may see "Lot #34 — one bowl." If you inspect Lot #34 at the presale exhibit, you may find it's a Limoges bowl, hand painted, and that the mark indicates it dates to the late 1800s. As each lot is sold, write the selling price beside it in your catalog.

Some houses publish more expensive catalogs for auctions featuring fine antiques and collectibles. These glitzy books are replete with colored pictures of the objects and contain complete descriptions of the items, including information about age, condition, rarity, provenance, and presale estimates. The presale estimate is no more and no less than an educated guess as to what an item will sell for at a specific auction. The higher purchase price of these heavily illustrated catalogs sometimes includes a post-sale list of prices actually realized at the sale.

How Much Is It Worth?

You may be looking for examples of a particular specialty, or you may have broader interests. Either way, when you inspect the treasures that are going to be sold, write down what you're willing to pay for each item you like. Whether you are a collector or a dealer, let your pocketbook and educated common sense be your guide. There are several things to take into account when deciding on price. More and more auctioneers charge a buyer's premium. This means that, over and above the price you bid for the merchandise you purchase, you'll also be charged a percentage of that price — usually ten percent. Auctioneers add the buyer's premium so that they can stay competitive and take a lower percent of the profits from the sellers of the merchandise. This, naturally, makes an auction house look more attractive to a prospective seller, and without merchandise to sell, an auctioneer has no business. Also, some states tack on a sales tax. Licensed dealers are exempt from paying the tax. Others should figure it in when deciding what they are willing to bid for an item.

Price guides help to determine value and resale prices. But consult these books judiciously. They were designed to be used only as guides. You must know your market. The region where you're selling or buying makes a big difference. There are places where primitives are hot items, for example, and other regions where you can't give them away. Does the piece need repairing before you offer it for sale or display it in your home? If so, subtract the cost of repairs from what you're planning to pay for the item.

A good, solid antique that has intrinsic value will probably be worth more five years from now than it is today. The collectibles market is, however, a bit more fickle. Something may be in one year and out, or on its way out, the next. You need to have your finger on the pulse of the business to know when to buy. A few years ago depression glass was all the rage, commanding extremely high prices. Depression glass has little intrinsic value; it was made to be given away during the depression. The market was suddenly glutted with depression glass that people had dug out of their attics and basements in an attempt to get in on the craze. New glass produced in depression patterns hit the market and was passed off as the real thing. Soon the prices plummeted. Dealers who had stocked up on depression glass found themselves stuck with an excess of inventory. Depression glass still sells, but not the way it did a few years ago. Our rule for investment-minded collectors and dealers is never purchase anything unless it's worth the price you pay for it in terms of quality, or, for dealers, unless you already have a customer for the item. However, if you're a collector and you've found the one rare piece that's missing from your collection, you may be willing to pay far more than the piece is actually worth.

Many collectors who love auctions are afraid to bid at an auction where there are too many dealers. They mistakenly think dealers have an advantage, but the opposite is true. If you're buying for yourself, you can pay top dollar. On the other hand, if you're a dealer, "What can I get for this?" must be your first consideration. Dealers must keep bidding low enough so that they can still make a profit.

Auction Action

Arrive at an auction early with your catalog in hand. Find out if you need a bidding number, usually printed on a card or a paddle-shaped device. Auction houses use bidding numbers to identify bidders. If you are deemed the highest bidder, you hold up your number and it's recorded with the amount charged against it. At the end of the auction, or when you choose to leave, you must pay the sum accrued under that number. Always keep track of what you've purchased, and be sure that your total matches the house total. Honest mistakes, and infrequently intentional mistakes, are made.

After you get your number, find a seat. Positioning yourself is a very personal decision. Some auction-goers prefer to sit in the back where they can see everything that goes on, and know who's bidding and to whom every item is knocked down (sold). Others prefer a middle position — closer to the merchandise but far enough back to get the flavor of the event. Still others, ourselves included, prefer the front row, as close to the auctioneer as possible. We can see the articles better, and we learn from the comments that we hear from the runners and others who assist the auctioneer. We've found that no matter how carefully we try to look at everything that's to be auctioned, there are always things that seem to be pulled from nowhere, especially at uncataloged auctions — and the vast majority of auctions are uncataloged.

Habitual auction-goers have their own individual ways of bidding. It's fun to watch. After the initial bid has been made and the auctioneer knows that some-one is bidding, that person may increase his bid by winking, moving one finger, nodding his head while looking away from the auctioneer, touching his ear, or a variety of other antics. However, it's difficult for auctioneers to keep track of these furtive bidders. In fact, some auction houses now insist that bidders hold up their bidding card or paddle in clear view of the auctioneer to avoid confusion.

Auctions are exciting and even the most seasoned auction-goers get carried away occasionally, bidding more than they intended. There are ways to avoid this. When a lot in which you're interested comes up for bid, stick with the top figure that you decided you would bid at the presale exhibit. We usually select an uneven number because we've found that most auction buffs home in on an even amount. For instance, we will go to $27.50 rather than $25.00 on a vase we want. This uneven number bidding has worked for us on many occasions.

Don't decide that the Limoges bowl, cast-iron doorstop, or that cute lamp must be worth a great deal because the man in the back, who always seems to know what he's doing, keeps bidding on it. The tempta-tion to outbid him and go home with the treasure is one you should resist. He may not be as knowledgeable as you think or he may have a special use for the item.

Since bidding is a big part of the fun of auctions, we recommend that you learn and follow the rules of disciplined bidding. But if you absolutely can't control your bidding, either have a friend bid for you or leave a bid with one of the auction house staff. Left, or absentee, bids are written bids on specific lots, usually submitted by people who can't attend an auction. A staff member will execute a left bid for you whether you elect to be at the auction or not.

Terms and Conditions of Sale

The auctioneer will often state the terms and conditions of a sale in the catalog or at the beginning of an auction. He'll explain important details like whether or not they accept checks or credit cards, or insist on cash. He'll also let you know if there are any reserves (prices below which an item may not be sold) or left bids and if telephone bids are allowed or expected. A telephone bidder makes a prior arrangement with the auctioneer to be contacted by phone when a specific lot comes up for bid. The telephone bidder, through a staff member who communicates his wishes, bids against the floor just as if he were there. As with the case of a left bid, when you are arranging for a telephone bid, discuss with the auctioneer how you'll pay for the item and when you can pick it up. If you want the item shipped to you, agree on the method of shipment and charges for packing and postage or freight.

Usually the auctioneer will say that you buy *on your own knowledge.* This means, for example, that if he says a plate is 16th-century Urbino and you find out later that it's a 19th-century copy of an Urbino plate, he's not liable. He's presenting each item with the best of his knowledge. Auctioneers, like the rest of us, can't be experts on everything.

The terms and conditions will probably include a proviso that you buy everything *as it is and where it is.* Some auctioneers refuse to take back any merchandise under any conditions — you buy it *as it is.* However, most auction houses will allow you to return a piece of glass or china within five minutes if you find that it's cracked or chipped. After all, you may have carefully inspected a glass or plate and found that it was perfect at the presale exhibit, and someone handling it later may have damaged it. Most other types of merchandise are considered sold no matter what you may find after the hammer, since it's unlikely that sturdy items like furniture, jewelry, or weapons would be damaged at the auction.

Where it is means that you are responsible for removing the items you purchase from the premises. Some auction houses may, for a price, deliver; others don't offer this service. Before you bid on a heavy empire chest, for example, be sure you have a way of moving it immediately, if necessary. In some instances, you may be allowed to leave the piece at the auction house for a limited amount of time, but some auctioneers insist that all goods be removed from the premises on the day or night of the auction to free up space for the next auction. Or, if the auction is held in a facility that the auctioneer has rented, he may have to clear it out when the auction is over.

Beware

The merchandise being offered at any given auction may come from an assortment of places or from a single source. "The items you see here come from a fine old estate," the auctioneer may tell his audience. And maybe every single article being brought up at that particular auction did, indeed, come from the estate of Mr. and Mrs. Smith, for example. But it's also possible that the auctioneer has brought in articles he's purchased or taken in from other sources on consignment. Some of them may be quite new. This practice is known as *salting.* Do honest auctioneers do it? Yes, sometimes they do. But they never try to pass off these items as old. When our favorite auctioneer brings up any new piece, he says something like, "This is newer but nice."

If you don't know and trust the auctioneer, try to see who you're bidding against. There are unscrupulous auctioneers who pull bids out of the air. We saw an auctioneer run a very green member of his audience up to 700 dollars on an item that couldn't have been worth more than 100 dollars. He kept looking to the back of the room and taking a bogus bid, forcing her to up her bid if she wanted the item. Sometimes auctioneers get caught at this when the "pigeon" stops bidding and the imaginary person at the back is supposed to get the article. Then you may hear something like, "Oh, didn't you raise the bid?" or "I didn't know you were out; where were we?" from the auctioneer, who will start the bidding again, this time honestly.

If you preview an auction and submit a left bid, your left bid is the highest amount that you have authorized the auction staff member bidding for you to go. If an auctioneer has more than one left bid on any given item, he may start the bidding at the second highest left bid. However, if there's only one left bid, the auctioneer should start the bidding from the floor.

Starting with a lone left bid — a highly unethical practice — might result in a lot bringing more than it would if a member of the audience started the bidding. For instance, say an auctioneer has a left bid of 100 dollars on a lamp. He starts on the floor and gets a twenty-five-dollar bid. He tops it with fifty dollars from the left bid. There's no more bidding, and the lamp is knocked down to the left bid at the price of fifty dollars. Now suppose the auctioneer is dishonest and starts the bidding for the same lamp with the left bid at 100 dollars. There are no more bids and the person who left the bid must pay 100 dollars for the lamp. If you leave a bid and find you've been successful in getting the item, but you had to pay the full amount of the bid, you may have cause to be suspicious that the auctioneer started with your bid.

Sometimes dealers get together and agree not to bid against each other. Each may pick out an item they want and the rest of the group will stand aside. In many states this practice is forbidden, because it puts the seller at an unfair disadvantage.

Detecting Reproductions and Fakes

One of the pitfalls of the antiques business for auctioneers, dealers, and collectors alike is mistaking a reproduction or fake item for the real thing. Paying the price for an authentic piece and ending up with a reproduction or fake can result in a substantial financial loss. It's something that happens to most people at some time during their antiques buying and selling, but a practiced eye and an awareness of what to look for minimizes the chance of being duped.

It's important to know that many reproductions are fairly desirable and have some age to them. For instance, it's quite all right to purchase a Remington restrike. Few of us can afford the original sculptures, and the restrikes are made from the same molds. But the seller should present the item as a restrike, priced accordingly, and the buyer should be aware that what he is purchasing is a restrike, not an original. There are also copies of Remingtons. These are far less valuable than the restrikes; in most cases, they lack the detail of an original Remington or a good restrike.

Antique guns, swords, armor, and related accessories are popular collectibles that have been copied. In the late 1800s, several German arms makers produced superb copies of guns and armor that dated back to the 1600s. Although these are reproductions, they're wonderfully made and coming across one is a real find. They're old enough to qualify as antiques in their own right. However, they should be sold as reproductions and not as original 1600s pieces.

Likewise, a chair in the Louis XIII style that is a copy of an original chair made between 1610 and 1643 might have been produced in the 1800s. It's an antique, but it's still a Louis XIII-*style* chair, not a Louis XIII chair. This type of reproduction is widely thought of as a legitimate copy rather than a fake.

Unfortunately, however, the antiques market is polluted with intentional fakes made specifically to fool the customers. There are even warehouses that specialize in selling "antiques" and "collectibles" hot off the assembly line. These places cater only to dealers. To gain admission, you must present a license to sell, a business card, or some other form of identification proving that you aren't just a retail customer in search of a bargain.

Wholesale warehouses are eye-opening — you'll see merchandise that, unless it is closely scrutinized, really looks old. Shelves of new iron doorstops that have been artificially aged sell for a small fraction of what a truly old doorstop would go for. Molds from old glass companies such as Westmoreland have been used to reproduce wares that can pass as originals. Brand new prints of works by Maxfield Parrish, Bessie Pease Gutman, Louis Icart, and other favorite artists from an earlier era line the walls. Many of these prints have been systematically discolored to make them look old. These warehouses are a boon to the unscrupulous dealer who can stock up on new "antiques" to sell to unsuspecting customers.

Armor and Arms

Each type of merchandise has its own kinds of fakes and forgeries. If your interest lies in collecting or selling armor or arms, you're delving into an area fraught with fakes and examples that have been extensively repaired with modern parts. Many new pieces of armor, swords, or guns have been artificially rusted or pitted to make them look older. The genuine antique should present uniform rust and pitting, which is difficult to copy. Reproduction armor tends to be a lighter color, and the insides are smoother to the touch than the insides of the older examples.

Guns should have locks and barrels that fit snugly into the wood of their stocks. If the fit looks bad, the pieces have been replaced. When a sword is the item in question, look for a tight fit at the base of the hilt and the shoulder of the blade. If there's a gap, the blade is probably a replacement. During the late 19th and early 20th centuries, some German companies, including Conrad, made replicas of very early, museum-quality pieces. These don't surface often for the average dealer, and they are extremely pricey. But it's good to be aware that they exist should you be offered what looks like a 16th-century piece.

Cast Iron

Cheaters sometimes leave newer cast-iron objects like doorstops in water or manure to create rust. New rust is a brighter, redder color than old rust, which has a dark brown or blackish hue. Copies of cast-iron articles have been made in aluminum, which is much lighter than the original cast iron. Modern screws on a supposedly old piece are a dead giveaway that the piece has been reproduced.

Ceramics

Newer ceramics are artificially aged by changing or altering their marks. A mark that's incised is usually valid because it was added to the piece before firing. There is less reason to suspect underglaze marks than overglaze marks, but there are underglaze marks that have been added. (One of the most frequently forged is the Meissen crossed swords.) If a mark is covered by a small patch of overglaze, thicker than what's on the rest of the piece, you're probably looking at a forgery and would be wise to pass it by.

Many early marks were done in gilt. Pieces from a much later period have been altered by grinding or sanding off the original, more recent mark and substituting an early gilt mark. When buying anything with a gilt mark, run your fingers over the bottom of the piece. If there is a slight indentation, the original mark may have been deleted. The indentation will not necessarily be right under the new mark; inspect the entire piece.

Before 1891, imported items bore only the name of the country of origin. The McKinley Tariff Act of 1891 dictated that all imported items be marked "made in" followed by the country of origin. Tricksters cover the words *made in* with a small design, creating the impression that the piece was made before 1891. There are many legitimate pieces circulating today that were made after 1891 but don't bear the words *made in.* Some were produced by small companies that simply ignored the McKinley Tariff Act and got away with it, because they were too small to be worth pursuing; others were purchased in their countries of origin by individuals who brought the wares back to this country.

Many Chinese pieces are marked with the six characters of an emperor who reigned during a much earlier period than that in which the piece was made. This was done to honor the emperor rather than to fool the public. Modern pieces are often marked with four characters, instead of the classic six, identifying them instantly as newer.

During the 19th century, French potters Charles Avisseau and Charles Pull produced earthenware figures and dishes that were made from molds of Bernard Palissy originals. Palissy was a talented potter of the 1500s. His followers produced his wares until the 17th century. The fakes are about six-sevenths the size of the originals — the result of unavoidable shrinkage that took place during the firing.

In 1845 Samson of Paris started making copies of works that bore the marks of Sevres, Meissen, Chelsea, and other notables. These were clearly marked with the Samson name as well as the original name. But some of the wares are being sold as originals by unscrupulous dealers who have had the Samson name removed. Again, feel for a slight indentation where the mark was ground off. Samson pieces are desirable for themselves, but don't command the prices of the originals.

Clocks and Watches

Since the mid-1600s, when English watchmakers were considered the best in the world at their craft, there have been imitations of their clocks and watches. Clocks are easier to fake, requiring less close work with skilled hands and tiny objects, so they've been forged more often than watches. Many clock forgeries are difficult to detect because the forger was a skilled craftsman and paid attention to detail. It's easier to recognize a clock of inferior quality that has been engraved with the name of a famous clockmaker. An expert will have no trouble recognizing the lack of quality. We recommend consulting one when the purchase is to be costly. Of course if you're attending an auction, you're going to have to rely on the judgment of the auctioneer or his staff, then make your own decision.

Copies of English watches were made generations ago using the tools available at the time. Dishonest watchmakers would sign the name of Daniel Quare (an English watchmaker) or Breguet (a noted French watchmaker) to these cheaper imitations. Although most of these fakes don't match the originals in quality and style, they are interesting, old, and quite collectible.

Furniture

When it comes to furniture, there are a few gray areas in determining what's a fake and what's actually an original. For instance, a dealer might replace a door on a dry sink; a drawer on a Sheraton piece; or a leg on an elegant, old table. These types of repairs are considered restoration and are deemed acceptable by most antiques buffs.

The amount of restoration that's allowed before a piece becomes a fake or forgery is open for debate. There are dealers who build an entire piece around one small part of an item. For instance, someone may find just the footboard of an old sleigh bed and have a cabinetmaker produce the headboards and side boards; or a dealer may have several drawers from a highboy and commission a craftsman to create a piece incorporating them. This new furniture is then passed off as antique — a shady dealer may take out one of the antique drawers, turn it over, and show a naive customer the obvious and legitimate signs of age. Anyone interested in antique furniture should learn what to look for and inspect the entire piece.

One way to determine if furniture is old is to look closely at the wood itself. The tools used years ago were hand tools, and the marks they made differ from those made by later power tools. And while marks on wood cut both by hand saw or in a more modern mill may be straight, those from the hand saw won't be evenly spaced. Lumber cut in a saw mill has marks that are uniformly spaced and are directly parallel to each other.

Beware of the furniture marriage. It rarely works, and even when it does, it seriously devalues the piece. Bookcases are frequently married to bureaus. China cupboards may be made up of tops and bottoms from different periods. Newer pedestals are commonly attached to lovely old tabletops or vice versa. A dealer who has only the top or bottom of a two-piece secretary may try to sell it as a complete unit. Look for signs that a part is missing, such as a buildup of finish where the other section fitted on. If you're buying a piecrust table, closely inspect the piecrust trim. It's often added to make a plain table into a fancier, more expensive one. This is not restoration; it's definitely faking.

Glass

Many glass objects have been copied. It takes practice to identify those that are masquerading as antiques. To those in the know, old glass is immediately recognizable by the tint. If you put the piece of glass in strong light, either electric or natural, then look down on the glass, an old piece will have a tinge of varying shades of gray around the rim. If you put a new piece of glass beside it, the difference is unmistakable. Look for signs of wear: The bottom of the old glass will show some dulling from sitting against another surface.

Jewelry

In the late 1700s and early 1800s, it was fashionable to create jewelry that copied the ancient Greek, Roman, Egyptian, and Etruscan styles. These copies are now sought for their own considerable value. However, other copies have been made to sell as originals at prices far greater than their actual worth. The cut of a stone and the workmanship in a piece usually reveal its age to an expert. But stones are not easy to assess unless they are removed from their settings. One of the tricks of the fake trade is to sandwich paste or some other colorless substance between layers of real stone. A purple paste has been quite successfully substituted for amethysts. Zircons and rock crystal are widely used to resemble diamonds. Even during the 1700s and 1800s, jewelers added fake stones to pieces with real stones to create desirable color combinations. The only way to safely purchase a piece of antique jewelry is to have it inspected by a trustworthy, expert jeweler.

Oriental Rugs

A machine-made rug is easy to distinguish from a hand-tied Oriental, so Orientals are not often faked. But occasionally a dishonest merchant will scorch the pile on a new rug, then brush it to give the appearance of wear. He'll even lightly burn the back of the rug to match the front. If you suspect that a rug is not as old as you're being told it is, or as it looks, try this test: Dampen a handkerchief and rub it quickly on a part of the carpet that looks worn. Immediately smell the handkerchief. If the carpet has been doctored, you should detect an odor of burned fabric on your handkerchief.

Pewter

During the 1930s, pewter enjoyed a surge of popularity, especially in England. There weren't enough old pewter pieces to supply the demand for them, so manufacturers started making new pieces from the old molds. They even used the same marks that had been used on the older pieces. Other pewter was made using newer designs. It was sold as ornamental and not passed off as old. Some very fine copies of antique pewter are made today and offered as what they are — reproductions. But there is still newer pewter being touted as antique. Old pewter usually shows scratches and other signs of wear, but these are easy to simulate. The mellow, aged patina of old pewter is the best tip-off that it's an authentic object. Handling many articles, both old and newer, is the best way to learn. In time, you'll know the difference.

Silver and Gold

One of the dishonest practices used to pass off a newer or inferior piece of silver as an older or better one is to cut the marks off a fine, old piece that has been damaged beyond repair and solder them onto the fake. In most cases the soldering is detectible even if a good job was done. Be suspicious of any silver marks with fuzzy edges. Some dishonest silversmiths copy marks from an old piece onto a new one; these marks seldom have the crisp outlines of the original. Being knowledgeable about silver marks and what they stand for is perhaps the best protection against being taken. For example, if you find a tea service with the mark used by a silversmith who made only spoons, you have discovered a fake.

Lovely, small gold boxes made in France during the 1700s and 1800s are often altered. Most of the authentically old and unaltered boxes bear three marks, because different makers produced different parts and each one added their own mark. These marks should, of course, be from the same period. Since it was easy to damage these delicate beauties, many of them didn't survive the centuries intact. Ingenious craftsmen have taken the undamaged parts and built new boxes around them, or they've combined the parts from several old boxes to make a marriage. Often the marks on these altered pieces are from totally different periods — a fact that screams fake to the knowledgeable collector.

If you become a regular customer of auctioneers or dealers who always operate from the same place, chances are you'll come to trust them and that they'll be worthy of that trust. They'll give you their best advice and share with you what they've learned about the field. But remember even the most honest professional doesn't know everything and may innocently sell you a reproduction or a fake, thinking it's legitimate. As with much in life, *caveat emptor* applies to buying antiques and collectibles.

A

Aalto, Alvar: (furniture) a furniture designer and architect who made bentwood furniture from the 1930s until the 1970s. His designs reflect the influence of the modern international style.

'abbasai talwar: (weapons) a Punjabi (India) saber with a slightly curved blade.

'abbasi: (weapons) a straight-bladed Rajput (India) sword with perforated supports at the back.

abrash: (floor coverings) a variation in colors (especially noticeable in the background color) found in many hand-woven carpets. Dyeing the wool in more than one batch causes the deviation in hue.

absolute auction: an auction at which all the merchandise is guaranteed to be offered and sold at the maximum bid. There is no reserve minimum bid on anything.

acanthus: (design) the conventionalized foliage of the acanthus plant, used as a decoration on furniture, silver, and china during the Renaissance period and again during the Victorian period.

accessories: 1. (decoration) a secondary or nonessential decorative object. **2.** (fine art) objects that appear in a painting which add interest but are subordinate to the main theme.

accidental rarity: (coins) a coin that was poorly struck, creating a flaw that makes it unique.

accordion: (music) a popular bellows-type instrument first developed by Freidrich Buschmann, a German musician (1805-1864). The early accordions were used chiefly for folk music.

achromatic lens: (scientific instruments) a lens made by combining two or more lenses of different focal powers to eliminate color fringes that distort images.

acid gilding: (ceramics) decoration achieved by printing the pattern on a porcelain piece with an acid-resistant material. The porcelain is then submerged in an acid solution that eats away, or etches, the material between the design. The process may be done in reverse by treating the spaces between the design with acid-resist material and acid-etching the design. The design is then banded over in gold and fired. This process was used most often on the borders of tableware. It was first used by Minton in 1863.

acid-polished: (glass) a piece of cut glass that has been polished by putting it in an acid solution.

acorn clock: a mantel or shelf clock about 24 inches high, with the upper portion shaped like an acorn. The design was common in New England during the early part of the 19th century.

acorn knop: (glass) an acorn-shaped form tooled into the stem of a drinking glass. The acorn is often inverted.

acoustic jar: (ceramics) a pottery vessel; often found embedded in the tops of the walls of the chancels in some medieval churches.

Adams, Robert (1728-1792): (furniture) Scottish architect who, with his brother James, had a major influence on furniture design during the last quarter of the 18th century. The brothers were greatly responsible for the revival of classical design and ornamentation.

Adams' Rose: (ceramics) a line of dinnerware that was produced by Adams and Son Pottery between 1825 and 1850. White blanks were hand painted with large, bright red roses and green leaves. Other companies copied this design, but in most instances the painting lacked the brilliance of the Adams' Rose and the white ware had a grayer tinge.

à deux crayons: (fine art) a drawing of two colors done in red and black chalk. Occasionally the red is replaced by another color.

advertising card: (paper) a small, colorfully illustrated cardboard card circulated during the 19th century by a merchant. Each one bears the name and address of an establishment and the merits of a particular product, as well as an attractive picture. Also called *trade card*.

advertising piece: any of the literature, signs, posters, and imprinted objects displayed or handed out by businesses and manufacturers to promote their services and goods.

adz: (tools) a carpenter's ax-like tool with the blade at right angles to the handle. Used to shape and dress wood.

adze: (weapons) a weapon with blades of jade and elaborately carved handles, used by Maori warriors (New Zealand).

aerogram: (stamps) a sheet of lightweight paper designed to fold into its own envelope, used for airmail stationery. Government issues are pre-stamped.

aeronautica: (collectibles) aviation memorabilia. There are two types of collectibles in this category: those that come from specific airlines and those that deal with personalities who made significant contributions to the field. The former encompasses everything from baggage stickers to model airplanes. The latter includes autographs, books, pins, plates, programs, photographs, and other souvenirs featuring such notables in aviation as Richard Byrd, Amelia Earhart, and Charles Lindbergh.

aerophilately: (stamps) the collecting of airborne postal material such as airmail stamps.

aerugo: (metal) the green corrosion that appears on copper or bronze.

Afghan stock: (weapons) the English name for an extremely curved gun stock with a deep, narrow butt; used in Sind (West Pakistan).

after-cast: 1. (metal) a figure made from a mold that was formed around an existing figure. **2.** (metal) a casting made from an original mold by someone other than the original artist or manufacturer.

agata: (glass) the gold and blue mottling that sometimes appears on New England peachblow glass. This type of decoration is achieved by applying a metallic stain to peachblow glass. Age has taken its toll on most of these pieces, which were made during the late 1800s, and in many cases the metallic decoration is quite worn. The more agata remaining on a piece, the more valuable it is.

agate: (marbles) marbles made from stone; usually translucent. Their bands of color alternate with white.

agate glass: glass made by pouring several colors of glass together and allowing them to swirl, but not blend, together; used to make molded or blown glassware. Popular in Venice and Germany during the Renaissance. Also called *schmelzglas*.

agate ware: (ceramics) a salt-glazed stoneware or lead-glazed earthenware resembling variegated natural stones. This style, which dates to the early 18th century, is accomplished by putting together different colors of clay. One of the most refined forms was produced by Josiah Wedgewood.

aigrette: (jewelry) a jeweled ornament that holds a feather in a lady's hair or in a cap. Aigrettes have been in use since the 16th century.

aiguillette: (jewelry, military) a knotted cord worn on the shoulder of a military aide's uniform during the 19th century. These are often adorned with jewels.

air twist: (glass) an elongated bubble of air in the stem of a glass.

akro agate glass: (collectibles) a thick glass made by the Akro Agate Company. They started operations in Akron, Ohio, in 1911. In 1914, the company moved their operations to Clarksburg, West Virginia. Until 1930, their only product was marbles. After that, they began to produce everything from ashtrays to vases. Their children's play dishes are particularly prized.

Alabama coon jigger: (black memorabilia, toys) a lithographed windup black man that dances. Made by Strauss in 1910 and widely copied.

alabaster: (materials) a hard substance used to carve artifacts such as statues, vases, boxes, and lamp bases. Alabaster comes from sulphate of lime.

alamani: (weapons) an Indian saber.

à la Poulaine Solerets: (armor) long, pointed foot guards worn with Gothic armor in the 15th century.

alarum: (clocks) seventeenth-century alarm clock. Also called *watch clock*.

Albert chain: (jewelry) a watch chain with a swivel end that holds the watch at one end and a bar at the other end. Worn by either men or women.

albumens: (photography) the first photographs printed on paper. Used after 1880.

album quilt: (textiles) a quilt with blocks that have been made by different individuals, each using her own style and theme. These quilts were often given as wedding gifts or to mark some other important occasion.

alchemy: (metal) an alloy of copper and tin used to make many spoons and plates dat-

ing from the 16th and 17th centuries.

alcohol colors: (fine art) colors made with an alcohol base and applied with an airbrush.

Alençon lace: (textiles) a delicate needlepoint lace that was made in Alençon, France. The industry started there in 1665 and was strongly influenced by the Venetian craftsmen who taught the French how to make lace. The Venetian influence was short-lived and soon Alençon was known for a finer Flemish pillow lace. In the 1700s, the area became famous for point d'Alençon, a narrow lace used mainly for borders and caps.

alexandrite: (glass) glass characterized by colors that go from pale yellow to rose and blue, introduced by well-known English glassmaker Thomas Webb. Other glassmakers mimicked Webb but they never achieved his high standard of quality. These inferior articles don't have the value of a Webb piece of alexandrite.

algrette: (jewelry) either precious, semiprecious, or costume jewels arranged in a setting shaped like a feather or feathers.

ali-ali: (weapon) a type of Malay knife.

alidade: (scientific instruments) a revolving sighting device used on nautical and surveying instruments.

alkaline glaze: (ceramics) a potash and sand glaze used on a vessel of clay.

allendale: (textiles) an English bedspread dating from the early 1800s.

alligator cracks: (fine art) age cracks that look like alligator skin on oil paintings.

alloy: (metal) two or more metals combined to form another metal.

altazimuth: (scientific instruments) a mounting used for astronomical telescopes that allows both horizontal and vertical rotation.

altered: (coins) a real coin that has been changed so that it appears to have a different (usually greater) value.

aluminum ware: (metal) during the 1930s through the 1950s, many novelty items, lamps, vases, serving trays, and pitchers were fashioned from aluminum. Russel Wright was one of the most prestigious designers who used this medium. The early aluminum objects are of spun aluminum. Many items produced in the 1950s are of hammered aluminum. Pieces that bear a company trademark are the most collectible.

amber glass: a popular brownish yellow colored glass used to make functional as well as ornamental objects.

amberina glass: an amber glass that shades to a deep red; used to make art glass. Amberina is produced by adding a gold powder to a batch of glass. The item to be made is heated on the top or the bottom until that portion becomes red. The earliest glass of this type was blown-molded, but both pressed and cut amberina are commonly seen now. Amberina dates from the 1880s, when it was developed by Joseph Locke at the New England Glass Company. Many of the most valuable pieces are signed "W.L. Libbey."

ambrotype: (photography) an underexposed wet-collodion negative on glass that becomes a positive when mounted against a black backing. Copies are not possible because the exposed negative is the finished print. From the late 1850s.

amen glass: a drinking vessel bearing either one or two verses from a Jacobite hymnal. The engraved message always ends with the word *amen*. The glasses have either a drawn stem or a baluster shape (resembling a vase).

Americana: antiques and collectibles that reflect the growth, culture, and character of American civilization.

American antique trader plate: (collectibles) an inexpensive commemorative plate.

American Belleek: (ceramics) Irish Belleek-style porcelain produced by several American companies from the last quarter of the 19th century until the 1930s. It is collectible and commands high prices since it is not easy to find. But it still is considered to be slightly inferior to its Irish counterpart. Some of the companies producing American Belleek were American Art China Company, Ceramic Art Company, Ott and Brewer, and Willets Manufacturing Company.

American coin silver: until the mid-1800s, solid silver was 9/10 silver and 1/10 other metals. Some marks used were "coin," "premium," "dollar," "pure coin," or "standard." Early coin silver was often marked with the initials of the silversmith, with his last name, or with his first initial and last name. Other examples have hallmarks mimicking those used on fine English silver. The letters *C* or *D* were also used. American coin silver is often overlooked and undervalued.

American Indian beading: (Native American) beadwork done by American Indians is highly prized. Each of the Indian nations (tribes) have their own distinctive way of working with the tiny beads they string on threads and use to adorn animal skins and clothing. Some Native Americans add animal teeth, fur, shells, and other decorative items from nature to the beading.

American sterling: (silver) sterling made in America is 925 parts pure and 75 parts other metal. It may be marked "925," "925/1,000," "sterling," or "sterling weighted." Pieces marked "sterling weighted" have a weight in the base. Because it is difficult to determine the actual silver weight in these pieces, they usually don't bring as much at auctions.

American Victorian: (furniture) the period between 1830 and 1900 that incorporates several styles of furniture, including Victorian Gothic, Victorian rococo, Victorian renaissance, and Eastlake.

amethyst glass: a purple colored glass, not to be confused with black amethyst. (Black amethyst appears to be black, but under strong light it is deep purple.)

Amish: (collectibles, folk art) followers of Jacob Amman who make up a religious sect that settled in Pennsylvania during the 1700s. Since that time, they've produced quilts and other primitive handcrafts that are highly prized collectibles.

amorini: (decoration) a decorative motif of cupids used on late-17th-century furniture.

amphora: (ceramics) a jar with a narrow neck and two handles used to carry wine or oil by the ancient Greeks and Romans.

amulet: (jewelry) an object worn on the body as a charm for good fortune against evil and injury.

anabori: (orientalia) very small, very deep carving.

ananaspokal: (table ware) a covered cup resembling a pineapple standing on a pedestal. Made in Germany in the 1500s and 1600s. Some examples are 30 inches high. Also called *pineapple cup.*

anchor escapement: (clocks) from about 1675, a standard device on all pendulum clocks named for the shape of the clocks' pallets — the steel surfaces that inter-

rupt the motion of the teeth on the scapewheel.

ancus: (tools) Indian elephant goad, shaped like a boat hook. The handle is short for handlers that ride, and long — about 5 feet — for handlers who walk beside the animal. Most are plain, but many are decorated with ivory, jade, gold, and precious stones.

andirons: (metal) a pair of brass or iron supports for holding logs in a fireplace. Also called *firedogs.*

aniline dye: (floor coverings) a dye made from coal tar. The colors range from red through purple and are subject to fading. First used in the mid-1800s.

aniline ink: (stamps) a water-soluble ink used to print earlier postage stamps. Stamps printed with this ink should not be soaked for removal from envelopes.

animated toy: a toy that is activated by one of several means such as winding, rubber bands, batteries, or electricity.

animated toy pistol: a cap pistol made in the form of an animal or person. The character was set into motion when the trigger was pulled and the cap exploded. Made mostly of cast iron from 1880 to 1910.

animation cel: (motion picture memorabilia) an original drawing used to create animated films and cartoons. Also called *production cel.*

anlace: (weapons) a medieval dagger with two edges.

annealing: (glass, metal) a process used to toughen flint glass and metals. This process, done in an *annealing oven,* involves heating the material to a high temperature and then cooling it gradually. As it cools, the material strengthens. Glass acquires an added brilliance during this process. Brittle metals, particularly silver, are softened when they are annealed.

anneau: (weapons) a ring guard on one, or both, sides of the guards on swords and knives. From early 16th century.

annoted print: a print that is dated and numbered.

annular-ringed clock: a clock with a stationary pointer; a band displaying the numbers revolves so that the numerals under the pointer change to give the time. (An ordinary clock works by moving hands around to fixed numbers.) Annular-ringed clocks were luxury items owned only by the wealthy. They are scarce and valuable.

annulate: (decoration) a design consisting of rings or circles. Also the circle of five-point stars that encompasses the Presidential Seal.

ansate: (decoration) having a loop or handle, such as the ansate cross.

anthemion: (furniture) a motif derived from the flower of the honeysuckle. Dates back to ancient Greece.

antia: (armor) the iron handle on a shield.

antic work: (furniture) carving imitating Roman antique wall paintings and stucco decorations found in underground tombs or grottoes. Also called *grotesques.*

antedated: (coins) coins made and dated later than the time of the regular issue.

antimacassar: (textiles) a decorative piece that was knit, crocheted, or embroidered and placed on the back of a chair or sofa to protect it from being stained. From about 1825 to 1875, it was fashionable for both men and women to use a hair oil called Macassar. When people rested their heads on the backs of chairs or sofas, Macassar left nasty stains. Antimacassars were still in use long after the hairdressing had fallen from favor.

antique: according to U.S. customs law, any object that is 100 years old or older. However, the term is commonly used to refer to items of an earlier generation, period, or era, and there are some authorities who say any item over fifty years of age should be considered an antique.

antique automobile: any car dating before 1930. Also, according to some judges, any car twenty-five years old or more. See also *classic automobile, milestone automobile, modern-day classic automobile.*

antique cut: (jewelry) a stone cut in a square or rectangle that has round corners. Also called *cushion cut.*

antiquity: usually refers to an object made during or before the Middle Ages.

Antwerp lace: (textiles) a strong, heavy-looking pillow lace. It is called pot lace, or *potten kant,* because of the two-handled vase or pot motif that usually appears in the lace. This motif was popular during the 18th century and was also used in Normandy lace.

aobie: (weapons) Japanese short bamboo sword.

aogai: (orientalia) mother-of-pearl made from thin, greenish-blue or reddish-purple iridescent shells, used as an inlay in Japanese lacquered articles.

A. O. P.: (glass, ceramics) stands for *all-over pattern.*

apocryphal: (silver, pewter) a fake. Dishonest silversmiths add marks to unmarked pieces of silver, silver plate, or pewter to dupe a potential buyer into paying more for an item.

Apollo harp: (music) a keyboard instrument developed in the late 1800s. It was popular with amateurs because it was easy to play. Professional musicians didn't use them.

apostle jug: (ceramics) a jug with figures of the apostles and an elaborate Gothic design. These jugs were made by Charles Meigh Company in the mid-18th century.

apostle spoon: (silver) spoons with finials depicting either Christ or one of the apostles in full figure. Made from the late 1600s until about 1850. A complete set of thirteen is extremely rare. Apostle spoons have been reproduced in recent years, so any apostle spoon should be purchased with caution.

apostle urn: (ceramics) an eight-sided urn for carrying water; made by Bennington Pottery. These urns bore figures of the apostles. Several English firms also made apostle urns as well as apostle pitchers and other items with like designs.

applewood: (materials) one of the hard fruitwoods used for furniture and picture frames. These woods are easy to work with and therefore lend themselves to turning and carving. None of the fruitwoods has the beauty of mahogany or rosewood, so they are often painted or gilded for picture frames. Other close-grained fruitwoods include cherry and pearwood.

applied decoration: an ornament or design added to an object after its manufacture, as by soldering, gluing, nailing, or painting.

applied handle: (glass, ceramics, silver) a handle that is made separately, then attached to a piece, instead of being formed as part of the piece.

applied stem: (glass) the stem of a glass object that is made separately and then attached using hot glass as the adhesive. Also called *stuck shank.*

appliqué: (textiles) to sew small pieces of material onto other pieces of material. Often done in quilt making. Also called *laid-on work.*

approvals: (stamps) stamps mailed to a customer by a dealer on speculation; the customer returns the undesired stamps.

apricot glass: a medium yellow glass lighter than amber. Apricot is a fairly common color of Princess-pattern depression glass.

apron: (furniture) the horizontal cross member where a piece of furniture connects with its legs. On a chair, it is the structure below and parallel to the seat. On case furniture, it is the horizontal surface below the bottom drawer.

aquamanile: (metal) ewers used to pour water over guests' hands after each course during a meal. These bronze ewers were made in various shapes, usually resembling animals. One of the most popular designs is a lion with a dragon on his back; the dragon serves as a handle. Since no utensils were used, these ewers were needed in the 13th to 16th centuries. Authentic examples are extremely rare, but there are quite a few reproductions.

aquatint: (prints) a method of etching several tones by altering the exposure time on different areas of a copper plate, resulting in a print that resembles an ink or wash drawing.

arabesque: (decoration) an inlaid, painted, or flat-carved intricate floral, geometrical, animal, fruit, or figural design; used on ceramics and other objects. Arabesques are thought to be an imitation of Islamic script.

arbalest: (weapons) a European crossbow of the Middle Ages.

arbrier: (weapons) the stock of a crossbow.

arcade: (furniture) a series of arches with columns or pilasters supporting them. As a motif, used on furniture in the 17th century.

arcanum: (ceramics) a term referring to a secret formula for making porcelain.

architrave: (furniture) the lower molding running under a frieze as on a mantelpiece or piece of furniture.

argent: (heraldry) a term for white or silver, which in turn signifies innocence and purity.

Argentan lace: (textiles) lace with a pointed floral (picotee) design. Originally made in Argentan, France, not far from Alençon, where the well-known Alençon lace was made. Argentan lace designs are bold and often worked over with small buttonhole stitches.

argentella lace: (textiles) needlepoint-type variation of point d'Alençon lace characterized by a large, dotted mesh.

argyle: (tableware) a gravy server made to look like a small coffee pot. Argyles were common from the late 1700s until the early 1800s. They have a hot-water heater — either a separate container or a space in the walls of the pot — to keep the gravy warm.

Argy-Rousseau, Gabriel: (glass) artisan who worked in the art deco style decorating jewelry, lampshades, vases, and the like during the early 1900s. Most of his work is marked "G-Argy-Rousseau."

armet: (armor) a helmet with hinged cheek pieces that overlap and fasten at the chin; used in the 15th and 16th centuries.

armillary sphere: (scientific instruments) an astronomical sphere with pathways of the planets in the solar system depicted by solid rings.

arming spurs: (armor) spurs worn with armor.

arming sword: (weapons) a short sword worn on the right side.

armlet: (weapons) an arm band, often with protruding points or sharp edges, used to strike or press against the opponent.

armoire: (furniture) a tall, large cupboard or wardrobe with doors.

armor: protective gear worn by those in battle from about 1500 B.C. until the present. Most collectible armor is from medieval times and is made of metal.

armorial: (heraldry) refers to heraldry or heraldic arms.

armorial fan: (fashion accessories, heraldry) during the period from about 1775 to 1800, fans featuring a coat of arms and a floral cartouche. The frames of these very popular fans were made of either tortoise shell or ivory.

arms: 1. (weapons) weapons. 2. (heraldry) a heraldic family seal or crest, or official insignia.

arm stump: (furniture) the front, vertical support of a chair arm.

arm support: (furniture) the curved or vertical upright supporting the front end of a chair arm. May be an extension of the foreleg or a separate piece rising from the seat rail.

arquebus (or harquebus): (weapons) originally a heavy matchlock gun, later the name was applied to wheel-lock guns. Finally, the term referred to guns of superior workmanship. From the late 14th century.

arras lace: 1. (textiles) a coarse pillow lace resembling Lille, but distinguishable by its scalloped edges. It is said that about 350 yards of it were used by King George I for his coronation clothing. 2. (textiles) a Flemish tapestry.

arriere bras: (armor) armor that covers the upper arms.

art deco: (design) an art movement dated from the Paris International Exhibition of 1925 that lasted through the

1940s. While art nouveau reflected nature with flowing lines, art deco embraced the lines of industry — straight, bold, and streamlined. New industrial materials, such as plastic and chrome, were freely used.

art doll: an often one-of-a-kind doll that was either designed by an artist or modeled after a figure in a painting.

art glass: glass objects made for decorative rather than utilitarian purposes.

art glass basket: a popular decorative accessory in the Victorian era, when glass blowers tried to outdo each other making them. The fancier a glass basket is the greater its value. There are many imitations being made today.

articulus: (toys) a paper toy depicting one of a variety of activities. Very much in vogue during the late 19th century. These paper articles were connected with wires and the wires were connected to an axle of a spinner that was activated by warm air. The connected items also had moving parts of their own. Stovepipes and hot-air registers supplied the energy needed to operate these fascinating, now collectible, toys.

artifact: an object that is representative of the time in which it was made. These objects were generally handcrafted.

art nouveau: (design) literally, new art (French). A style of art and design that began in the early 1890s and continued into the 1930s. It is characterized by sinuous, flowing lines and floral forms.

art pottery: pottery made primarily for decorative rather than utilitarian use.

Arts and Crafts: (design) the term covers a spectrum of design that began in England in the late 19th century in reaction to the mass-produced furniture and accessories of the Victorian era. True craftsmanship was the movement's goal. William Morris was its chief advocate. Elbert Hubbard, Frank Lloyd Wright, and the Stickley brothers were a few of the American proponents of the movement, which died out by the early 1920s. Furniture of the movement was influenced by both medieval structures and Japanese architecture, resulting in the dominance of simplified Gothic shapes and straight lines.

Ashburton goblet: (glass) drinking vessel featuring pressed patterns made in the 1800s. The most popular pattern was a heavy scallop design. The Sandwich Glass Company was one of the leading manufacturers of these goblets.

as is: a warning that the item is damaged and sold with that understanding. Therefore it is not returnable.

as it is and where it is: (auctions) a phrase used by auctioneers to inform their clients that there is no guarantee of condition for the merchandise they buy at the auction and that the buyer is responsible for removing any purchases from the premises.

asparagus tongs: (table accessories) tongs with small spikes that grip the asparagus. These handy tools, which were popular in the late 1800s, were designed to match the family's silver service.

Assisi: (needlework) an Italian embroidery with a background, usually red or blue, worked in a solid cross-stitch.

Astbury-type ware: (ceramics) pottery produced in the mid-1700s featuring a combination of red and white clay topped with a transparent lead glaze.

Astbury-Whieldon: (ceramics) lead-glazed Staffordshire earthenware statuettes, *ca.* 18th century. Named for noted Staffordshire potters John Astbury and Thomas Whieldon.

Astbury-Whieldon glaze is spattered with metallic oxide, making it slightly different from Astbury-type ware.

astragal: (furniture) a molding of small, convex beading.

astral lamp: (lighting) an oil lamp that has a central holder for oil, but the oil also runs into tubular arms with burners on the ends of them. The arms can be moved so that the burners throw light directly on a book or other object. Invented by Count Rumford.

astrolabe: (scientific instruments) a compact marine instrument dating from 150 B.C.; used to calculate the position of celestial bodies. Replaced by the backstaff and sextant.

à trois crayons: (fine art) a three-color drawing done in red, black, and white chalk.

attributed to: (fine art) a work of art that is of a certain artist's period and style. The work is thought, but not guaranteed, to be by that artist.

Audubon, John James: (prints) a Haitian-born artist and ornithologist who came to America from France in the early 1800s. His paintings of birds were compiled into a collection titled *The Birds of America*. The set consisted of 435 plates and was issued in a print run of only about 200.

Aunt Jemima: (black memorabilia) black female figure with long skirt and apron, scarf, and bandanna.

aurene: (glass) glassware developed by Frederick Carder, one of the founders of Steuben Glass Works, in 1904. This beautiful, iridescent glass was used to make objects ranging from ashtrays and toothpick holders to vases and candlesticks. Gold and blue are the most familiar colors although red and green were also used. Most of this very desirable glass has "aurene" or "Steuben" etched in the glass, but some of it was marked with paper labels.

Austrian ware: (ceramics) porcelain items imported from the Austro-Hungarian Empire (known as Bohemia) between the late 1800s and the beginning of World War I. Most Austrian ware is transfer-decorated rather than hand painted, but some pieces command fairly high prices. Because the factories were supported, to a large extent by American money, and the wares were made for export, the only mark appearing on most Austrian ware is "Austrian." However, some of the pieces do carry the mark of the manufacturer. These companies include M.S. Austria, Schmidt and Company, Victoria, and O. & E. Co.

authorized coin: a coin that meets the standards of the Coinage Act and that has been issued by the order of the director of a mint.

autograph quilt: (textiles) a quilt featuring autographs that have been done in pen or pencil and then embroidered. Some of these quilts are in blocks; others are one piece of fabric.

automata: (toys) self-propelled toys. They often can perform several different motions.

automobilia: (collectibles) articles related to automobiles. Hood ornaments and license plates are the most collectible automobile items, but books and catalogs about automobiles and automobile parts as well as car radios, horns, key chains, and old gear shift knobs are also sought after.

Autry, Gene: (collectibles) singer, movie star, and cowboy who was the subject of books, paper dolls, and photographs. His name appeared on cap guns, guitars, watches, and other memorabilia, all from his heyday in the 1930s and 1940s.

avant-bras: (armor) armor that covers the forearm.

avant-garde: (fine art, design) experimental, faddish, unconventional methods of expression. Often used in describing the style of a painting.

avant la lettre: (prints) signatures, overlettering, titles, and other marks added to a print after it has been proofed.

Ave Maria lace: (textiles) a pillow lace made in long strips; made in the first half of the 19th century in Dieppe, France.

aventurine: (glass) colored glass mixed with tiny bits of gold or copper. Gold aventurine was popular in the 15th century, while most examples with copper were done in the 17th century. The glass-making firm Miotti was the first to make aventurine glass. They perfected the process of spangling an opaque glass with particles of copper oxide during the early 1600s.

Avisseau, Charles: (ceramics) a 19th-century French potter who, with his partner, Charles Pull, produced earthenware figures and dishes from the molds of Bernard Palissy, a 16th-century potter.

awl-pike: (weapons) a shafted, spearlike weapon of German origin, but used throughout Europe in the 15th century. The head is long, slender, straight, and square to the point. There is usually a round or octagonal guard between the shaft and head.

ayda katti: (weapons) the national sword of the Coorgs (India). It has a very broad, heavy, single-edged blade, curved and wider near the end than at the hilt, with the cutting edge on the concave side. There is no guard, but the hilt has a large pommel. It is carried unsheathed, in a harness (*todunga*) on the back.

azagai: (weapons) a lance or javelin of Spain and Portugal. 15th century.

Azalea: (orientalia) a pattern of Japanese wares that is extremely popular and collectible in the United States. The Azalea pattern features pink and white flowers with yellow-green to dark green leaves. Collectors look for strong colors in this tableware.

azured: (books, leather) a tooling of parallel lines frequently used on old leather book bindings.

B

baby clout: (dolls) another name for a handmade rag doll.

baby doll: any doll that resembles a baby.

Baccarat: (glass) French glass company that has produced fine-quality glassware since 1765. They make all types of decorative and functional glassware, but their line of millefiori paperweights and their fine crystal cut-glass tableware are probably Baccarat's best. See also *Baccarat paperweight*.

Baccarat paperweight: (glass) an exquisite paperweight produced between 1845 and 1860 by Baccarat, the prestigious French glass company. Their paperweights are marked with the year they were made set in a line of red, blue, and green inside white lines. Some examples carry the letter *B* between the first two digits (18-) and the last two digits of the year. Baccarat began producing paperweights again during the 1950s. See also *Baccarat* and *millefiori*.

bachelor's chest: (furniture) a low chest of drawers with a folding top for writing. From mid-18th century.

backless binding: (books) a method of bookbinding used in the 1500s and 1600s. The spine of the book was covered in gilt so that the book appeared to have four gilt page edges and no spine.

back-of-book: (stamps) abbreviated as B.O.B., the term is used to describe all categories of stamps, other than regular issues, found on the back pages of a country's catalogs and albums.

backplate: 1. (furniture) a metal plate to which a handle is attached, as on drawers or the sides of a chest. **2.** (clocks) the rear or outer plate of two plates that secure the movement; usually engraved with the maker's name.

backstaff: (scientific instruments) a marine instrument that predates the sextant. So named because the navigator turns his back to the sun in order to measure the sun's altitude.

backstamp: (stamps) a postmark placed on the back of a piece of mail indicating the various post offices the piece passed through on its forwarding route. More common in earlier years.

backsword: (weapons) a saber with either a slightly curved or a straight single-edged blade.

bacon dish: (tableware) an oblong or oval dish for serving bacon. Usually made of silver or silver plate with a wood handle. Popular in the 1700s.

badelaire: (weapons) 16th-century saber with a short, broad, convex blade, straight hilt, ornamental pommel, and flat quillons — one curving back toward the pommel, and the other curved toward the blade tip.

badge: (collectibles) any of the shields that have been worn as a means of identification since the mid-19th century. Most of them are of brass or nickel. Law enforcement badges are the most desirable, but collectors look for other badges as well.

baff: (floor coverings) the knots in carpets.

bagh nakh: (weapons) an Indian weapon. The name means *tiger's claw*, which the weapon attempts to duplicate. It has two to five curved blades fixed to a bar that fits in the palm of the hand. Two rings on top of the bar fit onto the fingers.

bag sewing table: (furniture) a Federal sewing stand with a fabric bag hung from the lower drawer to hold work.

baguette: (jewelry) a thin, rectangular stone.

bail: (furniture) a half-loop handle or drawer pull.

bainbergs: (armor) protective coverings for the fronts of the legs. Usually made of boiled leather, but some were of metal plate. Probably of German origin, 13th century.

bait bag: (Native American) a bag used to carry fishing bait.

baize: (textiles) a cotton or wool material with a nap similar to felt. Usually green in color and used to cover gaming tables.

Bakelite: (materials) an early plastic with high chemical and electrical resistance; used for handles, radio cases, and a variety of other articles. From the turn of the century until the 1940s.

bakemono: (orientalia) decorations, sculptures, or figures featuring goblins or other unreal creatures in human form.

baku: (orientalia) a Japanese design featuring a beast with an elephant's trunk. This friendly monster is said to eliminate nightmares.

balanced design: (furniture) equal distribution of ornamentation on a furniture piece.

balance toy: a toy that moves by means of a weight either above, below, or in the body of the toy.

balance wheel: (toys) a small wheel that facilitates easy motion of a toy across a flat surface, such as the floor. Balance wheels are most often found on horses that are pulling a vehicle.

baldric: (weapons) a belt worn over the shoulder as a support for a weapon.

baleen: (materials) the hornlike material that forms plates in the upper jaws of whales. The plates filter plankton. Scrimshaw pieces are often made of baleen. Also called *whalebone*.

balista: (weapons) a machine for throwing projectiles such as darts and stone balls. Construction is similar to the crossbow.

ball-and-claw foot: (furniture) a claw or talon grasping a ball; used as a footing on cabinets, tables, and chairs by the Chinese and early Romans.

ball-and-ring: (furniture) a series of bead turnings alternating with flattened discs.

ball foot: (furniture) a ball-shaped turning with a flattened round sole at its base. Popular in 17th-century furniture.

ball joint: (dolls) a joint comprised of two concave parts with a ball in between that allows movement of the elbows, knees, and other joints of a doll. The parts are strung together, usually with elastic.

ballok knife: (weapons) a knife worn at the waist by priests in the 14th century.

balloon-back: (furniture) a hoop-shaped chair back created by Hepplewhite (d. 1786) and extensively used during the Victorian era.

ballot-box marble: a handmade marble, either black or white, with a pontil mark. The name evolved from their use in lodge elections.

baluster: (furniture) an upright, vase-shaped, turned post used to support a rail or balustrade.

baluster measure: (pewter) a pewter wine measure with a flat, hinged cover.

balustrade: (architecture, furniture) a continuous, ornamental railing and the row of posts supporting it. Adapted as a motif by 18th-century English furniture makers.

bandbox: (domestic) a round, covered box made of paper or very thin wood and used for storing small, often precious, items.

banded agate: (materials) any agate ware (pottery) or agate glass (used for jewelry) with bands of light and dark colors.

banderolle: (weapons) a small streamer secured to the head of a lance.

banding: (furniture) an inlay that provides a contrast in grain or color between the inlaid band and the surface it decorates.

band kit: (domestic) a large wooden receptacle for storing grains and other provisions. These barrels were also used for pickling. Also called *ben kit* and *bow kit*.

bandolier: (weapons) a waist belt or baldric with a number of pouches or containers attached, filled with powder and/or bullets. From 17th century.

bandy leg: (furniture) a leg that swells outward at the upper part (knee) and inward at the lower part (ankle) to create an S shape. Popular in the 17th and 19th centuries. Also called *cabriole leg*.

banister-back: (furniture) a chair back with vertical wood slats extending between an upper and a lower rail.

banjo: (music) a string instrument brought to America from Africa by slaves; the most notable to be used by old-time minstrels. Considered primarily a Southern instrument; used by folk musicians from the mid-1800s on.

banjo barometer: (scientific instruments) a barometer with a banjo-shaped case. Popular from *ca.* 1750 to *ca.* 1900.

banjo clock: a wall-mounted timepiece patented by Simon Willard (*ca.* 1765) and imitated by other makers. It has an eight-day weight-driven movement within a banjo-shaped casing.

bank: (collectibles) a receptacle for storing and saving coins. There are two basic types of banks: still and mechanical. Most still banks (those with no moving parts) are made of cast iron, but there are still banks of pottery and tin. Very early mechanical banks were made from tin or lead; later ones of cast iron. Cast-iron banks have been reproduced.

banker: (textiles) a tapestry used as a cover on furniture.

bank mixture: (stamps) a bulk lot of mixed, unsorted stamps still on paper. They are usually gathered from businesses, often banks, and are assumed to contain a large number of high-denomination stamps.

bantam work: (decoration) a form of japanning or lacquerwork featuring incised instead of raised designs.

bar-and-heart thumbpiece: (pewter) heart-shaped thumb-operated lever to raise the lid of a pewter tankard.

barber's dish: a large, round shaving dish with a cut-out that fits partway around the neck of a customer in a barber shop.

barbershop memorabilia: (collectibles) the barber chairs, beveled mirrors, hair tonic bottles, barber poles, razors, shaving mugs, and other articles that were the hallmark of the barbering profession. The oldest barber poles were red and white because originally barbers also were experts in the art of bloodletting. The red in the pole stood for the blood; the white for bandages. Later poles are red, white, and blue.

Barbie doll: 20th-century collectible doll. The first Barbie dolls, with white eyes, are the most valuable and the hardest to find. Since the Mattel Company made the first one in 1959, Barbie has had three face changes: in 1966, 1971, and 1976. Barbie's friends, including Cara, Christie, Ken, and Skipper, are also collectible.

barbotine: (ceramics) slip made by thinning potter's clay; used to decorate pottery.

bardiglio: (decoration) gray Italian marble with dark veins.

bargello: (needlework) embroidery created by working the thread in shades and stitches that form a sequence of peaks resembling flames. Also called *flamework, Florentine stitch,* and *Hungarian point.*

bargeman jug: (ceramics) a very rare type of Toby jug.

barometer: (scientific instruments) a device used to measure atmospheric pressure.

barong: (weapons) a large knife of the Moros (Borneo, Philippines). The blade is about 16 inches long by 21 inches wide. There is no guard and the hilt curves like a pistol butt.

baroque: (furniture) a 17th-century Italian architectural style characterized by prolific foliage and lavish use of curves, scrolls, volutes, and the like.

barrel-back table: (furniture) table with two leaves on either side of a cylinder the same length as the leaves. When the leaves are down, they resemble the covers of a book and the cylinder looks like the spine of a book. When the leaves are up, they meet in the center of the table and the cylinder is completely covered. Common between 1790 and 1870. Also called *bible-back table* and *book-back table.*

barrel helm: (armor) a large, barrel-shaped helmet that encloses the head; worn over a light helmet or hood of mail during battle. 13th century.

bars: (stamps) heavy, black horizontal lines used to block out a stamp's former value when its denomination is changed.

basal rim: (glass) the rim at the base of a paperweight with a concave bottom.

basalt ware: (ceramics) black, fine-grained, unglazed ware. The iron and manganese in this stoneware are what make it black, resembling the mineral basalt. Wedgewood perfected the method for making basalt ware. Many other companies including Palmer, Turner, Mayer, and Hollins copied Wedgewood and produced their own lines.

baseball cards: (collectibles) cards depicting baseball players from all the major teams. Those featuring superstars are the most valuable. Age and condition dictate price. Players in the Baseball Hall of Fame are particularly sought as are rookie cards, those from the first year of a player's career. Two of the companies that currently produce baseball cards are Bowman and Topps. Some of the older cards were giveaways with tobacco, gum, or candy.

baselard: (weapons) a dagger or short sword carried by civilians in the 15th century.

base metal: (materials) usually an alloy containing lead; used for inexpensive castings and/or as a base for plating with bronze, silver, or gold. See also *white metal.*

basin: (domestic) a bowl for washing hands and face. Larger size was used for laundry.

basinet: (armor) a 14th-century widely used light helmet.

basket-hilted sword: (weapons) a usually wide-bladed sword that has a basket-shaped handle that covers the hand. A favorite of the cavalry in the 1600s.

basketry: (Native American) light, durable baskets made in large quantities by Native Americans. Iroquois, Micmac, and Passamaquoddy nations still produce many splint and sweet-grass baskets. Pine needles and sugar cane are used by the Southeastern nations. The tightly coiled baskets made in the Southwest are by far the most prized. Quality and design are more important than age to the collector.

bas-relief: (decoration) a design carved or molded into an item, raised slightly from the surface of the object. Also called *basso-relievo*.

basse taille: (jewelry) jewelry with a transparent enamel applied over an engraved metal surface.

basso-relievo: (decoration) a design carved or molded into an item, raised slightly from the surface of the object. Also called *bas-relief*.

basting spoon: (kitchen) a large spoon or ladle used for pouring juices over cooking meat to keep it from drying out.

batardeau: (weapons) a knife carried in a pocket in the sword sheath. Late 16th century.

Batavian ware: (ceramics) a Chinese porcelain characterized by the famille rose pattern on a shiny brown background. Dates to early 1700s.

Batchelder: (ceramics) decorative tiles with designs that reflect the Arts and Crafts movement. Produced from 1900 to 1916 by Ernest Batchelder. The tiles are marked with a die stamp and are collectible.

Bateman, Hester: (silver) a leading 18th-century English silversmith. Hester Bateman's mark appears on all her pieces.

bath metal toy: a toy made of a copper and zinc alloy.

batik: (textiles) a method of printing cloth. Areas that aren't to be dyed are coated with wax so they'll reject the dye. Originated in Indonesia.

batsto: (kitchen) a fine type of ironware made from 1776 on in New Jersey. The wares included skillets, cookpots, and fish pots, and were considered better than the British ironware.

batter jug: (kitchen) jugs with a spout for pouring. Batter jugs were used to make cowlines, a treat similar in consistency to pancakes. The batter for cowlines was poured in a long line on a hot griddle, then it was cut in manageable lengths and served with syrup or preserves.

Battersea: (enamel) exquisite enamelware made from about 1754 to 1756 by Stephen Janssen in his factory at Battersea, England. Battersea is enamel worked over metal — usually copper. Boxes are the most common examples of this art. Many of them are signed. In 1756, Janssen declared bankruptcy. Much of his fine work, including snuffboxes, pictures, cases, perfume bottles, buttons, knobs, lids, and jewelry boxes, is still around. Enamelwork produced at a later time is sometimes passed off as Battersea, but the quality is inferior to the Battersea produced in the Janssen years.

battery works: (metal) an early term for a foundry where brass was made and brass objects were shaped.

battleship tray: (glass) a pressed glass box made in the shape of one of the warships owned by the U.S. Navy in the 1890s. The *Oregon* and the *Wheeling* are two of the ships portrayed. Originally sold as inexpensive novelties, these are now collectible.

baudekin: (textiles) a fabric that has a warp of gold thread and a woof of silk.

Bauhaus school: (design) founded in Germany by Walter Gropius in 1919, a school that attempted to blend the aesthetic with the practical in teaching architecture and design. The Bauhaus school brought together architects, painters, and designers to establish goals for the visual arts in the 20th century and, in response to industrialization and the Arts and Crafts movement, find ways to bring the high-quality aesthetics of handcrafts to the firmly established world of mass production. The Bauhaus style is characterized by clean, uncluttered lines with an emphasis on function.

Bavarian china: china made by many companies in the Bavarian section of Germany prior to World War II. Much of it was made for export to the United States, so there is no shortage of this fairly good-quality china at auctions, antiques shops, and even flea markets.

Baxter print: a print by George Baxter, who perfected the oil-color picture printing method in 1835. Blocks were inked and used to impress pictures on paper or canvas. Each block contributed a different color and a different part of the whole picture. The process gets its name from the oil-based ink that is used. Baxter continued his work until about 1860, producing hundreds of prints ranging from postage stamp to folio size. In 1837 he published *The Pictorial Album or Cabinet of Paintings,* a compilation of his work until that time.

beaded poke: (fashion accessories) a beaded bag or purse.

beading: (furniture) a decorative strip resembling a strand of beads or pearls.

bead molding: (furniture, architecture) a line of beads made of materials like wood, metal, or plaster; used to decorate furniture, frames, and architectural appointments. Enjoyed great popularity in the 18th century.

beaker: a large wide-mouthed drinking cup. Also a glass container with pouring lip used in laboratory work.

bearing: (armor) the figure within a heraldic design. Also called *charge.*

bear jug: (ceramics) a jug in the shape of a bear hugging a dog. The bear's head is removable and serves as a cup. First made in white salt glaze in Staffordshire during the early 18th century. In the latter part of the 18th century and into the early 19th century,

they were made in brown stoneware and in enamelware.

bears signature: (fine art) a piece of art that has an artist's signature on it, but which may not actually have been done by that artist.

beaten: (metal) brass, copper, or other metal objects with designs hammered out. Also refers to the older hand-worked method of beating molten brass into sheets or into objects such as bowls and hardware. Also called *hammered.*

Beau Brummell: (furniture) bedroom furniture designed for men, particularly a man's dressing table with a mirror and drawers.

beaufat cupboard: (furniture) a corner cupboard. Beaufats are usually built into the corner of a room, but some of them are portable pieces of furniture.

beaufat chair: (furniture) a chair built so that it fits snugly into a corner.

bec-de-corbin: (weapons) war hammer in use from the early 15th century.

becket: (furniture) a grip made of rope; used largely on early pioneer furniture.

bedouh: (weapons) an Arabic talisman found on sword blades. It is a square divided into smaller squares, each containing a letter or number.

bed pole: (furniture accessories) a long pole or wand used to even out sheets on high beds.

bedpost clock: a wall-hanging brass-cased clock affixed between a set of posts. *Ca.* 17th and 18th century.

bed steps: (furniture) movable steps used to climb onto high beds. They usually consist of three stairs.

bed warmer: (domestic) a long-handled round, oblong, or oval container for hot coals. The coal-filled metal container was passed between the covers to warm a bed. Silver bedwarmers are rare. Also called *warming pan*.

beefeater flagon: (pewter) a pewter vessel with a lid that resembles the headgear worn by the beefeaters at the Tower of London.

beehive chair: (furniture) chairs woven of rushes in a conical shape during the 1600s and 1700s. These early chairs resemble later wicker chairs.

beehive clock: a small shelf clock resembling a beehive or old-fashioned flatiron. *Ca.* 1860.

beer firkin: (domestic) a nine-gallon wooden container for beer.

beetle: (tools) an iron wedge used to split logs.

beggar's block: (textiles) a quilt made from scraps of material with little thought to design. The pieces used in the quilt were often contributed by friends and family, hence the name *beggar's block*.

belcher chain: (jewelry) a chain worn in the 19th century consisting of broad, equal-sized links.

bellarmine: (ceramics) a large drinking jug in the shape of a man with a pot belly and a bearded face. Said to be designed to resemble Cardinal Bellarmino. Made in Germany from 1700s to present.

Belleek: (ceramics) a delicate, translucent porcelain with a pearly glaze and intricate designs. First produced in 1857 at D. McBirney & Company in Belleek, Ireland. Lattice work, twig-shaped handles, and applied floral and leaf designs adorn much Irish Belleek. The factory is now called Belleek Pottery Limited. American Companies have copied Irish Belleek. Firms producing collectible American Belleek include American Art China Works; American Belleek Co., Inc.; Ceramic Art Company; Knowles; Taylor & Knowles China Co.; Lenox, Inc.; Ott & Brewer; and Willets Manufacturing Co.

bell flower: (decoration) ornamental floral bud design used on Victorian furniture.

bell ringers' jug: (pewter) a jug for serving ale to the men who rang church bells. These jugs were sometimes kept in the church tower, but were more commonly found in the home of one of the bell ringers where all the men congregated for a bit of cheer.

belly flagon: (barber shop memorabilia) a body-fitting vessel held in the laps of customers in barber shops to catch falling hair and shaving cream.

Belter, John Henry (1804-1863): (furniture) well-known American maker of rococo furniture in the late 19th century.

belt hook: (weapons) a flat hook on the side of a pistol or flask for hanging the object from the belt.

Belper pottery: a plain, brown ware made from 1750 until about 1834 in England. Much of it is incised with the word *Belper*.

Benares ware: (metal) an engraved, chased, and embossed Indian brass.

beni: (orientalia, prints) A substance obtained from saffron flowers and made into either pink or red pigment; used on Japanese prints. See also *beni-ye*.

beni-ye: (orientalia, prints) a Japanese print done in beni pink and one other color, generally green. See also *beni*.

ben kit: (domestic) a large wooden receptacle for storing grains and other provisions. These barrels were also used for pickling. Also called *band kit* and *bow kit*.

Bennett, John: (ceramics) artisan who decorated earthenware from his studios in New York City and New Jersey from 1876 until 1882. He used the experience he'd had working for Doulton in England to produce beautiful vases and other decorative pieces. His wares are marked "J. Bennett, NY" or "West Orange, NJ."

benoiton chain: (jewelry) a chain worn on the head that falls on both sides of the face and onto the chest in a circle.

bentwood: (furniture) wood made pliable by steaming, then bent into various shapes. The Victorian bentwood rocking chair is an example.

berdiche: (weapons) a poleax used in Europe and the Near East from the 15th to the 17th century.

bergere: (furniture) a French upholstered armchair with a loose, wide cushion. Mid- to late-18th century.

Berlin ware: (metal) a tinware made in Berlin, Connecticut, from the mid-18th to the mid-19th century.

Berlin wool: (textiles) a soft, thick wool used in hooking because it covers canvas well. Most examples are brightly colored. Popular in Germany in the 1800s.

Berlin work: (needlework) needlework featuring designs worked in — a popular pastime for Victorian ladies. So called because the wool and canvas usually came from Berlin, Germany.

berrettino: (ceramics) a blue glaze that could range from light to quite dark in tone; used on maiolica. Dates from the 16th century.

berry bowl: (tableware) a round bowl. Often there is one large or master bowl and a number of small, matching bowls for individual servings. Together the pieces are called a *berry set.*

besagues: (armor) plates laced over the openings between the shoulder and breast plates of armor at the armpits. 15th century.

bespoke tradesman: craftsman who carried no stock but made everything to order.

Beswick: (ceramics) Producer of collectible figurines. Although Beswick started producing dinnerware in 1890, it is the figurines produced since 1936 in which collectors are interested. John Beswick, Ltd., made series of animal figures such as dogs, horses, cats, wolves, and monkeys, as well as figures from children's film and fiction, including Beatrix Potter and Disney characters. In 1973, they became part of the Doulton Company. The mark "Beswick" is stamped on each figure.

Betty: a small vessel for holding whale oil.

beveled: (decoration) having edges that slant. Often used to describe book, mirror, or furniture edges.

bezanted: (armor) 14th-century armor made of small coin-sized plates of metal that are riveted or sewn to leather or cloth.

bezel: 1. (clocks) the metal surrounding the glass face of a clock or watch. **2.** (ceramics) the inside rim of a lid of a pot or other vessel. **3.** (jewelry) the setting for a stone in a ring.

bianco sopra bianco: (ceramics) literally, white on white. Used in reference to a white decoration on blue or gray pottery. It was first used in Italy, then adopted at delftware factories in Liverpool, Bristol, and Lambeth, England, in 1750.

bibelot: an attractive trinket, small object, or knickknack.

bible-back table: (furniture) table with two leaves on either side of a cylinder the same length as the leaves. When the leaves are down, they resemble the covers of a book and the cylinder looks like the spine of a book. When the leaves are up, they meet in the center of the table and the cylinder is completely covered. Common between 1790 and

19

1870. Also called *barrel-back table* and *book-back table*.

bible box: (wood) a box, either carved or plain, made to house a bible. They usually have a flat lid, although some have slanted lids. These boxes traditionally don't have locks, signifying that the bible should not be locked away from anyone who wishes to use it.

bicolor: (stamps) a stamp printed in two colors prior to the late 1950s, when multicolor stamp printing was introduced.

biddery: (metal) wares made of an alloy of copper, lead, and tin in India. The alloy was inlaid with silver and then the metal was blackened. It was imported to America just after the Revolution.

Biedermeier: (design) unpretentious, informal German furniture from the period from 1820 to 1850.

biggin: an early pint-size coffee percolator; used at *biggin time,* which was akin to our coffee breaks. A biggin holds enough coffee for one person.

Big Little Book: (books, collectibles) a thick, square children's book originally published by Whitman Publishing Company from the 1930s on. Big Little Books were forerunners of comic books and they fell from favor in the 1950s when comic books took over. Buck Rogers, Dick Tracy, Donald Duck, Terry and the Pirates, and Tom Mix are a few of the Big Little Book heroes.

bijin: (orientalia) the Japanese term for a lovely girl.

bijouterie: French jewelry box.

bilbao mirror: (furniture) a mirror with a wooden frame covered with a marble veneer. Made in France between the 1700s and early 1800s.

billet: a small lever above the hinge on a covered vessel that allows the lid to be raised by the thumb. Common to flagons and tankards. Also called *thumbpiece.*

bilsted: (furniture) the wood of the sweet gum or liquid amber tree; used in America as a substitute for mahogany in the latter part of the 18th century.

Binche lace: (textiles) a very closely woven, delicate pillow lace.

Bing and Grondahl: (ceramics) makers of porcelain plaques and figurines. Bing and Grondahl started business in Copenhagen, Denmark in 1853. They are still in business producing dinnerware and the underglazed, Copenhagen-blue annual Christmas plates and figurines for which they are famous. Most pieces are marked with "B&G," a castle, and the words "Made in Denmark."

bin label: (ceramics) a pottery label that was hung from a hook by a bin in a wine cellar. It identified the contents of that bin; used as early as the 1600s. Originally made at the Lambeth Potteries. Staffordshire also made bin labels.

binnacle: (marine) housing and stand that support the ship's compass.

birch: (materials) a close-grained hardwood of a whitish color; widely used in England and America during the 18th century for cabinet work.

bird-back chair: (furniture) a chair with a back that is carved to depict the silhouettes of two birds facing each other.

bird-cage support: (furniture) a support with a central pivot and four short balusters which allow the top to tilt and turn.

bird call: (ceramics) a whistle in a bird shape. Legend has it the bird call was built into chimneys to ward off evil.

bird's-eye maple: (furniture) a pattern of a wood grain found in some maple trees that suggests a bird's eye.

biscuit: (ceramics) a ceramic piece that has received one firing and has not yet been glazed.

bisect: (stamps) a stamp cut in half with each section retaining half the value of the stamp's denomination. To verify authenticity, bisects must be on covers. There are no official U.S. bisects.

bishop's bottle: (ceramics, glass) a glass or china bottle shaped like a coachman with a high hat. First made in the 1840s by Fenton. Also called *coachman bottle*.

bishop's mantle: (armor) a cloak of mail worn alone or over armor from the mid-15th to the mid-16th century.

bismuth: (metal) metal that is mixed with pewter to harden it.

bisque: (materials) an unglazed porcelain used for figurines and other art objects as well as for heads, feet, hands, and occasionally bodies of dolls. These objects are clearly distinguishable from glazed objects by their matte finish. Painted bisque figurines were popular during the Victorian era. Some are artist-signed or bear the factory mark, but most are unsigned. The more expert and detailed the features and decoration, the more valuable the piece.

bit: (coins) one-eighth of a Spanish dollar.

bitstone: (ceramics) a coarse, crushed quartz spread on the bottom of a sagger or kiln to prevent wares from sticking to the surface during firing.

bittlin: (kitchen) a milk bowl. It can be of china, glass, pottery, or wood.

black amethyst glass: a black glass that has a purple glow when held to strong light. Black amethyst glass is sometimes decorated, sometimes plain. It was, and still is, made by many glass houses. Few examples are marked.

black armor: armor that is painted or blackened to prevent rust.

black bottle: considered the ideal vessel in which to protect wines; widely used for this purpose during the 18th century. Black bottles are really brown or dark green.

black clockwork toy: (black memorabilia, toys) an animated black figure operated by interlocking gears and coil springs. Many of these toys portray blacks in unflattering roles. The most collectible were made from 1870 to 1900.

black-glazed pottery: black or brown glazed earthenware with a glossy finish. Originated in England *ca.* 1750.

blackjack: (leather) a tankard made of leather that sometimes has a silver rim. An original blackjack dates to the 1600s or 1700s, but these tankards have been reproduced — usually with more splendor than the old ones have.

black light: an ultraviolet light used by antiques and art dealers and collectors to detect repairs in porcelain, glass, furniture, figures, and other antiques, and to reveal overpainting, and added or deleted marks and signatures in art work. They work in the dark. When a black light is passed over an object, any defect or repair shows up black or purple.

black memorabilia: people of all races have become interested in collecting memorabilia that chronicles the role of African-Americans in American society. Some of these items are insulting to the black race and depict blacks in "Uncle Tom" situations; other pieces show blacks contributing to American heritage. Collectibles include magazines, figurines, cookbooks, records and sheet music, dolls, vases, toys, and games.

black metal: (metal) a poor quality of pewter.

black walnut: (materials) a dark, straight-grained wood popular with American cabinet makers in the early 19th century.

black work: (needlework) black silk thread embroidered in scrolls, leaves, grapes, and the like on a black or white ground, usually linen. Popular in the 16th and 17th centuries. Also called *Spanish work.*

blanc-de-chine: (ceramics, figurines) porcelain and figurines dating back to the Ming dynasty. Blanc-de-chine ranges in color from deep ivory to bluish white. The figures of Buddhist dieties were made at Te-Hua in the Fukien province. Some of these figurines depict Caucasians in typical Chinese settings.

blanket chest: (furniture) a large, rectangular wood chest for storing bedding.

blanket crane: (domestic) crane that served two purposes. First, the long tapered arm that swings out from either fireside or doorway was used to dry clothing and bedding on rainy or winter days. Second, a blanket was hung on the arm, which swung over the door or fireplace opening to keep drafts from the room.

blanking press: (coins) press used to cut or stamp coin blanks.

blazes: (glass) designs on glass made by cutting a series of upright or slanted lines in deep relief.

bleached: (furniture) darker woods that have been chemically blanched.

bleed: (prints) an image that extends beyond the edges of the paper on which it's printed, leaving the missing part of the image to the viewer's imagination.

bleu persan: (ceramics) pottery with an opaque white, oriental-stye design painted over a dark blue background. Originally made at the Nevers factory, then copied by English potteries.

blind: (furniture) nonfunctional facings resembling doors or drawers. Blind doors or drawers were built into pieces of furniture to make them look balanced or to decorate them.

blind printing: embossing.

blind tooling: (textiles, books) an impression made on textiles and book bindings and covers with a die stamp, a tool, or a roller. The design stands without any color.

block: (stamps) a group of four or more attached stamps, two or more rows across and deep.

block book: (books) a book in which the illustrations are done by wood engravings or woodcuts that were created the exact size of the page on which they were to be printed. Used extensively in the 15th century, especially to produce religious books.

blocked textiles: any textiles that have been decorated by means of block printing; used since 2500 B.C. See also *block printing.*

block foot: (furniture) a square foot at the base of a straight, untapered leg.

block front: (furniture) cabinetwork in which drawer fronts and doors have swelled projections instead of flat panels. The blocked, or protruding, area and the rest of the drawers or doors are cut from one solid piece of wood. Of particular distinction are the block-and-shell carved fronts by the Townsend and Goddard families of Newport. *Ca.* 18th century.

block printing: 1. (books) a design on the cover of a book or an illustration in a book that is achieved by the use of a piece of wood or metal with an engraved image. 2. (textiles) designs applied to materials by using blocks into which designs have been cut in relief. Sometimes a coppered block — a block with the design outlined in copper strips that have been hammered into the wooden block — was used. With this method, the areas that were used to print color were covered with felt material. See also *blocked textiles*.

block tinware: (kitchen) pure tin cooking and table utensils used from 1790 until about 1830.

blonde lace: (textiles) a French silk pillow lace made from the 1740s in the Arras, Lille, and Chantilly regions. Originally, it was made of unbleached silk. Black and white came later.

bloodstone marble: a green quartz marble with red flecks.

bloom: (glass) a dull, opaque film, sometimes found on old English or Irish flint glass; the result of high sulphur fuels used in making the glass.

bloomed gold: (jewelry) gold with a pitted look on a matte finish created by dunking the gold in acid.

blow hole: (metal) a small hole that is pierced in hollow handles, finials, and other applied parts. This hole allows air to be released when the part is heated; the air expands during the process of attaching it to a vessel.

blowing tube: (metal) a long metal tube that widens gradually to a large end that has a base that rests on the floor. The blowing tube was a forerunner of the bellows. To use it, a person placed the wider end near the spot that needed air and blew through a mouthpiece at the other, narrower, end.

blown glass: glass that is blown rather than pressed or molded. Blown glass has a pontil mark left by the pontil (a device for removing the blown object from the pipe). Much glass blown in the 18th century had a metallic content that made small, barely discernible flaws in the item. These provide a method for dating the object. Between 1820 and the 1850s, it was popular to blow glass into molds. Most of these molds were in three parts; the resulting items are called *three-mold* — for example, a three-mold tumbler.

blowpipe: 1. (glass) a long, hollow, iron tube used to blow molten glass. **2.** (weapons) a long tube of cane or wood in which darts are propelled by the breath of the user. Common to South America and Malayan countries.

blue-and-white stoneware: (ceramics) utilitarian items of blue-and-white pottery, made by many American potters from the late 1890s until about 1930. Burley Winter and Roseville were just two of the companies producing this now highly collectible ware. The pitchers, crocks, coffeepots, mugs, soap dishes, wash sets, and other domestic pieces were well-used and few survived without a ding or hairline crack. Perfect examples and those with clearly raised designs and strong color bring the most money.

bluebird china: (tableware) a transfer china dinnerware that was made, with some variation, by several American potteries from about the turn of the century until the 1930s. Bluebird china depicts bluebirds in flight amid a profusion of pink, flowering branches. Carrolton, Homer Laughlin, and Limoges of Sebring, Ohio, were a few manufacturers.

blue-dash charger: (ceramics) a decorative, tin-glazed earthenware plate adorned with figures or flowers and with blue dashes around the edges. These delftware plates were made from 1614 until about 1740.

blue milk glass: a light blue opaque glass. Also called *delphite glass*.

Blue Ridge: (ceramics) from 1935 until 1956, Southern Potteries of Tennessee produced Blue Ridge dinnerware in eight styles. In the 1940s, they added a line of designer plates and in the 1950s, they started making character jugs. All Blue Ridge is hand-painted underglaze. French Peasant is their most desirable pattern.

blue spatter ware: (ceramics) during the first half of the 19th century, blue spatter ware was made in the Staffordshire section of England for export to the United States. The outer edges of the pieces are decorated in a heavy blue spatter that lessens as it goes toward the center, which usually has a design on a plain background.

blue tint: (glass) a faint bluish cast that occurs sometimes in flint glass; caused when glass is made with lead oxide from lead mined in Derbyshire, England. Much old Waterford glass has this characteristic.

blunderbuss: (weapons) a short musket with a wide bore and a flaring muzzle. From 16th century.

board chest: (furniture) a plain, unadorned chest made of boards.

bobbin lace: (textiles) lace made by arranging pins in a pattern, then twisting threads from bobbins around the pins. Also called *bolster lace* and *pillow lace*.

bobbin turning: (furniture) turned chair legs, stretchers, and so on, with swellings that resemble a row of bobbins. Common on late-18th-century Windsor chairs.

bobeche: 1. (lighting) the collar on a candle socket to catch drippings. **2.** (lighting) the device that holds suspended prisms on a chandelier or candelabra.

bocage: (ceramics) a background of trees or foliage on decorated porcelain or earthenware. Popular in the 18th and 19th centuries.

boccaro ware: (ceramics) a name often used to describe Yi-hsing stoneware.

Boch Freres: (ceramics) from 1840 until 1907, the company that produced a line of art pottery that mimicked ceramics from the 18th century. Although the firm won worldwide acclaim for some of their sculptures in 1844, their products were sold mainly in their native Belgium. Charles Catteau was responsible for giving Boch Freres its reputation. Catteau became head of their art department in 1907 and changed much of the designing to reflect the art nouveau form. His designs were lauded at the Exhibit of Decorative Arts in Paris in 1925. Many of his pieces are signed with his name. He left the company, which is still in operation, in 1950.

Boehm: (ceramics) firm that produced figurines of animals, birds, and flowers. In 1953 Edward Marshall Boehm founded Osso Ceramics in Trenton, New Jersey. In 1969 Boehm died and his wife changed the company name to Edward Marshall Boehm, Inc. Today they produce collector plates as well as the figurines. Most pieces are marked "Boehm" with a horse head.

bogie rugge: a lamb's skin.

bogus: (stamps) a fictitious stamp of a real or fictitious country.

bog wood: (materials, jewelry) a natural product of the bogs in Ireland used during the Victorian era to make jewelry.

Bohemian glass: glass first produced in late-17th-century Bohemia. Most commonly ruby-colored, but blue, green, amber, and amethyst examples are also available. There are two types of Bohemian glass to be found on today's antique market. One has a color overlay that has been etched or cut to clear crystal to form a design. The second, more intricate Bohemian glass is made in three colored layers. When the layers are cut through, the design exposes all of the colors. This is often also decorated with colored enamels.

boite à portrait: (household accessories) small, ornate box used to store snuff during the 1700s. They had small portraits set in the tops.

Bokhara work: (needlework) a brightly colored embroidery featuring large floral designs done with a chain stitch or a diagonal oriental stitch; widely used on coverlets and sofa covers during the 1700s.

bolas: (weapons) an Indian weapon of the South American Plains. It consists of a cord with a stone ball attached to each end. There is usually a second cord with a smaller ball attached to the middle of the first cord. It is used as a handle to whirl the main cord and balls about the head. When the velocity is sufficient, the bolas is released to wrap around the legs of the animal being hunted, thereby disabling it. A similar, but lighter, weapon is used by Eskimos to catch ducks, geese, and other large birds.

bole: (ceramics) a red clay.

bolection molding: (architecture) the heavy molding framing a fireplace.

bolo: (weapons) literally Spanish for *knife*, but in the Philippines it applies to a sword or long knife. The word is most often used to describe a chopper or jungle knife.

bolster lace: (textiles) lace made by arranging pins in a pattern, then twisting threads from bobbins around the pins. Also called *bobbin lace* and *pillow lace*.

bolt: (weapons) the arrow for a crossbow. It is shorter and heavier than arrows used with the longbow. Also called *carreau* and *quarrel*.

bombazine: (textiles) an unglazed, very plain twill material.

bombé: (furniture) outswelling, curving, or bulging. Term used to describe a chest with a bulging front. In fashion from Louis XV period.

bonbon dish: an uncovered candy dish, named after the chocolate- or fondant- covered candies which are served in them.

bonbonniere: (household accessories) a small, decorated box used for candy. Made of materials like gold, silver, or porcelain.

boncours: (textiles) a tapestry material used in the 1600s.

bone china: (ceramics) a hard-paste porcelain containing up to 40 percent bone ash; used in English porcelain since 1800. Invented by Josiah Spode.

bone lace: (textiles) lace made using bobbins made of bone. Bobbins were called *bones*.

bones: (music) two pieces of wood struck together to produce a sound. (In spite of their name, bones are most often made of wood.) Considered the oldest of all musical instruments. They were popular in America in the 1700s and early 1800s and were used in vaudeville acts.

bonheur du jour: (furniture) a small writing table, usually with a cupboard above.

bonnet doll: a doll wearing a hat that is molded as part of its head. Also called *hatted doll*.

bonnet top: (furniture) a top made with a broken arch or pediment (the apex of the arch or triangle is absent).

Bonnin and Morris: (ceramics) a white, glazed earthenware decorated in blue, made by the Southwark Pottery of Philadelphia, Pennsylvania (the company was founded in 1762). This ware is scarce since it was made for only a short time. Marked with a capital *P*.

book-back table: (furniture) table with two leaves on either side of a cylinder the same length as the leaves. When the leaves are down, they resemble the covers of a book and the cylinder looks like the spine of a book. When the leaves are up, they meet in the center of the table and the cylinder is completely covered. Common between 1790 and 1870. Also called *barrel-back table* and *bible-back table*.

book desk: (furniture) a reading stand with a sharply slanted top. From the 1400s and 1500s.

book hinge: (metal) a hinge used on the lids of a jug or coffeepot. The back of this hinge looks like the spine of a book, hence the name. The pins in the hinges were covered with decorative caps.

book matches: (collectibles, advertising memorabilia) invented in the 1850s, book matches were first produced in 1897 by the Diamond Match Company. Since that time more than a million companies have used their covers and the matches themselves for advertising. The first match cover advertised Mendelssohn Opera Company, the second Pabst Brewery, and the third the American Tobacco Company. Those in good condition with all the matches are the most desirable.

book matching: (furniture) two sheets of veneer that are matched so the grain design on one appears to mirror the other.

Book of Hours: (books) a medieval prayer book with prayers assigned to be recited at different hours of the day.

book trough: (furniture) a small table with a V-shaped shelf for holding books.

boomerang: (weapons) a throwing stick, flat and curved with sharp edges, usually of wood. War and hunting boomerangs do not return. The returning boomerang is lighter and thinner with a slightly spiral twist, and confined to Australia. The weapon was used in ancient Egypt, and is still used in India, parts of Africa, and other areas of the world.

boot bottle: (ceramics) a pottery vessel in a novelty shape, such as a shoe or boot. Made in England from the 1700s on.

bootjack: (domestic) a metal or wooden device with a V-shaped notch to make the task of removing boots easier.

boot scraper: (domestic) metal, often ornate, devices that provided an edge on which people could scrape mud from boots and shoes before entering the house. Most doorsteps in the 1800s and early 1900s boasted a boot scraper.

borax: (furniture) cheap, mass-produced, gaudy furniture of poor quality. Made in the 1920s and 1930s.

borel: (textiles) a coarse, poor-quality wool cloth.

bosnian stitching: (textiles) a background or filler stitching consisting of straight stitches that meet at diagonal angles.

bosom bottle: (fashion accessories) a tiny holder of brass, glass, pewter, silver, tin, or other suitable material; used to hold flowers to be worn on a boot or discreetly placed between a lady's breasts. Fashionable in the 1700s.

boss: 1. (furniture) a round or oval knoblike swelling used as ornamentation. See also *embossed*. **2.** (books) a metal ornament used to protect the corners of books.

Boston and Sandwich Glass Works: glass company founded in 1825 by Deming Jarves in Sandwich, Massachusetts. The company continued in operation until 1888, producing fine glassware, including cut glass and Bohemian-type glass.

Boston rocker: (furniture) 19th-century American wooden rocking chair with an S- curved seat, high, spindled back, and usually a head-piece. Stenciled decorations over a black lacquer finish were common.

Boston Silver Glass Company (The): One of the leading manufacturers of mercury glass (hollow blown-glass objects filled with mercury).

boteh: (floor coverings) a popular Persian rug design featuring clusters of leaves.

bottle molding: (decoration) a round molding.

bottles: (collectibles, glass) old bottles have found favor among collectors. Barber's bottles, perfume bottles, figural bottles, ink bottles, medicine bottles, sarsaparilla bottles, liquor bottles, and the like are all desirable. Serious collectors only want examples made before 1900.

bottles slider: (tableware) a tray with wheels on it designed for sliding bottles and other containers across the dining table.

bouche: (weapons) a notch in the upper-right-hand corner of a shield for aiming the lance without exposing the arm. From the early 15th century.

bouchette: (armor) a large buckle on the Gothic breast-plate used to fasten together the upper and lower parts.

boudoir doll: large doll made as a decoration for a woman's bedroom; not a child's play-thing.

bough pot: (ceramics) pot made of porcelain or china fit-ted with a perforated cover to accommodate the stems of pussy willows, forsythia, fruit blossoms, and the like.

Boulle, Andre-Charles (1642-1732): (furniture) chief cabinetmaker to Louis XIV of France. See also *Buhl.*

boulting hutch: (furniture) a wooden hutch into which flour was sifted through a fine-meshed cloth.

Boulton, Matthew (1728-1809): (silver) a leading English silversmith. Boulton's mark appears on all his work.

bourdon: (weapons) a light, hollow 15th-century lance. Also called *bourdonasse.*

bourdonasse: (weapons) a light, hollow 15th-century lance. Also called *bourdon.*

bourse: (stamps) a market or fair where stamps are sold or traded.

bow: 1. (weapons) the oldest and most widely used weapon for shooting projectiles. The simple bow is a length of wood tapering from the middle to-ward the two ends, which are connected by a short piece of twine. The length of the bows ranges from 2 feet to over 8 feet — both extremes found in Japan. **2.** (weapons) the finger guard of a knife or sword.

bow kit: (domestic) a large wooden receptacle for storing grains and other provisions. These barrels were also used for pickling. Also called *band kit* and *ben kit.*

Bowie knife: (weapons) a large, single-edged fighting knife with a hilt and cross-piece. Designed by James, or his brother Rezin, Bowie; early 1800s.

bow-top chair: (furniture) a chair with a top rail that has one low, unbroken curve across its entire width.

box: a storage container, usu-ally rectangular, but may be round or of other shapes. Known since ancient Egypt and Rome. Many materials have been used to make boxes including, gold, silver, papier-maché, and wood.

box camera: (photography) the first camera to use a roll of film rather than a plate. Invented by George Eastman in 1888.

box comb: (fashion accessories) a comb for the hair made from boxwood.

box compass: (scientific instruments) a nautical compass suspended within a box by gimbals to keep it level.

box inkstand: (metal) an inkstand with a box that has one or two drawers supporting one or two inkwells. Made of brass, silver, pewter, or white metal.

box iron: (domestic) a late-19th-century flatiron used for ironing clothes. This type of iron was heated with hot metal slugs that were placed in the iron through a hinged door in the back.

box stretcher: (furniture) a square or rectangular brace connecting the legs of a chair, table, or cabinet.

bracer: (weapons) a wrist guard for archers to prevent injury from the recoil of the bow string. Made of wood, cloth, leather, horn, ivory, or metal.

bracket clock: originally, a clock that was hung high on the wall to allow its weight to hang down. After the spring drive was introduced, the term was applied to shelf or mantel clocks.

bracket foot: (furniture) a plain foot with ornamentation where it is joined to the stretcher or rail. The outer corner edge is straight and the inner edge is curved.

bracket rule: (kitchen) a device for holding bread to be toasted over hot coals.

braconiere: (armor) a narrow plate below the breastplate to which tassels were attached. 16th century.

Bradley and Hubbard: (metal, lighting) from the mid-19th century until around 1915, a company that fashioned household accessories such as lamps, andirons, and inkwells from metal. Many of their products were signed with a triangular-shaped logo bearing the company name and a lamp. The Bradley and Hubbard mark generally adds to the value of the piece.

braid loom: (textiles) a small loom used for braiding and for weaving narrow strips of fabric.

Brampton stoneware: (ceramics) stoneware made during the 1700s and 1800s at Brampton, England. This ware was produced by William Bromley, Robert Brambridge, and other potters of the era. There are two types of Brampton stoneware: one varies in color from buff to red and was made in the form of teapots, coffeepots, and Toby jugs; the other is chocolate brown and often has applied decorations. Many pieces made between 1820 and 1894 have a green glaze on the inside. These are generally dated.

brand: (weapons) a type of sword that hung from a saddle.

brander: (kitchen) a pierced-metal plate, usually with a hoop handle (for hanging it); used to make oatmeal cakes in Scotland.

brandestoc: (weapons) a hatchet with a long thrusting blade concealed in the handle.

brandreth: (kitchen) a metal tripod; used to hold a cooking pot over the fire.

brandy warmer: (kitchen) a tiny saucepan of silver or copper.

brass: (metal) a metal alloy of copper and zinc. It may have lesser amounts of other metals. Color is generally that of gold, but can range from reddish to gray or white, depending upon how much zinc is used. Brass is very ductile, or pliable.

brassard: (armor) plate armor that covers the entire arm. From 13th century.

brasses: 1. (hardware) hardware such as drawer pulls and plates used on furniture. **2.** (metal) brass grave monuments used in England during the Middle Ages.

Brastoff, Sascha: (ceramics) producer of artistic, unusual ashtrays, boxes, candlesticks, figurines, vases, and the like. Winthrop Rockefeller backed Sascha Brastoff by setting him up in business in 1948. At the height of his career, he had 150 employees. Pieces done personally by Brastoff are signed by him. Others are marked "Sascha, B."

brayette: (armor) a metal pouch or codpiece to protect the genitals, 16th century. Also a skirt or breech of mail.

brazier: 1. (metal) a circular receptacle holding a pierced plate on which charcoal is burned. A kettle or other receptacle is set on top to heat. **2.** (metal) one who works with brass.

bread-and-butter plate: (tableware) a plate for bread, usually 6 inches, that matches a set of dishes. Part of each diner's place setting.

breakfront: 1. (furniture) a desk, bookcase, or cupboard with three vertical sections. The center section projects forward, thus breaking the straight line of the front. **2.** (furniture) any cabinet that has a front with at least one recessed and two projecting sections, or two recessed and one projecting sections, creating "breaks" in the front of the cabinet.

breastplate: (armor) one or more plates covering the front of the body from the neck to below the waist. From the Middle Ages.

breath motivated: (toys) motion toys that are operated by blowing on or into them.

breechloader: (weapons) firearm loaded from the breech (rear of the barrel). Dating from the 16th century, breech-loading firearms were not a success until late in the 18th century.

breech of mail: (armor) a short skirt of mail (metal links). Late 16th century. Also called *broyette.*

Breguet: (clocks) a noted French clock maker who improved the mechanisms for pocket watches. Early 1800s.

breloque: (jewelry) an ornament hung on a watch chain or chatelaine.

Breton work: (needlework) embroidery done in colored silks and gold thread, usually in chain and satin stitches; used on borders of various garments and decorative items.

Breuer, Marcel: (furniture, design) Hungarian-born American architect and designer, inventor of the tubular steel chair, early 1900s. Breuer was a principal member of the Bauhaus school.

breweriania: (collectibles) articles connected with the brewing industry. Many collectors concentrate on just one brewery.

Brewster chair: (furniture) a 17th-century Pilgrim-style chair with decorative turned spindles and finials and usually with a rush seat.

brichettes: (armor) armor composed of culettes and tassets hung from the breast and back to protect the loins and hips.

bridal fan: (fashion accessories) a hand-painted fan that was a popular wedding memento. They usually depicted important events in the lives of the bride and groom. The best examples were designed by master fan makers of the day. Other, less costly bridal fans were made for, and presented to, the bride's attendants. Often made of silk, ivory, or paper. From 1720 until the turn of the twentieth century.

bride's basket: (glass, silver) popular decorative object during the Victorian era. These baskets ranged from rather plain to highly ornate, with fluted edges, cased glass, satin glass, enamel decorations, and the like. They were cradled in holders usually made of silver plate and, occasionally, sterling. Holders also ranged from the simple to extravagant, with much repoussé. Both Pairpont and Wilcox were responsible for some of the loveliest holders.

bride's quilt: a quilt with hearts in the design.

bridge fluting: (glass) an applied decoration used on drinking glasses from about 1750 until 1800. This ornamentation was at the point where the stem and bowl meet. Some examples have fluting that extends over part of the bowl itself.

bridge lamp: (lighting) a floor lamp made of wrought iron.

brigandine: (armor) a type of armor widely used in Europe from the 13th to the 15th century and later throughout the East.

bright-cut engraving: (silver) a style of engraving silverware. The metal is removed in a manner that leaves a beveled edge. This makes the design or engraving sparkle, hence the name *bright-cut.*

brilliant-cut: (jewelry, glass) a method of cutting gems or glass that produces the most facets and therefore, the greatest brilliance. Cut this way, diamonds have points at both ends. The best brilliant-cut stones have 58 facets. Diamonds cut in this style, which has been used since the early 1700s, are usually set in open-claw settings.

brilliant mint: (stamps) an early stamp in mint (unmarred) condition and lacking color fade.

briolette: (jewelry) a multifaceted gem in a teardrop shape.

brise fan: (fashion accessories) fan made solely from sticks of ivory, tortoise shell, or horn, joined together with silk ribbons. These fans were introduced in the late 17th century, and remained popular for about one hundred years. Designs were painted directly on the flat sticks or ribs so when the fan was open the entire motif could be appreciated. The tops of the ribs and end pieces of these fans are generally elaborately carved.

Bristol delftware: (ceramics) delftware dating from 1650. Unusual features include plates with straight sides and jugs with openwork necks formed by intersecting circles. The glaze used on this ware often has a lavender-blue tint. Borders often include sprays of leaves.

Bristol glass: made in Bristol, England, a semi-opaque opaline glass from which many English, French, German, Italian, and American companies made bottles, biscuit jars, dishes, vases, and the like to compete with the higher-priced glass that was being produced in the 18th and 19th centuries.

Bristol penny toy: a wooden toy with wheels. Made in the 1800s and sold on the streets of London.

Bristol porcelain: 1. a hard-paste porcelain made by Richard Champion at Bristol from 1770 to 1781, when he sold his rights to Staffordshire Potters. Champion's translucent wares are elegant. He favored leaf green and clear, deep red in the floral sprays. Unusual shapes, such as teapots that resemble inverted pears, are characteristic. He also made sets of figurines depicting Venus and Adonis, the seasons, and the elements. **2.** a soft-paste porcelain made by Benjamin Lund. Few pieces have survived the years since it was made in the mid-18th century — there are some figurines and an occasional sauceboat. These are generally marked "Bristol" or "Bristol 1750."

Britannia: 1. (coins) the seated female figure on British coins. **2.** (metal) an alloy similar to pewter; used to make objects common to pewter or as a base for silver plate.

broad arrow: (weapons) arrow with a broad, barbed head used at sea to damage sails and rigging. 14th and 15th centuries.

broadglass: a flat sheet of glass.

broadside: (paper) a large sheet of paper with printing on one side — an early notice, advertisement, or poster; used to convey information to mass audiences. Some are plain; others quite ornate. Value is determined by importance of subject matter and rarity.

broadsword: (weapons) a large cutting sword with a wide blade. May have two or four cutting edges. The term generally refers to the basket-hilted sword of the 17th- and 18th-century cavalry.

brocade: (textiles) heavy embossed fabric used for upholstery.

broderie Anglaise: (needlework) white-work embroidery with spaces cut or punched out, often with a stiletto. The edges of the holes are overcast. This work is now commonly referred to as eyelet. The best examples were made in the late 18th and early 19th centuries; used to adorn baby clothes, underwear, and the sleeves of dressy garments.

broken arch: (furniture) a cornice on a piece of furniture that lacks a central section. Also called *broken pediment.*

broken corner: (furniture) a corner cut off from the convergent sides.

broken pediment: (furniture) a cornice on a piece of furniture that lacks a central section. Also called *broken arch.*

bronze: (metal) a reddish brown alloy of copper and tin. Bronze was the first metal used by man. It is easily cast, chiselled, and engraved.

bronze disease: (metal) bright green spots that form on bronze caused by weather or salts in the atmosphere. The spots spread rapidly and can corrode the metal if not attended to.

brooch: (jewelry) a piece of jewelry that is attached to clothing with a back pin. Brooches are larger than pins.

brooch watch: (jewelry) a watch that is pinned, usually with a back pin, to clothing.

Brouwer: (ceramics) turn-of-the-century potter. In 1894 Theopholis Brouwer began making pottery in New York. He used fire painting, controlling the heat of the kiln. In 1925 he named his firm the Ceramic Flame Company. His beautiful wares bring high prices.

Brownie: (figurines, tableware, advertising memorabilia) an elflike creature with a triangular face, swollen belly, and an expression that mirror surprise; created by Palmer Cox. His characters include The Bellhop, The Chairman, and The London Bobby. Brownies were the delight of children and adults in the late 1800s. They appear on dinnerware and other useful items, and are the subjects of books. Also featured in advertising campaigns: The most notable of the products they represented was the Kodak Brownie Camera.

broyette: (armor) a short skirt of mail (metal links). Late 16th century. Also called *breech of mail.*

brush-stroked: (prints) prints that have been over-painted with a clear substance that leaves brush marks, creating the illusion that the print is actually an original painting.

Brussels lace: (textiles) both needlepoint and pillow lace made in Brussels. They date back to the 1720s.

bucket-form bowl: (glass) the straight-sided bowl of a drinking glass that resembles a bucket. In favor from the 1730s through the 1800s.

buckler: (armor) a shield, usually small and round, held in the left hand while fencing. From the 13th to 17th centuries.

buckling: 1. (fine art) bulges in a painting, usually caused by a canvas that's not correctly stretched. **2.** (fine art) a blister in an oil painting where the paint has raised from the canvas.

Buffalo Pottery: (ceramics) pottery company started by the Larkin Company, makers of soap, in Buffalo, New York, in 1902. Deldare, a tannish, transfer-decorated pottery, is the most popular of this ware. Pieces are marked with a buffalo and dated.

buff coat: (armor) a heavy, long, leather coat worn as armor in the 16th and 17th centuries. Back and breastplates were worn over the coat.

buffe: (armor) a faceguard of plate used with open helmets. From the 15th century. Also called *falling beaver.*

buffet: (furniture) a sideboard, side table, or cupboard used for the storage of china, glasswares, and other tableware.

buffet mirror: (furniture) a long, low mirror often divided into three or four sections. Also called *mantel mirror* and *landscape mirror.*

bugle beads: (decoration) small, cylindrical beads of glass or plastic used to trim clothing and accessories like gowns and purses.

Buhl (or Boulle): (decoration, furniture) a form of furniture decoration. The design is inlaid with tortoise shell, ivory, brass, and other metals of various colors. Also refers to furniture decorated in this manner. Developed by Andre-Charles Boulle. See also *Boulle, Andre-Charles.*

buisine: (music) a trumpet-type brass instrument with a bent tube. 14th century.

bukhara (or bokhara): (floor coverings) rugs with a pattern that is usually black-and-white octagons on red or brownish red.

bulawa: (weapons) a Russian mace.

bulb: (furniture) elongated, rounded form used on chair and table leg stretchers.

bullion: (metal) any precious metal, refined or unrefined, in bars.

bullova: (weapons) a type of fighting axe used in India.

bullroarer: (Native American) a wooden slat attached to a cord that makes a roaring sound when it is whirled about the head.

bull's eye: (stamps) a cancellation or postmark perfectly centered on the stamp.

bull's-eye mirror: (glass) a small, round mirror with either concave or convex glass. The frame is usually ornate and often has a candle holder on each side. These French or English mirrors were popular in the early 1800s.

bultos: (folk art) replicas of saints or religious figures.

bun elements: (furniture) furniture supports shaped like a slightly flattened sphere.

bungaknodori: (armor) a very early padded Japanese armor.

bureau: (furniture) in America, a chest of drawers. In England, a slanted desk.

bureau print: (stamps) a stamp printed by the U.S. Bureau of Printing and Engraving.

burgonet: (armor) a 16th-century open helmet with brim and comb(s). A buffe was usually worn with it.

burl: (furniture) a large, rounded outgrowth where a limb is joined to the trunk of a tree. Usually cut into thin pieces and used as veneer.

burnish: (metal) to polish or rub a piece of metal to obtain a glossy surface.

burst-off penny greenwork: (glass) bottles that have been knocked off the end of the blowing iron instead of being fire finished.

busar: (weapons) a Malayan crossbow.

butler's tray: (furniture) a serving tray mounted on legs or on an X-shaped folding stand. The tray is usually rectangular and fitted with a gallery.

butterfly table: (furniture) a small table with turned legs and drop leaves. The brackets, which swing out to support the leaves, are curved like a butterfly wing at the outer edge.

butter mold: (folk art) a carved wooden mold for butter. During the last half of the 17th century, decorating butter became quite fashionable in Europe. The practice was continued by American farmers who sold butter, along with other products, at farmers' markets. The farmers carved molds or had them carved, and the detail of the designs became fairly competitive. Butter molds portraying cows, eagles, fish, and roosters are the most valuable, but other animals or any mold with an unusual design is highly collectible and should command a good price.

butt-jointed: (furniture) a simple wood joint with the pieces attached end to end. Not very strong.

button: 1. (furniture) a simple, rectangular metal door fastener used on furniture. **2.** (collectibles) fasteners. Buttons may be made of brass, celluloid, china, glass, metal, pearl, plastic, silver, or other materials. Those with shanks and backmarks are considered the most desirable. Button collectors look for examples dating before 1918, the date the National Button Society considers the dividing line between antique and modern buttons.

buttonhook: (domestic) a device for fastening high-button shoes. These fashionable shoes came with a built-in problem — how to get the button through the tight buttonholes. Buttonhooks provided the answer. From the mid-1800s until around 1925, buttonhooks were a staple item in most homes. Many of them are decorative — some with repoussé or figural handles. Others carry advertising, perhaps from a local shoe store. The more elaborate the design and the more valuable the material from which it is made, the more a buttonhook is worth.

butt veneer: a decorative veneer cut from the base of a tree where the roots join the trunk. Also called *stump veneer.*

buyer's premium: (auctions) an amount, usually 10 percent of the purchase price, that a buyer must pay over and above the price he bids for an item at auction. An increasing number of auctioneers are charging a buyer's premium.

bygone: an object that is obsolete.

byrnie: (armor) body armor worn by the Danes in the 10th century.

C

cabaret set: (ceramics) a tea set complete with pot and tray, but having only one or two cups and saucers.

cabasset: (armor) an open helmet in use from the last half of the 16th century through the 17th century. It has a narrow brim and usually a point at the top. Worn by foot soldiers.

cabinet piece: (coins) a mint coin.

cabochon: 1. (jewelry) a highly polished, unfaceted, round or oval stone with a convex form. **2.** (jewelry) natural round stones, polished but uncut.

cabochon ornament: (furniture) oval or round ornament with a hand-carved scrolled-leaf design; used on furniture — most often, midway on legs of chairs — during the mid-18th century.

cabriole fan: (fashion accessories) named for a two-wheel carriage; a fan made of two or three arc-shaped bands of silk and decorated with a painted scene of a cabriole carriage, often carrying the owner of the fan.

cabriole leg: (furniture) a leg that swells outward at the upper part (knee) and inward at the lower part (ankle) to create an S shape. Popular in the 17th and 19th centuries. Also called *bandy leg*.

cachet: (stamps) a design appearing on an envelope or other postal cover, usually to promote or celebrate something of philatelic significance.

caddy spoon: (silver) a spoon used to measure tea kept in a tea caddy; often made in the form of hands, leaves, flowers, and other decorative shapes. Caddy spoons gained favor in better homes around 1780.

Cadogan teapot: (domestic) lidless porcelain or pottery teapot that is filled through a hole in the body of the pot. Made by factories in the Staffordshire section of England. The name "John Mortlock" is frequently incised on these teapots. They are named for the lady who first brought one from China to England.

Caen lace: (textiles) pillow lace made in the style of blonde Chantilly lace.

Cafaggiolo: (ceramics) a leading manufacturer of maiolica during the 15th and 16th centuries.

café au lait glaze: (ceramics) glaze with a soft brown hue; used on Chinese porcelain of the Ch'ing dynasty.

cagework: (gold, silver) an open floral or figural design made of silver or gold that forms a casing for a box or other receptacle. Especially popular in England and Germany in the mid-1700s.

Cairngorm: (jewelry) a yellowish quartz stone found in Cairngorm, Scotland; used in jewelry.

cake basket: (silver) a round or oval basket with reticulated designs; used to serve bread and fruit as well as cake. Cake baskets were introduced in the early 1700s. The earliest round baskets are the rarest. Later, in the 18th century, these baskets were made of wire and decorated with applied flowers or other forms. Still later examples have solid bodies.

cake mold: (kitchen) an aluminum or cast-iron mold in the form of a lamb, rabbit, Santa, or other fanciful shape. The more unusual the shape, the more valuable a cake mold is to a collector.

cake stand: (table accessories) a heavy, flat plate for displaying and serving cake, usually with either three feet or one pedestal. Made of glass, porcelain, or silver; usually round, although some are square.

cakewalk dancer: (black memorabilia, toys) a black

dancer in a swallowtail coat. He is made of tin and stands 9 1/2 inches high. Patented 1879 by J.M. Cromwell. Very valuable.

calash: (fashion accessories) a collapsible bonnet with a frame of wire stays. Worn by women in the 1700s.

caldron: (kitchen) a copper, iron, or brass cooking pot with a round shape, one or two pouring lips, and a bail handle; used over open fires.

calendar plate: (collectibles, advertising) a plate featuring the calendar for a specific year. Many of them were used as premiums and include the name of the business or merchant who gave them away. Those dated before 1920 are the most collectible.

caliber cut: (jewelry) small gems cut in a variety of shapes and used to set off a larger stone.

California Perfume Company: (collectibles) founded in 1886 in New York City, the California Perfume Company became Avon Company, Inc. in 1929. The bottles are highly collectible. Early bottles marked "Goettings & Co., New York," or "Goettings," or "Savoi Et Cie" are the most desireable.

caliver: (weapons) a matchlock gun smaller than a carbine. From late 16th century.

calligraphic drawing: (folk art) a drawing or sketch done with the thick and thin strokes used in calligraphy. Most weren't intended as works of art but were done to demonstrate the penmanship of the artist.

calligraphy: decorative handwriting.

calling card case: (fashion accessories) a Victorian-era case, similar to the business card case of today. Good Victorian manners dictated the use of calling cards, which were left with a maid or family member if the person a visitor

wished to see was not available. Some of these collectible cases are very elaborate and made of silver, ivory, or mother-of-pearl.

Callot figure: (ceramics, silver, gold) a small figure done in the style of Jacques Callot, a French engraver in the early 1600s, who specialized in depicting beggars and comedic figures.

calot: (armor) a steel coif (or cap) worn under a cavalry hat. Late 17th century.

calumet: (Native American) a ceremonial smoking pipe with a long stem and ornamentation; used by North American Indians. Also called *peace pipe*.

camail: (armor) a guard of mail fastened to the basinet to protect the neck and shoulders. From 14th century.

camak: (textiles) a 17th-century material woven of silk and camel hair.

camark: (ceramics) a line of wares similar to Weller. Jack Carnes started the Camden Art and Tile Company in 1926 in Camden, Arkansas. The company name was soon changed to Camark. They closed in 1983 and reopened under new owners in 1986. The wares are usually marked "Camark Pottery." See also *Weller Pottery*.

Cambridge glass: quality glass objects, from dinnerware to animals, produced by the Cambridge Glass Company from 1901 until 1958. Cambridge glass was clear until the 1920s, when color was introduced. Although the company used many marks through the years, the letter *C* in a triangle is the most common mark found on this popular ware.

Cambridge pottery: art pottery made from 1895 until about 1918 in Cambridge, Ohio. The brown-glazed ware has several marks including "Cambridge," "Oakwood," "Otoe," and "Terrhea." The company name was changed to Guernsey in 1904. At that time they started making a line of kitchen ware.

came: (furniture, lighting) a grooved strip of lead used as the divider between pieces of glass in a stained- or leaded-glass window or lampshade.

camel-back chair: (furniture) a chair with two or three humps on the back. On the three-hump chair, the middle hump is higher and dominates; on the two-hump chair, the division between the humps is in the middle of the chair back.

cameo: (jewelry) a stone, shell, piece of coral, or lava with two or more distinctive layers; the top layer is cut in such a way that it creates a design in relief against the underlying, exposed layer.

cameo glass: glass with delicate, multicolored designs made by carving into objects made of several layers of different colors of glass that are bonded, or eased, together. Although this art has been around for more than 2,000 years, it wasn't used extensively until the 18th and 19th centuries, when artisans in the Orient and Near East employed it to create magnificent objects. Originally all the carving was done by hand. Later, copper engraving wheels and acid were employed. Galle, Daum, and Thomas Webb are some of the names associated with fine cameo glass. By the late 1800s, many companies were producing a lower grade of acid-etched cameo glass. A hand-carved piece of cameo glass is quite expensive.

cameo habille: (jewelry) a cameo in which the relief design is the head of a female, and she is wearing jewelry that is actually set into the cameo.

campaign furniture: (furniture) chairs, beds, tables, and chests that either folded for travel or, as in the case of chests, were sturdily constructed to withstand the rough handling in transport under war conditions. *Ca.* 19th century.

campana vase: (household accessories) a bell-shaped vase with a thick pedestal on a square base. Campanas often have two handles. Originated in early 1800s.

Campbell kids: (advertising memorabilia) illustrations by Grace Drayton of chubby-cheeked children used for advertising by the Campbell Soup Company. The Campbell kids' first appearance advertising Campbell's Soup was in 1906. Grace Drayton's version of the characters was used until 1951. The kids have been resurrected, but they have a new, thinner appearance. It is the original Campbell kids that collectors seek. They are featured on salt and pepper shakers, cookbooks, dolls, plates, silver, and other collectibles.

camphene lamp: (lighting) a lamps from *ca.* 1835 to 1875 that was made to burn camphene, an explosive fuel made of alcohol and turpentine.

camphor glass: heavily frosted glass first made during the early 1800s at glass factories in Wheeling, West Virginia, and Pittsburgh, Pennsylvania, and later by other glass makers.

camp mug: (metal) a drinking mug made of pewter or silver; used by military men.

can: (metal, pottery) a cylinder-shaped container with a narrow neck; used to store liquids.

canary luster: (ceramics) pottery made of yellow clay topped with a yellow glaze and decorated with either silver or copper luster and black transfer designs. Produced in Staffordshire, England from *ca.* 1780 until the 1850s.

canceled to order: (stamps) stamps canceled in volume by the issuing country for sale to the trade as used stamps, without going through the mail.

cancellation: (stamps) a mark printed over the face of a stamp showing it has been used.

candelabra: (lighting) a pair of candlesticks each having a number of branches for holding candles. Plural of *candelabrum.*

candelabrum: (lighting) a candlestick with a number of branches for holding candles. Singular of *candelabra.*

candle box: (domestic) container used for storing candles. These square or round receptacles were made of wood or metal.

candle clock: an old and rare clock with a dial on which the numbers have been cut out. The dial revolves, and as the appropriate hour lines up with a square that has been cut from the body of the clock, a lighted candle from within the clock reveals the time. Also called *night clock.*

candle mold: (kitchen) a mold, usually of tin, used to form several candles at one time. Old ones are highly desirable but they have been extensively reproduced.

candle shears: (lighting) small shears for trimming candlewicks. There is a tiny box attached to the shears and the trimmed wicks fall into it.

candle shield: (lighting) a candle shade with pincers that hold the candle. First used about 1770, candle shields were made in many materials including horn, tin, and mica.

candlestick: (lighting) a holder with a cup or spike for candles.

candlewick: 1. (glass) glass items with beading that decorates the edges and forms the handles; made by the Imperial Glass Corporation (a subsidiary of Lenox, Inc.) from 1936 until 1982. Most Candlewick is clear glass, but a few later items are colored. Early candlewick has the most value. All

of this glassware was marked with paper labels. **2.** (needlework) embroidery done in tufts with a soft yarn.

candy container: (household accessories) glass and papier-maché candy dishes made in many shapes, from animals, cars, and other modes of transportation to guns, lanterns, and pianos. These containers were popular from 1876 until 1960 and in recent years have become collectible. They are being reproduced in quantity and it takes a practiced eye to discern the difference between an original and one of recent vintage.

cane: 1. (glass) the mixture of clear and colored glass rods that is basic to millefiori design. **2.** (materials) pliable material derived from any number of woody, flexible plants or trees and used in strips for wickerwork. **3.** (collectibles) a walking stick. Both useful canes and the beautiful glass canes created by glass blowers are collected. Walking canes are treasured for their age and for the gold, ivory, jade, sterling, and hand carving that are often part of them.

cann: (silver) a silver mug that stands on a molded base; most hold one pint.

cannelure: (weapons) grooves in a sword blade to lighten it.

cannon stove: (kitchen) a stove from the 1700s made in the shape of a cannon standing on its wider end.

canopic jar: (ceramics) an ancient Egyptian jar, vase, or urn used to hold the remains of the dead. Named for the ancient city of Canopus.

canopy: (furniture) a horizontal cloth covering used for protection or ornamentation. The rooflike covering over a four-poster bed. Also called *tester.*

Canova, Antonio: (fine art, ceramics) an Italian sculptor in the late 18th and early 19th centuries. Many Staffordshire potters have used Canova's portrait on their china.

cant: (furniture) a slanted edge or surface.

canterbury: (furniture) a stand with partitions to hold sheet music, portfolios, and the like.

Canton enamel: (metal) teapots, trays, bowls, tea caddies, and a host of other objects made of enamel on copper ware in the famille rose style. The best pieces date from the 1700s.

Canton ware: (ceramics) tableware with a blue bridge and other scenery gracing a white porcelain background; made in the area of Canton, China, from *ca.* 1780 until *ca.* 1910. The Chinese produced this ware exclusively for export to the Western world. It was so well received that manufacturers in England and the United States copied the blue-and-white motif on earthenware to give us the popular willowware. Original Canton pieces command a good price in today's market.

capacity mug: (ceramics) a measure made of salt-glazed stoneware from the late 1600s, and of mocha earthenware with a band from the late 1700s.

caparison: an ornamental cover for a horse's saddle or any ornamental clothing.

cap case: traveling bag or a hatbox.

capeline: (armor) a steel or iron cap worn by troops from the 13th through the 14th century.

capital: (architecture, furniture) the head or top structure of a pillar or column.

Capitol coverlet: (textiles) coverlets with a large repeat pattern depicting the Capitol building in Washington, D.C. Between 1835 and 1855, many of these coverlets were signed and dated. Other examples of this type of coverlet were used as blankets for prisoners.

Capo di Monte: (ceramics) originally a soft-paste porcelain made in Italy. While Italian Capo di Monte figurines and dinnerware dating from the mid-1700s are very desirable, the name — along with the original mark of a crown over an *N*—is being used on many items of inferior quality that are mass-produced in Germany, Hungary, and France.

cap of maintenance: (armor) a cap with the family crest mounted on it. Worn over helmets by 14th-century knights.

caramel slag: (glass) glass in shades of chocolate brown first produced in 1900 by Jacob Rosenthal of the Indiana Tumbler and Goblet Company. Other companies copied it. Also called *chocolate glass.*

carbuncle: (jewelry) a cabochon-cut garnet — a highly polished garnet cut in an oval, or round, convex shape without facets.

carcass: (furniture) the body of cabinetwork or joinery.

carcenet: (jewelry) a 15th-century necklace.

carda: (armor) a cloth used to make padded armor in the 13th century.

cardinal's hat dish: (pewter) a broad-rimmed, deep pewter dish.

cargan: (armor) a collar of mail; used in the 13th century.

caricature: (fine art) a sketch or painting of a person that exaggerates physical characteristics, making the individual appear humorous.

Carlsbad: (tableware, ceramics) tableware and accessories produced in Carlsbad, which has been both Austrian and German, changing as the countries' boundaries changed, and now is in Czechoslovakia. Most of this ware was produced after 1890. In addition to the mark of one of the many factories, pieces are usually marked with "Carlsbad," "Germany," or "Czechoslovakia." The oldest and most desirable pieces are Austrian.

Carlton: (ceramics) since 1890, English ware that usually has a black enamel background and is decorated with gilt birds, flowers, and the like. The company was originally called Wiltshaw and Robinson, but in 1958 it was renamed Carlton Ware, Ltd.

car mascot: (automobilia) a hood ornament on a car. Old ones are ornate and detailed and are being collected.

carnival chalkware: (collectibles) painted, plaster of paris figures given away at carnivals as prizes, primarily during the 1930s and 1940s. Some are dated. Because of the soft nature of the chalk, most carnival figures are not in good condition.

carnival glass: tumblers, pitchers, vases, bowls, candy dishes, lamps, and other objects made of iridescent glass so named because pieces were frequently give-aways at carnivals. First produced in America between 1905 and 1929 as an inexpensive substitute for higher-quality glass. Common colors are marigold, green, blue, and purple; the rarer white, opalescent aqua and peach, ice blue, and smoke are the most valued today. The Northwood Glass Company, Imperial Glass Company, Fenton, and Dugan Glass Company were the leaders in producing carnival glass. Designs range from roses to peacocks. The design and the degree of iridescence greatly affects value.

Carolean: (furniture, architecture) architecture, furniture, and accessories from the period of Charles I or Charles II of England.

carousel figure: (collectibles, folk art) an animal or other figure large enough to sit on while a merry-go-round re-

volves. Most figures were hand carved from wood during the late 1800s and early 1900s.

carpet balls: (toys) a set of large marble balls made of brown stoneware, earthenware, or agate and decorated with stripes, flowers, and other colorful designs; used for a Victorian parlor game. A set consists of one plain and six decorated balls.

carpet beater: (domestic) a long-handled instrument with a large, round or oval end usually made of wire; used to clean rugs before vacuum cleaners or carpet sweepers were invented. A rug was hung over a clothesline, then beaten with the carpet beater to loosen and remove dirt.

carpet runner: (toys) a train or other toy vehicle that has smooth wheels for easy running on a floor or carpet. Also called *floor runner.*

Carrara marble: (materials) a very fine Italian marble that varies in color from white to cream. It's often sculpted and has been in use since ancient times.

carreau: (weapons) the arrow for a crossbow. It is shorter and heavier than arrows used with the longbow. Also called *bolt* or *quarrel.*

carriage glass: a footless vessel carried in carriages and used for serving travelers.

carriage post: (folk art, metal) a large post with a ring for tethering a horse. Some of these were decorated by folk artists.

carrickmacross appliqué: (textiles) cambric from which a pattern is cut and the resulting holes filled in with needlepoint. The finished product is reminiscent of lace.

carrier's stamps: prior to 1860, United States postage stamps only covered the transport from one post office to another and private local carriers delivered to individual addresses. The government issued carrier's stamps to simplify the payment for this service.

cartes de visite: (photography) a small photograph, about the size of a calling card or business card, with a scene or portrait mounted on cardboard. Popular from 1854 until 1920 as calling cards. They were made by using a wetplate negative. Originating in France, they often featured a personal portrait, but sometimes pictures of subjects like animals, performers, sports figures, or military figures were used. The personal portraits are far more common and less collectible. A photographer's imprint adds to the value.

cartoon: 1. (fine art) a detailed drawing of decorations to be painted in fresco. **2.** (textiles) a painting from which a tapestry is woven.

cartoon characters: (collectibles) a variety of items using cartoon characters — not just cartoons — that are collectible. Early characters such as Li'l Abner, Betty Boop, Felix the Cat, and Little Orphan Annie are preferred to later ones. Sought-after items include games, books, figurines, bottles, greeting cards, soap, and toy pistols. Generally, the older an item, the more value it has.

cartouche: (furniture) a sculptured ornament shaped like an unrolled scroll.

cart-spring clock: an American thirty-day clock with a wagon spring instead of a weight. Also called *wagonspring clock.*

Carver chair: (furniture) a 17th-century chair with three horizontal rails and three vertical back spindles with turned finials on the posts. Named for Pilgrim leader John Carver and believed to have been brought to Massachusetts by him.

caryatid: (architecture, furniture) a column in the form of a draped female figure that supports an entablature.

cased: (furniture) enclosed with a cover or protective covering. Boxlike furniture such as cabinets and chests of drawers.

cased glass: two or more layers of glass bonded together. One layer is usually, but not always, white.

cash register: (collectibles) popular particularly with retail business owners who want to use them in their establishments. Condition is a prime factor: A fully restored cash register is the most desirable; a register with all its original parts is next; and if parts are missing, value is considerably less.

casino collectibles: poker chips, cards, dice, signs, postcards, and any other items printed or engraved with the name of a casino.

casque Norman: (armor) a helmet worn by the Normans in the 12th century. It is conical in shape with a broad, fixed nasal.

Cassel porcelain: porcelain tableware and figurines produced by a factory in Cassel, Germany, from 1766 until 1788. It wasn't until 1770 that these simple wares were marked. Two marks identify this porcelain: One is the letters *HC* in blue; the other depicts a heraldic lion with two tails.

cast: (metal) to form an object by pouring molten metal into a mold.

castel durante: (ceramics) tin-glazed maiolica in rich, bright colors made at Urbania, Italy, during the 16th century. Most of the decoration depicts scenes or characters from classical mythology.

Castellini, Fortunato (*ca.* 1800s): (jewelry) an important Roman jeweler in the mid-1800s. Castellini made fine jewelry in the Greek style. He applied gold grains to a gold base to get a grainy surface on many of his pieces.

Castelli majolica: (ceramics) a majolica earthenware that dates to the 17th and 18th centuries. Castelli majolica was made near Teramo in the Abruzzi. The dominant color was a grayish blue. The other hues were all rather drab. Many Castelli pieces featured historical or mythological scenes.

caster: 1. (furniture) a small, swiveled wheel or roller attached to the foot or base of furniture to facilitate moving. **2.** (tableware) a cruet for condiments and/or a stand for such bottles.

caster set: (tableware) a holder (often revolving) with three to six bottles for condiments; generally used at the table. The holder is usually of silver plate or pewter. Designs range from very plain with strictly utilitarian bottles to ornate with hand-cut bottles. Elegance and condition dictate worth. The earliest casters date to the 17th century, were in a cylindrical shape, and generally were fashioned of silver. Casters from the 18th century were often pear-shaped. By the late 18th century many caster bottles were made of cut glass with silver tops.

casting bottle: (domestic) a bottle of glass, brass, copper, or other material made for sprinkling, or casting, perfume around a room or in a bath. Popular in the 1600s.

cast iron: (materials) a brittle form of iron that can't be molded or forged, but is shaped by melting it and pouring the molten iron into molds. Cast iron contains about 4 percent carbon.

cast-iron toy: a toy that is usually cast in two pieces and then bolted together. Those from the late 1800s are most desirable. The most important

pieces were made in America, although some German and English toys are worthwhile. Some names to look for are Ives, Harris, Hubley, Stevens, and Wilkins.

castle: (armor) a closed helmet.

castwork: (silver) ornamentation that is cast in silver and applied to a silver piece such as a vase, compote, or teapot. The cast piece may be a finial, handles, feet, or the spout of a tea- or coffeepot. Some ornate silver pieces are completely cast.

Catalina Island: (ceramics) a company started in 1927 to make brick and tile, but best known for their dinnerware. The color of the clay is a clue to the period of a piece. Until 1930 it was brown or red; between 1931 and 1932, a variety of colors were used; and from 1933 to 1937 white clay was favored. Much of the ware was hand thrown. Most ware is incised "Catalina" or "Catalina Island." Pieces marked "Catalina Pottery," or "Catalina Rancho," were made after 1937, when the company was sold, and are not as desirable.

Catesby, Mark (ca. 1679-1749): (prints) an English artist and biologist who came to America in the early 1700s. Catesby was known as the father of American ornithology because of his remarkable bird pictures which he hand printed and tinted himself. All of Catesby's work appears in a two-volume work called *A Natural History of Carolina and the Bahama Islands*.

cathedral clock: an inexpensive clock made in the mid-1800s featuring steeples and other peaks.

Catskill moss ware: (ceramics) a light blue historic Staffordshire earthenware made by Ridgway of Hanley in the mid-19th century. It is decorated with American scenes and back marked "CC."

Caucasian rug: (floor coverings) an Oriental rug made in the Caucasian mountains between the Black and Caspian Seas, an area that produces Baku, Dagnestan, Gendje, Kazakistan, Kuba, Leshgi, Shirvari, Sumak, Talisn, and Tchi-Tchi rugs. The Ghiordes knot and geometric designs are generally used. Materials (highland wool) and workmanship are superior.

caudle cup: (tableware) a porringer named for caudle, a gruel often served in this type of cup.

Caughley ware: (ceramics) a product of the Caughley Coalport Porcelain Manufactory in England and produced by Thomas Turner. Much of this ware has the Blue Willow pattern.

cauldron: (domestic) round vessel with an open top used for cooking from early history. Cauldrons were originally made of bronze, then of cast iron, and can be found in a variety of sizes.

cauliflower ware: (ceramics) earthenware and porcelain in the forms of various vegetables and fruits made by Wedgewood, Whieldon, and other manufacturers. Dates back to the mid-1700s.

causeuse: (furniture) a settee, a small sofa for two people. Also called *marquise.*

cavity: (coins) the recessed impression of a coin in a die.

cedar chest: (furniture) a lift-lid chest for protecting garments, blankets, and other articles from moths. Made of cedar or cedar lined.

ceiler: (furniture) the fabric hung over a medieval bed like a tent; forerunner of the canopy.

celadon: (ceramics) a Chinese porcelain or semiporcelain of gray-white body with translucent glaze ranging from gray and blue-green to sea green and grass green. Produced from *ca.* 18th century.

celebrity doll: a doll made in the image of a well-known person. See also *portrait doll.*

celery dish: (tableware) serving dish for celery: either a flat dish with a long, narrow shape or a tall, cylindrical vessel in which celery stalks stand on end. The latter often has two handles.

cellaret: (furniture) a low, metal-lined cabinet used as a wine cooler. Also a wine case on legs.

Cellini, Benvenuto (1500 - 1571): (fine art) an Italian Renaissance sculptor and goldsmith. His autobiography describes intimate details of 16th-century daily life.

celluloid: (materials) an early, very flammable plastic made of camphor and guncotton; used extensively in jewelry, dresser sets, dolls, and other toys. Celluloid items are collectible, especially those that have escaped dents, tears, or burn marks. Widely used from 1890 until about 1920. Also called *French ivory, pyralin,* and *pyroxylin.*

celt: (tools) a chisel or axe head made of stone or bronze found in prehistoric European grave sites.

Celtic cross: (decoration) an upright cross with a circle or ring at the intersection of the shaft and crossbar.

censer: (metal) early incense burner that was suspended from a beam or ceiling by chains. Some are silver; others are made of bronze and lesser metals. They date to medieval times. Also called *thurible.*

centering: (stamps) the position of the printing on a stamp in relationship to its margins. Equal margins contribute to a stamp's value.

central device: (coins) the main figure or design on either side of a coin.

Ceramic Art Company: (ceramics) a company that made a fine-quality Belleek porcelain in Trenton, New Jersey, from 1889 until about 1906, when the company became Lenox. Many pieces are marked "CAC" or with the company name. Other examples had a paper label. Wares signed by an artist are the most desirable.

ceramics: clay items fired at a high temperature. May be glazed or unglazed.

cerbotana: (weapons) Italian and Spanish for *blowpipe*.

cerveliere: (armor) a steel scull cap worn under the coif (hood) of mail in the 13th century.

chaine de forcat: (jewelry) a man's heavy gold chain attached to a pocket watch or monocle. *Ca.* early 1800s.

chain-stich embroidery: (needlework) one of the oldest types of embroidery, done by pulling needle and thread in and out of material so it forms a chainlike line of stitches. The finished product resembles lace. When the stitch is done with a hook instead of a needle it is called *tambour work*.

chair-table: (furniture) a convertible chair with back that pivots to form a tabletop. From llth century. Also called *table-chair*.

chaise lounge: (furniture) a long, narrow seat used as a couch or settee, usually with a chair back at the head. Also called *day bed*.

chaldron: a 36-bushel measure.

chalice: a cup or goblet, usually of metal.

chalk silhouette: (decoration) a silhouette painted on a piece of chalk or plaster of paris.

chalkware: (household accessories) plaster of paris or gypsum molded into figures of birds, animals, people, and other familiar shapes, then painted with oils or watercolors. Chalkware enabled the middle and lower classes to own a form of art. Carnival chalkware was a cheaper imitation of chalkware which gained its name because it was given as prizes at carnivals. Carnival chalkware was popular during the last half of the 19th century.

Chamberlain Worcester: (ceramics) an English company started in 1786 that made a fine grade of porcelain.

chamber stick: (lighting) a flat, round base with an often pear-shaped candle holder rising from the center. The base is made with a handle for carrying from room to room. Many chamber sticks have snuffers and scissors for cutting candlewicks. Examples from the 1600s on are often made of brass or silver.

chamber table: (furniture) a dressing table designed to support a highboy. Also called *lowboy*. See also *highboy*.

chamfered edge: (furniture) a corner edge that is beveled or angled off.

champlevé: (decoration) a decoration made by incising a design into brass and filling it with enamel. Often confused with cloisonné and considered by some to be a form of cloisonné. The brass between elements of the design is generally thicker in champlevé pieces than it is on cloisonné, which is made by building designs with wire pieces and filling them in with enamel. See also *cloisonné*.

champnoine: (ceramics) an early pottery made before 1738 in Boston, Massachusetts.

champons: (armor) foot armor in use during the 13th century.

chandelier: (lighting) a hanging light with a series of candles. Incorrectly used in reference to electroliers and gasoliers (hanging lights fueled by electricity and gas).

chandry: (lighting) a box in which candles were stored.

chanfron (or champfron): (armor) the armor covering a horse's head.

changeling: (stamps) a stamp that exhibits natural changes in color from age or exposure, or from being chemically treated to duplicate natural changes for fraudulent purposes.

channeled: (furniture) routed grooves or furrows in wood. Also called *ribbed*.

channel setting: (jewelry) a series of like-sized stones set in a row between two strips of metal.

Chantilly lace: (textiles) a delicate, silk pillow lace named for Chantilly, France, where it was made.

chapbook: a short book or pamphlet originally distributed by salesmen (also called chapmen) in England. They covered a wide range of subjects from juvenile to educational and moral to sensational.

chape: (weapons, armor) a metal piece that strengthens the tip of a scabbard, belt, or girdle. Also called *crampet*.

chapel de fer: (armor) an open helmet of iron from the 12th century.

chapter ring: (clocks) the applied circle upon which the hour numerals are engraved on earlier clocks.

character doll: a doll modeled after a real baby or older child. Character dolls are a type of portrait doll. See also *portrait doll*.

charcoal iron: (domestic) a popular tool for ironing clothes in the mid-1800s; heated with hot coals inserted in the iron through a door in the rear.

charge: (armor) the figure within a heraldic design. Also called *bearing*.

charge coin: (collectibles) a forerunner of the credit card. Made of brass, celluloid, copper, silver, steel, and other materials, with the name of the store or business and a number printed on them. They were sometimes in die-cut shapes, like hats, birds, or stockings. Celluloid coins are usually the most valuable. From 1890 until the 1950s.

charger: (tableware) a large, shallow dish or platter.

Charlestown ironwork: (metal) intricate wrought-iron work done in Charlestown, South Carolina, during the early 1800s by MacLeishe, Ortman, Justi, Werner and other ironworkers of the time.

Charles II chair: (furniture) a Flemish- or Dutch-style chair with elaborate carving and a cane seat and back.

chase: 1. (furniture) a groove or slot cut in any object. **2.** (typography) the rectangular metal frame used to hold printing type. **3.** (weapons) the groove for the quarrel on a crossbow. **4.** (weapons) the part of a gun in front of the trunnions.

Chase Brass & Copper Company: (metal) a company that produced inexpensive art deco objects during the 1930s. They are highly collectible today.

chased: (decoration) metal decorated by hammering in small indentations.

chasing: (metal) a process of working over cast-metal objects with steel chisels and other tools to remove the rough edges and surfaces left from the molds. All the best bronzes and other fine metal are chased. Lack of chasing usually means an inferior product.

chatelaine: (domestic) a clasp for keys and other small objects that is attached to a chain. Worn by the housekeeper or mistress of the house.

chaton: (jewelry) the center and most important stone or ornament on a ring.

chausses: (armor) close-fitting armor for the legs. From the 13th century.

cha wan: (orientalia) a Japanese tea bowl.

checkered-diamond design: (glass) a design often used on glass objects that are blown in the mold. It features four small diamonds within a large diamond.

cheeks: (armor) pieces hung from an open helmet to protect the ears and sides of the face.

cheerio cabinet: (furniture) a cabinet to store liquor.

cheese dish: (tableware) a covered dish for storing and serving cheese. The top is usually higher than that of a butter dish to accommodate a wedge of cheese. The bottom is flat, usually with a rim to keep the cover from slipping. Often made of glass, porcelain, or silver.

Cheesequake pottery: a stoneware produced around the time of the American Revolution near the Cheesequake Creek in New Jersey. This stoneware, which mimicks English ware of the period, lost favor after the war, but it was made again in the early 1800s.

cheese scoop: (tableware) a short, curved blade, usually with a silver shaft and ivory or wood handle. *Ca.* late 1700s.

Chelsea: (ceramics) a very fine porcelain produced in the Chelsea section of London, England from 1745 to 1784. The earliest mark was an incised triangle with "Chelsea" and the year sometimes added. Later marks included an anchor in an oval, a red anchor, and a gold anchor — in that order.

Chelsea dinnerware: (tableware) white porcelain or pottery ware with relief patterns of grapes, ivy, fruits, and the like in tones of blue or violet. Made in Staffordshire, not Chelsea, England. Also called *grandmother ware*.

cheminee: (fireplace accessories) a fireplace screen with a center of tapestry or needlepoint; used extensively during the 16th and 17th centuries.

Ch'eng Hua (or Chenghua) period (1465 - 1487): (orientalia) The porcelain, with colored enamels over underglaze blue outlines, produced in China in this period is quite rare. The style was imitated from the 1600s on, and the reign mark used on later wares was used as sign of respect rather than as an attempt to counterfeit.

chenille: (textiles) a soft, tufted cording made of cotton, wool, or silk and used for fringing or embroidery work. Also, a material made of this cording.

chequer ornament: (furniture) an inlaid pattern of small, light and dark wood squares. *Ca.* 17th and 18th centuries.

chern: (metal) black decoration on light-colored metal such as silver.

cherrywood: (materials) one of the hard fruitwoods used for furniture and picture frames. These woods are easy to work with and therefore lend themselves to turning and carving. Other close-grained fruitwoods used for furniture are applewood and pearwood. Cherry is considered the most handsome of this group, although it can't compare to the beauty of mahogany or rosewood.

chestnut urn: elegantly curved, funnel-shaped, covered urns made of iron, pewter, tin, and wood; used to age fresh chestnuts during the 1700s and 1800s.

chest-on-chest: (furniture) a two-section chest of drawers supported on high legs. Also called *highboy* and *tallboy*.

chest-on-frame: (furniture) a chest that stands on a frame or table.

45

chest table: (furniture) the frame or table on which a chest-on-frame rests.

cheval glass: (furniture) a large rectangular toilet or dressing mirror that stands upright on four feet. The framed mirror pivots on pins or is raised or lowered by means of a counterweight. *Ca.* late 18th century to 19th century.

cheval screen: (hearth accessories) a decorative fire screen, often adorned with hand-painted folk art, carved and gilded crests, or needlework. See also *fire board.*

chevron: (decoration) a zigzag pattern, usually formed by inlay.

Chia Ching period (1522 - 1566): (orientalia) a reign of the Ming dynasty (1368 to 1644) noted for porcelain painted blue and white with a rich violet tone and brilliantly colored red, green, yellow, and turquoise enamel painting.

chiaroscuro: (fine art) the arrangement of light and shade in a painting.

chichi rug: (floor coverings) a Caucasian rug with small, jewellike designs in the center.

chiclaton: (textiles) a luxurious material made with gilt threads.

chiffonier: 1. (furniture) a tall, narrow chest of drawers, often with a mirror attached; *ca.* late 18th century. **2.** (furniture) a low cupboard with book shelves; *ca.* early 19th century.

chifforette: (furniture) a bedroom storage unit with drawers below and double doors above concealing sliding trays.

chifforobe: (furniture) a bedroom storage unit. Behind double doors are drawers on one side and hanging space on the other. A mirror is usually over the drawers.

chigai-dana: (orientalia) an arrangement of shelves which is used in one section of the main room of a traditional Japanese home.

chikuto: (weapons) a bamboo Japanese fencing sword.

chilanum: (weapons) a dagger of India with a double-curved, two-edged blade.

children's books: (collectibles) as with all books, first editions are the most sought. Collectors favor the Victorian era and look for color plates. Condition is very important.

chill: (lighting) earthenware oil lamp with a two-cup oil capacity; used in England before candles were invented.

chimera: (decoration) a Greek mythical animal with the head of a lion, body of a goat, and tail of a serpent.

chimney: (glass) a wide, three-plate mirror hung over the chimneypiece. *Ca.* early 18th century.

chimney crane: (domestic) a wrought-iron bracket for suspending a cauldron or teakettle over the fire.

china: earthenware or porcelain. Usually refers to tableware.

china clay: (ceramics) a white clay that results when granite decomposes; used in making porcelain.

china doll: a doll with a head, and sometimes hands, feet, and bodies, made of glazed porcelain. The porcelain was often dead white with the only color supplied by the hair and features. Easily discernible from bisque dolls, which have a matte finish.

Chinaman: (orientalia) name given to anyone who imported oriental porcelain or pottery.

china stand: (furniture) a stand for displaying figurines and/or flowers. Designs range from low pedestals on scrolled feet to three- and four-legged stools. *Ca.* late 17th century and 18th century.

china stone: (materials) material combined with china clay

46

and fired to form white, trans-lucent, hard-paste porcelain.

Chinese export: (ceramics) porcelain pieces made in China expressly for exporting to Europe, and later to America. Two of the most widely found patterns are Canton and Rose Medallion. From the 17th century until the late 19th century.

Chinese Imari: (ceramics) colorful porcelain, often with floral designs, originally Japanese. During the early 17th century, the Chinese produced copies of the popular Japanese Imari with its colors of red, blue, and sometimes yellow on a gray-white background.

Chinese Turkestan: (floor coverings) Oriental rugs that reflect Chinese design with patterns such as the Plate Medallion, Cloud Bands and Lotus, and Pomegranate. Coloring is unusual, with yellows, lacquer red, and blues in varied combinations. Most are from Khotan and Lashgar.

Ch'ing dynasty (1644 - 1912): the reign of Chinese emperors between the Ming dynasty and the Republican Revolution of 1916.

chingona: (weapons) a curved throwing stick of central Australia. Similar to a boomerang, but round with pointed ends.

chinkinbori: (orientalia) a Japanese lacquer ware that has a design incised in the surface of the lacquer and gold rubbed into the design.

chinoiserie: Chinese-style wares such as screens, figurines, and furniture with oriental motifs. Made in Europe and the United States; particularly popular in the early 1700s.

chintz: (textiles) glazed cotton fabric printed with a floral design.

chiollagh: (furniture) a stick chair made in the Isle of Man. Model for the Windsor chair.

chip carving: (furniture) a lightly cut surface ornamentation, usually on oak. Dates from the Middle Ages.

Chippendale, Thomas (1718 - 1779): (furniture) an 18th-century English cabinetmaker and furniture designer. His book of designs, *The Gentleman and Cabinet Maker's Director,* was first published in 1754.

chisa katana: (weapons) a Japanese sword of medium length with a lighter and shorter blade than most fighting swords.

chiseled-and-cut steel: (metal) the technique of engraving a steel surface by chiseling; used on articles as varied as snuffboxes and swords. Also called *faceted steel.*

chisel-edged: (weapons) a blade with one flat side; the other side of the blade gradually tapers almost to the edge, where the angle is more pronounced.

Chittenden bed: (furniture) popular mid-19th-century iron bed manufactured by S. Chittenden in New York. Some people refer to any iron bed as a Chittendon.

chocolate glass: glass in shadings of chocolate brown first produced in 1900 by Jacob Rosenthal of the Indiana Tumbler and Goblet Company. Other companies copied it. Also called *caramel slag.*

chocolate mold: (kitchen) a tin, copper, or pewter mold, smaller than an ice cream mold but similar.

chocolate pot: (silver, ceramics) pots for serving hot chocolate. Most chocolate pots are tall and thin. Old, silver chocolate pots have either removable finials or finials that slide to one side, revealing a hole through which a swizzle stick can be inserted for stirring the chocolate. Many porcelain chocolate pots have cups to match.

chodo-kake: (weapons) a Japanese stand that holds bows and arrows.

cho-ju: (weapons) a Japanese shotgun used to shoot fowl.

chopper: (weapons) a generic term for weapons with broad, heavy blades.

chrismatory: (religious) a vessel for holding chrism — oil used for Extreme Unction.

christening goblet: a footed, four-handled cup with a whistle attached to call for replenishment. English.

Christmas collectibles: mementos and decorations of the holiday. Items to look for include early Santa figures and cardboard angels sprinkled with gold; blown glass ornaments; Christmas lights, especially those made by Sandwich Glass Company; Kugel glass ornaments in round, fruit, or vegetable shapes; papier-maché and glass candy containers; and feather trees.

chrome: (metal) finish created by electroplating chromium over alloy steel.

chrome dye: (floor coverings) a synthetic dye that is popular with modern rug makers because it does not fade.

chromolithograph: (prints) a lithograph of more than two colors.

chromotype: (prints) maps and pictures that have some color printed on them and some color added with a stencil.

chronometer: (scientific instruments) a very precise clock or watch.

chuban: (prints, orientalia) a long, narrow Japanese print.

chu-ko-nu: (weapons) a Chinese repeating crossbow. Some are capable of firing two bolts at once. Used as late as the Sino-Japanese War in 1894 and 1895 by the Chinese.

chura: (weapons) a heavy knife-sword used by hill tribes of Afghanistan.

church fan: (religious) a fan depicting a biblical scene, usually done in soft tones. Church fans were sanctioned by the Bishop of London in the 1700s. They were supplied in, or carried to, churches during the summer months.

churn: (kitchen) a vessel in which milk or cream is agitated until it turns into butter. Early churns are made of wood; later models are glass.

ciborium: (religious) a gold or silver container with a pedestal bottom topped with a bowl and cover; used to hold the host or communion bread.

cigarette pictures: (paper) cards depicting actors, actresses, sports figures, and other celebrities that were included in cigarette packages during the late 1800s.

Cinderella: (stamps) non-postage stamps such as Christmas and Easter seals.

cinnabar: (orientalia) a color achieved by adding sulfide of mercury to lacquer. Sometime during the Han dynasty (*ca.* 200 B.C. to 200 A.D.), the Chinese started using colored lacquer as a protective finish; cinnabar was the first color used.

cinq trous: (textiles) the background pattern in Flemish lace, made up of threads crossing to form five small holes.

cinquedea: (weapons) a 15th-century Italian short sword or large dagger, with a flat triangular blade, five fingers wide at the hilt. Size ranges from 8 inches long to nearly the length of a sword.

cipher: (jewelry) two or three letters entwined to create a monogram.

circa: approximate, around the time of; such as *circa* 1900. Abbreviation: *ca.*

circle of an artist: (fine art) a work done in the same style and the same period of a well-known artist, but done by an associate rather than by the artist himself or herself.

circuit: (stamps) a method for buying and selling stamps through the mail within a limited group. The seller usually sends a book of mounted stamps with price to a rotating list of subscribers. Each subscriber takes out the stamps desired and leaves a mark indicating the purchase. The book is then sent on to the next person on this list. When the book has made its rounds, the seller processes the marks and bills the subscribers.

circular saw marks: (furniture) rounded or circular marks in wood that prove a piece was made after 1815, when the circular saw was invented.

circus memorabilia: (collectibles) the nostalgia items from Barnum and Bailey and Ringling Brothers circuses. Books, banners, calliopes, pennants, programs, tickets, and other memorabilia are desirable. Items from other circuses are collectible but far less desirable.

cistern: (domestic) a water container with a spigot usually used in the bedroom.

cistern barometer: (scientific instruments) the earliest type of barometer.

citrine: (jewelry) yellow semi-precious stone created by heating a black quartz stone. (The heat changes the stone's color.) Citrine resembles topaz.

cittern: (music) an early pear-shaped guitar. Popular in 16th-century England. Also called *pandora*.

clacket: (tools) a wheel with teeth that make a clacking noise when they hit a piece of wood (generally hickory) as the wheel turns; used to frighten birds from corn fields.

cladibas (or cladias or claidas): (weapons) a long, heavy sword used by the Celtic Gauls.

claire de lune: (ceramics) porcelain glazes in various shades of lavender blue created by adding small amounts of cobalt to clear glazes. Literally, French for moonlight.

clambroth: (glass) a semi-opaque, grayish white glass made during the Victorian era.

claret ground: (ceramics) a crimson background color introduced at the Chelsea Porcelain Factory in England in 1760.

claret jug: (glass) a glass ewer with either a wide or narrow neck and a spout; used in the 1700s and 1800s for serving claret.

clasp knife: (weapons) a knife that has a blade that folds back into the handle. A pocket knife.

classic: a unique or outstanding example of its kind, offering a standard of quality in design and/or craftsmanship.

classical: (design) as the word pertains to antiques, the design and form of antiquities; used most often in reference to ancient Greek or Roman articles.

classical style: (furniture) a style of design based on ancient Greek and Roman architecture; employed in England from the mid-1700s.

classic automobiles: certain cars limited in production that are unique in appearance and/or performance. According to the Classic Car Club of America, such cars were produced between 1925 and 1948 and include the Auburn, Cord, Duesenberg, MG, and Pierce-Arrow. See also *antique automobile, milestone automobile*, and *modern-day classic automobile*.

classification lamps: (railroad memorabilia) a pair of lamps mounted at the front of a locomotive to indicate the locomotive's running class; used during the era of steam locomotives.

clavel page: (fireplace accessories) a decorative wooden figure (sometimes painted, sometimes covered with a textile) placed beside the fireplace.

clavichord: (music) a 17th-century instrument similar to today's piano. Also called *clovichord.*

claw-and-ball foot: (furniture) a carved foot shaped like a ball held in a talon or claw.

claw setting: (jewelry) a round or square setting that secures a gemstone with prongs. See also *coronet setting.*

clay marble: a marble made of clay. There are some painted and some unpainted examples of these early marbles.

claymore: (weapons) originally the two-handed sword used by the Scots in the 15th and 16th centuries. The correct term is claidheamh-mor or Claidhmhichean-mhora. Claymore usually refers to a 17th-century Scottish broadsword copied from the Venetian schiavona.

clay ware: (paper) often confused with papier-maché, clay ware is a much tougher material made by laminating sheets of paper together, forming them into objects by placing them over a mold, baking them, and applying lacquer.

Cleminson: (ceramics) from 1941 until 1963, a producer of an inexpensive, colorful line of dinnerware, cookie jars, canisters, and novelties which have become collectible. The pieces are marked "Cleminson."

clepsydra: (clocks) an early clock (1649) energized by water running through it.

Clewell ware: (ceramics, metal) copper- and bronze-plated ceramic ware. From the early 1900s until his death in the 1960s, Charles Walter Clewell worked in his private studio plating ceramic objects with copper or bronze. The technique he used was his own discovery, and he took it to his grave with him. Most of his pieces are signed. His work is scarce and quite valuable.

Clews: (ceramics) earthenware by James and Ralph Clews who had a pottery in the Staffordshire section of England from 1817 until 1861. Most of their wares were decorated in blue-and-white transfer. They produced many series of wares, including one series called "Three Tours of Dr. Syntax," which has more than 70 different pieces. Clews ware is usually marked with the company name and a logo.

Clichy paperweight: (glass) a paperweight made in a factory in Clichy, a Paris suburb. They were not dated but are marked "C" and have a rose in the pattern.

clicker: (toys, collectibles) a small, metal or celluloid device that makes a clicking noise when the inner piece is pushed. Those with pictures are more collectible than those with just writing. Condition is important and scratches or dents decrease the value. They're divided into two categories: advertising and non-advertising.

Cliff, Clarice: (ceramics) from 1928 until 1935, the director of Wilkerson Pottery and Newport Pottery in Burslem, England. Her "bizarre ware" done in an art deco style was her best-received work. Many pieces are marked with her name.

clinquant: (decoration, metal) brass hammered very thin and applied to objects in place of gold leaf; used on objects like picture frames, boxes, and furniture.

clip: (jewelry) like a pin or brooch in design, an ornamental piece of jewelry that clips, rather than pins, onto clothing or accessories. Between 1920 and mid-1940, clips were very fashionable.

cloche: (glass) a glass dome used to keep dust off objects such as clocks, figurines, and artificial flowers.

clock fret: (clocks) a pierced, decorative wood or metal piece placed in the clock case to muffle sound.

clockwork mechanism: (toys) springs that uncoil to move interlocking gears that in turn move toys. This brass-and-steel mechanism was popular from 1862 until the 1890s.

cloisonné: (metal, enamel) a method of applying decorative enamel to metal. The best-known form of cloisonné is produced by soldering wires onto a metal object to produce a design outline. The outline is then filled in with colored enamel and fired. Other forms of cloisonné are wireless cloisonné, made by removing wires before firing; plique-a-jour, a transparent cloisonné produced by removing the metal form after firing; and foil cloisonné, achieved by using transparent enamel over a foil-covered object. See also *champlevé.*

close bed: (furniture) a folding bed that comes out of, and folds back into, a cabinet. Also called *press bed.*

close chair: (furniture) a boxed chair with a toilet bowl or chamber pot. See also *close stool.*

closed-handled: (glass, ceramics, silver) handles that are solid and protrude like tabs from the vessel.

close nailing: (furniture) the practice of placing nails in a line, so that each nail head touches the ones on either side. Brass nails with convex heads were close nailed on leather-covered trunks and chairs to secure the fabric.

close stool: (furniture) a boxed stool with a toilet bowl or chamber pot. See also *close chair.*

cloth-body doll: a doll with a cloth body and a bisque or glazed-china head — and sometimes hands and feet.

clothes tree: (furniture) an upright pole with pegs or hooks on which to hang clothing. Also called *hall tree.*

clovichord: (music) an early keyboard musical instrument. The instrument's soft sound is produced by pressing keys that are directly attached to tangents which strike horizontal strings. Also called *clavichord.*

club foot: (furniture) a circular foot that extends forward from the leg; the principal foot used with cabriole legs on Queen Anne furniture. Also called *Dutch-pad foot.*

cluster-column leg: (furniture) a Gothic chair leg shaped like a cluster of pillars. Popular in the mid-1700s, when a revival of medieval forms occurred.

Clutha: (glass) 19th-century opaque art glass with deliberate patterns of air bubbles; inspired by ancient glass; produced in Scotland. See also *Cluthra.*

Cluthra: (glass) glassware in which air bubbles are trapped between two layers of glass. Cluthra, a sophisticated form of Clutha, was perfected by Frederick Carder for the Steuben Glass Works, but it was used by other fine glass companies, too. See also *Clutha.*

coaching chair: (furniture) a folding chair used by ladies and gentlemen when they watched a hunt, a race, or other similar event. Coaching chairs were made in almost every period.

coaching glass: a round-bottomed glass that must be held until it is emptied — it cannot be set down without tipping and spilling. Used in the 1800s.

coachman bottle: a glass or china bottle shaped like a coachman with a high hat. First made in the 1840s by Fenton. Also called *bishop's bottle.*

coal box: (domestic) any covered container used to store coal; usually wood or metal.

coal carrier: (domestic) a covered metal pan, usually with a long handle; used to carry hot coals from one place to another.

coal hod: (domestic) an open wooden or metal bucket or pail used to carry or store coal.

Coalport: (ceramics) a factory that makes fine-quality, decorative dinnerware and accessories. Very early examples are soft paste. Founded in 1796 at Coalport in Shropshire, England, by John Rose; has changed hands several times and is now part of the Wedgewood group. Indian Tree and Hong Kong are two of the best-known Coalport patterns. Much Coalport made during the 1800s has a strong resemblance to Sevres. One of the most popular Coalport styles is a rococo rendering called Coalbrookdale.

coal scuttle: (domestic) a metal or wooden container for carrying coal, usually with a partially covered top.

coal vase: (domestic) an ornamental coal container used from the 1800s. Coal vases replaced coal scuttles, which were ugly and not usually displayed. The decorative coal vases had covers to conceal the coal they held.

coaster: (table accessories) a receptacle for moving food and drink on the dining table. It was fitted with a baize-covered base with small wheels, for ease of movement. *Ca.* 18th century. Also called *slider.*

coat of arms: (heraldry) any insignia of heraldic bearings,

usually blazoned on a tabard or surcoat.

coat of mail: (armor) any body garment of mail that opens down the front.

cobalt blue: (glass, ceramics) a deep, almost navy blue color. Some of the most popular depression glass was made in this hue, and it was popular as a transfer color on porcelain.

cobalt glass: glass of a deep blue color produced with a mixture of cobalt oxide and alumina.

cobbler's bench: (furniture) a bench used by shoemakers for plying their trade. There is a place to sit, compartments for small supplies, and a bin. Also called *cordwaine's bench*.

cobbler's candle: (lighting) a candle with a double wick invented by Benjamin Franklin.

cobirons: (metal) fireplace irons that are usually plain in design and have rows of hooks on the standards for the placement of spits.

Coca-Cola memorabilia: (collectibles) memorabilia from 1886, when the company was founded, until 1970, when the company changed its logo to include a twisted white ribbon. Advertisements, banks, banners, blotters, bookmarks, bottles, calendars, can openers, clocks, coasters, coolers, earrings, fans, glasses, knives, lighters, locks, pencils, pocket mirrors, post cards, posters, signs, thermometers, tip trays, trays, and watch fobs all have been made with the Coca-Cola logo. There are many reproductions, especially of knives, pocket mirrors, tip trays, and trays.

cockbeading: (furniture) a narrow, raised beading used as a border for drawer edges. *Ca.* 1730 to 1800.

cockfight chair: (furniture) a chair made to be straddled by the sitter. It has high arms and the back slants. Also called *pitside chair*.

cock's head hinge: (hardware) a curved H-shaped twin-plate hinge with four finials, each formed as a cock's head. For external use; always held in place by handwrought nails. *Ca.* late 1500s to early 1600s. See also *H hinge*.

cocktail table: (furniture) a low table for beverages and snacks, usually placed in front of a sofa. Also called *coffee table*.

Codd's patent bottle: (glass) a mineral bottle with a ball stopper; invented by Hiram Codd in the 1800s.

Codnor Park stoneware: stoneware bottles made from the clay from Codnor Park in England from 1821 until 1861.

coffee table: (furniture) a low table for beverages and snacks, usually placed in front of a sofa. Also called *cocktail table*.

coffer: (furniture) a chest or strongbox for carrying gold or other valuables. Rounded at sides and ends.

coffin tray: (metal) a deep, long, eight-sided, painted and stenciled tin tray. Its shape resembles that of a coffin.

cognizance: (heraldry) a crest or badge worn by a gentleman entitled to wear arms; usually the armorial bearings of the wearer.

coif de fer: (armor) a 13th-century steel cap.

coiffette: (armor) skull cap of iron. 11th and 12th centuries.

coif of mail: (armor) a hood of mail worn by knights under their helmet, and by lesser soldiers as their only head protection.

coin china: (ceramics) china objects sometimes decorated either with a transfer coin design, or with a coin design incised or in relief. *Ca.* 18th and 19th centuries.

coin glasses: wine glasses from the 1600s and 1700s with coins embedded in their stems.

coin-operated machine: (collectibles) a coin-operated entertainment or vending device dating from the turn of the century to the 1960s. Desirable collectibles include phonographs, juke boxes, vending machines, slot machines, pinball machines, and machines with characters that perform at the drop of a penny or a nickel, depending on how old the machine is.

coin silver: United States silver coinage has a fineness of 900, that is, 90 percent of the coin by weight is silver and 10 percent is copper. See also *sterling silver, eight hundred (800) silver*.

colfichet: (needlework) small embroidered pictures done in floss silk on paper so that each side had the same finished images. Used as bookmarks or kept between two sheets of glass. Originated in Italy in the late 1700s.

colichemarde: (weapons) a small sword blade, wide near the hilt, narrowing abruptly half way to the tip.

collage: (fine art) a picture made up of several pictures cut out and pasted to a common background.

collared toe: (furniture) the base, or foot, of a table or chair leg with an ornamental band.

collar lace: (textiles) a Venetian lace, usually in a geometric pattern, that was popular in the 17th century.

collectible: any item or classification of items that people collect. Some collectibles are antiques; others are of recent vintage. Collectibles tend to go in and out of fashion quite readily, especially if they lack intrinsic value.

collector's mark: (fine art, prints) a personal or identifying mark put on the backs of pictures and prints by collectors or museums to show ownership.

collet setting: (jewelry) the method of setting gem stones with a band of metal backed by foil to increase the stone's brilliance. Common until the beginning of the 19th century.

collier: (jewelry) a wide necklace popular in the 19th century.

collotype: (prints) a process by which fine reproductions are made photomechanically. There are no dots in this process as there are in offset prints.

colonial: an American object made during the period when the country consisted of 13 colonies.

colophon: (books) a publisher's trademark or emblem. Also the publisher's inscription giving facts concerning a book's publication.

colored lithograph: 1. (prints) a one- or two-color lithograph to which other colors have been applied by hand. **2.** (prints) a multicolor lighograph made from a number of lithograph stones, one for each basic color used.

color separation: (prints) a process by which each color in a print is put on its own plate. When the print is made, all the plates must be put together in perfect register so there will be no fuzzy edges.

Colt model P single-action revolver: (weapons) known as "the peacemaker," a revolver introduced in 1873, continuing in production until 1941. The demand was so great that production was renewed after World War II.

Colt percussion revolver: (weapons) the first breech-loading pistol; patented in Europe in 1835 and in the United States in 1836 by the American, Samuel Colt (1814-62).

combback chair: (furniture) an early Windsor chair with an extension top consisting of a cresting rail with spindles resembling a comb. Dating from mid-18th century, they were most often made of ash, beech, or elm.

combed ware: (ceramics) ware decorated with two or more colored slips (layers of thinned clay) brushed into a marbleized pattern. The pieces with more delicate combed patterns are called feathered ware. Combed ware was produced in Staffordshire, England, during the late 17th and early 18th centuries. See also *feathered ware*.

combination cover: (stamps) a cover bearing stamps of two or more countries.

combined weapon: a weapon such as a sword, axe, or spear combined with a gun. Popular in the 16th and 17th centuries.

comic books: (books, paper) collectible children's entertainment books. Nineteen thirty-nine to 1950 were the years when comics enjoyed a wholesome reputation and these are the years collectors seek. Adventure, humor, mystery, and westerns featuring Batman, Captain America, Superman, and other heroes found enthusiastic audiences. In 1954 the publishers of comics were accused of undermining the young, and the books almost disappeared until 1960, when the industry revived.

comic-strip marbles: a set of twelve marbles featuring the facial likeness of a comic-strip character on each one. These marbles, made by Peltier Glass Factory in Illinois, portray Little Orphan Annie, Kayo, Skeezix, Moon Mullins, and other popular comic characters of the period. *Ca.* 1920s and 1930s.

commemorative: (stamps) limited-edition stamps that honor a person, special event, or place.

commode: 1. (furniture) a low chest of drawers or cabinet. **2.** (furniture) a stand or cupboard containing a washbowl. **3.** (furniture) a chair with an enclosed chamber pot.

Compagnie des Indes China: (ceramics) Chinese porcelain imported by (and named for) the Compagnie des Indes, a French trading company, as well as other European trading companies, such as the English East India Company.

compagnie dessin: (ceramics) literally, company pattern. Refers to porcelain made for and imported by Compagnie des Indes, the French trading company.

compass: 1. (scientific instruments) a device for determining geographical direction, usually with a magnetic needle. **2.** (scientific instruments) a hinged instrument used to draw circles.

compass card: (scientific instruments) a circular magnetized disk marked with the points of the compass and the degrees of the circle. It freely pivots to point north. Also called *compass rose*.

compass rose: (scientific instruments) a circular magnetized disk marked with the points of the compass and the degrees of the circle. It freely pivots to point north. Also called *compass card*.

compensation clock pendulum: (clocks) a pendulum designed to offset the effects of temperature changes.

compo decoration: combination of alcohol, plaster, sawdust, and shellac worked into a hard plaster; used to make intricate decorations that were applied to furniture and other wooden objects. Used by Chippendale to make filigree.

composition doll: a doll with a molded body, head, and limbs made from combined materials (such as sawdust or wood pulp mixed with glue). Composition dolls are generally earlier and more desirable than plastic dolls.

composition toy: paper, wood pulp, sawdust, and other materials mixed with glue, then molded into the shape of a toy and decorated.

compote: (household accessories) a glass, porcelain, or silver open dish with a pedestal. Smaller compotes are used as candy dishes and larger ones as serving dishes, usually for pudding-type desserts. Some compotes are reticulated and used for fruit or strictly as decorative pieces.

compound perforation: (stamps) perforation of more than one gauge on the same stamp.

concentric circles: (glass) circles within circles that gradually increase or decrease in size.

conditions of sale: (auctions) the terms by which any and all pieces are sold. At an auction that usually means all items are bought in "as is" condition and that the purchaser is responsible for removing them from the premises.

conductor's lantern: (railroad memorabilia, lighting) a brass- or nickel-plated lantern, smaller and generally of a superior quality to a switchman's lantern. The globe is either clear or half colored and half clear. They rarely bear the railroad's name.

Conestoga wagon: a covered wagon named for the Conestoga Valley in Lancaster County, Pennsylvania; used extensively to transport goods in the late 1700s.

confidante: (furniture) a settee with additional seats at both ends that angle in toward the main section of the piece, making intimate conversations between several people possible.

conforming seat: (furniture) a seat shaped to fit, or conform to, a person when he or she sits in it.

Connecticut chest: (furniture) a decorative chest made

in Connecticut in the 17th and 18th centuries. A Connecticut chest often has one or more drawers, applied bosses, split spindles, and front panels with carved conventionalized flowers.

Conrad: (weapons) a German arms maker from the late 19th and early 20th century. The company produced museum-quality replicas of 15th- and 16th-century weapons.

conservator: an expert who restores furniture, art, textiles, dolls, photographs, paper, and other objects. Each conservator has his or her area of expertise.

consignment: giving an object or objects to a dealer to sell. At the time of the sale the dealer takes a percentage of the selling price — usually 30 to 40 percent.

consignor: the person or persons whose goods are being offered at auction.

console bowl: (table accessories) a bowl, often larger in diameter than in height, that serves as a centerpiece. Usually made of glass, occasionally of silver or porcelain. Often accompanied by matching candlesticks: the three pieces are called a console set.. See also *console set*.

console mirror: (furniture) a mirror that hangs over a console table.

console set: (table accessories) a bowl and matching candlesticks. The set serves as a centerpiece. Usually made of glass, occasionally of silver or porcelain. See also *console bowl*.

console table: 1. (furniture) a table designed to set against a wall; may be supported by brackets, or consoles, attached to the wall. 2. (furniture) an ornate bracket that supports a shelf or other object.

Consolidated: (glass, lighting) company that produced glass parts for lamps; established in Coraopolis, Pennsylvania, in 1894. In 1925, they started making vases, lamps, and the like from a sculptured glass similar to Lalique. This line was named "Martele." Phoenix Glass, also of Pennsylvania, produced a product almost identical to Martele. The only difference was that about 90 percent of Consolidated pieces were painted on the raised portions of the design only, and about 90 percent of Phoenix glass was painted on the background only.

constitution mirror: (furniture) a wall mirror in the Chippendale style having a scrolled-arch top with a bird or other finial, and a string of flowers or leaves on the sides; often partly gilded.

cont.: (books) a bookseller's term; abbreviation for *contemporary*. Sometimes used to state that the box or binding is contemporary with the original printing.

continental silver: silver from any of the European silver centers. There are thousands of continental silver marks. Each one denotes the region in which the item was made. This silver usually is 800/1000, or 8 parts silver to 2 parts of another metal. Continental silver is usually ornate, depicting wreaths, garlands, bows, and the like.

contour-framing: (ceramics) a way of isolating or highlighting an ornament with a white or uncolored outline. A decorative style derived from the Near East and used in Europe around the 16th century.

contreplatine: (weapons) a small ornamental plate on the stock of a gun or pistol opposite the lock. Also called *nail plate* and *side plate*.

conversation chair: (furniture) chair comprised of two seats, attached, side-by-side, facing in opposite directions. Popular in the 18th and 19th centuries. Also called *incroyable chair.*

convex frieze: (furniture, architecture) a molding of cushion-shaped sections. See also *frieze.*

convex mirror: (furniture) a round mirror with glass that bulges outward. Frames are usually gilt and often have a mounted eagle, vase, or basket design on top. When there are candle holders on either side, the mirrors are called *girandoles.* See also *girandole.*

cookie cutters: (kitchen) cookie cutters in a variety of shapes are being collected. The older the cutter and the more unusual the shape, the higher the value. Age can usually be determined by the depth of the cutting piece and the sophistication of the soldering job. One-inch- to 2-inch-deep cutters are usually from the late 1700s or 1800s. A neat soldering job usually indicates a fairly new, less valuable cookie cutter.

cookie jars: (collectibles) covered containers in a variety of whimsical shapes. Produced by companies such as American Bisque, American Pottery, Brush-McCoy, Fredericksburg Art Pottery, Hull, McCoy, Regal China, and Shawnee. Some people collect them by shapes; others collect only one company.

Copenhagen porcelain: 1. (ceramics) a soft-paste ware made at a factory at Copenhagen, Denmark, from 1759 to 1765. Not many examples exist today. **2.** (ceramics) hard-paste porcelain objects including annual plates and collectible figurines produced by the Royal Copenhagen factory, founded in 1774 and still in operation. Their various trademarks always include three wavy lines.

copper blank: (metal, enamel) paper-thin blanks of copper used as a form for applying enamel. The metal was cut and shaped before enameling on all sides and set with metal mounts.

copper luster: (ceramics) a shiny, copper-looking finish over pottery; the most plentiful of the lusters, first produced in Staffordshire, England, in the 1800s. Pitchers and bowls are the most common, but teapots and other items were made too. Copper luster usually has a hand-painted or transfer decoration. Also called *copper queensware.* See also *luster, pink luster, silver luster,* and *Sunderland.*

copperplate printing: (textiles) the use of engraved, flat copperplates to print color designs on textiles. *Ca.* 18th century.

copper queensware: (ceramics) a shiny, copper-looking finish over pottery; the most plentiful of the lusters, first produced in Staffordshire, England, in the 1800s. Pitchers and bowls are the most common, but teapots and other items were made too. Copper luster usually has a hand-painted or transfer decoration. Also called *copper luster.* See also *luster, pink luster, silver luster,* and *Sunderland.*

copperwash: (metal) liquid copper in a thin coat over tin.

Coptic art: (fine art) highly stylized art done in Egypt by the early Christians. Much of it was done on walls, but stone carvings and woven tapestries also were created. Natural subjects such as birds and plants were featured.

copy: (antiques, collectibles, furniture) a reproduction, or imitation, of an original object. The term does not indicate the lack or presence of quality. Also called *reproduction.*

coquillage: (decoration) an ornament fashioned after a sea shell and used extensively in rococo decorations, particularly on furniture and silver. *Ca.* mid-18th century.

coralene: (glass, ceramics) glass or porcelain with raised designs formed with beads or grains of glass. Made by several glass houses and porcelain manufacturers; easily recognized by its designs: seaweed (the most common design found on glass), flowers, and fish.

coralline point lace: (textiles) a Venetian, flat-point, needle-point lace with an elaborate pattern.

corbet: (architecture) a niche built into the wall of an American house with Georgian-style architecture; used to display statuary, vases, and other art objects.

cord: (glass) a slight irregularity on the surface of glass. A cord is usually not visible but can be felt with the fingers.

Cordey: (ceramics) figurines, lamps, and other ceramic pieces made by the Cordey China Company, started in Trenton, New Jersey, in 1942. Early wares are plaster; later pieces are made of a porcelain developed by Boleslaw Cybis called *Papka*. Cybis, one of the company's founders, designed figurines and in 1950 started Cybis Porcelain. Cordey was marked with a number and "Cordey." They ceased operations about 1955. See also *Cybis*.

cordial: (glass, silver) a small drinking vessel used to serve cordials, liqueurs, or aperitifs.

cordwaine's bench: (furniture) a bench used by shoemakers for plying their trade. There is a place to sit, compartments for small supplies, and a bin. Also called *cobbler's bench*.

core casting: (metal) a hollow metal casting made in one piece, rather than in halves that must be bonded together.

Corinthian candle holder: (lighting) a candle holder, usually of silver or brass, designed by Robert Adam after a classical Corinthian column. Popular in the last half of the 18th century.

Corinthian order: (furniture) the most ornate of the three classical Greek styles (orders) of architecture; more specifically, refers to a slender, fluted column with an ornate bell-shaped capital with acanthus leaves.

Cork Glasshouse Company: (glass) company that specialized in hollow, lightweight, blown-in-the-mold flint glass — especially bottles, many of which were black. Although it was founded in 1793, pieces from this factory weren't marked until 1812, when products bore the mark "Cork Glass Company." Expert glass cutters plied their trade at this factory before it closed in 1818, producing some of the best-quality flint glass made.

corkscrew thumbpiece: (metal) a thumbpiece with a twisted shape used on tankards in New York. *Ca.* 18th century. See also *thumbpiece*.

corner block: (stamps) a block of stamps from the corner of a sheet with the border attached on two edges.

corner chair: (furniture) a low-back armchair, usually diamond shaped, with the back and arms extending from the back corner to the two side corners. *Ca.* 17th and 18th centuries. Also called *roundabout chair*.

corner cupboard: (furniture) a triangular cabinet that fits into a corner. Some have open shelves; others have shelves enclosed by doors.

cornet: (jewelry) a small crown worn by nobles under the rank of sovereign.

corn husk doll: (Native American, folk art) a doll with a body made of a corn husk. These toys were widely made in the eastern and midwestern United States, and those made by settlers were always dressed in a bonnet and pioneer gown.

cornice: (furniture) horizontal crown or top molding of an entablature.

coromandel lacquer: 1. (decoration) an Oriental technique of incising a design into a lacquer surface. Objects with this finish were introduced in England in the late 1600s. See also *japan*. **2.** (materials) type of ebony wood from East India.

coronet setting: (jewelry) the means of securing a gemstone with prongs usually in a round setting. See also *claw setting*.

corset busk: a thin, flexible stay of metal, wood, whalebone, or plastic used to stiffen the garment. Often decoratively carved on whalebone (scrimshaw) by sailors at sea as gifts for wives.

corset cors: (armor) breastplate, from 14th century.

cosmos: (glass) distinctive milk glass featuring relief-molded flowers in blue, pink, and yellow. Produced by the Consolidated Lamp and Glass Company from the late 1800s to the early 1900s. Most was in the form of tableware such as syrup pitchers, creamers, spooners, and butter dishes, but it was also made into lamps and perfume bottles.

costrel: a bottle with handles to which a cord was attached for ease in carrying; used by travelers.

costume miniature: (fine art) a miniature portrait, usually of a lady, done on copper or silver with several sheets of mica. Parts of a costume were painted on the sheets of mica. The artist "dressed" the lady by placing the mica sheets over the portrait. Also called *talc*.

cottage clock: modern term for any of an assortment of small Connecticut spring clocks with modern cases made during the last half of the 19th century.

cottage furniture: mass-produced 19th-century furniture with a simple utilitarian style.

couched work: (needlework) embroidery with the thread laid on the material and held in place by stitching.

counter box: cylindrical container used to hold coins in the 1600s.

counter-guard: (weapons) the parts of a sword between the hilt and the quillon.

countermark: (coins) a symbol or letter punched into the surface of a coin.

counterpane: (textiles) a bed cover or other textile article made up of embroidered pieces of material sewn together.

counter-proof: (fine art) a print made from a damp impression that reveals the subject in reverse. Artists used counter-proofs to aid them in making changes on printing plates, which also show in reverse.

country furniture: informal furniture produced in America by country craftsmen from 1690 to 1890.

court chimney: (domestic) a small, portable fireplace used in the 16th century.

court cupboard: (furniture) an early cupboard with doors and drawers below and a smaller cupboard above; the top is supported by heavy turned columns at the corners.

court dish: (tableware) not a dish, but a cup of the finest quality made of china, glass, gold, silver, or other fine material.

courting mirror: a small ornately framed, crested mirror, often bearing a picture or design painted within the cresting. A courting gift in 18th-century New England.

courting pitcher: pitchers decorated with romantic figures, sentimental poems, and the like. Popular from *ca.* 1790 to 1830.

coustil à croc: (weapons) a 15th-century short sword with a double-edge, straight blade.

cover: (stamps) an envelope with cancellation marks and stamps intact.

Cowan, Guy: (ceramics) artisan who operated a pottery in Ohio from 1912 until 1931. Striving for quality, he perfected some fine glazes on his tiles and artware. The better pieces are incised with the name "Cowan," or "Cowan Pottery." Other mass-produced, but still quality, pieces are marked with an incised "Lakewood."

cow pitcher: (ceramics, silver) a pitcher in the shape of a cow with the mouth as the pouring spout and the tail forming a handle. The pitcher is filled from a hole in the cow's back. Generally used for milk.

cozy chair: (furniture) an upholstered wing chair designed to keep the person sitting in it comfortably protected from drafts.

cracked-ice pattern: (ceramics) decoration resembling cracks in a sheet of ice; used on Bristol delftware. Late 18th century.

Cracker Jacks: (collectibles) snack food product that has been packaged with toy prizes since 1912. Some of these collectible prizes are marked "Rueckheim Brothers," others "Reliable Confections." Until 1948 prizes were made of clay, metal, paper, or wood. In 1948 plastic took over. All are collectible, the earlier the better.

cracker jar: (domestic, advertising) glass, earthenware, or porcelain jar that resembles today's cookie jars in size and form. Originally sold with crackers or cookies in them. Many are collectible as advertising pieces.

crackle: (ceramics) porcelain decorated by controlled crazing, a technique introduced into Europe from China in the 19th century. See also *crazing*.

crackle glass: glass with a crackly appearance that is achieved either by rolling hot glass in ground glass particles and then refiring it or by dunking a hot piece of glass into cold water. Although most crackle glass that surfaces today is from the 1800s or later and was made in the United States or Europe, the process originated at an earlier date in Vienna.

crampet: (weapons, armor) a metal piece that strengthens the tip of a scabbard, hilt, or girdle. Also called *chape*.

cranberry: (glass) glass the color of cranberries produced by adding molten gold to amber glass. A cheaper cranberry with a purple cast is achieved with copper instead of gold. Popular in the middle to late 1800s. There are many reproductions.

crane: (domestic) an iron arm used over a fire to support a kettle or other cooking vessel.

craquemarte: (weapons) a heavy 17th-century cutlass used at sea.

crayon engraving: (prints) method of combining etching and engraving to reproduce chalk drawings.

crazing: (ceramics) a network of fine cracks developing in the glaze of pottery caused by unequal shrinkage of the glaze and the body. Old pieces usually show crazing. However, crazing is not a guaranty of age; it can occur on any piece that was fired at low temperatures when it was made.

crazy quilt: (textiles) a patchwork quilt made of irregular shapes of material all fitted together in a perfect rectangle. Expensive materials, such as velvet or satin, were often featured. Decorative stitching was often used.

cream basket: (domestic accessories) a boat-shaped basket or vase, usually in silver and often pierced. *Ca.* late 1700s.

creamer: (tableware) a small pitcher or jug to hold cream.

cream soup: (tableware) two-handled glass or porcelain dish used to serve bouillon or consommé.

creamware: (ceramics) very delicate, often reticulated earthenware first made by Wedgewood in the mid-1700s. Although it has been widely reproduced, later examples are heavier and lack the grace of the original creamware.

creche: (religious) a miniature nativity scene first used by the Nestorian Christians or Greek Church. Moravians introduced the custom of exhibiting creches to America. Materials include china, plaster, and wood.

credence table: (furniture) table with a top that folds in half, one half on top of the other, and legs that swing out to support the top when the table is open. In use as early as the 14th century.

credenza: (furniture) a buffet or sideboard, usually without legs; used as a serving table. From 15th century.

crenel: (armor) the peak of a helmet.

Creole earring: (jewelry) a hoop earring that is thick at the bottom and narrows toward the lobe of the ear.

cresset: (lighting) a metal cup or basket attached to a rod for burning pitch, oil, or wood for a torch.

crested mirror: (furniture) a mirror, usually of Queen Anne or William and Mary style, with an ornament on the top, above the frame. The design is often heraldic.

cresting: 1. (furniture) decorative carved ornament on the center or top rail of a chair or settee. **2.** (ceramics) the decorative edging on a pot or bowl.

cresting rail: the top rail on the back of a chair.

cretonne cloth: (textiles) an unglazed chintz printed with large designs; used for curtains and upholstery.

crewelwork: (needlework) first done in England around 1600, needlework renderings of elaborate trees, exotic fruits, animals, flowers, and similar motifs worked in a stylized manner in two-ply wool or yarn on linen or a coarse, textured material.

cricket stool: (furniture) a small stool put by the hearth to warm one's feet.

cricket table: (furniture) a table that resembles a stool.

crimper: (kitchen) any tool used to press corrugated ridges along the edge of pastry. Also called *jagging wheel*.

crimping: (glass) a knobby, ridgelike design made in handles of glass pitchers, vases, and other glass objects.

crinoline: (fashion accessories) a full, stiff underskirt worn to make an overskirt stand out. Also called *hoopskirt*.

crizzling: (glass) small surface cracks that alter the color and shine of a glass object.

crochet: 1. (jewelry) a jeweled ornament similar to a brooch that is fixed on a straight pin. *Ca.* 18th century. Also called *croshett*. **2.** (needlework) hooked-needle knitting first done in Ireland where the finest examples were done.

crocket: (furniture) a small, carved, curling foliage-shaped form; used on spires and pinnacles.

croft: (furniture) a small filing cabinet with numerous small drawers and a writing top; made to be easily moved in the library. *Ca.* late 18th century.

Croix à la Jeannette: (jewelry) a heart with a cross — French peasant jewelry popular in the early 1800s.

crooks: (music) detachable loops of tubing in various lengths; used by horn players to reduce or increase the tube length before the advent of valves.

croshett: (jewelry) a jeweled ornament similar to a brooch that is fixed on a straight pin. *Ca.* 18th century. Also called *crochet.*

crosier: (religious) a staff with a cross or crook at the upper end; carried as a symbol of office by abbots, bishops, and archbishops.

cross bar: (furniture) a horizontal piece joining two sides.

crossbow: (weapons) a bow mounted horizontally on a stock grooved for the arrow and fitted with a trigger mechanism, allowing it to be discharged from the shoulder position. Records indicate that the crossbow was used in Europe about the 4th century, but its use was not widespread until the 10th century.

crossbow bolt: (weapons) a short, heavy arrow.

crossed the block: (auctions) a phrase meaning an item has been sold at auction.

crossrail: (furniture) the horizontal bar or splat (flat, thin piece) in a chair back.

cross-stitch: (needlework) a stitch resembling small, X-shaped crosses; used on samplers, linens, and other handwork.

cross-stretcher: (furniture) an X-shaped brace with straight or curved lines; used on some side tables and chairs around 1700.

crotch grain: (furniture) wood cut from the forked, or V section, of a tree.

crotch-grain veneer: (furniture) a thin strip of wood cut from the forked, or V section, of the tree, where limbs and branches develop. Graining is often featherlike in appearance.

crouch ware: (ceramics) a brown salt-glazed stoneware. Most made in Staffordshire, *ca.* 1750.

crouke: (ceramics) an earthenware pitcher.

Crowen desk: (furniture) fine desks made by combining mahogany and rosewood with papier-maché. Crowen Company produced them in England from about 1840 until 1855.

crowfoot: (furniture) a simple form of the ball-and-claw foot.

crown glass: an optical glass with low refraction containing a soda-lime-silica mixture. Also window glass made by whirling a glass bubble into a flat disk — a bull's-eye remains in the center from the craftsman's rod.

crown jug: (ceramics) a jug with four spouts that meet in a common space on the top of a vessel. The spouts resemble a crown, hence the name.

crown Milano: (glass) an opaque, elaborately decorated glass featuring enamels on light backgrounds. First made by the Mount Washington Glass Company in 1884; usually marked "CM," often with a crown.

crown setting: (jewelry) an open setting that holds the stone in place with a circle of points.

crown weight: (glass) a blown-glass paperweight that is hollow in the middle.

crozier: (religious) a bishop's staff.

cruciform: (glass) early wine bottle made in the shape of a cross.

cruet: 1. (tableware) a bottles for condiments (vinegar or oil) often kept in pairs in a caster (stand). **2.** (religious) a vessel for wine or water; used during Eucharist.

crumb mortar: (kitchen) a mortar made of wood; used for making bread crumbs from stale bread and for crushing herbs.

crystal: (materials) term that usually refers to quality, clear flint glass. True crystal is a variety of transparent rock quartz.

cuchillo: (weapons) a Spanish clasp knife with a broad leaf-shaped blade; used for throwing.

cuir bouilli: (armor) leather boiled and molded in shape then allowed to dry and harden; used throughout Europe and the East for armor. Also called *quierboyle*.

cuisse: (armor) knee guard. First made of padded material and boiled leather (cuir bouilli), then of metal plate. Mid-14th to 17th centuries.

culet: (armor) a skirt of joined plates attached to the backplate to protect the loins. From mid-16th to mid-17th century.

cultured pearl: (jewelry) a pearl grown inside a mollusk under artificial (man-made) conditions.

culvertail: (furniture) a form of dovetailing so fine that once a piece is put together it is almost impossible to take it apart.

cupboard-top highboy: (furniture) a highboy (tall chest of drawers on legs) with several drawers on the bottom and a cupboard on the top (where a classic highboy would have more drawers). Also called *Westchester highboy* and *press-top highboy*.

cup-hilt rapier: (weapons) a 17th-century sword with a circular bowl-shaped guard and a straight quillon; used in Spain and southern Italy.

Cupid's bow: (furniture) a bow made up of two convex curves with recurved ends; form of the top rails of Chippendale chairs.

cup plate: (domestic accessories) a 3- to 4-inch saucer first made of pottery, then of glass. Until the mid-1800s, etiquette allowed ladies and gentlemen to pour hot tea from their cups into their saucers to cool. They then sipped the tea directly from the saucers and set their cups on the cup plates. By the mid-1800s, the most popular cup plates were made of glass, primarily by the Sandwich Glass Company.

curfew: (hearth accessories) a metal fireplace cover in the shape of a quarter-sphere with a handle in the middle; used to cover a fire and keep it alive overnight.

curio cabinet: (furniture) a high, narrow cabinet with shelves to display small collected items. Also called *pier cabinet*.

Currier and Ives: (prints) lithographs depicting life in America during the middle and late 1800s produced by Nathaniel Currier and James Ives. Their output was greater than all of the other lithographers in the country put together. They published more than 7,000 different prints. Currier and Ives have been extensively reproduced.

curule chair: (furniture) a chair supported by carved, X-shaped rails. Also called *Dantesque chair*.

cushion cut: (jewelry) a stone cut in a square or rectangle that has round corners. Also called *antique cut*.

cushion frieze: (furniture) a cushion-shaped form incorporated into case furniture cornices in the late 17th century.

custard glass: glassware first made in England in the 1880s that got its name from its color, which resembles that of the pudding. Real custard glass will glow when put under a black light because of the uranium used in its production. By the turn of the century, Harry Northwood had started producing custard glass in the United States; other companies soon followed his lead, making souvenir mugs, glasses, bowls, and the like.

cut corners: the rounded corners on playing cards — not legal before 1862.

cut glass: glass with the pattern ground into it with a metal or stone disc. See also *pressed glass*.

cutlass: (weapons) a variety of backswords dating from the 15th century. From the 18th century on, the term applied to a saber with a short, curved, single-edged blade used at sea.

cut velvet: (glass) cased glass with a smooth inner layer of glass topped by a relief-molded layer, usually in a quilted or ribbed pattern. Made in the late 19th century.

cutwork: (needlework) embroidery used on tablecloths, napkins, dresser scarves, and the like. Patterns are cut out of the fabric and the cut edges are bound with an overstitch.

Cybis: (figurines, ceramics) fine-quality figurines and plaques produced in the United States from the 1930s until the present. Originally designed by Boleslaw Cybis for the Cordey China Company. See also *Cordey*.

cyclas: (armor) a 14th-century garment worn over armor. The front is shorter than the back.

cylinder music box: a box with a brass cylinder that hits steel pins and makes music as it revolves. Originated in Switzerland; popular from the mid-1800s until about 1910. The finer the tone of the music, the more valuable the box.

cylinder-top desk: (furniture) a writing table or desk with a curved panel that conceals the writing surface, drawers, and compartments when closed. Differs from a roll-top desk only in that the curved panel is solid rather than slatted.

cyma curve: (furniture) a double curve that forms an S. See also *cyma recta* and *cyma reversa*.

cyma recta: (furniture) a molded cornice having two curves, the upper a concave form, and the lower a convex form. See also *cyma curve* and *cyma reversa*.

cyma reversa: (furniture) a molding or corner piece with two curves, the upper a convex form, and the lower a concave form. A reversed molding from cyma recta. See also *cyma curve* and *cyma recta*.

cymbalet: (music) a small instrument resembling a tambourine; used in America for a brief time during the late 19th century.

cymric: (jewelry) term used by Liberty and Company for the jewelry and other articles the company imported from English manufacturers. *Ca.* 1899.

D

dabus: (weapons) an Arabian mace studded with nails.

dagger marks: (weapons) marks struck by members of the Cutlers' Company in London. Found on knife blades beside the manufacturer's mark.

daguerreotype: (photography) the earliest photographic process, dating from 1839. The impression was made on a copperplate coated with silver and developed by mercury vapors. The finished print is clear and brilliant, but must be held at an angle to view because the silver reflects light so easily. The image can easily be smudged or rubbed off, so it should be covered by glass. The plate and print are the same, so only one print is possible.

daisho: (weapons) a pair of swords, one large and the other small, carried by the Japanese military class.

dalle de verre: (glass) thick glass used in stained-glass windows.

damascene: (metal, weapons, furniture) decorated metal surface (steel, iron, brass or copper) with gold and/or silver inlaid or etched in wavy patterns. Dates back to antiquity, but it was during the last half of the 16th century that this art form was most in demand. Milan, Italy, produced the most and best, although other European centers also manufactured damascene on a limited scale.

Damascus steel: (weapons) bars of hard and soft steel doubled and welded several times, then etched; used to make swords, knives, and gun barrels. Experts claim that the finest steel ever produced was made this way by early Japanese swordsmiths. Also called *watered steel*

Damascus sword: (weapons) a sword made or traded in Damascus. Although some swords were made in Damascus, it is believed that most of the swords traded there from the 10th century on originated in India or Persia.

damask: (textiles) a firm, lustrous, patterned fabric similar to brocade. It is reversible and comes in one or two colors; one side is satiny, the other has a dull finish. Often used to upholster furniture.

damaskeen: (decoration, metal) an engraving done on metal; used on watches as well as early armor.

dance card: (paper) a small card used by a Victorian lady to record the names of the gentlemen with whom she danced. Usually attached to the wrist or to a dress sash with a ribbon or cord. The men would ask the girls for a dance at the beginning of the festivities, and a lucky girl started the evening with her dance card filled. These bits of nostalgia are collectible.

dancing jack: (toys) a figure made of cardboard with the arms and legs cut separately and joined together with string so that the figure "danced" when jiggled.

dandy's stick: walking stick made of ash, teak, mahogany or some other fine wood with carved head of Chinese, Turk, or Moor person; used by dapper gentlemen in the early 1800s.

dangle-spit: (domestic) a long metal rod with hooks on the end from which meat was hung. The other end of the rod was hung by a chain, dangling the meat over a fire. The chain twisted from side to side, ensuring more even cooking.

danpira (or dambira): (weapons) the Japanese term for sword.

Dantesque chair: (furniture) a chair with curved, X-shaped supports. Named after Dante, the Italian poet. Also called *curule chair*.

Darby-Joan settee: (furniture) a settee with two chair backs. Popular in Queen Anne, Georgian, and Chippendale styles.

d'argental: (glass) an art-nouveau-style cameo glass made in France between 1872 and about 1920. Shades of brown and tan were dominant colors.

Daric: (coins) a gold coin depicting a king with a bow. Named for King Darius.

darky with alligator: (black memorabilia, toys) cast-iron pull toy of a black man pulling an alligator. Patented in 1903.

date: (armor) Japanese for a helmet crest; usually in the form of an animal or mythical monster.

dated: a piece of fine art or a decorative object that has a date which is thought to be accurate and to have been added at the time the art or decoration was done.

date letter: (silver) alphabetical mark used on silver by the English Assay Offices to identify the year of hallmarking. Not used on United States silver.

date nails: (railroad memorabilia) small nails used on railroad ties from 1900 on. Most were made of steel, but aluminum, copper, and plastic was also used. Each nail has the last two digits of the date it was made either raised or incised on the head.

Daum Nancy: (glass) cameo-type glass in the art nouveau style, featuring pictorial nature designs. Made from the late 1800s until the early 1900s by Jean Daum, who operated a glassworks in Nancy, France. Most pieces are signed and command prices in the thousands of dollars. The factory still operates under the name *C'ristalleries de Nancy*.

Davenport: (pottery, porcelain) wares, including willow and flow blue, made from 1793 until the late 1800s by Davenport and Company in the Staffordshire area of England. Their marks always contained the word *Davenport*.

davenport: 1. (furniture) a large sofa. **2.** (furniture) a chest of drawers with a slanted top for writing. Dated from early 1800s.

davenport table: (furniture) a long table that can be placed behind a davenport.

day bed: (furniture) a long narrow seat used as a couch or settee, usually with a chair back at the head. Also called *chaise lounge*.

day-of-the-month clock: a clock that indicates the date as well as the time.

dealer: one who buys and sells antiques and/or collectibles. (The term, of course, also applies to anyone who deals in other merchandise.)

death's head burgonet: (armor) a heavy (up to twenty pounds) helmet with round openings for the eyes and projecting hoods over the openings. From 17th century.

decal: (decoration) a design or picture printed on transparent material that can be transferred to glass, pottery, wood, or metal. Developed in the 19th century, it replaced earlier forms of transfers using gelatine and tissue paper. Also called *decalcomania*.

decalcomania: (decoration) a design or picture printed on transparent material that can be transferred to glass, pottery, wood, or metal. Developed in the 19th century, it replaced earlier forms of transfers using gelatine and tissue paper. Also called *decal*.

decanter: (household accessories) a glass, porcelain, or silver bottle, usually tall and with a stopper; used for serving wine or other alcoholic beverages. Decanters for hard liquors are shorter and fatter.

deckle edge: (prints, paper) an irregular, torn-looking edge on a print or any other paper item.

decorative art: art used to enhance a useful item that otherwise would appear plain.

decoy: (collectibles, folk art) a hunter's lure made to look like a duck, loon, or other game bird. Some were made to float and others were used on shore. Widely used from the 1880s until 1910. Originally hand carved. Some canvas and papier-maché decoys were produced. Many decoys were mass produced. Hand carving and original paint add to the value.

Dedham Pottery: company best known for its pottery with blue designs on a grayish, crackleware background. A rabbit was their most popular motif and was used in their marks from 1895 until they closed in 1943. They started business as Chelsea Pottery in Chelsea, Massachusetts, in 1860 but moved to Dedham a few years later. Reproductions have been produced at a Concord, Massachusetts, pottery since 1977. Reproduction rabbit is a slightly different style; original plates were crackle-glazed on the front only; reproductions are glazed on both front and back. New pieces are marked with a star, the painter's initials, the year it was painted, and "U.S.A."

deerfoot handle: (metal, tableware) handles made in the image of deer hooves; used as handles on 17th-century eating utensils. Also called *hoof handles.*

defect: (stamps) a stamp with serious damage.

definitive: (stamps) one of the regular (not special-issue) stamps of a country.

Degenhart glass: paperweights and other quality glass objects made by the Crystal Art Glass Factory, opened in Cambridge, Ohio, in 1947 by John and Elizabeth Degenhart. John died in 1964 and his wife continued operation until her death in 1978, when the company was sold. At that time the logo, a heart with a *D,* was discontinued. Collectors are primarily interested in items with this mark.

de Lamerie, Paul (1688-1751): (silver) a leading English silversmith.

delatte: (glass) a French cameo glass made up of contrasting colors. Made in the 1920s.

delft: (ceramics) a tin-glazed pottery decorated with blue on a white ground. Delftware has been made since the 1600s. Pieces marked "Holland" were made after 1891 and are not as desirable as earlier examples.

delphite glass: a light blue opaque glass. Also called *blue milk glass.*

demi-lune tables: (furniture) half-round tables that were customarily placed at each end of a rectangular table to make a long, oval dining table. Also called *half-moon tables.*

demi-parure: (jewelry) a small, usually two-piece set of matching jewelry. For instance, a brooch and earrings, a necklace and bracelet, or earrings and a necklace.

demi-placcate: (armor) the lower part of a Gothic breastplate.

demi-poulaine solerets: (armor) foot guards with pointed toes, moderate in length. From 15th century.

demitasse: (tableware) a small glass or porcelain cup with a saucer; used for serving after-dinner coffee.

demonetize: (coins, stamps) to divest a coin or stamp of its monetary value. This rarely occurs, and then usually years after the coin or stamp has been removed from sale or circulation.

de Morgan, William Frend (1839-1917): (ceramics) an English potter who was especially known for his tile designs in the late 1800s. He often used the style of early majolica in his work.

denga: (coins) a silver coin first issued in the 1300s in Russia. The most common ones have an image of a horse and rider.

denomination: (stamps) the face value of a stamp.

dentil molding: (furniture, architecture) a form of molding made of small rectangular blocks set at equal distances from each other.

Denver: (ceramics) brownware with an underglaze decoration produced by the Denver China and Pottery Company. William Long started the company in Colorado in 1901. Pieces are marked "Denver" or "Denaura" and usually are dated.

departmental stamp: an official postage stamp authorized for use only by a single department of the government. In the 19th century, nine United States departments had their own stamps.

Depression: in the U.S., the years between 1929 and 1940 characterized by high unemployment, low wages, and a generally impoverished economy.

depression glass: mass-produced, inexpensive glass made in a variety of colors, patterns, and objects that added a bright note to the Depression era, when it was available by mail-order and at stores, and given away as premiums by gas stations, food stores, and movie houses. This glass has become a popular collectible in recent years; some patterns and pieces command high prices.

Derby: (ceramics) tableware, figurines, candlesticks, and the like produced by Derby Pottery. Founded in Derby, England, in 1756 and still operating, the company has changed names several times, which helps in dating wares. From 1756 to 1769 it was Derby Porcelain; from 1769 to 1785 it was Chelsea Derby. Royal Crown Derby is the modern name.

Derbyshire pottery: pottery or porcelain that was manufactured at any of a number of factories in Derbyshire, England.

derringer: (weapons) a small mid-19th-century pocket pistol with one or two barrels, each about 1-1/2 inches long. First made by Henry Deringer of Philadelphia.

Deruta maiolica: (ceramics) an Italian maiolica best known for the blue-and-yellow Deruta luster ware produced during the 1500s.

desk box: a slant-topped box that was used as a writing desk. The top opens to store paper and other writing supplies. Sometimes ornate, sometimes plain, they were almost always made with locks and placed on stands or tables. *Ca.* 16th and 17th century. See also *devenport*.

desserte: (furniture) a tiered serving table.

detonator: (weapons) device for sparking the charge in a gun. Ignition was by percussion; however, the fulminate was either shaped like a pill or small ball or contained in a tube or backed by paper. Introduced after the flintlock and before the percussion proper. Also called *pill lock.*

Deutsche blumen: (decoration, ceramics) literally, *German flowers.* A style of painting first used at Meissen in the early 1700s.

de Vaucanson, Jacques: (toys) one of the first inventors of mechanical figures. One of his first creations was a man playing a flute. His work advanced automata greatly in the 1700s.

DeVez: (glass) an acid-cut cameo glass from the early 1900s.

devenport: (furniture) a desk box and the cabinet on which it sits. The cabinet has drawers and the box slides forward on it when in use. See also *desk box*.

device: (design) a decorative pattern, design, symbol, or figure, such as those used in heraldic arms or embroidery.

De Vilbiss: (glass) a top manufacturer of perfume atomizers. De Vilbiss operated from 1888 until 1968. Some of their atomizers were marked; others had paper labels. De Vilbiss is prized by collectors.

Devon: (ceramics) an English firm that produced majolica and earthenware items from 1879 until the mid-1900s. Their art deco vases are particularly sought.

Devonia lace: (textiles) a lace featuring raised flower petals. Popular in the mid-1800s.

Devonshire pottery: slipware pottery made in North Devonshire, England, from the 1600s until the early 1900s.

dexter: (heraldry) the right side of a shield.

diamond ornament: (furniture) a diamond-shaped design that was carved frequently into the doors on cupboards, the fronts of chests, and the legs of other pieces during the 1600s.

diamond-point engraving: (glass) designs scratched onto glass items with the point of a diamond. Popular from the 1500s until the end of the 18th century.

diaperwork: (furniture, design) a surface decoration made up of regular repeats of a design; often done with geometric figures.

dibble: (tableware) a pewter plate — often an underplate.

die: 1. (metal) a metal press used to cut, form, or stamp shapes and designs into metal. **2.** (stamps) the original metal engraving for a stamp from which the printing plates are made.

die-cast: (toys) inexpensive, mass-produced toys made by pressing metal alloys into molds. Details of the toy are clearly defined by this method.

dinanderie: (metal) brass items made in the Flemish town of Dinant until the 16th century. Candlesticks, cooking pots, jugs, basins, and fonts are among the many items produced in Dinant. The presence of large zinc deposits there made it possible to produce brass when other areas were using bronze.

dinar: (coins) an Islamic gold coin dating back to the 7th century.

dining car collectibles: (railroad memorabilia) the silverware, glassware, china, linens, menus, swizzle sticks, coasters, and other objects from railroads dining cars. They are marked with the name of the railroad on which they were used. Usually the smaller the railroad, the more valuable the piece.

Dionne quintuplets: (collectibles) any item featuring the widely-publicized quintuplets, born in Canada on May 28, 1934. The siblings' likenesses were used to promote many products. The Madame Alexander Dionne quintuplet dolls are the priciest and the most desirable of the dolls.

dipped seat: (furniture) a concave seat with the middle and front lower than the sides. Also called *dropped seat*.

dipped pottery: pottery with either a plain brownish finish, with or without a colored band, or pottery that appears marbled. Most examples are from the 1800s, but dipped pottery actually dates from the early 1700s.

Directoire: (furniture) furniture from 1795 to 1799, when the Directoire governed France. This furniture had the following characteristics: simple designs; a strong Greek influence in the form; fairly heavy; made of solid mahogany; chair tops with a rolled-backward design; the use of French-revolution scenes or symbols for ornaments; and Egyptian motifs. The American Directoire period was 1798-1804.

dirhem: (coins) Islamic silver coins.

dirk: (weapons) a dagger like that carried by the Scotch Highlander, which has a heavy single-edged blade, thick at the back and tapering from hilt to point. There is no guard.

disappearing darky: (black memorabilia, toys) black Jack-in-the-box. The man pops out of a chimney and thumbs his nose. Made in Germany *ca.* 1910.

discharge printing: (textiles) a fabric with a white or natural design on a colored background. The design is achieved by first dyeing the fabric and then printing the design with a bleach that removes the color. This process was first used in the early 1800s.

disclosed: (heraldry) an eagle with inverted wings spread out and pointing down.

disc music box: (music) music box that plays steel discs. Considered superior to the cylinder music box. First made in Germany in the 1880s, but American companies soon followed suit. Popular until *ca.* 1920.

dish top: (furniture) a tabletop with a plain, raised rim. Mid-1700s.

dished corner: (furniture) a table corner slightly scooped out to hold a candlestick.

Disneyana: (collectibles) any item portraying a Disney character. Those made during the 1930s have the greatest value.

disparate parts: parts taken from different objects and assembled to create a complete object like a clock or lamp.

displayed proper: (heraldry) an eagle with upraised wings.

distlefink: (decoration) a brightly colored, painted or carved bird motif; used extensively by the Pennsylvania Germans (called Pennsylvania Dutch) in their crafts.

distressed: (furniture) the result of deliberately marring a surface to simulate age.

ditty bag: (marine) small bag in which sailors kept personal items. See also *ditty box.*

ditty box: (marine) small chest in which sailors kept personal items. See also *ditty bag.*

divan: (furniture) a long backless, upholstered couch.

Doccia porcelain: porcelain made from 1735; usually marked with an impressed star of blue, gold, or red. Originally soft-paste, but by the early 1800s hard-paste porcelain was being produced at the Doccia factory, which reproduced the works of many other factories.

documentary stamp: a revenue stamp used on legal, official, or business papers.

dogane: (weapons) a wide collar of metal around the middle of a Japanese knife or sword.

dogcart: (vehicles) a horse-drawn cart seating two persons back-to-back. See also *dos-a-dos.*

dog collar: (jewelry) a wide necklace that fits right to the neck.

dog ear: (architecture, furniture) a projecting rectangular ornament at the top of door frames, paneling, and mirror frames. Common in early Georgian pieces. *Ca.* 1714-1760.

dog's foot: (furniture) a brass furniture foot resembling a dog's leg and foot. Used mostly on chairs. Also called *dog's paw.*

dog's paw: (furniture) a brass furniture foot resembling a dog's leg and foot; used mostly on chairs. Also called *dog's foot*.

dogusuri-iro: (weapons) a Japanese powder flask.

dokyu: (weapons) a Japanese repeating crossbow. A close copy of the Chinese chu-ko-nu. See also *chu-ko-nu*.

dombay: (weapons) a rifle used in the Caucasus.

dolls: (toys) old and new dolls are collectible. Some of the names to look for are Armand Marseille, Barbie, Bru, Effanbee, Horsman, Ideal, Jumeau, Kestner, Lenci, Madame Alexander, Schoenhut, Shirley Temple, Steiner, and Vogue. Materials include composition, cloth, porcelain, and papier-maché.

dolphin candlesticks: (glass) glass candlesticks in the form of dolphins first made by the Boston and Sandwich Glass Company, *ca.* mid-1800s. They were produced in vaseline, clear, and white. Dolphin candlesticks have been copied by many companies.

dolphin console: (furniture) a tabletop that is held up by wall brackets shaped like dolphins.

dolphin foot: (furniture) the feet and legs of mid-18th-century furniture shaped like dolphins' heads and scaly bodies.

domed foot: (glass, silver) a dome-shaped support for the stem of a vessel.

domino tray: (glass) a tray for serving sugar cubes. The tray has a slightly raised ring for a creamer. The ring keeps the creamer from sliding as the tray is passed.

Donaldson, John: (fine art, decoration) an artist in the 1700s who was considered one of the most important producers of miniatures and enamels.

Donegal carpet: (floor coverings) a coarse carpet woven in Donegal, Ireland, since 1898.

door furniture: (metal, ceramics) door accessories, including door handles, key plates, and finger plates. Considered an important part of a room's decor during the 18th century.

door knocker: (metal) a device found on most front doors before the invention of the doorbell. Made in many shapes and sizes, and usually of cast iron. Those made in England are particularly desirable. The more unusual the shape, the higher the price.

doorstop: (domestic) heavy device placed on the floor to keep a door open. Cast-iron doorstops are by far the most popular. They have been used in this country since just after the Civil War. Age, condition, shape, and size all influence price. They have been widely reproduced.

doré: (metal) the French term for gilding over brass or bronze.

Doreurs, Corporation des: (decoration) the craft guild responsible for gilding in France.

Dorflinger, Christian (fl. 1865): (glass) maker of very fine cut glass in his factories in New York and Pennsylvania from the mid-1800s until his death in 1915. President and Mrs. Lincoln were among the famous people who had cut-glass treasures made by Dorflinger. This rare glass was usually marked with a paper label.

dormand: any permanent part. For example, a dormand beam in a house or a dormand top on a table.

dos-à-dos: 1. (books) the binding of two books together back-to-back with a common lower board. Used for small devotional works in the 16th and 17th centuries. **2.** (furniture) a sofa for two people with a centered back so the occupants face away from each other. **3.** (vehicles) a carriage, such as a dog cart, that seats two persons back-to-back. See also *dogcart*.

double cruet: (tableware) a pair of cruets that are permanently joined together, each with its own spout and each with its own holding space.

double-lens camera: (photography) camera that produced two pictures at once which, when viewed, looked like one three-dimensional image.

double-scroll handle: (furniture) a handle design with the lines of an *S* or pair of reverse curves.

double stretchers: (furniture) two stretchers on chairs where one is usually used. The second stretcher is for added strength and/or for decoration.

double-struck: (coins) a coin with a portion of its design repeated.

doublet: (jewelry) a counterfeit gemstone with a thin layer of the authentic gem covering a glass or paste back.

dough tray: (kitchen) a deep boxlike trough with sloping sides used for kneading yeast dough and allowing it to rise. The trough is sometimes on legs.

Doulton: (ceramics) company that originally produced industrial salt-glazed stoneware. Doulton Pottery began in 1815 in Lambeth, England. Early wares include jugs, bottles, flasks, whistles and pitchers. By 1902 they were known as Royal Doulton.

douters: (lighting) a scissorlike implement with flat, oval blades for extinguishing candle flames. Differs from snuffers, which have cutting edges to trim the wick.

dovetail joint: (furniture) a tight interlocking joint formed by a tenon fitted into a corresponding mortise.

dowel: (furniture) a wooden pin used to fasten two pieces of cabinetwork together.

dower chest: (furniture) any storage chest used to hold the trousseau and linen of a future bride. Also called *dowry chest* and *hope chest*.

dowry chest: (furniture) any storage chest used to hold the trousseau and linen of a future bride. Also called *dower chest* and *hope chest*.

dragonware: (ceramics) Japanese pottery made during the 1940s and 1950s depicting a dragon in raised white (moriage) on a gray, orange, and lavender, or orange and brown background. See also *moriage*.

draisiana: (vehicles) an arrangement, much like a bicycle without pedals, of two wheels held together by a frame that is straddled by the rider. The draisiana was propelled by the feet and, when it got going, the rider could coast. It was invented in 1818 in Philadelphia.

drake foot: (furniture) a three-toed club foot found on early furniture originating in Philadelphia and the Delaware Valley. Also called *duck foot* and *Dutch foot*.

dram cup: two-handled bowl similar to a wine taster. It has not been in fashion since the late 1700s.

dram glass: (glass) small vessel for serving liquor. The various forms in which these glasses were made helps date them. As a rule, those with four feet are from the early 1600s; short, molded stems and cup-shaped bowls date from 1675 to 1750; a straight-sided glass on a flat knob was used from 1690 to 1710; a trumpet bowl on a short stem puts a piece between 1710 and 1850.

draw leaves: (furniture) table leaves that store under the top and are pulled out and adjusted to provide a level extension of the tabletop.

drawn work: (needlework) embroidery in which threads are pulled from a fabric and the resulting holes are stitched.

draw table: (furniture) a long, narrow table with underleaves that pull out and up to extend the surface. Also called *refectory table*.

dredger: 1. (kitchen) a small, cylinder-shaped pot used in the 18th century to hold pepper. **2.** (desk accessories) small box for sand, or pounce, found on inkstands. Also called *pounce box*. See also *pounce*.

Dresden: (ceramics) any porcelain produced in any of the numerous factories in Dresden, Germany, during the 1700s and 1800s. Each piece bears the mark of the factory in which it was made. Crossed swords on a Dresden piece indicates it was made in the prestigious Meissen factory.

dressing box: (furniture) a small box with an adjustable mirror and compartments inside for combs, cosmetics, and the like.

dressing glass: (furniture) an adjustable shaving mirror attached to a set of drawers. Popular from the 1600s to the 1800s.

dressing table: (furniture) a table with one or more mirrors at which a woman can sit to apply cosmetics and comb her hair. Also called *vanity table*.

drill: (textiles) twilled linen.

Drissell, John: (folk art) an American painter who lived in Bucks County, Pennsylvania, where he decorated small wooden objects in the late 1700s.

drop-center vanity: (furniture) a three-section dressing table with a lower center section.

dropped seat: (furniture) a concave seat with the middle and front lower than the sides. Also called *dipped seat*.

drop spindle: (domestics) a sticklike spindle with a disc-shaped weight known as a whorl on one end. It relied on the force of gravity for operation. Drop spindles have been used for centuries, beginning with primitive societies.

drollery: (fine art) a humorous picture or illustration often featuring animals taking human roles.

drum table: (furniture) a round table with drawers all around the edges. Old ones are rare, but they were copied in the mid-20th century.

drunkard's chair: (furniture) a chair, just large enough for two people, made in Chippendale and Queen Anne styles. Also called *lover's chair*, *sparking chair,* and *sporting chair*.

Dryden: (ceramics) pottery produced by James Dryden who founded a factory in Ellsworth, Kansas in 1946. By the late 1950s he had moved his pottery to Hot Springs, Arkansas. Artus Van Briggle made some of Dryden's pieces. Most Dryden pottery is marked with "Dryden" or "Ozark Frontier." The earlier pieces are made of dark tan clay and those made in Hot Springs are white clay.

dry mount: (prints) the process of mounting a print on a board or other surface using a sheet of dry glue and heat.

duck box: (accessories) boxes made in animal shapes. The oldest ones were made in China of jade or crystal. So named because ducks were the first shapes produced.

duck foot: (furniture) a three-toed club foot found on early furniture originating in Philadelphia and the Delaware Valley. Also called *drake foot* and *Dutch foot*.

duck stamp: (stamps) a popular name for the United States Hunting Permit revenue stamp issued yearly since 1934.

ductile: (metal) flexible or malleable during the shaping process.

dudgeon: (weapons) a dagger with a wooden hilt made from the box tree root.

dueling sword: (weapons) a special sword for dueling that evolved after the carrying of swords was abandoned. It had a simple hilt, a shell guard, and a triangular blade.

dulcimer: (music) a quadrilateral stringed instrument with only two parallel sides; played with light mallets.

dulcimore: (music) a three- or four-stringed American folk instrument placed in the lap and strummed or picked.

dumbwaiter: (furniture) a dining room stand with shelves. English, early 1700s, with a tripod base supporting a center post holding three circular trays of graduated sizes, the largest on the bottom. Later versions were of various designs.

Dummer, Jeremiah: (silver) the first silversmith born in America. Dummer apprenticed with John Hull in Boston during the 1600s. Most of his work imitated the English style.

dummy board: (hearth accessories) flat, wooden cutout figures painted to represent animals or soldiers, children, maidservants, and other persons. 17th and 18th centuries.

Duncan and Miller: (glass) producers of pressed-glass dinnerware, opalescent vases, and glass candy boxes. The most famous pattern produced by Duncan and Miller is Three Faces, designed by John Ernest Miller, a top glass designer of the 1800s. While it is collectible, this glass usually does not command very high prices — a few patterns, such as Three Faces, are the exceptions.

Durand: (glass) an art glass produced in New Jersey that is similar to Stueben Glass. Most Durand Glass was not marked. Pieces marked with the company name bring much higher prices than unmarked ones.

dust board: (furniture) a wooden partition between the drawers of a chest of drawers for protection against dust and theft.

Dutch foot: (furniture) a three-toed club foot found on early furniture originating in Philadelphia and the Delaware Valley. Also called *drake foot* and *duck foot*.

Dutch gold: (decoration) a copper and zinc alloy used as a substitute for gold leaf in decoration. Also called *Dutch metal*.

Dutch metal: (decoration) a copper and zinc alloy used as a substitute for gold leaf in decoration. Also called *Dutch gold*.

Dutch oven: (kitchen) an oven with an open front, placed before the fire for baking. Made of iron, brass, or pottery.

Dutch-pad foot: (furniture) a circular foot that extends forward from the leg; the principal foot used with cabriole legs on Queen Anne furniture. Also called *club foot*.

dwarf candlestick: (metal) a low candlestick of brass or silver.

Œ

eagle, American: 1. (furniture) adopted as the national symbol in 1786, the bald eagle has been a popular furniture ornament ever since. **2.** (coins) a former United States gold coin with the face value of ten dollars.

eagle and star: (furniture) motif inlaid on many pieces of American furniture. The number of stars used is indicative of the date. For example, if there are fourteen stars, it was made after 1791, when Vermont became a state; fifteen stars means after 1792, when Kentucky entered the union, and so on.

eagle volant: (heraldry) an eagle in free flight.

Eames, Charles: (furniture, design) American architect and designer who strongly influenced modern furniture design. His modern plastic and metal furniture set trends in the 1940s and 1950s.

eared dagger: (weapons) a 15th-century Italian dagger with disks attached to the pommel that stand out like ears. Modified from Oriental models. Also called *estradiot dagger*.

ear flaps: (armor) a forerunner of the visor, they first appeared on 11th-century helmets. Also called *ear guards*.

ear guards: (armor) a forerunner of the visor, they first appeared on 11th-century helmets. Also called *ear flaps*.

early Victorian: (furniture) furniture made from 1830 to 1860 with a French influence. Also called *second rococo*.

earthenware: (ceramics) pottery that is by definition at least 50 percent porous. There are two classifications of pottery — earthenware and stoneware; and there are two classifications of earthenware — glazed and unglazed. Objects such as bricks are unglazed earthenware, while an earthenware plate may be glazed, thus making it semi-porcelain. See also *stoneware*.

East India Company China: denotes Chinese porcelain imported into Europe by the East India Company or the French Compagnie des Indes.

Eastlake, Charles Lock (1836-1906): (architecture, design) an English architect who expounded a return to simple and sturdy furniture during the period 1868 to 1880 — late Victorian period.

Eaton, Moses: (folk art) the best-known itinerant American stencil artist.

ebonized wood: (furniture) wood stained black to look like ebony.

echinus molding: (furniture) a quarter-round molding.

eclectic: (furniture, design) a mixture of various styles.

ecrevisses: (armor) armor made of overlapping plates.

ecuelle: (tableware) a porcelain or silver shallow, circular, covered soup bowl with flat side handles. French, 17th and 18th centuries.

Edkins, Michael: (glass) a fine English glass painter from 1760 until 1787.

Effanbee: (dolls) collectible dolls depicting babies, small children, and adults. Made since 1910 by a company founded by Bernard Fleischaker and Hugo Baum.

effigy: (decoration, coins) the image of a person.

EFO: (stamps) term referring to stamp errors, freaks, and oddities.

egg-and-dart: (decoration) ornamentation made up of alternating figures of an egg and a dart or arrowhead; used on furniture, silver, and jewelry from the late 1500s.

egg-and-tongue: (decoration) ornamentation of alternating egg and tonguelike motifs. Used on furniture, silver, and jewelry during the 17th and 18th centuries.

eggshell porcelain: an extremely thin porcelain, first made in China in the early 15th century. Japanese and European factories have produced eggshell-thin porcelain since the 19th century.

eggshell ware: (ceramics, collectibles) a very thin porcelain ware made by the Rozenberg factory in the Netherlands in the late 1800s and early 1900s. Highly prized by collectors.

eglomise: (decoration) glass painted with gold leaf. Process first used by French decorator Glomi for whom it is named.

Egyptian black: (ceramics) a name used to describe basalt ware, a black stoneware. See also *basalt ware.*

eight hundred (800) silver: European alloy of 800 parts silver and 200 parts copper. See also *coin silver* and *sterling silver.*

eight-legged table: (furniture) a table with four stationary legs and four mobile legs, two on each side, that pull out to support leaves.

elastolin: (toys) a composition material that was molded around wires to form the shape of a toy. Made in Germany. Not very durable.

elbow chair: (furniture) armchair.

elbow cop: (armor) elbow guard of plate. From the late 14th century. Also called *elbow piece.*

elbow gauntlet: (armor) a long steel or leather glove that reaches to the elbow. From the 16th century.

elbow guard: (armor) a large plate guard worn over the regular armor on the left arm during tournaments in the 15th and 16th century.

elbow piece: (armor) elbow guard of plate. From late 14th century. Also called *elbow cop.*

electrolier: (lighting) the correct term for what is commonly called an electric chandelier.

electroplate: (metal) to coat a thin layer of metal by electric current (electrodeposition) onto a second metal. The technique was patented in the 1830s, and, in the case of silver, replaced Sheffield plate.

electrum: (jewelry, metal) a metal golden-color alloy obtained by mixing 80 percent silver and 20 percent gold.

Elfinware: (ceramics) a line of small porcelain articles made in Dresden style from the early 1900s until about 1940. Raised flowers were very often used on these pieces. Many are marked "Elfinware" and "Germany."

Elgin cutlass pistol: (weapons) a combination single-shot percussion pistol and bowie knife, patented in 1837 by George Elgin. They were used by the United States Navy for a short time but civilian interest was nil.

Elizabethan: (design) applies to designs and objects made during the reign of Quenn Elizabeth I of England, 1558 to 1603.

ell: (textiles) the measure formerly used to measure material, particularly tapestry. The English ell is 45 inches, the French 46 3/4 inches, and the Flemish 27 inches. Originally, *ell* meant *forearm,* and the distance between the elbow and the extended middle finger was the accepted measure.

elliptical: (furniture) oval shaped.

Ellis, Harvey: (furniture) a New York designer hired by Gustav Stickley to design mission furniture.

émail ombrant: (ceramics) similar to lithophane, émail ombrant has an intaglio decoration that is enhanced with a glaze of a single color in a variety of tones. Green was the most popular choice for émail ombrant. See also *lithophane*.

embay: (decoration) to confine or enclose.

emboitment: (armor) breastplate made of two or more overlapping plates made flexible by sliding rivets or straps.

embossed: (decoration) a relief design often used on metal, wood, and pottery achieved by molding, carving, or adding to the surface, or by hammering and stamping from the underside. See also boss.

embossing: (textiles) a design or monogram worked or stitched in relief, often with several layers of thread worked over each other.

emission: (stamps) the issuance of a stamp.

empire mirror: (furniture) a name incorrectly given to a tabernacle mirror that was popular from 1800 to 1840. These mirrors are of American design.

Empire style: (design) evolved from Directoire style, a furniture style that became popular during the reign of Napoleon I. Later the term was applied to the heavy furniture with coarse carving of the early 19th century. See also *Directoire*.

enamel: (decoration) a heated glass which, when applied to metal, may be either opaque or translucent.

enarmes: (weapons) the straps used to secure a shield to a warrior's left arm during the Middle Ages.

encased overlay: (glass) a design laid on a glass surface that is covered by another layer of transparent glass.

encased stamp: (stamps, coins) a stamp enclosed in a transparent holder and used as money. Encased stamps have been used during coin shortages — during the Civil War and in some European countries during World War I, for example.

encaustic: (ceramics) a method of painting and firing decoration on earthenware by applying colored beeswax, then hardening it with heat.

enchasement: (stamps) any very elaborate design used to decorate a stamp.

encoignure: (furniture) a low, elegant corner cupboard of French design.

encrier: (desk accessories) French for *inkwell*.

encrusted cameo: (glass) an early glass paperweight made by embedding an unglazed white china plaque with a design in relief, in glass. Also called *sulphide*.

endboards: (furniture) vertical support boards for Gothic stools and chests.

end matching: (furniture) sheets of veneer matched end to end.

end-of-day marble: a multicolored glass marble.

endpapers: (books) the double leaves of paper at the front and back of a book. The outer leaves (paste-downs) are glued to the inner sides of the cover and the inner leaves (free endpapers) form the first and last pages of the book. When the endpapers are of silk or other nonpaper material, they are called *linings*.

end table: (furniture) a small table placed beside an armchair or sofa, usually to hold a table lamp.

en esclavage: (jewelry) a necklace with strands that are bound together at both ends but hang separately in the middle.

engine: (weapons) any device used for throwing arrows, stones, or other missiles. Engines include balistas, catapults, trebuchets, and crossbows.

engine-turned: (decoration, metal) engraving created with a lathe; used to decorate metal objects.

English plate: (metal) silver plated on copper. This term was first used by the Sheffield platers who favored this plate to the silver on a white metal used by the Germans.

English sterling: (silver) highly desirable sterling wares made in England. Pieces are marked with either four or five hallmarks: a lion facing to the left, signifying sterling; a guild mark representing the town or city where the piece was made (a leopard's head means London; a harp, Dublin; a castle, Edinburgh; an anchor, Birmingham); a letter in a shield that denotes the year a piece was made; and initials of the silversmith. Hester Bateman, Matthew Boulton, Paul de Lamerie, and Paul Storr are among the most familiar English silversmiths. The fifth mark, which may or may not appear, depicts a reigning queen or king. See also *sterling silver.*

engobe: (ceramics) a heavy slip used for decorating pottery. See also *slip.*

engraving: 1. (decoration) decorating by cutting or carving the surface of an object. **2.** (prints, books) a print made from an engraved block or plate.

en plein enamel: (decoration) opaque enamel painted in bright colors; applied to various objects for decoration. This method was popular in France, Germany, and England for a short time in the mid-18th century. Most examples are French.

ensho-ire: (weapons) a Japanese powder flask.

ensign: a national flag carried aboard a vessel. Originally the term referred to all flags, banners, standards, and the like; later, to the colors of the infantry, carried by an ensign, a junior officer rank abolished by the army in the early 19th century.

entablature: (furniture) the section above the capital of a column consisting of three parts: the architrave, frieze, and cornice.

entre le dish: (tableware) a covered serving dish made of silver. Some have covers with detachable handles so the covers can be used as separate dishes.

envelope table: (furniture) a triangular table, or a square table with four triangle-shaped leaves.

epaul de mouton: (armor) a large, curved guard worn over the regular armor in tournaments to protect the right arm. Also called *polder mitton.*

EPBM: (metal) the abbreviation for *electroplate (silver) on Britannia metal*. Initials imprinted on objects.

EPC: (metal) the abbreviation for *electroplate (silver) on copper.* Initials imprinted on objects.

epee: (weapons) a long, narrow dueling sword carried by 18th-century gentlemen. Originally the sword had a flat blade, which was too flexible; the blade later became triangular for rigidity. The modern fencing epee has the same blade with a blunt point. Both weapons have a bowl-shaped guard. See also *foil* and *saber.*

epergne: (household accessories) a large porcelain, glass, or silver serving bowl, basket, or dish, usually with compartments or several smaller containers branching out from the center container; used as a centerpiece. Often very elaborate; commonly used for flowers.

ephemera: (paper) paper items that were produced as throwaways, but that have become collectible. Newspapers, product labels, ticket stubs, and sales literature are a few examples.

EPNS: (metal) the abbreviation for *electropated nickel silver* — a silver layer electroplated on a nickel alloy. Initials imprinted on objects.

epreuve: (prints) a proof.

EPWM: (metal) the abbreviation for *electroplate (silver) on nickel with white metal mounts* (feet, handles, finials, and the like). Initials imprinted on the object.

Erphila: (ceramics, collectibles) porcelain novelty items made in Czechoslovakia and Germany. Pieces, including boxes, figurines, Toby mugs, and vases, are all marked with the country and "Erphila."

errata: (books) errors discovered in a book after printing. If the mistakes are identified before binding, they may be acknowledged on a spare page or partial page; if not, they are printed on a separate slip and tipped in.

error: (stamps) a broad term that covers any mistake detectable on the stamp. It can be a flaw in the design, paper, ink, printing, or perforation; or the result of an addition, omission, or inversion.

esclopette: (weapons) a 17th-century short wheel-lock gun with a hinged stock that folds back. It was carried in a holster. Also, other similar folding guns with updated ignition, used much later, usually for unlawful purposes, because they were easy to conceal.

escritoire: (furniture) a secretary cabinet with a fall front for writing. The upper section has drawers and pigeonholes, while the lower portion is a chest of drawers or a stand with legs. From the late 17th century. Also called *scrutoire*.

escutcheon: 1. (furniture) the metal plate of a keyhole. **2.** (heraldry) a shield-shaped emblem bearing a coat of arms.

E. S. Germany: (ceramics) porcelain made from 1860 until 1925 in Suhl, Germany, by Erdmann Schlegelmilch, the founder of the factory. Pieces are marked "E. S. Germany." Erdmann Schlegelmilch also made E. S.

Prussia in Saxony, Prussia. See also *E.S. Prussia*.

espadon: (weapons) a large 15th-century sword.

espagnolette: (decoration) a lady's head carved of wood with a stiff collar of lace. Used often as a mounted furniture decoration in the 1700s.

espallieres: (armor) shoulder guards formed of metal strips (lames) flexibly attached; 16th century.

E. S. Prussia: (ceramics) porcelain made in Saxony, Prussia, in the late 1800s and early 1900s. The E. S. is for Erdmann Schlegelmilch, founder of the factory. Pieces are marked "E. S. Prussia." Erdmann Schlegelmilch also made E. S. Germany in Suhl, Germany. See also *E.S. Germany*.

essay: (stamps) a proposed stamp design not yet accepted.

estate auction: an auction offering the entire, or most of, the contents of a home.

estoc: (weapons) a sword with a long, narrow, quadrangular blade for thrusting. Originally hung from the saddle or, when on foot, carried in rings on the belt.; later they were carried in scabbards. From 13th to 17th century.

estradiot dagger: (weapons) a 15th-century Italian dagger with disks attached to the pommel that stand out like ears. Modified from Oriental models. Also called *eared dagger*.

etagere: (furniture) an open shelved unit, sometimes with a drawer or enclosed cabinet below, to display small objects.

etched: 1. (glass) glass items that have a design cut into them, usually with acid. **2.** (metal) metal with a design impressed with acid.

eternity ring: (jewelry) a ring set with a complete circle of stones. Given to a loved one to symbolize never-ending love.

Etling: (glass) company that produced glass made in the style of Lalique during the 1920s and 1930s in France.

Etruscan art: (fine art) sculpture and murals by people from Etruria in central Italy, now known as Tuscany. Their murals and terra cotta statues depicted a happy life. Even the life-size statues that guarded the tombs were smiling.

Etruscan majolica: (ceramics) tin-glazed pottery made by Griffin, Smith, and Hill in Phoenixville, Pennsylvania, from 1879 until 1889. Pieces are marked "Etruscan Majolica."

etui: a small case used to hold scissors, bodkins, and other items used by women.

everlasting cloth: (textiles) a woolen fabric that lasts a long time. Also called *perpetuana*.

evolute: (decoration) a repetitive wave motif for frieze or band decoration; used on furniture.

ewer: (kitchen) a large pitcher with a wide spout.

ewery: (furniture) a plain, basic kitchen cupboard.

excelsior desk: (furniture) a desk made in the 1800s for college girls. It has a top that folds over a writing surface which pulls out to expand the work area.

exergue: (coins) the area on the reverse side of a coin or medal below the central design, often giving the date and mint mark.

ex-library: (books) a book that has been in a lending library. Such a book has less value.

ex libris: (books) Latin term meaning *from the library of*, used on bookplates with the owner's name.

expertising: (stamps) the appraisal of a stamp or other philatelic item.

exploded: (stamps) the cover and leaves of a stamp booklet separated and mounted individually for display in an album.

extended: (books) the restoration of the inner margin of a book leaf. The renewal of one to three outer margins is called *remargined,* and the renewal of all four margins is called *inlaid.* See also *remargined* and *inlaid.*

F

Fabergé: (jewelry, household accessories) a Russian jewelry company started in St. Petersburg in 1842. The gold pieces, eggs, buckles, icons, jugs, and the like fashioned by Fabergé are highly prized and very expensive.

fable-painted: (ceramics) tableware decorated with characters from *Aesop's Fables* during the 1750s. This work has not been attributed to any one potter or artist.

fabric: (coins) the metal and surface characteristics created by the production of a coin.

fabris: (ceramics) exquisite figurines made in Bassano del Grappa, Italy, starting in 1875. These limited-edition individual figurines and groups were done in the fashion of famous paintings. They are marked with a red anchor. The early molds were used again in an issue called "The Museum Collector," made from 1980 to 1982. These pieces are marked with a gold anchor.

face: to cover a surface with a different material.

face different: (stamps) stamps of differing design and/or color.

face piece: (metal) a decorative piece of brass that was suspended so it fell on the forehead of a horse.

facet: (jewelry) any flat, polished surface on a cut gemstone.

faceted steel: (metal) engraved steel. Also called *chiseled-and-cut steel*.

facon: (weapons) a Spanish throwing knife of about 24 inches.

faience: 1. (ceramics) a bright, thick glaze used on pottery such as majolica; named for the Italian town of Faenze, where earthenware has been produced since the 1500s.

2. (ceramics) wares with faience glaze.

faience parlante: (ceramics) heavily glazed French earthenware from the 1800s adorned with inscriptions, including sayings, proverbs, or records of special family times.

fairings: (ceramics) small, ceramic figures or groups of figures depicting courting situations, often bordering on the risqué. Purchased by English fair-goers from 1840 until about 1900. Larger examples were made from 1840 to 1860 and had embossed manufacturers' and artists' names. In 1860 marking was discontinued and size diminished. In 1870 marking was reinstated, then 1880 marks were again discontinued. In the 1890s German potters bought the molds. German pieces usually have holes in the base.

fake: (stamps) a stamp that has been repaired, or redesigned in a way that makes it look like a different, usually more expensive, issue. Or, any object that has been altered or is not genuine.

falchion: (weapons) a short, single-edged sword with a curved blade. Dating from the 12th century.

faldestool: (furniture) a very early upholstered chair usually made of turned wood and often draped with fabric.

fall front: (furniture) the lid on a desk that drops down, forming a writing surface.

falling beaver: (armor) a face guard of plate used with open helmets, from the 15th century. Also called *buffe*.

false edge: (weapons) a sharpened area for more effective thrusting near the point on the back side of a single-edged sword.

false face: (Native American) carved medicine-man mask made by the Iroquois of New York.

famille jaune: (ceramics) literally, yellow family. Chinese porcelain with yellow figuring prominently — often as the background color. Many of these pieces are in animal shapes.

famille noire: (ceramics) literally, black family. Chinese porcelain that has a black background.

famille rose: (ceramics) literally, red or rose family. 18th-century Chinese porcelain vases, tureens, and the like decorated predominantly in shades of pink, rose, and red. Decorative motifs include Oriental and European people, animals, and birds.

famille verte: (ceramics) literally, green family. Chinese porcelain that features varying shades of green.

fanam: (coins) a variety of small gold and silver coins of southern India, Malabar Coast, and Ceylon, issued between the 10th and 18th centuries.

fan back: (furniture) the back of a Windsor chair with the spindles flaring out like an open fan.

fan guard: the two outer pieces to which the fan is attached. The bottom of the fan guard is the handle.

fantasy box: a name given to sculptural boxes, perhaps because some of the designs seem to be artists' flights of fancy.

farm memorabilia: (collectibles) farm implements such as hay forks, chicken feeders, and grain scoops made before 1940. Signs of wear are indications that the article in question is legitimate. Some examples have been varnished or refinished, which detracts greatly from their value.

farthing: (coins) a British coin originally struck in silver, later in copper.

farthingale chair: (furniture) a chair that developed during the first quarter of the 17th century to accommodate the farthingale-hooped dress. It was armless with a wide, high seat.

fashion doll: a doll dressed in the fashion of the time in which it was made.

fast food memorabilia: (collectibles) cardboard and plastic premiums made to promote the fast food chains.

fats: (lighting) candles made to be used on pricket candlesticks (candlesticks with spikes on which to impale the candles). As the name implies, fats are thicker than conventional candles.

fausse-montre: (jewelry) a fake watch worn in the late 1700s on one end of a chatelaine to balance the real watch worn at the other end.

fauteuil: (furniture) an armchair with open arms.

faux: false or fake.

favrile: 1. (glass) handmade iridescent art glass patented by Louis Comfort Tiffany in 1880. **2.** (glass) any piece of glass made in the Tiffany Studios under the direction of Louis Comfort Tiffany. **3.** (household accessories) infrequently, non-glass items produced at Tiffany Studios. See also *Tiffany glass*.

FDC: (stamps) first-day cover.

feather-edging: (decoration) a feather design of veneer or marquetry banding on furniture.

feathered ware: (ceramics) slipware finely marbleized. See also *combed ware*.

feather staff: (weapons) a concealed weapon carried by off-duty officers in the 17th century. Similar to a cane in appearance, it had one long and two short blades hidden within the shaft which could be ejected from the tip with a jerk.

Federal style: (furniture) furniture made in the United States between 1785 and 1830. These years represent the early years of the Republic but no definite style, for the influence of Hepplewhite, Sheraton, Directoire and early Empire can all be seen in the furniture of the era.

fede ring: (jewelry) a ring with two clasped hands. Often used as an engagement ring.

Federzeichnung: (glass) brown glass sections on a satin glass with trails of gold. Made in Germany in the late 1800s.

feeder: (domestic) a shallow, oval-shaped bowl with a long, tapered end; used for feeding infants and invalids. Made of silver and other materials from the early 1700s. Also called *pap boat* and *pap dish*.

feeding cup: (domestic) a small, porcelain or silver panlike cup with handles and a spout designed for feeding invalids or children. Dates from the mid-1600s.

fels: (coins) Islamic copper coin, dating from early 8th century.

felspar china: (ceramics) a china decorated with a purple transfer made by Josiah Spode in the 1820s. Pieces are marked "Felspar Porcelain" and "Spode."

felspathic glaze: (ceramics) glaze containing felspar rock; used on all glazed porcelain and some stoneware.

fencing gauntlet: (armor) a glove for the left hand designed for parrying or grasping an opponent's blade.

fender: (hearth accessories) a narrow, horizontal metal shield running the length of a fireplace to prevent ashes from spilling over.

Fenton: (glass) glass objects made by Fenton Art Glass Company, founded in 1905 in Ohio. Within two years the company had moved to Williamstown, West Virginia. Until 1970 their glass was marked with a paper label. Since then an oval trademark has been stamped in the glass.

ferroniere: (jewelry) French word for a chain worn around the head with a jewel centered over the forehead.

ferrotype: (photography) a positive image made directly on a thin iron plate covered with sensitized film. From the 1850s. Also called *tintype*.

fescule: a wooden pointer.

festoon: 1. (decoration) a string of flowers, leaves, ribbon, or similar material formed in a curve between two points. **2.** (decoration) decorative festoonlike motif used on furniture or sculpture.

fetish: (Native American) object believed to have magical power.

fiberboard: (materials) a bonded material made of wood or other fibers, compressed into rigid sheets; used to back chests and cabinets.

fiddleback chair: (furniture) a modern term for a chair that has a violin-shaped slat in the back.

field: 1. (coins) the background portion of a coin, or the object surrounding the design. **2.** (stamps) the entire printed area.

field bedstead: (furniture) bed frame with half-high posts that support a canopy with netting or cloth.

fielded panel: (furniture) a raised panel with beveled edges used on 17th-century drawer fronts.

Fiesta: (ceramics) a line of dinnerware featuring solid, bright colors and incised, concentric circles produced from 1936 until 1973 by Homer Laughlin China Company of West Virginia.

figurehead: (folk art) a carved figure attached to the bow of a ship. Original figureheads are of wood. Reproductions of fiberglass are plentiful.

filigree: (jewelry, furniture) delicate and intricate ornamentation, especially when done with gold, silver, or other fine, twisted wire.

fillings: (textiles) the intricate, open stitches used in the pattern spaces in needlepoint lace and pillow lace.

fillet: 1. (textiles) a narrow strip of ribbon. **2.** (decoration) a thin, flat strip of molding used to separate sections of ornate molding on furniture.

filo: (weapons) the cutting edge of a sword.

filoselle: (textiles) a delicate, spun silk made of thread with from two to six strands.

Finch, Kay: (ceramics) animal and bird figures made by Kay Finch and the small company she formed in California in 1939. The company, which also produced a line of tableware, closed in 1963. Most Finch pieces are marked.

Findlay Floradine: (glass) a line of rose satin glass decorated with white flowers made from Dalzell, Gilmore, and Leighton Glass Company's Onyx molds. It was produced from about 1891 until 1901. See also *Findlay Onyx*.

Findlay Onyx: (glass) a line of glass made of two layers of glass with a pattern (usually floral) decorated with a metallic luster in between. Made by Dalzell, Gilmore, and Leighton Glass Company of Findlay, Ohio, from 1889 until about 1891. Generally white, but occasionally amber, lavender, or rose; colored pieces are much more valuable than white ones. See also *Findlay Floradine*.

fine art: art, such as oil paintings, watercolors, and sculptures, which is created for its own sake rather than to decorate and be subordinate to a useful item.

fine drawings: (textiles) the delicate stitches used to join lengths of lace net.

fineness: (metal) the degree of purity of a precious metal.

finger bow: (weapons) the part of a sword hilt that pro-

tects the fingers from a cross cut. It may simply be recurving quillons, or one or more plates connecting the quillons to the pommel, or a basket. Also called *finger guard*.

finger guard: (weapons) the part of a sword hilt that protects the fingers from a cross cut. It may simply be recurving quillons, or one or more plates connecting the quillons to the pommel, or a basket. Also called *finger bow*.

finger molding: (furniture) a wooden trim that edges the ornate curves of the upholstered part of a sofa or chair.

finger roll: (furniture) concave roll cut into the border of a piece of furniture.

finial: 1. (furniture) the crowning ornament used at the top of an arch. **2.** (lighting) the ornamental nut screwed on top of a lamp to hold the lamp shade in place.

finishing mold: (glass) the second of two molds used to make modern bottles. The first, called a parison, forms the bottle, then the bottle is transferred to the finishing mold for final details. See also *parison*.

firearm: (weapons) a weapon capable of propelling a missile by using an explosive charge. From the 14th century.

fire back: (hearth accessories) a cast-iron sheet placed at the back of a fireplace to reflect heat.

fire board: (hearth accessories) a decorative fire screen often adorned with hand-painted folk art, carved and gilded crests, or needlework. Also called *cheval screen*.

fire bottle: (glass) a small bottle for keeping phosphorous to start fires. The phosphorous was covered with water. In order to start a fire, a small splinter of wood was dipped into the phosphorous and struck on a rough, dry surface.

fire box: (hearth accessories) a metal box with two compartments; one for a container of sulphuric acid and the other for wood splinters that had been dipped in chlorate of potash. The wood splinters ignited when they were dipped in sulphuric acid. Fire boxes were usually kept on the hearth.

firedogs: (hearth accessories) a pair of brass or iron supports for holding logs in a fireplace. Also called *andirons.*

fired on: (glass, porcelain, pottery) a factory-applied design painted, then baked to ensure durability.

fire-fighting memorabilia: (collectibles) nostalgic items ranging from hats, badges, axes, tickets to firemen's balls, fire-engine lanterns, buckets, and brass hoses to the old fire engines themselves. Hand-painted leather fire buckets are highly prized.

fire fork: (hearth accessories) a tool made of iron or brass with a long handle; used to move burning logs in a fireplace.

fireglow: (glass) a light tan opaque glass that glows red when held to the light.

firelock: (weapons) originally, a wheel-lock musket; later, a flintlock.

fire mark: (advertising) a plaque issued by an insurance company to be placed on the front of a home or business to indicate that the building was insured. Each company had its own mark. Fire fighters could collect money from the insurance company in question if they saved the building. These signs became obsolete in the 1860s.

fire point: (hearth accessories) a fire poker.

fire polishing: (glass) the process of reheating a piece of glass, once it is complete, to remove any marks left from handling it with tools.

fire screen: (hearth accessories) an adjustable screen that affords protection from the heat and sparks of an open fire. First used in the 1600s.

firkin: a small wooden cask or a British measure.

first-day cover: (stamps) a piece of mail with a postmark bearing the date of the first day the cancelled stamp on it was issued. See also *first-flight cover.*

first-flight cover: (stamps) similar to a first-day cover, but it applies to the first flight of a new airmail service, and not the issue of a new stamp. See also *first-day cover.*

Fischer, Moritz: (ceramics) founder of a pottery in Herend, Hungary, in 1839. The factory made copies of pieces by Leeds, Meissen, Sevres, and others. In 1948 it was taken over by the state.

Fisher, Harrison: (prints) illustrator whose work appeared in the Hearst papers, books, and magazines. His prints of illustrations of the Fisher Girl and his other creations are collectible. One of his best-known works is a series of six pictures called *The Greatest Moments in a Woman's Life.*

fishing memorabilia: (collectibles) fishing rods, lures, and reels made from the early 1800s on. Reels and lures are the most desirable. Condition is important. Some of the companies to look for are Creek Chub, Heddon, Pflueger, Shakespeare, South Bend, and Winona Boyer.

fish-scale work: (needlework) embroidery in which dried fish scales have been worked into the design.

fish-skin appliqué: (textiles) garments decorated by Eskimos with strips of dried animal intestines (usually from seals) that have been painted with designs. Other adornments such as beads, fringe, and fur may be added.

fish tail: (decoration) a carved motif used on furniture, especially chair backs, that resembles a fish tail.

fissure: (coins) a small crack in a die or die blank. (A narrow crack in any object.)

five and ten: (stamps) early name for the first two United States stamps. Issued in 1847, they had five- and ten-cent face values.

fl.: (books, fine art) abbreviation of *flourished;* indicates the period an artist or author is known to have worked; used when the artist's dates of birth and death are unknown — fl. is followed by a date or dates.

flag-bottom chair: (furniture) a chair with a rush seat.

flag fan: (fashion accessories) a fan with the blade on one side of the handle rather than centered.

flagon: (domestic) a large metal or pottery vessel with a handle and spout; used for holding wine or liquors.

flail: (weapons) a metal or wood handle with a ring at the tip that secures a bar or chain, usually armed with studs.

flambé: (ceramics) a brilliant red-and-purple ceramic glaze produced by the oxidation of copper in an iron-based glaze.

flame finial: (decoration) a top, knob decoration in the shape of a flame.

flame work: (needlework) embroidery created by working the thread in shades and stitches that form a sequence of peaks resembling flames. Also called *bargello, Hungarian point,* and *Florentine stitch.*

flashed on: (glass) a thin layer of color added over glass. This color is fragile and wears off easily, unlike color that has been fired on. See also *fired on.*

flat chasing: (jewelry) a low relief decoration on precious metal.

flats: (toys) two-dimensional soldiers made of lead.

flatware: (tableware) tableware such as knives, forks, spoons, flat dishes, and trays. See also *hollowware.*

flaw: (stamps) an insignificant imperfection on a stamp that does not effect its quality.

Flemish foot: (furniture) a double-scroll design with one scroll turned in and the other turned out; used on Jacobean furniture. *Ca.* 1603 to 1625. Also called *Flemish leg.*

Flemish leg: (furniture) a double-scroll design with one scroll turned in and the other turned out; used on Jacobean furniture. *Ca.* 1603 to 1625. Also called *Flemish foot.*

Flemish scroll: (furniture, architecture) an ornate form with a curve that is broken by an angle.

fleur-de-lis: (decoration, heraldry) stylized likeness of the iris flower, usually with three petals. A symbol of royalty.

flint glass: glass that contains lead oxide and has a high refractive quality. Also called *lead glass.*

flintlock: (weapons) a gun lock with flint embedded in the hammer, which produces a spark when released, igniting the charge. Dating from the early 17th century.

flirty-eyes doll: a doll with eyes that travel from one side of the eye socket to the other in a flirtatious manner.

floating off: (stamps) removing stamps vulnerable to water from paper by one of two methods. The stamp is floated upright on lukewarm water, allowing the paper, but not the stamp, to become soaked. This softens the glue so the stamp can be pulled off. Or, the stamp is placed in a humidifier until the glue softens.

floating signature: (fine art) a signature that's been done over the varnish on a painting rather than under it. Most of these are forgeries.

floor runner: (toys) a train or other toy vehicle that has smooth wheels for easy running on a floor or carpet. Also called *carpet runner*.

Florence Ceramics: figurines made in the 1940s and 1950s in Pasadena, California. Pieces are backstamped with the company name and the name of the figurine is usually incised on each piece.

Florentine cameo: (glass) a white substance applied in a design to the surface of glass objects which, at first glance, resemble cameo glass. Made in England or France; usually unmarked, but may be signed "Florentine."

Florentine stitch: (needlework) embroidery created by working the thread in shades and stitches that form a sequence of peaks resembling flames. Also called *bargello, flamework,* and *Hungarian point.*

Florin: (coins) a coin minted in Florence from 1252. St. John the Baptist is depicted on the face, and on the reverse side, a lily and the arms of Florence.

floss: 1. (textiles) short fibers or waste silk from the silkworm cocoon that cannot be reeled. **2.** (needlework) the soft, loosely twisted thread used for embroidery. **3.** (needlework) a lightweight knitting yarn.

flow blue: (ceramics) tableware and other items with cobalt blue designs on white backgrounds. Produced by many English potters including Alcock, Meigh, Podmore, and Walker. Wares are usually ironstone and the patterns on them are numerous. The deeper the blue and the more it smudges and melts into the white, the more desirable the piece.

flower horn: (household accessories) a horn-shaped vase. May either hang on a wall or be put in a base with a flat bottom to sit on a piece of furniture. Popular in the 1700s.

flue cover: (household accessories) a round painting, either under glass or reverse painted on glass; used to cover the hole left when the stovepipe was disconnected from the chimney in the spring. Children, flowers, pets, and women were the most popular subjects portrayed.

flute: (glass) a medium-sized drinking glass with a tall bowl; often used for champagne.

fluted: (decoration) a border that resembles a scalloped edge; used as a decoration on furniture and glass, silver, and porcelain items.

flute harmonica: (music) a cross between the flute and the harmonica; popular with children and folk musicians from 1880 to about 1920.

flying shuttle: (domestics) a mechanically operated shuttle that traveled back and forth between both sides of a loom.

flyspeck: (stamps) an imperfection on a stamp that is so tiny that it is almost imperceptible. Usually these flaws do not alter a stamp's value.

flyssa: (weapons) a Kabyles (Morocco) sword with a long, straight, single-edged blade and no guard.

fob: (jewelry) an ornamental piece worn on a chain — often a watch chain — along with a watch.

foible: (weapons) the weaker section of a sword blade — from the middle to the tip. See also *forte.*

foil: 1. (weapons) a light, modern fencing sword with a thin, flexible, tapered blade and a circular, often cuplike, handle. See also *saber.* **2.** (metal) a thin sheet of metal, or the coating of metal applied to a plate of glass to create a mirror. **3.** (jewelry) a leaflike design in glass or stone. **4.** (jewelry) a thin layer painted on the back of a stone; used in costume jewelry to make the piece have more luster.

foining: (weapons) any weapon used to thrust.

folded foot: (glass) the foot of a drinking glass that has been folded under to reinforce the area most likely to be damaged in use.

folded rim: (glass) the thick rim of a glass vessel — usually twice as thick as the rest of the body.

folio: 1. (books) a large sheet of paper folded once to form two leaves, or four pages. **2.** (books) a book or manuscript with folio leaves that are about 15 inches high.

folk art: paintings, crafts, and decorations on everything from furniture to tinware that were produced by people who had no formal training. Some of these works show a poor use of space and balance, but all are sought for their quaint charm and historical significance. Also called *primitives*. See also *naive art*.

Folwell, John (fl. 1775): (furniture) a Philadelphia cabinetmaker, active around the time of the American Revolution. He has been called "the Chippendale of America" because of the Chippendale influence on his style.

foot bank: (domestic) a pottery, tin, or soapstone receptacle designed to hold charcoal or hot water; used on chilly days in homes, churches, or carriages to warm a person's feet. They are sought both by collectors and people who want to ward off winter's chill. Also called *foot warmer*.

football cards: (collectibles) cards produced since the 1890s that depict professional football players. Not as popular with collectors as baseball cards.

footman: (hearth accessories) a four-legged trivet for the hearth. Made of wrought iron and/or brass, usually with cabriole-style legs. From the mid-1700s.

foot warmer: (domestic) a pottery, tin, or soapstone receptacle designed to hold charcoal or hot water; used on chilly days in homes, churches, or carriages to warm a person's feet. They are sought both by collectors and people who want to ward off winter's chill. Also called *foot bank*.

fore shaft: (weapons) the section of an arrow or spear between the head and shaft.

forgery: any item intentionally made to appear to be something other than what it actually is. Usually accomplished by adding a false signature on a piece or by treating an object to make it look older than it is.

format: (stamps) the general organization of the elements of a stamp, including its size, shape, design, graphics, and margins.

form watch: (clocks) any watch with an unusual shape — for example, the shape of an animal, a musical instrument, or a flower.

forte: (weapons) the stronger portion of a sword blade, from the hilt to the middle. See also *foible*.

forty-leg table: (furniture) a table with drop leaves and usually six stationary legs and two additional legs which swing out like a gate to hold up the drop leaves. Also called *gateleg table* and *hundred-leg table*.

Fostoria: (glass) pressed-glass items — tableware, figures, lamps, and the like — in an array of colors and patterns made from 1887 to 1986 by the Fostoria Glass Company. At one time they produced more handmade glass than any other factory in the world. This glass is plentiful and fairly inexpensive.

four-poster: (furniture) a bed with tall corner posts, originally to support a canopy or curtains.

four-way matched veneer: (furniture) the combination of book- and end-matched sheets. See also *book matching* and *end matching*.

fowling piece: (weapons) a gun, such as a shotgun, intended for shooting birds.

fox-head cup: (household accessories) a cup in the shape of a fox head. The fox's mouth and ears form the feet on which the cup stands. *Ca.* 18th century.

foxing: (prints, paper) staining, usually brownish-yellow spots, from mildew on paper stored in a damp environment.

Fraktur: (folk art) a letter style used in German manuscripts and documents. Also the documents, such as birth, baptism, or wedding certificates, issued in the German-speaking communities of the United States during the 18th and 19th centuries, that bore such lettering. Frakturs were often done by members of the clergy or teachers.

frame: 1. (stamps) the outer border of a stamp's design. **2.** (stamps) the method of displaying mounted album pages at shows.

Francesware: (glass) swirl or hobnail glass pieces, either clear or frosted, with dark rims. Made in the 1880s by Hobbs, Brockunier and Company in West Virginia.

franchise stamp: (stamps) a special-issue stamp supplied cost-free to various humanitarian institutions or organizations. Issued from time to time by several European countries.

Franciscan: (ceramics) dinnerware made by Gladding McBean and Company in their plant in Glendale, California, starting in 1933. The company had been making tiles and garden crockery since 1875. Their most popular patterns are Apple, introduced in 1940; Desert Rose, introduced in 1941; and Ivy, introduced in 1948. In 1979, Wedgewood purchased Franciscan.

Frankart: (household accessories) white metal ashtrays, bookends, candlesticks, lamps, and the like with a green, black, or gray finish produced by Frankart, Inc. in New York. Their work features nudes and other art deco motifs. Some are unmarked; others are stamped "Frankart, Inc." with the year they were made. *Ca.* 1920s.

franking: (stamps) privilege provided officials that allows them to use their signature or initials in place of paid postage. Members of the United States Congress have this privilege.

Franklin clock: a shelf clock with wooden movements made by Silas Hoadley in Plymouth, Connecticut, between 1825 and 1830. Hoadley named the clock Franklin, it is assumed, after Benjamin Franklin.

Franklin stove: (domestic) a cast-iron stove shaped like a fireplace; invented by Benjamin Franklin. Metal baffles increase its efficiency.

Frankoma: (ceramics) a company that produces decorative pieces from figures to vases. Originally called Frank Pottery when it was founded in Oklahoma in 1933; the name was changed to Frankoma in 1934. From its inception until 1956, pieces were fashioned of cream-colored clay; after 1956 red clay was used. They have produced several series, including Christmas plates and bottle vases. The factory is still in business.

Fraunfelter, Charles: (ceramics) founder of the Ohio Pottery Company in 1915. The company made hard-paste porcelain items for chemical laboratories until 1923, when they began to make brown-and-white tableware called *Petrascan*. The company name changed to Fraunfelter China Company in 1923 and closed in 1939.

freak: (stamps) a stamp with an abnormality. The particular variance is limited to one or very few stamps and does not affect the value.

free-blown glass: glass blown and shaped using hand tools instead of being blown into a mold.

freedom box: a small, hinged box, usually of gold or silver, bearing the arms of a city and containing a small scroll that promises the hospitality of the city to the recipient. Given to visiting dignitaries, usually in England, during the 17th and 18th centuries.

freedom quilt: (textiles) a quilt made from the dresses of a young man's various girl friends and given to him on his twenty-first birthday. When the man married, the quilt went to his bride.

French foot: 1. (furniture) in Chippendale furniture, a scroll terminating a cabriole leg. **2.** (furniture) in Hepplewhite furniture, a delicate bracket foot.

French ivory: (materials) the earliest form of plastic, invented by John Wesley Hyatt in the 1860s. Highly flammable. Also called *celluloid*, *pyralin*, and *pyroxylin*.

French jet: (jewelry) a fancy name for black glass from any country.

French pie mold: (kitchen) a round, hinged mold with a removable bottom. Made in a variety of sizes from about 5 inches to 12 inches in diameter; used for making pies. Dates from 1800s on.

French polish: (furniture) a high-gloss finish obtained by hand rubbing boiled linseed oil and shellac onto the surface; used for several hundred years, but no longer in vogue.

French provincial: (furniture) a very sophisticated style of furniture similar to the furniture made in the French provinces during the 17th and 18th centuries. *Ca.* 1940s.

fresco: (fine art) a painting executed on the wet plaster surface of a wall or ceiling.

fretwork: (furniture) an ornamental network usually in relief made up of small, straight bars intersecting one another.

Frey furniture: (furniture) primitive Chippendale-style furniture made in the late 18th and early 19th centuries by Jacob Frey in Pennsylvania.

friable: (metal) brittle; easily broken or crumbled.

friendship quilt: (textiles) a quilt made of squares done by a number of people, usually to present to a friend as a wedding gift or housewarming present.

Friesland clock: an eight-day clock with a decorative case. Made in the Netherlands in the 1500s and 1600s.

frieze: (architecture) a decorative band just below the cornice.

frog: 1. (household accessories) a heavy glass, porcelain, or metal device with holes for holding flowers upright in a floral arrangement. The frog is placed in a bowl or vase, then the stems of flowers and greens are stuck in the many holes. Some frogs are figural and the figure appears among the blooms; others remain entirely hidden under water, covered by the flora. **2.** (weapons) a leather sleeve used to attach a scabbard to the belt.

front: (stamps) the part of a cover or envelope containing the address and postmarked stamps when it is detached or cut away from the rest of the mailer.

frosting: (decoration) a matte, white finish on glass and silver produced by acid fumes or scratch brushing.

frozen Charlotte: (dolls) a doll with no moving parts; made of one solid piece of bisque or glazed porcelain. Supposedly named after a girl in an 1860s ballad who was so pleased with her new dress that she forgot to don her coat before rushing out into a blustering, freezing cold night. Her body was found frozen stiff. Also called *pillar doll*.

fruit cooler: (kitchen) a set of two bowls: One large, deep bowl holds ice. The second bowl is placed over the ice and filled with fruit.

fruit-crate art: (collectibles, paper) colorful paper labels used on fruit crates from 1880 until about 1945. They must be in mint condition to attract a collector.

fruit jar: (glass) a canning jar. The oldest dates back to 1829. Several thousand types have been produced since then. Black, amber, and cobalt are very desirable colors. Condition, color, and scarcity are the leading considerations in determining value.

Fry: (glass) producers of fine cut glass starting in 1901. The H. C. Fry Glass Company of Rochester, Pennsylvania, later produced oven ware and an opalescent glass with colored decorations called *Foval*. The factory closed in 1933. Most pieces were not marked but "Fry" in a shield was sometimes used.

fuddling cup: (ceramics) three or more cups interlocked with internal passages between them. *Ca.* 17th and 18th centuries.

fugitive ink: (stamps) non-fixed ink, usually soluble in water or other fluids; widely used in the 19th century for printing stamps and postmarking. Seldom used today.

full crystal: (glass) crystal made with potash and containing approximately 30 percent lead. Also called *lead crystal*.

fulminates: (weapons) fulminate of mercury, an explosive salt; used to ignite gunpowder since the early 19th century.

Fulper Pottery: (ceramics) line of art pottery produced by the American Pottery Company since 1910. The Flemington, New Jersey, company was originally founded in 1805 to produce bottles and jugs. The company became known for its glazes, especially the famille rose glaze. Fulper made dolls' heads, powder boxes, and perfume lamps during World War I. Wares were marked "Fulper," "Flemington," "Prang," "Rafco," and "Vasekraft." Paper labels were sometimes used. In 1929, Martin Stangl bought out Fulper and changed the name to "Stangl."

fumbari: (weapons) the part of a blade nearest the hilt of a Japanese sword.

fumed oak: (furniture) a dark oak finish created by exposing the furniture piece to ammonia vapors.

fundame: (decoration, orientalia) a gold lacquer background with a matte finish. Achieved by using fine gold powder.

fuse: (metal) to bond or join together by heat.

fusee: (weapons) a flintlock gun. Also called *fusil*.

fusil: (weapons) a flintlock gun. Also called *fusee*.

fustian: (textiles) pile fabrics other than velvet.

futa-suji-hi: (weapons) the double groove in a Japanese sword blade.

G

gadlings: (armor) spikes and knobs on the knuckles and backs of gauntlets. From the 14th century.

gadroon: 1. (furniture) a carved band of fluted or reeded convex molding; used on furniture during the 16th to 18th centuries. **2.** (silver) a band of fluted or reeded convex molding; used on silverware from the late 17th century on. Also called *knulling*.

galatea: (textiles) a durable cotton material, usually striped; used for making clothes.

Gallé, Émile (d. 1904): (ceramics, glass, furniture) founder of a firm in Nancy, France, in 1874 that produced pottery, enameled glassware, cameo glass, and furniture. Best known for his cameo glass and furniture. He used marquetry to decorate furniture with art nouveau designs depicting nature. During the 1890s his cameo glass also reflected the art nouveau movement. Although the glass bears his signature, much of it was actually done by his employees. Galle died in 1904. Glass made after that has a star before the signature. The factory closed in the 1930s.

gallery: (furniture) a rail or rim of fretwork or bars at the back of sideboard tops or surrounding tabletops.

gallipot: (ceramics) an apothecary jar — a small earthenware pot with a tin glaze; often used for ointments. Also called *gleypot*.

galloon: (textiles) the narrow outer border of a fabric or tapestry.

gally paving tiles: (ceramics) tin-glazed earthenware tiles; used to decorate walls.

Gama Sennin: (orientalia) a Taoist hermit; depicted with a toad in art and on figurines.

gambeson: (armor) a sleeveless garment. Made of leather or sturdy, quilted material; worn under armor during the Middle Ages.

gambling memorabilia: (collectibles) old poker chips, cards, games of chance, dice cups, gaming tables, gambling wheels, and other gaming articles. Condition is all-important.

game boards: (collectibles) boards with brilliantly colored and intricately fashioned designs. Hand crafted during the 1700s and 1800s; mass produced from the late 1800s on. The early factory-made boards are collectible, but they don't command the price that the hand-crafted boards do. Condition and sophistication of design are important considerations in determining value.

game plate: (ceramics) a plate adorned with pictures of game animals, fish, or birds; used to serve wild game during the 1700s and 1800s. Sometimes hand painted and sometimes transfer designed. A full set includes six to twelve plates and a platter. Collectors look for single plates as well as sets.

gaming table: (furniture) a table with a folding top made for playing cards. Older tables often have holes for candles on the corners and small wells on each side to hold counters. First gaming tables date to the 1700s.

gapestick: (kitchen) a wooden cooking spoon so large that if the cook wanted to take a taste of her creation the spoon stretched her mouth.

garden carpet: (floor coverings) a Persian carpet with a floral design that includes animals.

Gardner's porcelain: (ceramics) figures of Russian peasants made in Moscow in the late 1700s by an Englishman named Francis Gardner. Mark is similar to Meissen.

garnish: (pewter) a set of pewter ware consisting of 12 bowls, platters, and saucers.

gasolier: (lighting) the correct name for a gas chandelier.

gateleg table: (furniture) a table with drop leaves and usually six stationary legs and two additional legs that swing out like a gate to hold up the drop leaves. Also called *forty-leg table* and *hundred-leg table*.

gather: (glass) the formless blob of glass at the end of the blowpipe before the glass has been blown.

gaudy Dutch: (ceramics) the popular name for gaily decorated pottery made in Stafford, England, for export to the United States between 1810 and 1830.

gaudy ironstone: (ceramics) ironstone decorated by F. Morley and Sons in the mid-1800s. The ware resembles gaudy Dutch with its big, bold, colorful patterns.

gaudy Welsh: (ceramics) the popular name for pottery made in England for export to the United States between 1830 and 1865.

gauffered edges: (books) the pattern or design stamped or blocked on the edges of a book.

gauffrage: (prints) an 18th-century Japanese printmaking method that produced an embossed effect in black and white.

gauntlets: (armor) armor covering the hands that first appeared at the end of the 13th century or beginning of the 14th century as leather gloves covered with leather scales or mail. By mid-century the hand and wrist were protected by a single plate.

Geisha girl: (ceramics) late-1800s Japanese-export tea sets, salt and pepper shakers, chocolate pots, nut sets, and the like with designs that feature a Geisha girl. Some of the designs were hand painted, some transfer with a touch of hand painting, and some transfer designed. This inexpensive ware, often given as premiums, has been reproduced.

gembi: (weapons) the guard on a Japanese sword.

Genovino: (coins) a gold coin struck in Genoa from the 13th century.

genre: (fine art) a style of art depicting people participating in everyday activities that typify the period. Usually done in realistic style.

geode: (collectibles) a piece of stone with a hollow that's filled with crystals.

Geometric period: (fine art) a period from 900 to 700 B.C. when vases and urns were decorated in geometric patterns. Late examples may include animal designs.

Georgia Art Pottery: (ceramics) Georgia company that produced vases, mugs, pitchers, ewers, and the like with a fine glaze starting in 1935. Early pieces are marked "GAP."

Georgian: (furniture, architecture) the furniture and architectural styles prominent during the years from 1714 to 1811, when English kings George I, II, and III were in power.

Georgia white: (fine art) an American marble used for sculpting. Polishes to a high sheen.

German silver: (metal) the old term for nickel silver, a compound of nickel, copper, and zinc. It contains no silver.

gesso: (decoration) a parchment, gypsum, or plaster of paris and glue mixture used in bas relief. Popular from the late 1600s to the mid-1700s.

geyser: (domestic) hot-water heater powered by gas.

Ghiordes knot: (floor coverings) the knot formed by pushing the ends of a pile thread down over the outer sides of two warp threads, then pulling both ends up between the two threads. Found on Oriental carpets from Djoshagan, Herez, Kurdistan, and some from Tabriz, Shiraz, and Herat.

Ghiordes rug: (floor coverings) a very fine quality Turkish rug with fine yarns and warp; often of silk.

Gibbons, Grinling (1648-1721): (decoration) artisan born in Holland who moved to England, where he gained fame carving picture frames decorated with a profusion of natural subjects such as birds, fruits, foliage, and shells. Many people copied his work.

Gibson Girl: (fine art) the idealized sketches of the American girl in the 1890s by Charles Dana Gibson. She is usually portrayed in a long skirt and a tailored shirtwaist with leg-of-mutton sleeves.

gilded ceramics: ceramic objects adorned with gold. The earliest gilding was a base of honey mixed with a gold powder that was applied to ceramics before the piece was fired. The firing process dried and hardened the honey. By the early 1800s, amalgam of mercury replaced honey.

gilding: (fine art) applying thin layers of gold to a surface.

Gillinder: (glass) small, decorative glass pieces made by William Gillinder at his factory in Philadelphia starting in 1863. Many examples are marked "Gillinder."

gilly pot: (kitchen) a small pot.

gilt tops: (books) the top edges only of a book are gilded. Commonly used abbreviation is *T.L.G.*

gimbal: (scientific instruments) a device with two rings mounted on axes at right angles to each other, allowing an object such as a ship's compass to remain suspended horizontally regardless of motion.

gimp: (textiles) a narrow cord or braid of fabric; used to trim clothes, drapes, or upholstered furniture.

giobu: (decoration, orientalia) a technique used by the Japanese; lacquer and odd-shaped bits of foil are applied to an item to give it a mottled appearance.

girandole: 1. (furniture) a branched candle holder usually attached to a mirror. **2.** (decoration) any structure with a radiating form. **3.** (jewelry) a piece of jewelry such as a necklace, brooch, or earrings featuring one large central stone from which three smaller, long, narrow stones hang.

girdle plate: (kitchen) a flat, iron sheet on which Scottish cooks made oat cakes.

Gladdings McBean: (ceramics) architectural terra cotta, garden pottery, and tile produced by Gladdings, McBean and Company. In the early 1900s, this company was the leading tile producer in the United States. In 1934 they added lines of artware and dinnerware. Much early ware is marked "G Mc B" in an oval.

glassine: (stamps) a thin, strong, translucent paper; used as windows in business envelopes, and for philatelic use. There are glassine envelopes ranging in size from 1-3/4 inches by 2-7/8 inches to 4-1/2 inches by 10-3/8 inches.

glass knobs: (furniture) fashionable furniture accessories between *ca.* 1800 and 1860. They may be blown, cut, or pressed; plain or decorated.

glass silhouette: (decoration) a silhouette painted on the back of plate or convex glass.

glatton: (textiles) flannel material made in the 1700s by the Welsh weavers of Pennsylvania.

glaze: (ceramics) the application of a thin, smooth, glassy coating to earthenware and porcelain, leaving it impervious to liquids. The glaze may be dull or brilliant, translucent or opaque, and may contain bright colors.

gleypot: (ceramics) an apothecary jar — a small earthenware pot with a tin glaze. Often used for ointments. Also called *gallipot*.

glory: (heraldry) cloud puffs clustered to form a halo around a symbol.

glost: (ceramics) a kiln in which a glazed piece of pottery is fired to fix the glaze. This is always a first glaze over which the decoration is done. Pieces are always fired again.

glyptograph: (jewelry) an engraved inscription or design on a precious stone.

gnomon: (scientific instruments) an object, such as the style in the center of a sundial, that casts a shadow used as an indicator.

goat-and-bee jug: (ceramics) a jug decorated with a goat or goats in relief and with an incised bee in the base. Made at Coalport in the mid-1800s.

goblet: (glass, metal) a drinking vessel with a tall stem supporting the bowl.

Goebel, F.W.: (ceramics) German figurine manufacturer. In 1871 he started the Hummelwork Porcelain Manufactory. They are still in business making Goebel figurines, plates, and the like, as well as the famous Hummel figurines. See also *Hummel*.

gofun: (decoration, orientalia) decoration achieved by using powdered oyster shells; found on some Japanese objects.

gold: (metal) soft, yellow metal; corrosion-resistant; the most malleable and ductile of metals. It is usually alloyed for strength.

golden agate: (glass) a pressed glass with holly leaves in amber-colored glass shading from tan to brown. Made by the Indiana Tumbler and Goblet Company for a brief time in 1903. Also called *holly amber glass*.

gold-filled: (metal) having an outer layer of gold and an inner layer of a base metal.

gold foil: (metal) a thin sheet of gold, thicker than gold leaf.

gold leaf: (metal) very thin sheets of gold; used for gilding.

Goldscheider: (ceramics) porcelain figurines, lamps, music boxes, and the like produced by the Goldscheider family in the pottery they established in New Jersey in the 1940s after leaving Vienna. They also founded a business in the Staffordshire section of England. Most pieces are marked with the company name.

goldstone marbles: clear glass marbles with gold-colored, copper specks.

gold-tooled binding: (books) the hand decoration of leather book bindings by using tools impressed in gold. From mid-16th century.

golf memorabilia: (collectibles) books and pictures featuring golf, and golfing equipment, including bags, balls, and clubs. Scarcity dictates value. Examples before 1850 are quite rare. Those made from 1850 to 1900 are more available but still collectible. Any golf items after 1900 are plentiful and not sought by collectors.

gol henai: (floor coverings) floral pattern frequently found in Persian rugs.

golliwogs: (black memorabilia) black characters introduced in books by Florence K. Upton, published around the turn of the century. There are golliwogs in the shapes of dolls, figurines, banks, and pins; their likenesses also appear on playing cards, plates, and other wares.

Gombroon (or Gombron) ware: (ceramics) any of the pottery produced at a factory in Gombroon (Iran), established by the English East India Company in the 17th century. Native Persian ware as well as Chinese porcelain were imported into England from the factory — both are referred to as Gombroon ware.

Gonder: (ceramics) producer of inexpensive figurines, lamps, vases, and the like, starting in 1941. Much of this ware has an Oriental motif. The glazes used by Gonder Art, Inc. include a Chinese crackle glaze and a 24K gold crackle glaze. Most lamp bases are marked "Eglee." Other items are signed "Gonder."

gong: (clocks) a steel wire that has been wound in a spiral on which the hour is struck; first used in the late 1700s.

goofus glass: inexpensive glass bowls, plates, vases, and the like. Made by several American companies from 1900 until about 1920. Goofus glass has an embossed design on the reverse side of the item. This design is painted usually with gold and red, blue, purple, or green. Gold-and-red is the most common combination.

gorget: (armor) armor to protect the neck. From the 15th century.

gossip bench: (furniture) a small table with space for the telephone, a directory, and a seat or bench that may be attached. Also called *telephone set*.

gossip pot: (kitchen) a pot with two handles.

gotch: (ceramics) a large stoneware jug.

Gothic armor: a modern term for 15th-century plate armor with slender lines.

Gothic style: (architecture, design) an architectural style of the Middle Ages prevalent in Western Europe between the 12th and 16th centuries. Also refers to other art forms derived from Gothic architecture.

gouache: 1. (fine art) opaque watercolors mixed with gum. **2.** (fine art) a painting executed in gouache.

Gouda: (ceramics) wares made in Holland since the 1600s. Most Gouda found today comes from either the 18th-century Zenith Pottery or from Zuid-Hollandsche, a company in business from the late 19th century until the mid-20th century. The latter marked their wares "Gouda."

gouge work: (furniture) decoration achieved by scooping out the wood with a troughlike chisel; used extensively on oak furniture in the 1600s.

gourd cup: a tall, gourd-shaped cup made of silver. These cups, produced during the 1500s and 1600s, often have stems shaped like gnarled trees.

grace cup: a small silver goblet with a high stem. From 16th and 17th centuries, and again in the early 19th century.

Graham, George (fl. 1715): (clocks) the London clockmaker who invented the deadbeat escapement, which made clocks more accurate.

graining: (furniture) the imitation of natural wood grains by applying paint or stain.

grandfather chair: (furniture) a high-backed chair with side pieces or wings that protect the sitter from drafts. Also called *wing chair*.

grandfather clock: (clocks) a tall floor clock with hanging weights and pendulums. Also called *long-case clock* and *tall-case clock*.

grand guard: (armor) a large plate covering the left shoulder and lower part of the face. It was worn over regular armor in tournaments. From the 16th century.

Grandma Moses: (folk art) the most famous 20th-century American folk artist. Her work was first discovered in a drugstore by a collector when Grandma Moses was in her seventies. Her real name was Anna Mary Robertson.

grandmother clock: a small, long-case clock measuring 6-1/2 feet or less.

grandmother ware: (tableware) white porcelain or pottery ware with relief patterns of grapes, ivy, fruits, and the like in tones of blue or violet. Made in Staffordshire, England. Also called *Chelsea dinnerware.*

grangerized: 1. (books) a book illustrated with drawings, engravings, or prints from other books. Named for James Granger, an 18th-century writer who illustrated his history book this way. **2.** (books) a book with its illustrative material clipped out. **3.** (stamps) a fake stamp created from pieces of genuine stamps.

granite ware: (ceramics) a durable and inexpensive white earthenware sold in the United States during the mid-1800s.

grapeshot: (weapons) a cluster of small iron balls encased so they could be fired as a single shot and break up upon impact.

graver: (tools) a tool used for engraving.

graybeard: (ceramics) a large stoneware jug with a grayish finish. Often decorated with a bearded mask in relief.

grease pan: (lighting) a circular drip pan below the nozzle of a candlestick; used to catch the grease and wax from the burning candle.

greaves: (armor) armor for legs below the knees. Worn by the Greeks and Romans; also worn in Europe from the 11th to the 17th century.

Greek cross: (decoration) a cross with four limbs of equal size; used as a motif for furniture and jewelry.

Greenaway, Kate (1846-1901): (books, ceramics) a children's book illustrator, starting about 1866. Her work has appeared in magazines and on greeting cards and porcelain items. The images of cute children dressed in 1800s clothing are recognizable and collectible.

green opaque: (glass) ware made of soft green glass with a band of gold produced for less than a year by the New England Glass Company. Dates to 1887 and is hard to find.

Greentown glass: glass made by the Indiana Tumbler and Goblet Company at their factory in Greentown, Indiana, from 1894 until 1903. They made pressed glass items but are most famous for the chocolate glass perfected by Jacob Rosenthal in 1900.

Greenwich armor: armor made at the only English Royal workshop, founded by Henry VIII at Southwark in 1511 and later moved to Greenwich Palace, where it remained in operation until *ca.* 1635.

grenade: (weapons) an explosive shell thrown by hand.

greyhound jug: (ceramics) a vessel named for its greyhound-shaped handles; decorated with sporting scenes done in relief.

grid-iron: (domestic) a grid made up of parallel bars; placed over the fire for cooking.

griffin: (decoration) a winged, mythological figure with the head of an eagle and the lower body of a lion; used on furniture, textiles, and accessories.

grill: (stamps) a tiny grid pattern cut into the fibers of stamp paper; used in the United States in the late 1860s and early 1870s to prevent the removal of cancellation marks. It absorbed the ink into the broken fibers so that the ink could not be eradicated.

grill plate: (tableware) a glass or china plate divided in sections (usually three); designed to keep foods separated from each other. Part of each diner's place setting.

grisaille: (fine art) a monochromatic painting done in shades of gray.

groat: (coins) an English silver coin with the value of fourpence; used from the 14th to the 17th centuries. Scottish groat, from the mid-14th century.

Gropius, Walter (1833-1969): (design, architecture) a German leader of modern functional architecture and design, Gropius was the director of the Bauhaus school from 1919 to 1928. See also *Bauhaus*.

grosgrain: (textiles) a heavy silk or rayon fabric with narrow horizontal ribs.

gros point: (needlework) a large embroidery cross-stitch covering two vertical and two horizontal threads worked with needlepoint on 8- to 12-to-the-inch mesh; used for chairs and settee covers.

grotesques: (decoration) a method of decoration taken from Roman wall paintings. Grotesques feature motifs like leaf and flower designs, half figures, masks, and fruits. Also called *antic work*.

ground: (textiles) any background to a lace pattern.

ground colors: (ceramics) the background of colored glaze upon which a decoration is painted or gilded on porcelain or pottery.

grounded lace: (textiles) lace with a mesh background.

ground stopper: (glass) a glass stopper that has had the part that fits in a bottle ground so that it resembles frosted glass.

Grueby: (ceramics) hand-thrown pottery tiles, vases, bowls, and the like with a soft, dull glaze in blue, brown, gray, green, and yellow made by the Grueby Faience Company of Boston, Massachusetts. Pieces were painted in the Arts and Crafts style. The

company, which started in 1894 and closed about 1920, marked its wares "Grueby Pottery, Boston, USA," "Grueby Faience," or "Grueby, Boston, Mass."

guardant: (decoration) an animal with its body shown from the side and its head turned toward the viewer; motif used in furniture and jewelry.

guard chain: a long chain hung from the neck to hold keys or toilet articles.

Gubbio maiolica: (ceramics) a tin-glazed earthenware made by Giorgio Andreoli at his workshop in Gubbio, Italy; famous for the ruby pigment Andreoli used. From the 1500s. See also *maiolica*.

gueridon: (furniture) a small, round table or stand, usually for candles.

Guernsey measure: (metal) a baluster-shaped pewter measure with two bands around a heart-shaped lid, and an acorn thumbpiece.

Guiennois: (coins) a large gold coin issued in Guienne, France, by England's Edward III (1312 to 1377) and the Black Prince (1330 to 1376).

guilder: (coins) a silver Dutch coin during the 17th and 18th centuries.

guilloche: (decoration) a decorative band or border that resembles a line of interlocking circles.

guinea: (coins) British gold coin valued at one pound, one shilling. Issued from 1670 to 1813.

gulail: (weapons) an aboriginal pellet bow of India, Burma, and Nepal. It has a double string with a pocket in the middle for a missile of baked clay, stone, or other material. At the instant of release, the bow must be moved to the left or the missile will hit the thumb.

gules: (heraldry) the color red, indicated by vertical lines.

Gunderson glass: a fine peachblow made from 1952

until 1957 by the Gunderson-Pairpoint Glass Works in New Bedford, Massachusetts.

gunmetal: an alloy of 90 percent copper and 10 percent tin; popular in the late 1800s for jewelry and other objects.

gunner's stiletto: (weapons) a knife with a scale on the blade for measuring gunshot.

gupti: (weapons) an Indian sword cane.

gusoku: (armor) a complete suit of Japanese armor.

gusoku bitsu: (armor) a Japanese box made of wood or papier-maché; used for storing and transporting armor.

Gutman, Bessie Pease: (prints) an American artist and illustrator who worked from the late 1800s to the mid-1900s. Her most popular illustrations were those featuring children, and they were widely used in children's books. Original Gutman prints are collectible, but her work has been extensively reproduced.

gutta-percha: (materials) hard rubber substance made from the sap of a Malayan tree beginning in 1840; used to make jewelry, statues, furniture, and other objects. Particularly popular for making small photograph cases, usually designed to hold two pictures.

gutter: (stamps) the unprinted space left between the individual panes on a full press sheet of stamps.

gutter pair: (stamps) any pair of stamps separated by a gutter, horizontally or vertically.

gwafu: (orientalia) a book of Japanese sketches.

ℋ

ha: (weapons) the cutting edge of a Japanese blade.

habaki: (weapons) the metal ferule that surrounds the blade adjacent to the guard on a Japanese sword. It secures the blade in the scabbard, preventing damage to the edge.

Hadley chest: (furniture) a distinctive dower chest with incised carvings of tulips, vines and leaves covering the entire front. Originated in the area of Hadley, Massachusetts, *ca.* 1690 to 1710.

Hague, The: (ceramics) hard-paste porcelain made at The Hague from the late 1700s under the guidance of German workmen. Marked with a blue stork under or over the glaze.

haiku: (fine art, books) a Japanese poem of seventeen syllables. Also called *hokku.*

hairline: (stamps) a fine-line flaw on a stamp. The defect is usually the result of a minute scratch on the printing plate, which can either cause an unwanted line to be printed, or the loss of a detail.

hairline crack: (glass, ceramics, metal) a fine line caused by trauma such as stress, heat, or age. It may be restricted to the surface or penetrate the material.

hair pencils: (fine art) brushes of many sizes called, according to size, *crow, pigeon, duck, goose, extra small swan, little swan, middle swan,* and (the largest) *big swan.* Also called *quill pencils.*

hairpin lace: (textiles) lacy crochet work done on a hairpin loom.

hairwork jewelry: jewelry woven from a girl's or woman's hair. Fashionable *ca.* 1800s and early 1900s. Much of this work was set in gold. It became a popular craft (just as quilting and knitting were) and many women's groups gathered to weave their hair as they exchanged tidbits of gossip.

hakase: (weapons) Japanese for *sword.*

halbard: (weapons) a spearlike weapon consisting of a long shaft with an axe blade, a peak point opposite it, and a long spike or blade at the end. From the 13th to 18th centuries.

halberd: (weapons) an axlike blade with a steel spike mounted on the end of a long pole. Fifteenth and 16th centuries.

half armor: (armor) suit of armor that covered only the body and arms, or only the body. From the 17th century, when guns had become the major weapon.

half-bound: (books) a book that has the spine and outer corners covered with leather. The remainder of the book is covered in cloth. See also *leather-bound* and *quarter-bound.*

half crown: (coins) a British coin formerly valued at two shillings and sixpence.

half doll: a porcelain figure from the waist up; used from 1900 until 1930 as the tops for pincushions, clothes brushes, perfume bottles, and other functional objects. The bottom, functional part was usually made in the form of a skirt.

half-hanger: (weapons) a type of guard used on a saber.

half-hull model: (marine) model of one side of a boat hull, usually in a scale of 1:20 or 1:40, mounted on a board; originally used as a model from which the full-scale boat was built.

half-lead crystal: (glass) crystal containing about 15 percent lead.

half-moon tables: (furniture) half-round tables that were customarily placed at each end of a rectangular table to make a long, oval dining table. Also called *demi-lune tables.*

halfpenny: (coins) **1.** British copper coin since 1672; **2.** a silver coin during the Middle Ages.

half tester: (furniture) an early folding bed that is hinged to the headboard; used from the late 1700s to *ca.* 1840.

half title: (books) the page preceding the main title page with the title and/or volume number of the series if any. The verso may be blank or carry the printer's imprint; in modern books, other books by the author may be listed. The half title can be at the top of the first page of the text. If so, only the title is printed.

Hall China: (ceramics) an East Liverpool, Ohio, company best known for their teapots. In business since 1903; in 1920 they began making teapots, then dinnerware — Autumn Leaf is the most popular pattern. Pieces are marked with the company name.

hallmark: (metal) a mark stamped on a silver or gold object in England designating its standard of quality and the Hall or Assay office where it was assayed. Broadly used, the term refers to any mark indicating quality.

hall tree: (furniture) an upright pole with pegs or hooks for hanging clothing. Also called *clothes tree.*

Hamadan: (floor coverings) rugs with a long pile and a rather coarse texture. The colors are bright and animals are frequently used in the designs.

Hamada, Shoji: (orientalia, ceramics) producer of Oriental rural pottery both in England in the early 1920s and later in Japan. He is the most respected Japanese potter and his wares are highly prized.

Ham and Sam: (black memorabilia, toys) lithographed windup toy of two blacks, one at a piano and the other playing a banjo. Made by Strauss in 1920.

hamidashi: (weapons) a Japanese dagger with a small guard only slightly larger than the grip.

hammered: (metal) brass, copper, or other metal objects hammered into shape or decorated by hammering. See also *beaten.*

hammered aluminum: (tableware) handmade and machinemade Arts-and-Crafts-style metal ware that was introduced in the 1920s and remained popular through the 1950s. Items include trays, silent butlers, coasters, and serving pieces.

hammer price: (auctions) last amount that has been bid when an auctioneer pounds his hammer or gavel and announces an item is sold. Any bidder coming in after the hammer is considered too late.

Hampshire pottery: (ceramics) redware and stoneware churns, crocks, flowerpots, and the like produced by the Hampshire Pottery Company when they opened in 1871 in Keene, New Hampshire. By 1878 the company was making majolica. Cadmon Robertson joined the firm in 1904. He perfected the matte glazes in blue, brown, green, and red for which the company became known. Some of these pieces are marked "M" in a circle. The company closed in 1923.

hand-and-a-half sword: (weapons) a 15th-century sword with a long, straight blade, plain cross guard, long grip, and rounded pommel. Ordinarily used with one hand, the long grip provided grasp for fingers of the left hand for added power.

handback: (stamps) a cover hand canceled at the post office and returned to the customer instead of being sent through the mail.

handcooler: (glass) a glass egg said to be used by ladies to cool their hands when they were in a frenzy of anticipation over an expected kiss. Between kisses handcoolers had the more practical task of being used to darn socks.

Handel, Philip: (ceramics, glass) since 1885, producer of art glass objects in his factories in Meriden, Connecticut, and New York City. Lamps in the Tiffany style and reverse-painted lamps are what the firm is best known for. Most pieces are marked "ANDEL" inside a large H.

handkerchief table: (furniture) a small, single-leaf table with the top and leaf each triangular in shape. With the leaf down, the table fits into a corner; when open it is square shaped.

hand-lapped: (metal) a steel piece hand polished with an oil stone.

hand-pressed: (glass) any glass object made in a hand-operated press instead of a machine press.

handstamp: 1. (stamps) cancellation by hand instead of by machine. **2.** (stamps) the rubber stamp used to apply the hand cancellation.

hanger: 1. (weapons) a short, light, curved single-edged sword, originally hung from the belt. **2.** (weapons) the triangular sling attached to the belt that held a rapier. Late 1500s and early 1600s.

han kyu: (weapons) a small Japanese bow.

hardi: (coins) a gold coin issued in the French possessions by the English Black Prince (1330 to 1376).

hard-paste porcelain: (ceramics) porcelain with kaolin, a fine white clay, as the main component. It is harder and more durable than soft-paste porcelain, so more of it survives intact. It originated in China and was not made in Europe until the early 1700s.

hard pewter: (metal) an alloy of copper and antimony. Harder and of a whiter color

than ordinary, tin-lead-antimony pewter.

harinuki: (paper) the Japanese name for *papier-maché*.

Harker: (ceramics) pottery from a company founded by Benjamin Harker in 1840 in East Liverpool, Ohio. Harker produced yellow ware from the clay in the region. White ware and a brown-glazed pottery were added later. In 1931 the company was moved to West Virginia. In 1971 Jeanette Glass Company bought Harker. It closed in 1972. Most ware is marked "The Harker Pottery Company" with an arrow.

harleian: (books) a style of binding in leather that features a tooled border and usually a central diamond-shaped design.

harlequin: (decoration) a variegated parti-colored pattern inspired by the dress of a comedy character with the same name; used in textiles, jewelry, furniture.

Harlequin: (ceramics) dinnerware made by the Homer Laughlin China Company of West Virginia. Decorated in strong colors such as blue, maroon, mauve-blue, spruce green, turquoise, yellow, red, and cobalt. First made in 1938. Woolworth had the exclusive rights to sell Harlequin. In the 1950s animal figurines were added. They are the most highly prized.

harmonica: (music) a mouth instrument first produced in an attempt to simulate organ music. Most of those available are poorly made.

harmonium: (music) a type of organ.

harness: (armor, weapons) the term used for armor, and sometimes weapons, during the Middle Ages.

harpsichord: (music) an instrument with three or four strings for each note; played by plucking the strings with a quill. A forerunner of the piano.

harquebus (or arquebus): (weapons) a heavy, portable matchlock gun. *Ca.* 15th century.

hash dish: (tableware) a round silver or silver-plate dish with straight sides, loop or drop-ring handles, and a cover; used in the 18th and 19th centuries to serve hot food. Some are on an open frame with a spirit lamp to keep food warm.

hasp: (hardware) a hinged strap with a pin or lock; used to secure a chest or door.

hat badge: (fashion accessories) an ornament worn on a man's hat during the Renaissance. Some had cameos, some mythological characters, and some religious scenes.

hatching: (stamps) a background of parallel or crossed lines for decoration or shading; more common on earlier stamps.

hatchment: (textiles) a coat of arms embroidered on a black background; hung on the door to announce a death in the house.

hat pin: (jewelry) a long pin used to fasten a lady's hat to her hair. Many of these pins have ornate heads.

hat-shaped: (glass) a dish, vase, toothpick holder, or other small accessory shaped like an upside-down top hat.

hatted doll: a doll wearing a hat that is molded as part of its head. Also called *bonnet doll.*

hauberk: (armor) a long coat of mail worn over a quilted gambeson by knights. From the llth to 13th centuries.

haussegen: (folk art) a decorative wall hanging with a religious motif, usually a psalm. A house blessing.

Haviland: (ceramics) dinnerware and art pottery produced by the Haviland family companies. In 1840 David Haviland founded the Haviland Company in Limoges, France, where the extraordinary clay attracted many similar companies. Theodore Haviland left the company to form a firm of his own, and in 1941 he moved his business to New York. Dinnerware predominated Haviland's output, but in the 1880s and 1890s, the company also made a fine line of art pottery. Early Haviland made in Limoges is marked "H & Co"; after 1890 the company name with "France" or "Limoges" was used. Theodore Haviland marked some of his early pieces "Mont Mery"; after his move to New York, his wares were marked "Theodore Haviland, N.Y." or "Theodore Haviland, Made in America." Most collectors prefer Limoges Haviland.

Hawkes, Thomas (d. 1913): (glass) one of the masters of cut glass. He created lovely pieces in his factory in Corning, New York. His company, which opened in 1880 and closed in 1962, cut blanks made at other glassworks. Many pieces are signed with a fleur-de-lis and two hawks in a trefoil.

haystack: (metal) a pewter measure made in sizes from a pint to several gallons; used in Irish taverns.

heading sword: (weapons) a two-handed, broad, straight, two-edged sword; used for executions in Europe from the 16th to the early 19th centuries.

head vase: (ceramics, collectibles) a vase portraying a woman from the shoulders up; used by the florist industry from the 1930s to the 1960s. The most elaborate of these were made in the 1950s and 1960s. Some of these ladies wore necklaces and earrings while others were plainer. Larger ones are more valuable than smaller examples.

Hearty Good Fellow jug: (ceramics) a Toby jug portraying a drunken man holding a jug.

heaume: (armor) a 13th-century headpiece of plate.

height of the device: (coins) the thickness of the image above the coin's surface.

Heisey: (glass) dinnerware and glass animals and birds produced by H. Heisey and Company in Ohio from 1896 until 1957. Color was a late addition to their wares. In 1957 Imperial Glass Corporation bought some of the molds from the failing firm. Very early Heisey is unmarked; most Heisey Glass is marked with an "H" within a diamond. In 1968 Imperial dropped the Heisey trademark.

helm: (weapons) a large helmet that covered the head, face, and neck to the collarbone. Late 12th through 16th centuries.

hen dish: (ceramics, glass) a basket-shaped, shallow dish with a cover in the shape of a hen. When the cover is on, the dish looks like a hen sitting on a nest.

Hepplewhite, George (d. 1786): (furniture) an 18th-century English furniture designer whose style was characterized by simple, but elegant forms, as found in his shield-back chair.

heraldic: (decoration) a shield-shaped motif carved on furniture.

heraldic eagle: (decoration) an eagle with legs and wings spread apart.

heraldry: the history and description of armorial bearings, accessories, ensigns, insignia, and the like.

Herat carpets: (floor coverings) Persian carpets of an excellent quality with an allover design usually featuring a fish motif or a leaf and rosettes. Background is generally dark blue, often with a soft green border.

herb mortar: (kitchen) a wooden mortar used for pulverizing herbs.

hermaphrodite: a mixed match — a combination of contradictory or diverse parts.

Heubach: (ceramics) doll heads, piano babies, figurines, and novelties produced by Gebroder Heubach in Germany since the mid-1800s. Most of their items are marked "H" in a sun over "C."

heyazashi: (weapons) a short Japanese sword or knife carried in the house.

Heywood Brothers: (furniture) the five brothers of the Heywood Company in Gardner, Massachusetts, which produced wicker in the late 19th century.

H.G.E.: (metal) initials that stand for *hard gold electroplated*. A piece marked "H.G.E." is made of a base metal with a thin coat of gold applied by electroplating.

H hinge: (hardware) a hinge similar to the cock's head hinge, but with straight lines; used on 16th- and 17th-century cupboards. See also *cock's head hinge.*

Hicks, William: (folk art) an early folk artist famous for his many renditions of *The Peaceable Kingdom,* portraying animals of many species living tranquilly with humans.

Higbee glass: pressed glass made by J.B. Higbee Company in Pennsylvania for a brief time around 1900. Though mostly clear glass was used, some colored pieces were made. Some pieces are marked "HIG" inside a bee.

highboy: (furniture) a two-section chest of drawers supported on high legs. Also called *tallboy* and *chest-on-chest.*

high-wrap tapestry: (textiles) tapestry woven on an upright loom. Considered finer than other old tapestries.

himotoshi: (orientalia) the holes made in netsuke so they can be strung on a cord or belt. See also *netsuke.*

hinge: (stamps) a small, thin piece of gummed paper; used to mount a postage stamp in an album.

hipped knee: (furniture) the carving on the knee of a cabriole leg that extends up to and onto the seat rail.

hiramakie: (orientalia) Japanese lacquered ware with designs in low relief.

Hispano-Moresque maiolica: (ceramics) tin-glazed earthenware made by Moorish craftsmen in Spain, first in Granada and later in Valencia. *Ca.* 1400 through the 1500s.

historical glass: glass bread trays, plates, pitchers, and the like depicting historical events in clear or colored glass. Popular in the 1800s.

Hitchcock chair: (furniture) a chair with inclined round legs and a pillow-back top rail, usually painted black with gold or colored stenciling of flowers and fruit. Adapted from an 19th-century chair by Lambert Hitchcock of Hitchcockville, Connecticut, who made a large number of the chairs between 1820 and 1850.

Hobbs, Brockunier: (glass) a company in Wheeling, West Virginia, that made amberina, peachblow, and other fine glass from about 1875 until the turn of the century. They also produced receptacles for use by druggists.

hobnail glass: a glass with very pronounced bumps all over it. Made by many companies from clear glass, colored glass, milk glass, carnival glass, and the like.

hodden gray: (textiles) a garment woven from black and white sheep's wool.

Hoechst Porcelain: (figurines) hard-paste porcelain figurines, often in the Meissen style, produced in Germany from 1750 until 1798. From 1765 most figures were depicted on a base that looked like a grassy mound. Most pieces are marked with a six-spoked wheel.

hokku: (fine art, books) a Japanese poem of seventeen syllables. Also called *haiku*.

Holbeinesque: (jewelry) jewelry designs inspired by the art of 16th-century German painter Hans Holbein the Younger; the rage in 1870s England.

hold-to-light postcard: (paper) a postcard that has a message or picture that can only be seen when the card is held up to the light.

holey dollar: (coins) Spanish dollar with its center removed; used as official coin by other countries.

hollow cast: (toys) a method of casting toys by pouring molten metal into a mold, then moving it around to coat the sides of mold, producing a hollow figure or toy. Also called *slush cast*.

hollow cutting: (glass) the cutting or grinding of a design on glass with a convex-edged tool.

hollow stem: (glass) a hollow glass cylinder that forms the stem of a drinking glass. Popular in the late 1700s.

hollowware: (silver) serving pieces such as pitchers and bowls, usually made of silver or silver plate. See also *flatware*.

holly amber glass: (glass) a pressed glass with holly leaves in amber-colored glass shading from tan to brown. Made by the Indiana Tumbler and Goblet Company for a brief time in 1903. Also called *golden agate glass*.

holly work: (needlework) a white-work embroidery done on babies' clothing from about 1715 to 1800. This delicate needlework was inserted in holes that were cut in material.

holy water sprinkle: (weapons) a large head of wood or iron studded with spikes mounted on a shaft; used in Europe and the Orient from about the Middle Ages through the 17th century. Also called *morning star*.

Homer Laughlin China Company: (ceramics) from 1871 until the present, a company that produces dinnerware and other ceramics in Newell, West Virginia. Fiesta and Harlequin wares are two of the company's creations. They also released many popular patterns including their version of the willow pattern. Most pieces are marked "HLC" followed by a number.

homespun: (textiles) a loosely woven wool or linen fabric made from yarn that was spun at home.

Honan ware: (orientalia) Chinese porcelain with a black or brown glaze. From the Sung dynasty.

honzogan: (metal) the Japanese inlaying of metal.

hood: 1. (clocks) the upper section of a long-case clock that encloses the face. It is removed by sliding it forward. **2.** (furniture) the hood-shaped top of any cabinetwork.

hoof foot: (furniture) a chair or table foot in the form of an animal hoof; used with the cabriole leg from *ca.* 1695 to 1720. It was the forerunner of the club foot.

hoof handle: (metal, tableware) handle made in the image of a deer hoof; used as handles on 17th-century eating utensils. Also called *deer-foot handle*.

hooked rug: (floor coverings) a decorative American rug handmade by pulling yarn through a mesh backing to form a pile.

hoop-back: (furniture) a chair back with uprights and top rails that continue in one unbroken curve.

hoopskirt: (fashion accessories) a full, stiff underskirt worn to make an overskirt stand out. Also called *crinoline*.

Hoosier cabinet: (furniture) a free-standing kitchen cabinet with enclosed storage sections and drawers above and below a porcelain-enameled metal counter. Storage sections include pullout bins for flour, sugar, coffee, or other dried goods, a pullout breadboard, and a bread drawer. Made between the late 19th century and World War II by several firms including the Hoosier Manufacturing Company of New Castle, Indiana. Hoosier was so successful that their name became generic for the cabinet.

hope chest: (furniture) any storage chest used to hold the trousseau and linen of a future bride. Also called *dowry chest* and *dower chest*.

horagai: (music) a Japanese shell trumpet.

hornbook: (books) a sheet of parchment on which a child's primer is written. The sheet of transparent horn used to cover and protect it is responsible for the name.

horn salts: (tableware) salt-cellars made from the horns of animals.

horo: (armor) a cape worn over armor by the Japanese.

horology: (clocks) the measurement of time and the making of time pieces.

horse brasses: (metal) round, brass adornments for horse harnesses. Made first in the mid-1700s. They had either cast or stamped designs including likenesses of soldiers, lions, griffins, and politicians. The age and grade of brass are important factors in determining value.

horseman's hammer: (weapons) a 15th-century war hammer with either a short or long handle.

horse pistol: (weapons) any type of large pistol carried by a horseman.

horseshoe-back chair: (furniture) a Windsor chair with a hoop back.

hostess cart: (furniture) a small table with wheels used for food and beverages. Also called *hostess wagon, tea cart,* and *tea wagon.*

hostess wagon: (furniture) a small table with wheels used for food and beverages. Also called *hostess cart, tea cart,* and *tea wagon.*

hosting harness: (armor) armor designed for use on the battlefield as distinguished from that intended for use in tournaments.

hound handle: (decoration) handle in the shape of a running hound; used on pitchers and ewers.

Hubbard, Elbert (1856-1915): founder of Roycroft, a publishing house, school, and factory for furniture and household wares in the Arts and Crafts style. Hubbard authored *A Message to Garcia* in 1899, which sold over 40 million copies. See also *Roycroft.*

Hull: (ceramics) a pottery operating in Ohio from 1905 until the present. The firm produced commercial wares until 1917 when they added a line of art pottery. In 1940 they added the Little Red Riding Hood line and a new line of matte-finish art wares. In 1950 they experimented with a high-gloss finish. Pieces are usually marked "Hull USA."

Hull, John (fl. 1652): (silver) noted 17th-century Boston silversmith. Hull worked in partnership with Robert Sanderson to create useful silver articles. Most of them are marked and many have survived, although they are quite costly.

humidifier: (stamps) a small air-tight container for removing paper from stamps or separating stamps that are stuck together. The stamps and a moistened pad are placed in the container for about fifteen minutes.

humidor: (household accessories) a cabinet or container designed to keep tobacco moist and fresh.

Hummel: (ceramics) figurines, plates, bells, and other decorative pieces produced by Franz Goebel using designs created by Berta Hummel, a Franciscan nun whose religious name was Sister M. Innocentia. The first figurine was made in 1935. Pieces were first marked with a crown; from 1950 until 1959, they were marked with a full bee in "V"; from 1959 until 1964, with a stylized bee in "V"; from 1964 until 1972, the stylized bee with three lines of print; and in 1970, "V" with the bee between the *b* and *l* of "Goebel." In 1979 the bee was dropped. Age, condition, and size are very important to collectors of the figurines. See also *Goebel.*

hundred-leg table: (furniture) a table with drop leaves and usually six stationary legs and two additional legs that swing out like a gate to hold up the drop leaves. Also called *forty-leg table* and *gateleg table.*

Hungarian point: (needlework) embroidery created by working the thread in shades and stitches that form a sequence of peaks resembling flames. Also called *bargello, flame work,* and *Florentine stitch.*

hunting carpet: (floor coverings) a Persian carpet that vividly depicts an elaborate hunting scene.

hunting case: (jewelry) a watch case with a cover that conceals the face of the watch. You press lightly on the top of the case to flip it open and reveal the time.

hunting sword: (weapons) a short, light saber carried on the hunt.

hurdy gurdy: (music) stringed instrument operated by turning a wheel, usually with a crank, so it strikes the strings. Dates from the mid-1700s.

husk: (decoration) an ornament resembling the bell flower or the husk of a wheat ear; often used on furniture and silver.

hutch: 1. (furniture) a cupboard with open shelves above, drawers in the middle, and doors below. **2.** (furniture) a chest with doors in front.

Hutschenreuther: (ceramics) producer of porcelain in Selb, Germany, from the early to mid-1800s until the present. They make dinnerware, figurines, and limited edition collector plates. The wares are usually marked with the company name and a lion.

I

Icart, Louis: (fine art, prints) a French artist that started his career as a fashion artist in the early 1900s. During World War I, he sketched and etched in his spare time while he served in his country's army. Those sketches were produced in limited editions and are very collectible. High-fashion art deco and art nouveau females were his favorite subjects.

ice cream molds: (kitchen) pewter ice cream molds produced in many shapes, including apple, banana, basket, cat, cradle, dog, duck, elephant, football player, horn of plenty, pear, valentine, and wedding ring. There are also molds that were made in the image of insignias of various organizations.

ice cream scoops: (kitchen) small and large cone-shaped or lever-operated scoops of pewter, tin, aluminum, or nickel-plated brass. Among the names to look for are Gilchrist, Benedict Indestructo, and Hamilton Beach.

ice glass: glass that has the look of cracked ice; produced by immersing hot glass in water and later reheating it.

ice lip: (glass, china) a part of a pitcher that is molded over the lip, leaving a hole that allows the liquid to be poured while it keeps the ice in the pitcher.

icon: (religion, fine art) a picture of a religious subject, usually painted on a small wooden panel; used in devotion by Eastern Christians.

illuminated book: a 19th-century book with plates and initial letters gilded and colored in the fashion of medieval illuminated manuscripts.

image toys: (ceramics) pottery figures made at Staffordshire, England, in the mid-1700s.

Imari ware: (ceramics) Japanese enameled porcelain exported by Dutch traders from the seaport of Imari in the late 17th century. Rich colors make the ware unique: soft orange, red, pale primrose yellow, grass green, turquoise green, lilac-blue, and gilding. Imari with a brocaded design in blue, red, and gold greatly influenced later English china and earthenware patterns. One style of Imari with irregular designs in blue, red, gold, and to a lesser degree, other enamel colors, inspired the English to produce gaudy Welsh for the American market. After Japan was opened to the West in the 1860s, a large volume of Imari was exported until 1900; it is this 19th-century Imari that is sought by most collectors. Imari ware is still being made.

imbricate armor: European armor with overlapping scales attached to cloth or leather. Eleventh and 12th centuries.

impasto: (ceramics) color that is put on so thickly that it stands out from the surface of the vessel to which it has been applied.

imperf: (stamps) a stamp issued without perforation. Also called *imperforate*.

imperforate: (stamps) a stamp issued without perforation. Also called *imperf*.

Imperial Glass: glass company best known as makers of candlewick glass. Opened 1901 in Bellaire, Ohio; by 1910 they were a leading maker of carnival glass and in 1916 introduced a line of stretch glass called Imperial Jewels. In 1931 the company closed. It reopened shortly as Imperial Glass Corporation; now owned by Lenox. Imperial made reproductions from molds purchased from Central Glass Works and Cambridge and Heisey; most of these are marked "I" over "G." See also *candlewick* and *stretch glass*.

Imperial Porcelain: a company best known for its American Folklore Miniatures and its numbered Blue Ridge Mountain Boys series of figurines. It also made mugs, planters, and miscellaneous novelty items, all of which are collectibles. In business from 1947 to 1960.

Imperial St. Petersburg: (ceramics) a Russian porcelain factory that produced statues, busts, bisque portrayals of groups, and dinnerware. Started in 1744, but gained importance in the 1760s. Many pieces are decorated with Russian scenes. In the early 1900s the factory started making wares in the art nouveau style. Imperial changed its name to Lomonosov in 1925. Until 1917 pieces were marked with the initials of the monarch in power at the time.

imperial yellow: (orientalia) a distinctive yellow enamel so named because it was perfected in the 1400s in the Chinese Imperial kilns.

important: (auctions) a piece that is of high value and usually rare.

impression: (coins) the reverse design on a die pressed into another die to be stamped.

imprint: (books) the publisher's name and address, date, and edition on the title page. Also the printer's name on the copyright page.

Ince and Mayhew: (books) cabinetmakers who published *The Universal System of Household Furniture* in the 1700s. It contained more than 300 furniture designs.

incense boat: (metal) boat-shaped vessel in which incense was kept before it was placed in a burner. Sometimes made of precious metal and often set with precious stones.

incidit: (decoration) engraved.

incised design: (decoration) a design that is cut, carved, or engraved into the surface of an object.

incised stem: (glass) a drinking-glass stem with a spiral groove. Most popular from the late 1600s through the 1700s.

inclusion flaw: 1. (glass) a flaw that happened during the making of a glass object. **2.** (jewelry) a naturally occurring flaw in a precious stone.

incroyable chair: (furniture) a chair with two seats that are attached side-by-side, facing in opposite directions. Popular in the 18th and 19th centuries. Also called *conversation chair*.

incunabulum: 1. (books) a book printed with moveable type in the 15th century. **2.** an artifact from an early period.

incuse: (coins) a design hammered, stamped, or pressed into a coin.

independent decorator: (ceramics) an 18th- or 19th-century professional artisan who purchased plain white-ware porcelain (blanks) from porcelain manufacturers and skillfully enameled and painted the pieces to sell to London dealers. Some fine examples of Coalport, Swansea, and Nantgarw, as well as some salt-glazed stoneware, were decorated by these artists.

index: (scientific instruments) a device that indicates the value or quantity of a measurement.

Indian artifacts: (Native American) crafts created by North American Indians. Among the desired articles are baskets, beaded bags and belts, blankets, clothing, dolls, headdresses, horns, jewelry, moccasins, and rugs. The Navajo, Cherokee, Hopi, Crow, Sioux, Apache, and Penobscot are just a few of the tribes whose work is sought.

Indian beadwork: (Native American) work done in clear and colored beads mostly by the Northwest American nations during the late 19th and early 20th centuries. The larger the piece the more value it has. Colored beads are more desirable than clear ones.

Indian blankets: (Native American) colorful handwoven blankets. The most sought-after are those made on upright looms by the Navajo nation. The Zuni and Hopi also make fine examples.

Indian carving: (Native American) chests, eating utensils, masks, totems, and other articles carved from wood. Examples by the Haida, the Kwakiutl, and other Northwestern nations are especially collectible. Pre-1940s examples are rare.

Indian Ische Blumen: (decoration) literally, Indian flowers. A porcelain decoration featuring chrysanthemums and leaves. Copied from East Indian porcelain.

Indian mask: (decoration) a mask motif complete with plumes; a popular decoration for the tops of mirrors from the mid-1700s to the mid-1800s.

Indian pottery: (Native American) dishes, bowls, figures, and other articles made by members of Native American nations. Examples from New Mexico and Arizona are made of coiled clay and decorated with abstract, geometric designs either painted on or scratched into the article.

Indian swirl marble: a black glass marble with a swirl of color. The marble often has an irregular shape.

Indian Tree: (ceramics, decoration) a common dinnerware pattern featuring the branch of a tree laden with pink blossoms; used by several manufacturers including Coalport. First produced in the early 19th century.

India ware: (ceramics) the name given Chinese porcelain that was imported in England during the 18th century. This ware got its name because it was sold at auction in India House in London.

ingot: (coins) alloyed or pure metal that has been molded from molten metal into a bar or other specific form.

ink bottle: (desk accessories) a bottle to store ink dating to the 1900s. In an effort to make untippable ink bottles, the manufacturers of ink came up with decorative and distinctive bottle shapes. Earlier glass or pottery bottles are of a plainer design. Those made through the beginning of the 20th century are collectible.

inkstand: (desk accessories) a stand that holds an inkwell and pens. See also *inkwell.*

inkwell: (desk accessories) a receptacle that holds ink for writing with a quill or pen. Seventeenth- and 18th-century examples were for use with quills; the dip pen replaced the quill in the 19th century. The advent of the ballpoint pen in the 1930s eliminated the need for inkwells. Examples in styles like art deco, art nouveau, and Victorian were made of glass, silver, gold, brass, bronze, wood, and porcelain. See also *inkstand.*

inlaid: (books) the restoration of the four margins on a book page. See also *remargined* and *extended.*

inlaid bookbindings: (books) leather-bound books with different colored slips of leather inlaid in a mosaic pattern.

inlaid to size: (books) a smaller page or illustration mounted on a larger page.

inlay: (decoration) to create a design by cutting out shapes from a surface and replacing them with contrasting material.

inner stripe: (floor coverings) the stripe that is woven between the border and the middle of a Persian rug.

inro: (orientalia) furniture and jewelry decorated with a lacquer derived from the exuded sap of several varieties of the ash tree, found only in Asia.

Made in China and Japan prior to the 20th century. See also *Japanese inro.*

inscribed copy: (books) a book autographed and/or inscribed by its author.

inspector's lamp: (railroad memorabilia, lighting) a hand-carried lantern with a large lens; used by railroad workers when they checked the trains.

insulators: (collectibles) glass, pottery, and wood items used on telegraph and telephone wires. They date back to 1844, when the telegraph was invented. Thousands of different types were produced over the years. Scarcity and color determine value.

intaglio: 1. (decoration) a figure or design impressed into a surface. **2.** (decoration) a carved design hollowed out from the surface of a gem or glass.

intaglio eyes: (dolls) eyes that are formed by incising (cutting into) the head.

intarsia: 1. (furniture) a detailed, elegant form of inlay featuring pictorial scenes done in Italy. **2.** (jewelry) stones cut in shapes and inlaid into a larger stone, usually forming a picture or scene. Bone, wood, shell, and metal were also used.

interchangeable cylinder box: (music) a music box with more than one cylinder so it can play a greater selection of tunes.

interlaced heart design: (furniture) heart-shaped forms joined with an oval on the back of a chair.

in the style of: a piece that has features similar, but not identical to, an original. It may also have the added features not present in the original. Not a reproduction. See also *reproduction.*

invert: (stamps) a stamp with part of the design printed upside down.

ipek: (floor coverings) Turkish silk used in weaving rugs.

Irish Belleek: (ceramics) a delicate porcelain with a creamy finish first made in the 1850s. From that time until 1946, Belleek had several marks — all black. From 1946 until 1980 the marks were green. Since 1980 a gold mark has been used. Some of the older Belleek pieces are worth thousands of dollars. Belleek also produced earthenware, although it is not as popular or well-known.

iron red: (ceramics) a red paint made from iron oxide; used for decorating ceramics.

ironstone: (ceramics) a heavy, fairly durable pottery first made in the early 1800s by William and John Turner of Caughley, and Josiah Spode. Other manufacturers quickly followed suit. May be hand painted or decorated with transfer designs. A great deal of ironstone was decorated in flow blue. Some pieces are unmarked. Others are marked "Ironstone" and also have a factory mark.

Isahan carpet: (floor coverings) a multi-colored Persian carpet with likenesses of vases or medallions in the design.

ishimatsu: (decoration) the Japanese pattern of alternate squares of contrasting metals such as silver and copper.

ishime: (orientalia) a Japanese method of applying lacquer so that it resembles stone in texture.

ishi-zuri: (orientalia, prints) Japanese name for *stone print.*

isnik pottery: white, Turkish earthenware with a clear glaze; decorated with formal floral designs and scrolled borders done in vibrant reds, blues, and greens. It was made during the 16th century.

Ispanky, Lazlo: (design) designer of figurines and other objects of porcelain, stone, metal, and wood since 1966. He has designed collectibles for Cybis and Goebel. His work is growing in value.

issue: (stamps) one or more stamps put out as a single series.

issuing authority: (coins) the government or bureau that authorizes a coin.

istoriato: (ceramics) pictorial painting used on ceramics, especially maiolica, during the 15th, 16th, and early 17th centuries. The picture generally covers the entire surface of a plate and depicts a biblical, historical, or mythological scene. This method was copied in the 19th century. In Italian, *istoriato* means *with a story on it.*

Italian comedy figure: (ceramics) a figurine of an actor from the Italian theater. Produced during the 1700s by the Chelsea Porcelain Factory in England.

itinerant craftsman: (decorating) an artisan who moved from place to place plying his craft.

ittobori: (orientalia) Japanese carving style; angles are achieved with single cuts of a knife.

ivory: (materials) material that has been used for centuries to make fine carvings. The only true ivory is from the tusks of elephants. Since they are an endangered species, it becomes less and less available. However, to those who aren't purists, walrus, whale, and hippopotamus teeth and tusk are classified as ivory. Vegetable ivory, bone, horn, and plastic are used to simulate ivory.

J

jabot pin: (jewelry) a lady's stickpin, attached to a blouse or dress.

jack: 1. (clocks) the mechanical figure that strikes the external bell of a clock. **2.** (armor) body armor, either padded or interlined with mail plate or horn. Worn by foot soldiers in the 15th and 16th centuries.

jack boots: (fashion accessories) large, heavy boots reaching the knee. Worn by horsemen in the 16th to 18th centuries.

Jackfield: (ceramics) a red clay earthenware with a black glaze, often decorated with raised flowers and incised scrolls. This ware was produced by several potters in the Staffordshire region of England in the late 1700s.

Jack-in-the-box: (toys) an American-made toy with a figure that springs out of a box when a handle is turned.

Jack-in-the-pulpit vase: (glass) a vase made in a trumpet shape to resemble the flower of the same name. Popular during the late 1800s and early 1900s. They were made in every conceivable color, some plain, some ornate.

Jacobean, early: (furniture) English furniture produced during the reign of James I (1603 to 1625). A continuation of Elizabethan style, early Jacobean furniture was made of oak and massive.

Jacobean, late: (furniture) English furniture produced during the reigns of Charles II (1660 to 1685) and James II (1685 to 1689). Made of walnut, less massive than early Jacobean, often gilded or inlaid, with a continental influence. Also called *Restoration*.

Jacob, Georges (1739-1814): (furniture) a French cabinetmaker particularly known for his production of chairs. His work is from the late 1700s and early 1800s and is marked with a stamped "G Iacob" — it was carried on after his death by his sons, Georges II and François.

Jacobite glass: a drinking vessel with a motto and emblem to promote the Jacobite cause in the late 1600s. The most common design was a six-petal rose, emblem of the House of Stuart. See also *Jacobite pottery*.

Jacobite pottery: rare salt-glazed stoneware and earthenware pieces that bear mottoes and illustrations to support the Jacobites. See also *Jacobite glass*.

Jacquard: (textiles) figured fabric created on a special loom invented by Joseph Jacquard (1752-1834).

jade: (materials) material used to make jewelry, figurines, and accessories. Before 1700 all jade pieces were made from nephrite, which ranges in color from white to light green to dark green. Nephrite has a waxlike feel and appearance. During the 18th century, jadeite, with a more glasslike look, came into use. In addition to the colors of nephrite, jadeite also is found in yellowish brown and violet. The most desirable jade pieces are from 1736-1795.

jagging wheel: (kitchen) a wheel with corrugated ridges used to crimp the edges of pastry. Also called *crimper*.

jambeaux: (armor) leg armor made of leather. Fourteenth century.

jamb hook: (hearth accessories) a large metal hook; used to hang fire tools from the jamb near the fireplace.

jambiyah: (weapons) a dagger with a blade that curves sharply almost forming a right angle. Of Arabian origin.

japan: 1. (decoration) a durable, glossy black finish of enamel or lacquer. **2.** (decoration) to decorate and varnish wood or tin objects in the Japanese manner. **3.** (decoration) a base coat of paint in preparation for decoration. **4.** (ceramics) Oriental design used on ironstone and porcelain by English potters during the 18th and 19th centuries.

Japanese inro: (orientalia) a small lacquered or carved box with from one to five compartments; used by the Japanese to carry seals, medicines, and other little necessities. The inro was carried on the end of a cord that was attached by the other end to a Japanese garment. If an inro has a signature, it is probably from the 1800s. During the 1700s inros were seldom signed. See also *inro.*

Japanese luster: (ceramics) china with a pearllike finish of blue, tan, or white with a (usually) hand-painted design; often given away as prizes during the 1920s. Salt and peppers, tea sets, and condiment sets are common.

japon: (prints) a Japanese paper used for art prints.

Jaquet-Droz et Leschot: a factory famous for its automata (mechanicals) during the 1700s.

jardiniere: (household accessories) a planter and stand, or a larger planter without a stand.

Jarves, Deming: (glass) founder of the Boston and Sandwich Glass Company in Salem, Massachusetts, in 1820. The company was among the first to produce pressed glass items such as cruets, cup plates, and salts. Well-known for opalescent, cut, and hobnail glass. The company closed in 1888. See also *Sandwich glass.*

Jaseron chain: (jewelry) necklace comprised of a delicate gold chain and a gold cross. Very fashionable in the early 1800s.

jasper: (jewelry) an opaque quartz, reddish brown or yellow in color.

jasper dip: (ceramics) white jasper ware that has been colored by dipping it in a solution. See also *jasper ware.*

jasper ware: (ceramics) a fine, hard, close-grained, white stoneware invented by Josiah Wedgwood. It can be stained with metallic oxide to create a variety of colors and shades. Much of the ware is colored with a raised, white design.

jaune jonquille: (ceramics) a warm, vibrant yellow enamel used as a base color on Sevres porcelain from 1753 on.

jaunie: (paper) the yellowing of prints and other paper items due to aging.

jaw: (weapons) the viselike part of a flintlock that holds the pyrites (flint).

jazerant: (armor) garment made of plates or strips of horn, leather, or metal attached to leather or cloth. From 14th-century Europe.

jedburg axe: (weapons) a poleax that is nearly 9 feet long; used in Scotland in the 15th to 18th centuries.

jelly bag: (kitchen) a bag of coarse, porous cloth often with a handle at each end. Runny jelly is poured into the bag and it is squeezed to eliminate excess liquid.

Jervis, W.P.: (ceramics) operator of a pottery in Oyster Bay, New York, that made mostly bowls and vases from 1908 until 1912. Many of his pieces were slipware with the designs scratched into them (sgraffito). Most pieces were incised "Jervis" on the bottom.

Jesuit china: (ceramics) Chinese porcelain depicting Christian missionaries. Dates from the beginning of the 1700s. The designs were done in famille rose or black monochrome.

jet: (jewelry) a lightweight coal by-product, actually fossilized wood, that came largely from Whitby, England, where it was made into lockets, necklaces, brooches, bracelets, and other jewelry. Since jet is black or very dark brown, this jewelry was often worn by 19th-century ladies when they were in mourning. Gutta-percha, onyx, and black glass are often mistaken for jet.

jet-enamelled ware: (ceramics) wares transfer-printed in black. First produced by the Worcester Porcelain Factory in the 18th century.

jewelled tole: (metal) good-quality tinware enhanced with colored beads.

Jew's harp: (music) a small harp-shaped instrument played with the mouth and fingers.

jezail: (weapons) an Afghan gun with a long barrel and a crooked stock. Originally matchlocks, many were converted to flintlocks with European locks.

jigger: (ceramics) a stick that fits into a pottery mold. While the mold is spinning on a potter's wheel, the stick forms a vessel by pressing the clay firmly against the inside of the mold.

jigsaw mirror: (furniture) a mirror with a frame that has been decorated by piercing in an interlaced design (fretting).

jinto: (weapons) a Japanese war sword.

Joel, Betty (*ca.* 1930): (furniture) London designer in the 1920s who made laminated wooden furniture in the art deco style.

Johnson Brothers: (ceramics) owners of factories in England that have produced an inexpensive line of earthernware tableware from 1883 until the present. They have been owned by Wedgewood since 1968. Wares are marked "Johnson Bros."

joined chest: (furniture) a chest that has been made in the very finest way — with dovetailed drawers and doweled joints.

joined stool: (furniture) a stool that is made so it fits together without the use of nails or screws. Fine construction.

jointed-body doll: a doll with some parts — usually the head, arms, or legs — that are moveable.

joint stool: (furniture) a small stool with legs connected by stretchers.

joney: (ceramics) an English pottery dog; used as a chimney ornament.

journal rack: (furniture) a rack with several sections that spread out like a fan; used in the 18th and 19th centuries for magazines and periodicals.

jousting chest: (furniture) a chest with hunting or jousting scenes carved in high relief. Although originals are from the 14th and 15th centuries, they were extensively copied during the 19th and 20th centuries.

jubilee: (coins, stamps) a coin or stamp issued to mark the anniversary of the accession of a British sovereign.

Judaica: (religious) articles created throughout the world by members of the Jewish faith. Through the ages, Jews have resided in many countries. Items created express their religious and cultural beliefs and unity and also reflect the country in which they were made. Most articles have a religious theme. The most highly prized are of silver but art, engraving, literature, and other creative expressions are also collected.

jug: (kitchen) a fat, round, metal or pottery container with a small, short neck and handle.

jugate: (collectibles) picture of a pair of political candidates together. May be on a poster, a button, or other political advertising medium. Very popular with collectors.

Jugtown: (ceramics) a pottery started at Jugtown in

Moore County, North Carolina, in 1920. Their work is reminiscent of the pottery that was made in North Carolina as far back as the early 1700s. They produced both country wares and Oriental-style pieces. Glazes used include orange, natural clay, buff, white, black, frogskin green, and Chinese blue. Orange was used most frequently, but the Chinese blue (really a turquoise) is the most stunning and the most valuable. They also made a salt-glazed ware with cobalt designs. The pottery closed in 1958 but reopened in 1960. The newer pieces do not have the lovely glazes of the originals and aren't as desirable.

julep cup: a short silver or glass tumbler; used to serve mint juleps.

Jumeau, Émile: (dolls) from 1876 until 1899, maker of expensive French dolls. He was the first one to produce dolls with sleep eyes.

junk auction: an auction at which household goods and miscellaneous items are offered rather than antiques or collectibles.

juval: (textiles) a huge bag, usually about 40 by 45 inches, in which nomads stored their belongings. Generally made of carpeting material.

ju ware: (ceramics) Imperial Chinese porcelain with purple-blue crackle glaze over a tan ground. Ju ware was made in the 12th century and is extremely rare today.

K

Kabistan rug: (floor coverings) a fine carpet made in the Baker section of Russia: either a Kuba rug, depicting individual floral blossoms, palms and eight-point stars or, a Hila rug.

Kabuki: (prints) prints of famous Japanese actors in the roles they performed in the Kabuki plays — dramas that were popular in the late 1600s.

kabuto: (weapons) a Japanese helmet.

kachina: (Native American) a mask or full figure carved from cottonwood by the Southwest Pueblos.

Kaendler, J.J.: (figurines) chief modeler at the Meissen factory in the early 1700s; among the first to make figurines out of hard-paste porcelain. His Italian comedy figures are his best known work.

kakemono: (orientalia) a Japanese picture that is long and narrow and can be rolled up for storage.

kakiemon: (decoration) an asymmetrical style of enamel ornamentation; used on Japanese porcelain and freely copied by French, German, and English factories in the 1700s.

kalemdam: a case for carrying a pen.

kale pot: (kitchen) a pot for cooking cabbage.

kaltemail: (ceramics) German term for the 16th- and 17th-century technique of decorating with cold enamel as a substitute for fired enameling; used on pieces that would be damaged by heat or were too large to fit in the kiln.

kantschar: (weapons) a Russian sword with a narrow blade and short quillons curved toward the tip. From the 17th century.

kaolin: (ceramics) a fine clay; used in making ceramics.

karako: (orientalia) the use of the likenesses of Chinese children in Japanese art and wares.

karat: (metal) The proportion of fine gold to alloy metal used in an object. A karat is 1/24 part by weight of the object assayed. A ten-karat piece has a ratio of 10 parts of gold to 14 parts alloy metal, while a twenty-two-karat piece has a ratio of 22 parts gold to 2 parts alloy.

kard: (weapons) a dagger with a straight blade; of Turkish or Persian origin.

kas: (furniture) a large, Dutch-style, high-case wardrobe with paneled doors, overhanging cornice, and ball-front feet. Many are painted with lively designs. Made in the Hudson and Delaware River valleys from the last quarter of the 17th century to mid-18th century.

kasak rug: (floor coverings) a deep-pile carpet with bold, masculine designs done in strong, bold shades of blue, red, and yellow.

Kashan (or Keshan): (floor coverings) Persian carpets made in the area of Kashan, Iran. The all-silk Kashan is considered supreme.

Kashmir: (floor coverings) rugs that come from the Kashmir area in northern India. They may be wool or silk.

katar: (weapons) an Indian dagger with a sharp, pointed blade.

Kayserzinn: (pewter) pewter with art nouveau designs in relief made in Germany during the 19th century. Pieces are marked "Kayserzinn."

keep: (kitchen) a cabinet for storing meat — a meat safe.

keeper ring: (jewelry) a heavy gold ring with chased decoration.

keeping room: 17th-century term for living room.

kelim: 1. (floor coverings) the part of the fringe on a rug that is between the knot and the carpet itself. **2.** (floor coverings) flat rugs without pile.

Kelleyeh: (floor coverings) a carpet that is about three times longer than it is wide.

kelt: (textiles) a gray wool cloth made by combining white wool and black wool.

Kelva: (glass) glass produced in Meriden, Connecticut, by the C.F. Monroe Company. Pieces are painted (usually in pastels) and decorated with floral or scenic designs. Hand-painted examples are worth far more than those with transfer designs. Manufactured from 1900 until the beginning of World War I.

Kenare: (floor coverings) a Persian runner used in a long hall or beside the main carpet in a large room.

Kentucky Derby glasses: glass and (later) plastic drinking vessels issued to commemorate the anniversary of the Kentucky Derby each year since 1940.

Kentucky rifle: (weapons) a gun made in Pennsylvania from *ca.* 1750; named for its use in Kentucky by such men as Daniel Boone.

kepi: (militaria) a military cap with a flat, circular top and a small visor.

Kermes: (floor coverings) a Persian carpet that is predominantly red.

Kestner, Johannes D.: (dolls) craftsman known as the king of German dollmakers. He made dolls with heads of bisque, celluloid, leather, or wax in his factory in Walterhausen. His trademark is a crown with streamers.

kettle: (kitchen) a deep receptacle for cooking foods or boiling liquids.

kettle front: (furniture) a swelling or bulging front with sharper curves than those found on bombé fronts.

kettle tilt: (hearth accessories) a wrought-iron device that holds a kettle above the fire. By using the tilt's long handle that extended outside of the fireplace, the unit tilted the kettle for pouring hot liquid.

Kew-Blas: (glass) iridescent glass produced by the Union Glass Company of Somerville, Massachusetts, from 1890 until the 1920s.

kewpie: (collectibles) one of the little winged creatures created by Rose O'Neill in the early 1900s. They made their debut in the *Ladies Home Journal.* Dolls, pictures, vases, plates, and tea sets soon featured their likenesses. All kewpie items, especially the dolls, are collectible.

khandar: (weapons) a two-edged sword of Indian origin with a long handle meant to be gripped with both hands.

Khorassan carpet: (floor coverings) an elegant Persian rug with delicate stitching done in a soft, luxurious yarn. Not as durable as other Persian rugs.

kiathos: an ancient Greek container shaped like a teacup and used for pouring.

kibble: (domestic) a wooden bucket used to draw water from a well.

kibosh: wooden or sculpted objects onto which cement or plastic has been blown.

kick: (glass) a pointed indentation. Found in the bottoms of some very early glass objects such as bottles.

kick-up base: (glass) the pushed-up bottom of a bottle. The bottom was indented so that when the pontil was broken off, leaving ragged edges, the bottle would still have a firm base.

kidderminster: (textiles) a coarse fabric made of linen and wool; used as an early type of carpeting.

kidney dagger: (weapons) a dagger with the guard formed by the lobes.

kidney-shaped: (furniture) any piece of furniture with a top shaped like a kidney. Usually a table.

kiku: (decoration, orientalia) the chrysanthemum design; used extensively on Oriental ware.

kiln: (ceramics) an oven for firing hard-paste porcelain.

kiloware: (stamps) a package of mixed stamps from one foreign country.

kimono: (orientalia) a long, loose Japanese robe with wide sleeves, worn with a sash.

kindjal: (weapons) a short double-edged dagger with no quillon.

King's Rose: (ceramics) a soft-paste ware decorated with a red-orange rose with leaves of various colors. Manufactured from *ca.* 1820 to 1830 in Staffordshire, England.

kingwood: (materials) a hardwood with a purplish tinge; used mainly for veneers.

kinji: (orientalia) a Japanese technique for decorating lacquer ware. Powdered gold is applied to a lacquered surface and burnished.

kirikane: (decoration) the Japanese technique for decorating lacquer ware with embedded squares of gold leaf.

Kirman rug: (floor coverings) a rug named for the district of Persia where it was made. The medallion and tree patterns are the most popular designs.

Kir-Shehr rug: (floor coverings) a Turkish rug, usually with an angular tree motif that fills the center, which is surrounded by a border. Red is a popular color for these carpets.

kitchen collectibles: kitchen tools, each designed for a specific job, that flooded the market during the 1800s. Today those items, including kettles, egg cups, ice buckets, graters, grinders, clothes sprinklers, and egg beaters are collectible. Most are fairly inexpensive.

knee: (furniture) the uppermost curve of a cabriole leg.

knee carving: (furniture) the carved decoration on the curve, or knee, of a furniture leg.

knee-hole desk: (furniture) a tabletop with an open space below and drawers at each side; used as a dressing table or desk. Also called *knee-hole table*.

knee-hole table: (furniture) a tabletop with an open space below and drawers at each side; used as a dressing table or desk. Also called *knee-hole desk*.

knife: (weapons, collectibles) any medium-sized to large knife in very good to mint condition made before 1970. Small knives are of little value to collectors. Those manufactured in the United States are vastly preferred to foreign knives. Case is the most popular manufacturer.

knife case: (household accessories) a cutlery storage box kept in the dining room. Until the late 1700s, made of wood or leather with sloping, hinged tops, convex fronts, and varying degrees of ornamentation. Inside, they are divided into sections for the different types of cutlery. Later knife cases are cylindrical with a center stem on which the cover can be raised or closed.

knife rest: (tableware) a table-setting accessory on which 18th-century ladies and gentlemen rested the soiled tips of knives during a meal. Often made of solid glass, usually cut or pressed, and shaped like a barbell.

knob turning: (furniture) a turning with a series of knobs or balls; common on 17th-century furniture legs and stretchers.

knocked down: (auctions) auctioneer's term for *sold*. When a successful bid is reached on an item at an auction, the item is *knocked down*.

knocker latch: (hardware) a door latch that is also a door knocker; widely used in the 1700s. Twisting the knocker opens the door latch.

knopped stem: 1. (glass) a knob — the swelled portion of a stem on a cup, goblet or other drinking glass. **2.** (glass) a drinking glass stem with numerous knobs. Common in the 18th century.

Knox, Archibald (*ca.* 1900): (design) a designer who created art nouveau silver and pewter items for Liberty's, a posh London store.

knuckle: (furniture) a design that looks like the knuckles on a fist; often carved on the arms of Windsor or Chippendale chairs.

knulling: (decoration) a short, fluted design; used on silverware from the late 17th century on. See also *gadroon*.

koban: 1. (coins) a thin, oval gold coin issued in Japan from the late 1500s to the early 1800s. **2.** (orientalia) a small Japanese print.

kogo: (orientalia) a Japanese box for storing incense.

kopek: 1. (coins) a 16th-century Russian silver coin. **2.** (coins) during 18th century and later, 1/100 of a ruble.

koro: (orientalia) a burner used for incense.

Kosta: (glass) Swedish glassware and sculptured glass dating from the 16th century until the present. Kosta 20th-century art glass is being collected.

koto: (music) a Japanese instrument in the shape of an oblong box with thirteen strings stretched over it for plucking.

kovish: (tableware) a boat-shaped, Russian drinking cup made of wood or silver. *Ca.* 1600s.

K.P.M.: (ceramics) a mark used by several potteries for hard-paste porcelain during the 18th and 19th centuries. The most collectible pieces were made in Berlin. These high-quality figurines, vases, and dinnerware items command good prices.

krater: a Greek vase with a wide mouth and handles on either side.

kreuzer: (coins) a German coin made of billon (copper and silver) in the 16th and 17th centuries, and copper or silver in the 18th century. Circulated in Austria and German states.

kugel: (glass) a glass Christmas ornament characterized by its heavy weight. Some are plain balls; others are in the shapes of fruits and vegetables. Dating from the early to late 19th century. They were made in a range of sizes from small, 1-inch balls to 15-inch examples.

kukri: (weapons) a heavy, curved sword from Nepal with small knives or daggers attached to the sheath.

Kurdish rug: (floor coverings) coarse-textured carpet woven by nomads. Runners were done more often than area rugs.

kurk: (floor coverings) very soft wool that comes from the sheep's chest; used for making rugs.

Kutani: (ceramics) colorful Japanese ware made from the mid-1600s into the 1800s. Most of what is found in the United States today was made for export in the 19th century. Red, gold, and black are predominant colors in many of the later pieces, which featured warriors, birds, flowers, and animals. Kutani from before 1800 is extremely rare.

Ku Yueh Hsuan: (ceramics) eighteenth-century Chinese porcelain often done in famille rose and with a poem printed on the body of the ware.

kwaart: (ceramics) a combination of sand, potash, salt, and lead; used as a finishing glaze on ceramics.

kwacho: (fine art, orientalia) Japanese pictures featuring images of birds and flowers.

Kyoto: (ceramics, orientalia) a Japanese pottery with overglaze enamel decoration. Kyoto ceramics were first produced in the early 1600s in Kyoto — Japan's capital city at that time — by many local potters. Most of it is fine quality. Eiraku, Hozen, and Ogata Kenzan are among the favored artisans associated with Kyoto.

L

labeled furniture: any piece of furniture with a paper label bearing the name of the maker.

Labino, Dominick: (glass) producer of a variety of blown-glass pieces in his studio in Ohio from the 1950s until 1985. He had many styles, from conventional to very modern. His pieces are signed and dated. After Labino's death in 1986, E. Baker O'Brien continued his work. O'Brien's wares are signed "Labino Studios, Baker."

lace-edged tray: (household accessories) a fancy tray with a hand-painted or pierced edging that resembles lace. The finest examples are fashioned of silver. Fashionable at the time of the Revolution; some were done by Paul Revere.

lace glass: (glass) clear glass with embedded strands of white glass forming involved patterns in the object. Also called *vetro di trina*.

lacis: (textiles) designs darned on netting. Popular in the 1500s.

Lacloche Freres: (jewelry) jewelers in Paris, France, who were famous for art nouveau designs.

lacquer: (orientalia) a Chinese and Japanese technique of coating wood or metal with many thin layers of varnish.

lacquered brass: (metal) brass objects with a thin coat of varnish that prevents tarnishing.

lacy glass: pressed glass made in the first half of the 19th century with detailed relief patterns on a lacy background; used to make such articles as plates, lamps, salts, and candlesticks. Sandwich Glass Company was the first, but not the only, company to produce lacy glass.

ladder-back: (furniture) a chair back that has horizontal cross rails instead of a vertical splat.

ladik box rug: (floor coverings) Turkish carpet with a lily design.

ladle: (tableware) a long-handled spoon with a deep bowl; used for serving soup, punch, and other liquids.

lady bird cage: (household accessories) a bird cage shaped like a woman, with a wooden head and a bust and skirt of wires; used in the 1600s and 1700s.

lady doll: a doll with a full figure and made-up face, created in the image of an adult female.

Lafayette salt: (tableware) a boat-shaped open glass salt cellar. Made by Boston and Sandwich Glass Company (1830-1888).

laid-on work: (textiles) small pieces of material sewn onto other pieces of material. Often done in quilt making. Also called *appliqué*.

lake: (stamps) the deep red color frequently seen on stamps.

Lalique, René (1860-1945): (glass) a French glassmaker who produced molded, pressed, and blown glass, usually with a frosted finish. The most valued pieces are marked "R. Lalique" and were made before his death in 1945. After 1945, the Lalique company dropped the "R." from the mark. Lalique still makes quality perfume bottles, vases, hood ornaments, and other glass items.

lambrequin: 1. (decoration) a hanging-drapery motif on metal or wood. **2.** (household accessories) a valance.

lames: (armor) overlapping strips of metal used to form portions of armor.

laminated: (materials) several layers of wood, paper, or fabric that are bonded or glued together.

lampas panel: (textiles) a two-colored damask material; used for upholstering furniture and for wall hangings.

lamp teapot: (tableware) any teapot in the shape of an early Roman lamp.

lance: (weapons) a horseman's spear. From the Middle Ages.

lancet: (furniture) a sharp, pointed arch; found on early Gothic furniture.

lancet clock: a spring-driven clock with a pointed top; popular in the late 18th and early 19th centuries.

landscape: (fine art) artwork depicting scenery with or without people, animals, or buildings which, if they are present, are subordinate to the scenery.

landscape mirror: (furniture) a long, low mirror often divided into three or four sections. Also called *mantel mirror* and *buffet mirror.*

Lange Leisen: (ceramics) tall, thin male and female figures; used to decorate some Chinese porcelains made for export. Also called *Long Eliza.*

laniers: (armor) leather straps used to fasten together different parts of armor. From the 16th century.

Lannuier, Charles-Honoré (fl. 1780-1819): (furniture) a superior French cabinetmaker who plied his craft in New York from 1800 to 1820. The Directoire style was his specialty. Some consider his work better than Duncan Phyfe's.

lantern: (lighting) an oil or gas lighting fixture with the flame enclosed in glass.

lantern clock: a 17th-century weight-driven English clock. Seldom made to run more than thirty hours.

lanthorn: (lighting) a lamp made of horn peeled to a translucent density.

larin: (coins) a thin, fishhook-shaped silver bar; used as a coin along the coast between the Persian Gulf and Ceylon in the 16th and 17th centuries.

latch: (weapons) the 16th-century English crossbow.

Latin cross: (decoration) a cross with a long descending bar — the basic cross associated with Christianity.

latten: 1. (metal) a brass-colored alloy of copper and zinc, hammered thin and used in the manufacture of church vessels. **2.** (metal) any thin sheet of metal.

lattice: (decoration, furniture) wood or metal lathes crossed diagonally to make diamond patterns.

latticinio: (glass) opaque threads of various colored glass in a random network melted onto clear glass; widely used on paperweights. From the late 1500s.

latticinio core swirls: (marbles) an inner lattice of colored swirls radiating through the center of a glass marble.

lavabo: (domestic) a basin used for washing hands; normally placed under a wall-mounted cistern.

lavaliere: (jewelry) one or more pendants hanging from a decorative chain necklace, often ending with a baroque pearl. The pearl was particularly popular from the late 1800s to the early 1900s.

law enforcement memorabilia: (collectibles) badges, billy clubs, holsters, handcuffs, leg irons, and other memorabilia from the 1800s and early 1900s.

lazy Susan table: (furniture) a dining table with a revolving tray for condiments or food at the center.

lead crystal: (glass) crystal made with potash and containing approximately 30 percent lead. Also called *full crystal.*

leaded-glass motif: (furniture) a decorative motif used in a cabinet door. Made by securing individual glass shapes together with strips of lead.

lead glass: glass that contains lead oxide and has a high refractive quality. Also called *flint glass.*

lead glaze: (ceramics) an early glaze used in several forms including liquid lead glaze and colorless lead glaze. Lead is also used in tin glaze and salt glaze.

lead mirror: (furniture) an early mirror made by heating a sheet of glass and pouring a thin layer of melted lead on it.

leadwork: (metal) ornaments such as sundials, figures, cisterns, and other popular objects for the formal garden. Popular during the early 1700s.

leather-bound: (books) a book completely covered in leather. If the spine and full corners are covered in leather, it is three-quarters-bound. If the spine and narrow corners are covered in leather, it is half-bound. If only the spine is covered in leather, it is quarter-bound. See also *half-bound* and *quarter-bound.*

lectern: (furniture) a stand or desk with a slanted top to hold the books or notes of a speaker.

Leeds Pottery: (ceramics) cream-colored, painted, often salt-glazed ware. Most Leeds Pottery is not marked, but some later pieces are signed "Leeds Pottery — Hartley Green and Co." Pieces with a greenish glaze and twisted handles are early. Blue edging on a creamy base came later.

left bid: (auctions) a bid left with an auctioneer by someone unable to attend an auction, but who wants to bid on an item. The bid is executed by the auctioneer or a member of the staff on behalf of the customer. Bidding should start with the floor (those attending the auction) unless there is more than one left bid, in which case the auctioneer may start with the second highest left bid.

left-hand dagger: (weapons) a dagger with arched quillons designed to be used with a sword to entangle an opponent's sword blade.

Lefton: (ceramics) inexpensive porcelain imported from Japan for sale in the United States by the Lefton Company starting in 1940. Items are generally marked "Lefton" and are being collected.

legend: 1. (books) an explanatory text or caption accompanying a chart, map, or the like. **2.** (coins) the inner edge of a coin just below the border which is inscribed within the specifications of the Coinage Act.

Legras: (glass) cameo and enameled glass made in St. Denis, France, from 1864 until the early 1900s. All pieces are signed.

Lenci: (dolls) exquisite dolls with full, rounded bodies and painted eyes, glancing sideways, on felt heads topped with mohair wigs. First made by Eleanora Scavani in the early 1900s. The factory is still operating today.

leni croich: (armor) a padded or quilted garment made of yellow cloth; used in Scotland.

Lenox: (ceramics) the official china of the White House since 1917. Lenox has been in business since 1906 when Walter Scott Lenox left the Ceramic Art Company to start his own firm. The creamy white color of most pieces is easy to recognize. Older factory-decorated Lenox with a green wreath mark and the hand-painted pieces with a green palette are the most desirable.

leontine chain: (jewelry) a long watch chain, usually gold. Popular in the 1800s.

Levant Morocco: (books) a coarse-grained, highly-polished, elegant bookbinding made of goat skin.

Le Verre Français: (glass) a mottled cameo glass made in France from 1920 to 1933. The name "Le Verre Francais" is incised on the pieces.

LeVerrier, Max: (design) designer who executed bronze and spelter figures in the art deco style.

Libbey Glass Company: a company started in 1878 in Toledo, Ohio. They produced fine examples of art glass and cut glass. The company opened after the New England Glass Works of W. L. Libbey and Sons of Massachusetts closed. In the 1930s it was purchased by Owens-Illinois and is still in operation today, making practical glassware for the average consumer.

library step-chair: (furniture) a Chippendale-style chair with a set of steps that swings out from the bottom of the chair. The steps were used to reach books on high shelves.

library table: (furniture) a large, rectangular table on which books can be stacked.

lighthouse coffeepot: (kitchen) a tall, round, tapered pot made in the 1600s, 1700s, and 1800s; made of tin, pewter, or silver.

Lille lace: (textiles) eighteenth-century English pillow lace with patterns heavily outlined in flat thread and set in mesh. Sometimes found in black.

lily pad decoration: (glass) glass formed into designs resembling lily pads by pouring molten glass over an existing glass object.

lime glass: a clear glass resembling lead crystal, but not as heavy or resonant. Developed by William Leighton in the mid-1800s.

lime seat: (furniture) a chair seat of woven fibers from the bark of the linden tree.

limited edition: (books) an edition of a book limited to a stated number of copies.

limited edition collector plates: (ceramics, collectibles) a series of decorative plates issued by companies specifically for collectors. The first annual Christmas collector plate was issued by Bing and Grondahl in 1895. Royal Copenhagen followed suit in 1908. Since then, and especially from the 1960s to the present, many manufacturers have issued collector plates. Some of them are worth far more than the issue price, but others do not bring anywhere near the original cost. The first year of any series is the most prized.

limner: (folk art) amateur artist.

Limoges: (ceramics) French town famous for its porcelain manufacturers. At the height of its success, Limoges had about forty-five porcelain companies using the kaolin from the area to make porcelain. Haviland is the best known of these businesses. Since *ca.* 1740, hundreds of companies have produced lovely tableware and accessories mostly for export. The white ware was either transfer decorated at the company that produced it, hand painted by them, sold to a decorating firm, or sold as white ware for amateur painters to decorate. With rare exception, the most valued is hand painted in the factory.

line bracelet: (jewelry) a flexible bracelet of single stones set in a line around the wrist.

line engraving: (books) a hand-engraved metal plate used for illustrations in the 17th and 18th centuries.

linenfold carving: (decoration) carving on a furniture panel that resembles a formal linen fold.

linen press: (tools) a press consisting of two boards; used for removing wrinkles from linens during the 17th and 18th centuries.

line pair: (stamps) two stamps on a roll that have a

line appearing on or beside the perforation between them. This line is found between every twenty-fourth or twenty-fifth stamp on a roll. Line pairs are very collectible.

ling lung: (orientalia) pierced openwork found mostly on blue-and-white Chinese porcelain bowls and vases from the 1600s and 1700s.

lining paper: colored paper printed with black floral, scenic, or heraldic designs; used to line the insides of boxes during the 1500s and 1600s.

Linnell, John: (furniture) a carver and cabinetmaker working in the Chippendale style from 1760 until 1790. Some of his furniture is in the Victoria and Albert Museum.

linsey-woolsey: (textiles) an inferior grade of coarse woolen goods.

linstock: (weapons) a pike with brackets on each side of the blade to hold lighted matches for firing a cannon. From mid-16th century.

lion: (coins) a gold Scottish coin with Arms of Scotland or St. Andrew on cross.

lion mask: (decoration) an ornament used on furniture, silver, and jewelry from 1700 to about 1750 and again from 1795 to 1830, during the Regency period.

lion sejant knop: (decoration) a finial or knob in the form of a seated lion.

lion's paw foot: (furniture, silver) carved foot in the shape of a lion's paw; used on chairs and side tables during the Regency period (1795 to 1830). They generally terminated cabriole legs. Silversmiths also employed this decoration on many of their footed creations during this period.

lithography: (prints) a printing process invented in 1797, utilizing the principle that oil and water do not mix. The design was drawn on a flat, limestone surface with an oil crayon. A thin layer of water was applied next, and then a roller with greasy ink was rolled over the surface. The water repelled the ink, but the crayon markings absorbed it, and an impression was made. Modern lithography uses chemicals and zinc or aluminum sheets. See also *original lithograph.*

lithophane: (ceramics) translucent porcelain with an impressed design; first produced in Germany early in 1800s. Panels, lamp shades, and tea cups are some of the objects made with lithophane. The design can be seen only with backlight. See also *émail ombrant.*

lithotint: (prints) an advanced form of lithograph that produced tinted pictures ranging from black to brown; widely used from 1840 to 1860.

lithyalin glass: an opaque, colored, marbleized glass with the appearance of precious stones. Invented in Bohemia in 1828.

Liverpool: (ceramics) ivory-colored ware decorated with patriotic American scenes generally done in transfer prints. Made in Liverpool, England, for export to the United States from the late 1700s until about 1825.

livery cupboard: (furniture) a 17th-century hanging cupboard with two pierced doors.

Lladro: (figurines) good-quality porcelain figurines and plates made in Spain since 1951. The older figures are sought by collectors.

Lloyd's loom: a loom used to weave man-made fibers into sheets of wickerlike material from which "wicker" items were made. From 1917.

lobby chest: (furniture) a small chest of drawers; most often used in halls or studies.

Lobmeyer: (ceramics) nineteenth-century enamel-decorated pottery adorned with images of people in 18th-century dress. Made in Vienna, Austria.

lobster-tail helmet: (armor) a 17th-century helmet with a back piece resembling the tail of a lobster.

locals: (stamps) stamps issued by private post offices and businesses from 1844 until 1861, when the United States Government took over the production of stamps. They were only good within specified areas.

lock: (hardware, collectibles) any of the mechanical key-operated devices first made in early Rome. Yale, Sargeant, Winchester, and Keen Kutter locks from the 1800s and early 1900s are among the most collectible. Brass and bronze locks are preferable to steel and iron locks.

Locke art: (glass) etched glass from a small glassworks founded in Pittsburgh, Pennsylvania, during the 1880s by Joseph Locke, who had worked in many American and English glass houses. His pieces are signed "Joe Locke" or "Locke Art." The mark is worked into the design.

locking gauntlet: (armor) a gauntlet with very long fingers that could be locked to the wrist with the sword or mace locked in the hand to prevent the user from being disarmed.

lock plate: 1. (hardware) the plate that covers a keyhole or a lock. **2.** (weapons) a flat plate screwed to a gun at the end of the barrel to support the gun's firing mechanism.

locomotive builder's plates: (railroad memorabilia) metal plates affixed to all locomotives bearing the name of the manufacturer, the serial number, location of works, and year of completion. Plates were usually placed on each side of the smoke box. Those from steam locomotives are collectible. Most are cast bronze.

locomotive chair: (furniture) a three-wheeled wheelchair.

Loetz: (glass) cameo and other glass in the Tiffany style made in the factory of J. Loetz Witwe, who left the Tiffany factory in the 1840s to start his own glassworks in Klostermule, Austria. The company closed in the 1930s. Many pieces are marked.

log: 1. (books) a record of a ship's course, speed, and other important events. **2.** (scientific instruments) a device trailed from a ship to measure distance and/or speed traveled.

loggerhead: 1. (desk accessories) a round inkstand surrounded by a flat base. **2.** (kitchen) a ball of iron on a long rod. The ball was heated and put into mugs to heat the contents.

lohan: (orientalia) depictions of the disciples of Buddha used in art and in decorating porcelain and the like. Also called *rakan*.

Lomonosov: (ceramics) fine porcelain miniatures and vases made in Russia since 1744. Most of the miniatures are numbered.

long-case clock: a tall floor clock with hanging weights and pendulums. Also called *grandfather clock* and *tall-case clock*.

Long Eliza: (ceramics) tall, thin male and female figures used to decorate some Chinese porcelains made for export. Also called *Lange Leisen*.

long ladies: (lighting) tall candles.

long-playing musical movement: a music box with a large spring or several springs that enable the mechanism to run for a long time before it needs rewinding.

Longwy: (ceramics, enamel) a French pottery that started in 1798 and marked its wares "Longwy," either incised or under glaze. Their best work was produced in northern France during the art deco era.

They also produced oriental-style items.

Lonhuda: (ceramics) a slip-decorated, brown-glazed pottery made by Lonhuda Pottery Company from 1889 until 1901, when the company moved from Ohio to Denver, Colorado, and the name was changed to the Denver China and Pottery Company. Early ware was marked "LPCO" with the company name; the next mark was an Indian; then came an Indian head. Denver examples are usually marked "LF" in a diamond.

looking glass clock: (clocks) any clock with a mirror as a prominent part of the case. Also called *mirror clock*.

loom: a frame used for weaving yarn into cloth by holding threads going in one direction so that threads can be woven through them at right angles.

loop-back chair: (furniture) a kind of Windsor chair.

loopings: (glass) glass threads of colors that are in contrast to the body of the glass object. The loopings are wrapped around the object, pulled up to make a wavy pattern, then embedded.

loo table: (furniture) a gaming table. Usually circular or octagonal; supported by a pedestal.

lorgnette: (fashion accessories) opera glasses or eyeglasses with a short handle on one side.

loriner: (metal) a metalsmith who made the metal sections of tack (horse harnesses).

losset: (kitchen) a wooden dish or platter.

lost wax: (metal) a method of casting brass; used from the Middle Ages to the early 18th century. A model of the object was made of wax, then covered with clay. The clay mold was allow to harden, then heated to a high temperature that burned up (lost) the inner wax mold. Molten brass was poured into the then empty clay mold. After the brass had cooled, the clay mold was broken away, leaving the cast object.

lotus ornament: (decoration) representations of the sphinx, the lotus, and other Egyptian motifs; used on furniture, silver, and ceramics in the early 1800s.

Lotus Ware: (ceramics) a thin porcelain reminiscent of Belleek. Made by Knowles, Taylor, and Knowles Company in East Liverpool, Ohio, between 1890 and 1900. Early pieces are marked "KTK." Later ones are marked "Lotus Ware."

louis: (coins) a gold French coin first issued by Louis XIII in 1640 and continued until the Republic (1792).

Louis XIV: (furniture) important furniture designed in France during the later years of the reign of Louis XIV (1643-1715). Characteristics include straight, rectangular lines; elaborate carvings; very heavy pieces with underbracings on most; and the use of tapestries and velours featuring intricate designs.

Louis XV: (furniture) furniture characterized by curved backs, curved legs, and graceful, flowing lines. The cabriole leg was used exclusively. Pieces were lighter and more graceful than those from Louis XIV, and underbracings were not used. Mahogany and walnut were the most popular woods; inlaid decorations, gilding, and rococo and naturalistic ornamentation were used (1710-1744).

Louis XVI: (furniture) during this period (1774-1789) furniture became less formal and smaller in size than in the earlier Louis XIV and Louis XV periods. Dining room tables came into use. Less ornamentation was used. Straight lines replaced curves. Rectangular shapes returned. Much of the furniture was painted. Pieces were fragile.

lover's chair: (furniture) a chair just large enough for two people — a love seat. Made in Chippendale and Queen Anne styles. Also called *drunkard's chair, sparking chair,* and *sporting chair.*

love seat: (furniture) the popular name for an upholstered settee large enough for two persons.

loving cup: a trophy. Originally an oversize ceremonial cup for wine that was passed from person to person during communion.

lowboy: (furniture) a dressing table designed to support a highboy. Also called *chamber table.* See also *highboy.*

low case of drawers: (furniture) a bureau; not a lowboy.

Lowestoft: (ceramics) softpaste porcelain pieces, mostly small, made in Lowestoft, Suffolk, England, from 1757 to 1805. Many of the wares are dated. Some are marked numerically in blue underglaze.

low tiles: (ceramics) handcrafted and machine-made tiles of a fine quality by J. and J. G. Low Art Tile Works from the late 1800s until the early 1900s. They are signed "J. & J. G. Low."

lozenge: (decoration) a diamond-shaped figure or motif.

luckenbooth brooch: (jewelry) a brooch depicting a heart and often a crown. Named for the street booths, called *luckenbooths,* in Edinburgh, Scotland, where the brooches were sold.

luggage stickers: (railroad memorabilia) stickers for luggage given to rail travelers by railroad companies with the names of the railroads, and often names of vacation or tourist spots, on them. Popular during the heyday of rail travel. Those from the era of the steam locomotives are the most desirable.

lug handles: open knobs protruding from opposite sides of an object. Leather straps were attached to the knobs to make a handle with which to "lug" the piece. Often used on trunks.

lullaby: (furniture) a crib on rockers — a cradle.

lunar clock dial: (clocks) a dial showing phases of the moon.

lunch boxes: (collectibles) tin boxes used from the late 1800s on to transport food. Those being collected date from the 1930s through the 1970s. The thermos must be in perfect condition, and the box itself should have a perfect handle and show no signs of rust. Superheros and TV stars are common subjects for the decoration on these boxes. Early, square lunch boxes with metal handles, *ca.* 1900, were sold by tobacco companies full of their product. Around 1930 Ohio Art Company sold decorated oval lunch boxes; by 1950 lunch boxes were rectangular and the Aladdin company had begun making lunch boxes featuring Hopalong Cassidy, Joe Palooka, or Roy Rogers. Some of these are diepressed, with characters in relief.

lunette: (decoration) a decorative piece in a half-moon shape. Often made of metal but also carved in wood in a continuous design.

lunt work: (weapons) a type of matchlock used in Scotland.

Lu Ray Pastels: (ceramics) dinnerware first produced in 1940 by Taylor, Smith, and Taylor in Ohio in an array of solid colors. It has become collectible in the past few years.

luster: 1. (glass) glass prism that hangs from a lamp, chandelier, or candle holder. **2.** (ceramics) a glaze that employs metallic oxides to give a shiny, metallic finish in copper, silver, or pink tones; used on porcelain, china, and earthenware.

lute: (music) a stringed instrument used as early as 2500 B.C. Lutes were most popular during the 13th century A.D.

and were made in a variety of woods at that time.

luting: (ceramics) the process of applying parts of a molded piece, such as a handle or molded decoration, by using liquid clay, or slip, as the bonding agent.

Lutz: (glass) art glass with the threaded and striped design perfected by Nicholas Lutz of the Boston and Sandwich Glass Company and made there by him from 1870 to 1888. His work was widely copied and the term is now a generic one. Lutz's own pieces are not signed.

Lutz marble: a glass marble with alternating bands of solid color and bands flecked with copper.

lye dropper: (domestic) a small box perforated in the bottom so that water poured over wood ash will run out. This process was used to obtain lye.

lyre: (furniture) a decorative motif resembling the stringed musical instrument of the same name; found on chair backs and table bases.

lyre-back chair: (furniture) a chair with a square back with the splat carved in the shape of a lyre. An Adams design of the late 1700s.

lyre clock: a banjo clock in the shape of a lyre.

M

Maastricht: (ceramics) a pottery at Maastricht, Holland, established by Petrus Regout in the 1830s. They produced mostly one-color, transfer-decorated earthenware. The early wares are marked "MAASTRICHT" and "P. Regout" in an oval. In 1878, when Petrus Regout died, his sons changed the mark to "Petrus Regout" and "Maastricht" within a sphinx logo. Early dinnerware patterns include Mythology, Pleasure Party, Wild Rose, and Willow. The company is now called N.V. Konmklijke.

mace: (weapons) a heavy, spiked medieval war club.

macramé: (textiles) knots tied in geometrical patterns, usually with a coarse thread or rope.

maculated: (prints) marked with undesirable spots.

Madame Alexander: (dolls) American doll company started by Beatrice Alexander in 1923. The first Madame Alexander doll, "Mildred," was made in the image of Beatrice Alexander's daughter. Madame Alexander had expanded her company to three factories by 1959. The company is still making dolls.

madder: (floor coverings) a deep reddish brown dye; used in Oriental rugs.

madeira: (textiles) fabric with small eyelet holes embroidered with overcast stitches.

made up: (furniture) a piece of furniture that has been put together from parts of other pieces of furniture.

made-up copy: (books) one complete book made up from two or more copies of the same book — a book that is made complete by replacing missing pages with corresponding pages from another volume of the same book. This greatly lessens the value.

Magen David: (religious) a six-point star formed by placing two triangles together, one inverted over the other. They may be interlaced. Also called *Star of David* and *Solomon's Seal.*

magenta: (stamps) nickname for the British Guiana one-cent stamp. Only one is known to exist, and it is considered the most valuable stamp in the world.

magnum: (glass) a paperweight of 3-1/4 inches or more.

mahogany: (materials) a rich brown hardwood used extensively in furniture making both in solid form and as a veneer. Particularly popular in 18th- and 19th-century England.

maidenhead: (decoration) a decoration in the form of a female bust; used on spoons in the 1400s.

mail: (armor) armor made of interlocking rings. In use from the 2nd century B.C. until the 17th century A.D.

maintaining power: (clocks) a spring that keeps a clock going while it is being wound.

maiolica: (ceramics) tin-glazed, brightly decorated earthenware made in Italy and Spain during the 15th, 16th, and 17th centuries. Many of these plates, ewers, and other pieces depict historical and religious scenes and were painted by fine artists. Urbino and Caffaggiolo were two of the leading manufacturers of this early ware. This should not be confused with Victorian-era majolica. See also *majolica.*

majolica: (ceramics) lead or tin-glazed earthenware from the Victorian era. Majolica was produced by many manufacturers both in the United States and abroad. In the United States, Griffin, Smith, and Hill; Edwin Bennett; The New York City Pottery Company; and the Chesapeake Pottery Company were among the leading producers.

Wedgewood, Minton, and George Jones were some of the notable English companies who contributed majolica to the market. Usually brightly decorated, in a variety of unusual shapes and designs such as animal pitchers, shell and seaweed tea sets, and fan-shaped platters. This should not be confused with maiolica. See also *maiolica*.

maker's mark: (metal, jewelry) a goldsmith's identification mark struck on each piece from his workshop.

malachite: 1. (materials) a dark green mineral called carbonate of copper; used for stoneware. Also a source of copper. **2.** (ceramics) parian ware with the color of malachite stone. See also *parian ware*.

malachite glass: an art glass in shades of green. Many of the designs are done in relief.

malicorne: (ceramics) earthenware made to resemble Quimper; produced near Paris in the Sarthe region from about 1875 until 1897. It's marked "PB."

Maltese lace: (textiles) pillow lace first made in the early 1800s. The best known Maltese lace motif is a Maltese cross.

mammy: (black memorabilia) mature, black female figure with full skirt, apron, bandanna, and scarf.

manchette: (jewelry) a bracelet popular in the 19th century.

Manchu dynasty: (orientalia) reign of the Ch'ing emperors of China (1644 to 1912). The last dynasty.

mandala: (decoration) a circular design symbolic of the universe.

Mandarin china: (ceramics) porcelain imported from China to the United States and England from the late 1700s on. The wares were predominantly decorated in pink, gold, or red enameled flowers or figures with blue scrolls.

Mandarin square: (textiles, orientalia) a badge worn by a Chinese official, either civilian or military, to indicate rank. By the 1800s wives of officials wore the ranks of their husbands, but the women's badges were mirror images of the men's — that is, reversed.

mandolin: (music) a lute-type instrument with a pear-shaped body, a fretted neck, and from four to six strings.

mandora: (music) old form of the lute.

maniere criblee: (prints) method of printing done with metal plates in which groups of dots have been punched in the background areas of the design; used in the 15th and 16th centuries and again at the end of the 18th century.

manivelle: (music) a hand-cranked music box.

mannerist style: (decoration) a design or decoration that depicts forms and space in an unnatural, unrealistic way. For instance, human forms are elongated. Used in the 16th century.

manner of: (fine art) a piece of art done in the style of a certain artist, but appearing to have been executed at a later date than that of the artist in question.

mannheim gold: (metal) an alloy of copper, zinc, and tin.

Mansell, Sir Robert (*ca.* 1618-1649): (glass) a financier who controlled most of the glass industry in England during the early 1600s.

Mansion House dwarfs: (ceramics) figurines of funny little men. Made in Staffordshire, England.

mantel clock: a clock, usually footed, made to stand on a mantel or shelf. Also called *shelf clock*.

mantel lusters: (lighting) a pair of lamps designed to be used on a mantel. They usually had prisms that reflected the light, making them lustrous.

mantel mirror: (furniture) a long, low mirror often divided into three or four sections. Also called *landscape mirror* and *buffet mirror.*

mantel tree set: (household accessories) a set of two to five decorative pieces; used on a mantel over a fireplace. Items varied from sets of vases or bowls to groups of figurines or animals.

Manton, John: (weapons) one of the most famous English gun makers of the 1800s.

Manwaring, Robert: (furniture) an English furniture maker who wrote several books about his craft in the 1700s.

maple: (materials) a light-colored wood first used in North America for furniture. Popular grains include bird's-eye and tiger-eye.

maple sugar molds: (kitchen) hand-carved wooden molds in a variety of shapes; used for molding the sweet confection made from maple syrup.

maps: (paper) all types of maps including celestial, geographical, military, railroad, and street maps. The first printed maps date from the mid-1400s. Those made prior to 1850 are desirable. Errors in maps make them more valuable.

maquette: (household accessories) a miniature room furnished with rugs, pictures, and furniture, and displayed in a glass case.

marbled paper: (books) paper that is decorated with an all-over pattern resembling marble; used as endpapers on books published since 1800.

marbled ware: (ceramics) pottery decorated with various colored slips blended into a marble or a natural stone pattern. Some early marbled ware made in China was achieved by rolling together different colored clays to form a marbleized pattern.

Marblehead: (ceramics) hand-thrown pottery first made in 1905 as a form of occupational therapy in a sanitarium in Marblehead, Massachusetts. The pottery was converted to a money-making business a few years later and closed in 1936. Most pieces are in matte glazes of gray, yellow, rose, brown, or Marblehead blue. The mark is a stylized sail boat with "M" on one side and "P" on the other.

marbleize: (decoration) painting a surface to resemble marble.

marbles: (collectibles) popular toys since about 1850. Glass is the most common material used for marbles, but clay, metal, stone, and wood were also used. The first glass marbles were made from small pieces broken from glass rods. The pieces were heated in sand and charcoal, and stirred until they were round.

marble-top table: (furniture) a fine wood table with a marble surface. Rare and of the highest quality during the 1600s and 1700s. By the 1800s they were being mass-produced and most from this era aren't quite as fine as earlier examples.

marcasite: (jewelry) a mineral of iron disulfide, a man-made material fashioned into stones, beads, and the like; extensively used during the Victorian era. Also called *white iron pyrites.*

Marcolini: (ceramics) period from 1774 until *ca.* 1804 at the Meissen Porcelain Factory when Count Camillo Marcolini was director of the works. Wares are marked with crossed swords and a star.

margin: (stamps) the outer borders on both sheets of stamps and on individual stamps. Before the advent of perforated stamps, margins were often destroyed when stamps were cut. This, as well as off-center perforation, can cut into a stamp's design and lower the value.

margin block: (stamps) a block of stamps from the edge of a sheet with the border attached.

Marieberg porcelain: (ceramics) Swedish porcelain made near Stockholm from 1768 until 1788. Incised mark "MB" in blue or red.

marine antiques: anything pertaining to ships, such as figureheads, scientific instruments, ships' lanterns, and items like scrimshaw handcrafted by sailors at sea.

Marinot, Maurice: (glass) from 1922 until 1937, producer of sculpted molten-glass art objects. His method of building up layers of glass with bubbles in between characterizes his work.

marker lamps: (railroad memorabilia, lighting) a pair of marker lights displayed on the end car to indicate the train's classification; used during the era of steam locomotives and passenger and freight trains.

Marlborough leg: (furniture) a square leg often ending with a block foot.

marotte: (dolls) a mechanical doll with a head and upper body and a stick instead of legs. When the doll revolves it, plays a tune or sings a song.

marqueterie sur verre: (glass, decoration) a method of pressing lumps of colored glass into the warm, soft surface of a newly made glass object.

marquetry: (furniture) a veneer made of thin pieces of wood arranged and glued in a geometrical pattern on the surface of furniture.

marquise: 1. (furniture) a small sofa for two. Also called *causeuse.* **2.** (jewelry) an oval stone that is pointed at both ends. A popular choice for rings and brooches during the late 1700s and early 1800s.

marquisette: (textiles) a sheer fabric used for clothing, curtains, and netting.

marriage: the union of two separate decorative or furniture pieces to form one new, less valuable piece.

Martha Gunn jug: (ceramics) a Toby jug portraying Martha Gunn, who lived from 1727 to 1815 and was known as "the Brighton bathing woman."

Martha Washington chair: (furniture) an armchair with upholstered low seat and high back. From mid-18th century.

Martha Washington mirror: (furniture) wall mirror in the Georgian style, with gilded moldings, leaves, fruit, or flowers down the sides, a scrolled top, and a bird finial. Made in the United States during the last half of the 18th century.

Martha Washington sewing stand: (furniture) a sewing cabinet with drawers in the center and convex storage spaces with hinged, flat tops at the ends.

Martinware: (ceramics) fine, salt-glazed stoneware produced by Southall Pottery from 1877 until it closed in 1912. Named for the four Martin brothers who owned the company. Decorated by engraving, incising, or carving designs into the salt glaze. Blue, brown, gray, and yellow are the most common colors. All Martinware has an incised signature.

martlet: (decoration) a bird depicted without feet.

Marx: (toys) a company that made all types of toys except dolls from 1921 until 1976. They put out quality at a reasonable price.

Mary Gregory glass: glass items decorated with white enamel figures of children. From 1856 until 1908, Mary Gregory worked at the Boston and Sandwich Glass Company. Legend has it that during that time she designed and decorated these glass items, which were so popular that they were widely copied. This story is countered by people who claim Mary Gregory only worked at the company for two years and didn't decorate glass. Whatever its origin, Mary Gregory glass is sought by collectors. If the children have tinted faces or clothes, the piece is probably European. Cranberry is the most desirable color; amethyst is next, followed by blue. The other colors command considerably less. This glass has been widely copied and is now often referred to as Mary-Gregory-type glass.

maselin: a cup made of maselin, a metal alloy.

mask: (decoration) a full face depicting humor, an animal, or the grotesque; used as a form of ornament on furniture.

mask-face doll: a doll with a face made from cloth that has been treated with wax and then molded into facial features.

Mason: (ceramics) ironstone produced from 1814 until 1848 in the Staffordshire section of England. This sturdy tableware made in quantity for the middle class was the inspiration of Miles Mason. He was joined in business by his sons Charles and George. The oldest Mason ironstone reflects the Oriental designs favored by Miles Mason. Most of the decorations are transfers, but many are highlighted with enamel touches. Wares are marked "Fenton Stone Works" or "Mason's."

Massachusetts shelf clock: clock with eight-day brass movements. Made by Simon Willard and other clocksmiths between 1800 and 1830.

Massier: (ceramics) earthenware decorated with metallic lustre. Made in France from 1881 until 1917. The art nouveau shapes were embellished with plants, flowers, and other designs from nature. Most pieces are marked with an incised "Massier" or "CM."

master die: (coins) a die used for making working dies but never used for striking coins.

masticator: (kitchen) a device to tenderize meat. Often made of wood with a series of sharp projections. When these are pressed into the meat, they break down tendons and tissues, thus tenderizing the meat. Some date from the 1800s.

mat: (prints) a decorative border used around a print inside the frame.

matapan: (coins) a silver coin issued in Venice from the late 1100s.

Matchbox: (toys) die-cast toy cars made since 1953 by Lesney Products Corporation. They are exact replicas made 1/75 of the original size of the cars. Highly collectible.

match covers: (collectibles, paper) the paper covers in which book matches are contained. Collectors remove the matches and flatten the cover for display. The first matches of this type were produced in 1892.

match holder: (kitchen) a hanging container for holding wooden matches.

matchlock: 1. (weapons) a firing mechanism in which powder is ignited by a "slow match" — a slow-burning cord. **2.** (weapons) a musket using a matchlock firing mechanism. Introduced in the late 15th century.

match safe: a container for storing and/or carrying matches. Many have strikers built into the covers. Those that were designed to be carried are made of brass, silver, pewter, tin, and horn. Those for home use are often made of porcelain.

matte glaze: (ceramics) a dull glaze that produces a flat, non-reflecting finish.

matting: (silver) a dull, rough surface on silverware produced by hammering with a burred tool. Popular in the mid-1600s.

mauchline box: a wooden, hinged box decorated in black or full tartan, and depicting Scottish scenes. Originated in Laurencekirk in the late 1700s.

Maundy money: (coins) silver coins given out to beggars on Maundy Thursday. Originally official currency was used, but King George II minted special coins with his portrait on one side. Other monarchs followed suit, using coins with their images.

Maximilian armor: a late term for the fluted or crested armor that came into use in Italy and Germany during the reign of Emperor Maximilian I (1493 to 1519).

mazarine: (kitchen) a flat dish with holes in it; used for straining fish. Usually made of silver.

Mazarine blue: (ceramics) a dark blue color used on porcelain and earthenware. Named after Cardinal Guilio Mazarine.

mazer: (tableware) a medieval drinking bowl made of maple wood.

McCoy: (ceramics) makers of kitchen artware, including a line of collectible cookie jars. J.W. McCoy founded McCoy Sanitary Stoneware Company with his son in 1910. In 1933 the company became Nelson McCoy Pottery Company. The best known McCoy pieces were made after 1940. Early McCoy majolica pieces are marked "NMUSA." Newer pieces are marked "McCoy." This company should not be confused with the J. W. McCoy Pottery, also started by J.W. McCoy. See also *McCoy, J.W.*

McCoy, J.W.: (ceramics) a pottery first called the J.W. McCoy Pottery when it opened in 1899. In 1911 owner J.W. McCoy took a partner and the company became Brush-McCoy. They made majolica ware and pottery kitchen items and also produced Mt. Pelee, a line of art pottery with a matte green or iridescent gray glaze. Most of this ware is unmarked but some pieces are signed "Loy-Nel-Art," and others "McCoy." This company should not be confused with McCoy Sanitary Stoneware Company, also founded by J. W. McCoy. See also *McCoy.*

McKee: (glass) manufacturers of depression glass and a line of opaque glass dinnerware called Rock Crystal, which was fashionable in the 1920s. The company started in 1853 in Pittsburgh and moved to Jeanette, Pennsylvania, in 1988.

McKinley Tariff Act of 1890: a United States law that went into effect on March 1, 1891, which dictated that all imported items be marked with the country of origin. In 1914, and again in 1921, the act was modified: objects after 1914 had to be marked "made in" followed by the country of origin; after 1921 the country of origin had to appear in English.

Meakin: (ceramics) earthenware and ironstone produced at Alfred Meakin, Ltd., in Hanley, England, from 1877 until the present. The ironstone isn't marked, but the earthenware pieces are backmarked "Alfred Meakin/England."

measure: (kitchen) a cup or pitcher marked to measure liquids.

meat fork: (kitchen) a two-pronged, long-handled fork; used when cooking meat.

mechanical bank: a bank with one or more moving parts. See also *still bank.*

mechanical bird: (household accessories) birds that, at the push of a button or turn of a switch, spring to life and sing. Popular from the 15th century until the present. Marie Antoinette treasured a life-size bird in cage that sat on top of a clock and sang on the hour. Tiny birds fit into snuffboxes. They raised their heads, moved their wings and tails, and sang when the boxes were open. Watches were made with singing birds, as were pistols from which a bird emerged singing when the triggers were pulled.

mechanical picture: a picture with a figure or object that moves by mechanical means.

mechanical toy: a toy that can move about with the aid of a (usually internal) mechanical or electrical device.

medallion: (furniture) a large, oval or circular medal with a figure or inscription in relief.

medallion carpet: (floor coverings) a Persian rug that includes the medallion shape in its design.

medallion fan: (fashion accessories) a fan made of fine silk painted all over with a light background color and decorated with three scenes, each in a medallion shape. The center one is usually larger than those flanking it. The background often has beads or sequins. Sticks are generally adorned with mother-of-pearl. From the late 18th century.

medallion quilt: (textiles) a quilt with a large central design often surrounded by subordinate designs.

medicine bag: (Native American) a satchel carried on the body which contains several objects, such as bones, feather, shells, and stones, that are particularly meaningful to the bearer and are believed to have magical powers.

Medici porcelain: (ceramics) European porcelain produced first by Francesco de' Medici in Italy during the late 1500s. The ware is marked with a cathedral cupola and "F." This mark is underglaze in a flowing blue.

meerschaum: (materials) a soft mineral from which pipes are carved; also used for carving figurines.

Meigh: (ceramics) a company that was in business from 1805 until 1901. Their white stoneware jugs with relief Gothic designs produced in the 1840s are their best-known works. In 1842 Meigh released the Minister Jug — their most famous work.

Mei P'Ing: (ceramics) a Chinese vase with a small opening designed to accommodate one spray or blossom.

Meissen: (ceramics) excellent quality figurines and tableware first made by the Royal Saxon Porcelain Works in Meissen, Germany. The company started in 1710, producing the original Meissen pieces. Because they were copied, in 1731 Meissen started marking their pieces with crossed swords. Today, any porcelain that came from the city of Meissen is called "Meissen." Much of it lacks the quality of the original. The Onion Pattern made by several manufacturers originated in the Royal Saxon Porcelain Works.

melon bulb: (furniture) a swelling on the legs or posts of furniture.

memento mori: (jewelry) reminders of one's mortality worked into pieces of jewelry. Motifs include skulls, coffins, tombstones, and skeletons. Literally, *remember you will die.*

memorabilia: items from another period that bring to mind events of that time.

mennecy porcelain: (ceramics) soft-paste porcelain made in France between 1735 and 1785; used to produce vases, coffeepots, tea sets, and figures — many in the Sevres style. Some pieces are marked "DV."

Mennonite: (folk art) a religious sect that settled in Germantown, Pennsylvania, in 1683. Well known for their handmade quilts and other primitive crafts.

mercury glass: glass objects blown or molded so that they are made of two layers of glass with a space between them. This space is filled with a mixture of mercury, tin, lead, and bismuth. The result is a silver color. Occasionally blue or gold was added to the mercury solution. Popular in the late 1800s.

mercury head: (coins) term used in reference to the Winged Liberty cap dime, minted in 1916.

mercury pendulum: (clocks) a pendulum invented by George Graham in 1726. Temperature changes affect the mercury, which keeps the clock running.

merese: (glass) the round, button-shaped piece of glass between the bowl and the stem of a glass.

mermaid bottle: a glass or pottery bottle in the shape of a sea horse. Produced in the 1700s and 1800s. Bennington Pottery made some of the pottery mermaid bottles.

Merrimac Pottery: (ceramics) company founded in Newburyport, Massachusetts, in 1897 that produced ceramic tiles, crocks, and a line of artware. Their pieces are marked with the company's name and a fish.

merryman plates: (ceramics) a set of six tin-glazed earthenware plates. Each plate in the set is inscribed with one line of a six-line poem. One example is: (plate one) "When thou sit down to meat," (plate two) "Give thanks before thou eat," (plate three) "Be sure that thou conceive," (plate four) "The mercies thou receive," (plate five) "That such favours may be," (plate six) "Repeated unto thee." Late 17th century and well into the 18th century.

metal: 1. (materials) any of several ductile, malleable, fusible substances; used alone or in combination with other metals (alloy). **2.** (glass) glass in its molten state.

metamorphic library chair: (furniture) a chair with a four-step ladder that folds under the seat. See also *library chair.*

Metlox: (ceramics) a company that made figurines and dinnerware in California starting in 1927. They are best known for their collectible artware done by Carl Romanelli during the 1930s and 1940s.

metropolitan slipware: (ceramics) red earthenware with applied inscriptions of a moral nature done in trailed white slip. Many jugs, mugs, chamberpots, and bowls were done in this ware during the 1600s.

Mettlach: (ceramics) a company founded by Nicholas Villeroy and Eugene Boch in Mettlach, Germany, that produced steins, plaques, tiles, and vases from 1836 until 1921. Most examples of this pottery are marked "Mettlach" with an incised castle, although other marks were used.

mezzotint: (prints, books) the engraving of copper or steel plates by scraping and burnishing areas to create light and shadow; used in the 18th century for reproducing paintings in monochrome.

mica marble: a colored or clear-glass marble with flecks of mica. When the marble is rolled, the mica looks like silver.

micrometer: (scientific instruments) a device that measures minute distances, especially an instrument adjusted by rotating a finely threaded screw.

midband: (silver) a molded band placed just below the center of a silver tankard to strengthen and decorate it; first used in Boston in the early 1700s.

midshipman jug: (ceramics) an early, crude Toby jug measuring 6 1/2 to 8 inches high.

midwestern glass: glass produced from 1814 by any of the many glass manufacturers in the midwestern United States.

Mies van der Rohe, Ludwig: (architecture, design) the second director of the Bauhaus school and an influential designer of modern, chrome-plated steel furniture in the early 1900s. His art deco furniture was popular in the 1920s. See also *Bauhaus school.*

mihrab: (floor coverings) a niche in a wall facing Mecca; often used as a design element in Turkish rugs.

milestone automobiles: certain cars produced between 1946 and 1970 such as the 1955 to 1957 Thunderbird, 1957 Chevrolet, and 1965 Mustang. Also called *modern-day classic automobiles.*

militaria: (collectibles) anything having to do with the military. Some collectors are interested only in memorabilia from one country; some collect only one type of item, such as helmets or medals, regardless of where they are from; others are interested in any war souvenir. See also *war memorabilia.*

militariana: (toys) military toys. Lead soldiers, especially British, are highly collectible because they're extremely well made.

milk glass: opaque white glass originally called opal ware. Made first in England in an attempt to imitate porcelain. The most desirable has intricate designs — in most cases hand painted — and was made during the last half of the 19th century in England, France, or the United States. Most newer milk glass is of inferior quality.

milk paint: a paint made of milk, oil, lime, and color; used on furniture and interior woodwork during the 1700s. One of the most durable paints ever invented.

millefiori: (glass) literally, *a thousand flowers* in Italian. A form of glass achieved by putting together a group of glass rods so they resemble flowers; first used in Venice in the 1500s. In 1845 a factory in Paris started producing millefiori paperweights; in 1846 Baccarat began making them. Other glassmakers have since followed suit.

mille fleurs field: (textiles) a design employing leaves and flowers scattered in the background of medieval scenes on 16th-century tapestries.

millegrain setting: (jewelry) the mount of a gemstone decorated with a band of tiny metal beads.

Millville art glass: a company in Millville, New Jersey, that produces collectible glass objects like cups, plates, bottles, and paperweights depicting memorable events. They use the marks "HCB," "MAG," or holly leaves.

Ming dynasty: (orientalia) the dynasty that ruled China from 1368 to 1644, a period marked for great achievements in scholarship, art, and in particular, porcelain.

mingei: (orientalia) Oriental folk art.

miniature: a small scale replica of an item.

miniature paperweight: (glass) a paperweight that is 2 inches in diameter or smaller.

Minkus: (stamps) publishing company that produces catalogs of stamps from all countries. These references have been released in the United States each year since 1954.

minneteppich: (textiles) tapestries depicting romantic love scenes.

minogame: (orientalia) a long-tailed turtle; its image is used in Oriental art and decoration.

minor arts: all forms of art other than fine arts

minor coinage: (coins) coins with a face value of one cent or five cents, or their equivalent.

minor variety: (stamps) a slight deviation in color or design from other stamps in the same issue.

mint: 1. (stamps) condition of an unused stamp with its original gum and not mounted. **2.** a generic term that means *like new*.

mintage: (coins) all of the coins issued by a mint or a government during any one year.

mint mark: (coins) a small symbol or letter(s) on the coin indicating where it was struck.

Minton: (ceramics) a company started in the Staffordshire section of England in the 1790s making earthenware dinnerware — mostly Blue Willow. By 1805 they were producing highly decorative porcelain tea sets and other table accessories. In 1820 they added stoneware items. Some old Minton pieces are marked with crossed *Ls*. Others mimic the crossed swords used by Meissen. Starting in the 1860s, all Minton ware was marked with, "Minton" or "Mintons." The factory is still in operation.

mint set: (coins) an uncirculated set of coins.

miquelet: (weapons) a flintlock with a cocking mechanism in which the sear (catch) hits against lugs instead of a tumbler.

mir: (floor coverings) a Persian rug with a central motif featuring palm leaves.

mirror clock: (clocks) any clock with a mirror as a prominent part of the case. Also called *looking glass clock*.

mirror knobs: (hardware) ornate knobs used to hold a mirror in place on a wall. Each knob was attached to one end of a long screw. The knobs were screwed into a wall, and the bottom of a mirror was

rested on them. Made of many materials including brass, glass, porcelain, and battersea enamel. Most date from the mid-18th century to the mid-19th century.

mirror painting: a picture made by coating glass with tin and mercury to create a mirror. The design was then sketched on the coating and the parts to be painted were carefully scraped off. The design or scene was then filled in with appropriate colors, leaving a mirror background. Popular in the 18th century.

misericord: (weapons) a narrow, medieval dagger used in the mercy killing of a seriously wounded knight.

Mission furniture: a late-19th-century furniture style, massive and plain, usually of oak and upholstered with cushions. A spin-off of the Arts and Crafts movement.

mission mixture: (stamps) an assortment of cancelled stamps. Also called *mixtures*.

Mission Ware: (ceramics) a marbleized pottery made by Niloak Pottery and signed with their name.

miter cutting: (glass) cutting glass with a V-edged grinding wheel. The double miter wheel was used to cut complicated diamond patterns.

miter joint: a joint with two beveled surfaces, usually at 45 degree angles.

mixing table: (furniture) a small sideboard in the Federalist style — a mixing table that has compartments at both ends in which to store liquor; used in the southern United States during the late 1700s.

mixture: (stamps) an assortment of cancelled stamps. Also called *mission mixtures*.

mizpah ring: (jewelry) a ring with *mizpah* written on it. Given to close friends during the 1800s. The message meant, "May the Lord watch between me and thee while we are absent one from the other."

mocha: (ceramics) thick, beige pottery made in England for export to the United States in the 1800s. The ware is decorated in a variety of colors and patterns.

mock tapestry: (textiles) heavy cloth that has been painted to resemble tapestry.

modello: (fine art) an oil sketch that is used as a model for a painting.

modern automata: (collectibles) toys made since 1950, mostly in Japan, that are either windup or battery-operated. Collectors seek examples in mint condition and complete with their original boxes.

modern-day classic automobiles: certain cars produced between 1946 and 1970 such as the 1955 to 1957 Thunderbird, 1957 Chevrolet, and 1965 Mustang. Also called *milestone automobiles*.

mohair: (furniture) hair from the Angora goat; used for upholstery and blankets, often with a mixture of cotton.

moiré: (textiles) a heavy silklike fabric with a wavy (watered) variation throughout; used for upholstery, drapes, and dresses. See also *moreen*.

mokumé: (orientalia) a form of lacquer work used by the Japanese to simulate wood grain.

mold: 1. (glass) form for making glass articles. They usually have two sections, although many glass items have been made in three or four molds. The hot glass is poured into the mold and allowed to set. You can tell how many molds were used by feeling the lines between molded sections of a piece. **2.** (kitchen) a pan or bowl used to shape food. For example: a candy, jelly, cake, or vegetable mold.

mold-blown glass: glass objects made by blowing a gather of molten glass into a mold. There are one-, two-, and three-piece molds; the two- and three-piece molds allow for more ornate decoration.

molded-hair doll: a doll with hair that is molded, along with the features, as part of the head.

molded-teeth doll: a doll with an open mouth and teeth that are molded into it, leaving an opening into the doll's head.

molding: (architecture, furniture) an edging on a building or furniture piece that emphasizes the difference in planes or provides a decorative band.

molten: melted by high temperatures, as with metal or glass.

monart glass: glass decorated by dropping colored enamel into molten glass. Made by John Moncrief in the glassworks he opened in 1924. It was marked with paper labels.

monax: (glass) a very thin white glass.

money buckles: (fashion accessories) shoe buckles made of coin silver.

Monkey Orchestra: (ceramics) small porcelain figures depicting monkeys playing a variety of musical instruments. Produced by the Chelsea Porcelain Company in the mid-1700s, and earlier by the Meissen factory. These miniature musicians have become quite valuable.

Monmouth: (ceramics) a pottery company that made salt-glazed crocks, churns, and other items. Founded in Monmouth, Illinois, in 1892. In 1906 they were bought out by Western Stoneware Company. Most pieces are marked "Monmouth" printed across a maple leaf.

monogram: (decoration) a design composed of one or more letters.

Monot and Stumpf: (glass) from 1868 until 1892, a firm that made fine art glass items.

monotype: (fine art, prints) a print made by painting with a slow-drying paint on glass or a polished metal plate, then transferring the art to a sheet of paper by placing the paper over the plate and rubbing. Only one print of a painting can be made this way.

monstrance: (religious) a vessel for displaying the host either in a procession or at an altar. Most are splendidly ornate with enameling and jewels. Size varies widely.

monte à cage: (decoration, metal) a gold or silver framework that surrounds some snuffboxes, compacts, and other fine articles forming a cagelike cushion.

monteet: (household accessories) a cooler for wine glasses.

monteith: (household accessories) a silver or silver-plate punch bowl with indentations for hanging wine glasses upside down; first used in the late 1600s. Early monteiths are one piece; later examples have removable rims.

month clock: a clock that will run for thirty to thirty-two days with one winding.

Mont Joye glass: acid-cut cameo glass decorated with enamel flowers. Made in the late 1800s and early 1900s by the Cristallerie de Pantin, France. Most of this glass is frosted.

monumental candlesticks: (lighting) brass or silver candlesticks with high feet topped with large columns. Fashionable in the 17th century .

moonlight luster: (ceramics) a marbled luster achieved by mixing gold, pink, gray and other colors and used on earthenware. Developed by Wedgewood.

moon's age clock: a clock with moons rotating on a disk over the dial. It has a globe on either side of the moon. When the moon passes behind a globe, the moon appears as

new, first quarter, and so on. The disc revolves completely in twenty-eight days.

Moorcroft: (ceramics) a pottery in Bursalem, England, founded by William Moorcroft in 1913. He produced vases, bowls, lamps, and other decorative pieces, mostly in the art nouveau style, with hand-done, slip-trailed decoration. His early pieces are marked "Moorcroft Bursalem." In 1919 the mark was changed to "W. Moorcroft." In 1921 "Made in England" was added to pieces intended for export. All pieces, except those done in salmon color, were marked. Since 1945, when William Moorcroft died and his son Walter took over, the ware has been marked "Moorcroft."

Moore, Bernard (?1670-1726): (ceramics) producer with his son, Bernard Joseph, of decorative porcelain and earthenware pieces with a variety of glazes. From 1905 until 1915, Bernard Moore operated a firm in Stoke-on-Trent, England. Their wares were decorated by some fine artists; most of them signed their work. The pieces are also marked either "BM" or "BERNARD MOORE."

Moore, James (?1670-1726): (furniture) an early-18th-century cabinetmaker who decorated many of his pieces in gilt bas-relief. Some of the furniture in Blenheim (Churchill's boyhood home) was created by Moore. Much of Moore's work is signed with his name incised.

moquette: (textiles) a fabric similar to velvet but of a coarser weave; used for carpets and upholstery since the 16th century.

Mor.: (books) an abbreviation used in book catalogs indicating that a book is bound in Moroccan leather.

Moravian work: (needlework) needlework portraits done in memory of the deceased during the 18th century. This originated in Moravia.

moreen: (textiles) a heavy, silklike fabric; used for upholstery, drapes, and dresses. When it has a wavy, or watered, variation throughout, it is called *moiré*. See also *moiré*.

Morgan, Matt (fl. 1850s): American lithographer, designer of theater posters which were in vogue at the end of the 19th century.

Morgan, Matt: (ceramics) owner of Matt Morgan Art pottery in Cincinnati, Ohio, producers of fine art pottery from 1882 to 1885. The vases, chargers, and other pieces are in vibrant colors and many have gold trim. Much of this ware has a Rookwood look. The pieces that weren't marked with a paper label bear the company name.

moriage: (decoration) a raised clay decoration used on some Japanese pottery. Some of it is quite detailed.

morion: (armor) a metal helmet with a crest on top and a curved brim that peaks in front and back. *Ca.* 16th and 17th centuries.

morning star: (weapons) a large head of wood or iron studded with spikes mounted on a shaft; used in Europe and the Orient from about the Middle Ages through the 17th century. Also called *holy water sprinkle*.

Morocco: (books) leather bookbindings made of goatskin. When the term was first used, all the leather came from Moroccan goats. However, the term now refers to all goatskin. Morocco grains include Hardgrain, Levant, and Niger.

Morris chair: (furniture) easy chair with adjustable back and removable cushions named after William Morris, who first manufactured it. See also *Morris, William*.

Morris, William (1834-1896): the English "apostle" of the Arts and Crafts movement who advocated a return from factory production to honest craftsmanship in furniture, housewares, and art objects with simple, functional lines, and durability. He was an artist, writer, printer, and socialist. His firm, Morris and Company, established in 1861, used medieval craft techniques.

mortar and pestle: (kitchen) vessel-and-tool set used to pulverize chemicals for apothecaries, to grind condiments for cooking, and to mix pigments for artists. The first mortars were of stone or pottery. By the Middle Ages, bronze was used. Many fine 14th- to 18th-century examples have survived. They are often inscribed in raised letters and usually are dated. Later cast pieces are easily distinguished by their poor quality.

Mortens Studio: (figurines) producers of a line of animal figurines made of plaster molded over wire designed by Oscar Mortens during the 1940s. Mortens opened the studio in Arizona with Gunnar Thelin. The work portrayed hundreds of animals, both domestic and wild. The studio name appears on most examples.

mortise: (furniture) a hole cut or routed in a piece of wood to receive a tenon. See also *tenon*.

mortise lock: (hardware) a lock that can't be seen because it fits into the door's edge. Only the brass knob is visible in early mortise locks; the keyholes were covered by a moveable escutcheon. In later examples, the keyhole is visible.

Mortlake Tapestry: (textiles) tapestries woven at Mortlake, England, from 1618 until 1665. More than fifty weavers worked designs created by such notable artists as Rubens and Van Dyck.

Morton Pottery: (ceramics) wares from any of the six potteries opened at various times by members of the Rapp family: Morton Pottery Works and Morton Earthenware Company — both operated from 1877 until 1917; Cliftwood Art Potteries, Inc. and Midwest Potteries, Inc. — in business from 1940 to 1944; Morton Pottery Company — operating from 1922 to 1976; and American Potteries — from 1947 to 1961.

mortuary chair: (furniture) a mid-17th century chair with a scrolled back that has a carving depicting a bearded man's head in the middle, said to be a likeness of Charles I of England.

mortuary sword: (weapons) a 17th-century sword with a straight blade and a shell guard (a shelllike protective shield).

mosaic: (decoration) a design made up of small pieces of glass, stone, or tile and joined together with cement or another adhesive.

mosaic binding: (books) a bookbinding in several colors that has been achieved either by applying thin leather pieces to the leather cover, by painting the leather cover, or by cutting colored leather pieces and inlaying them into the leather cover where corresponding shapes have been cut out.

mosaic gold: (metal) a metal alloy of various mixtures of copper and tin or zinc that resembles gold in appearance. Also called *ormolu*.

Mosaic Tile: (ceramics) company founded in 1894 that produced tiles and novelty items until it closed in 1967. Their wares are marked either "MT," "MTC," or "Mosaic Tile Co."

Moser Glass: glassware designed by Ludwig Moser and Son between 1857 and 1938. Many of their designs reflect nature; Moser is best known for depicting birds in flight.

Their work features heavy, bright enameling, and sometimes jewels were applied to the designs. Few pieces of this art-nouveau-style glass are marked.

Moser, Kolomann: (design) graphic artist and cofounder of Wiener Werstatte, Vienna workshops that designed art nouveau furniture, glass, metal objects, and other accessories from 1901 until 1932.

Moss Rose: (decoration) a very popular pattern for dinnerware from 1808 until around 1900. Produced by many Staffordshire firms as well as by the Wheeling Pottery of West Virginia. The design features pink and green flowers.

mother-of-pearl glass: glass with a pearlized finish made both in England and the United States, mostly from 1850 to 1900. The most valued pieces feature a rainbow of colors, combining white, yellow, blue, and rose. Diamond Quilted, Raindrop, and Herringbone are the most popular patterns of this glass.

motif: 1. (fine art) a repeated design in artwork of any style. **2.** (decoration) the basic theme or distinctive feature of a period or object.

mount: (furniture) a handle, escutcheon, or other ornamental metalwork.

Mount Washington Glass Works: (glass) from 1837 until the late 1890s, producers of art glass first in South Boston, Massachusetts, then in New Bedford, Massachusetts. In the 1890s they merged with Pairpoint Manufacturing Company. The two companies had few rivals in the blowing and cutting of glass. They made cameo glass, Burmese glass (yellow with a pink tinge), amberina (ruby glass shading to amber), and peachblow (glass resembling a peach in color).

mourning collectibles: (folk art) pictures and samplers depicting tombs, weeping willows, people in black, and pertinent facts about deceased persons. Often done by grieving widows and mothers during the 1700s and 1800s.

mourning fan: (fashion accessories) a fan decorated in black, gray, white, and brown, often with the ivory sticks painted brown and overlaid with silver. These fans sometimes have a picture of the Queen of Sheba painted in white on a gray background.

mourning jewelry: black jewelry worn by people in mourning during the 1800s. It was a common practice to have an allowance written into a will to be used for this jewelry. The jewelry was then handed out at the funeral to close friends of the deceased. The value of the jewelry depended on the financial status and generosity of the deceased.

mourning locket: (jewelry) a gold or silver locket worn during the 1700s and 1800s by a woman who had lost a loved one. The locket contained a lock of hair, a picture, or other small memento of the deceased.

Moustiers faience: (ceramics) earthenware with blue monochromatic designs produced in Provence, France, which at the time was considered one of the leaders in faience. Early 1700s.

mouton: (coins) a 14th- and 15th-century French gold coin with Lamb of God and Cross on one side and a floral cross on the reverse.

movie memorabilia: (paper) books, display cards, magazines, posters, photographs, and other printed material about early movies and the stars who acted in them. Condition is of utmost importance.

mower's ring: (bottles) a large, doughnut-shaped bottle used during the 19th century by workers in the field. These circular water bottles had a hole in the middle large enough for a man to put his arm through it and carry the bottle over his shoulder.

Mr. and Mrs. Caudle: (ceramics) a brown stoneware flask with relief decorations depicting Mr. and Mrs. Caudle in bed on one side and Miss Prettyman on the other. Made by Doulton during the mid-1800s. The characters were from Douglas Jerrold's *Punch Papers*.

Mucha, Alphonse (fl. 1880s): (design) a Czechoslovakian artist who worked in France and the United States; known for his intricately designed art nouveau posters.

mud: (floor coverings) a finely woven, geometric Iranian rug.

mudjur: (floor coverings) a woolen prayer rug of Turkish origin.

muff chain: (jewelry) a chain passed through the opening in a muff and worn around the neck to keep the muff in place when it was in use.

muffineer: (kitchen) a large metal or glass container with a pierced top; originally used to sprinkle sugar on muffins.

mulberry china: (ceramics) ironstone with purplish transfer designs produced by many potters in the Staffordshire region of England in the mid-19th century. The color is reminiscent of mulberry juice. Many of the same patterns were also made in flow blue.

mule chest: (furniture) an oak or walnut chest from the 1600s that has either one long drawer or two short ones side-by-side at the bottom of the chest.

mull box: a standard Scottish snuffbox. Made from a ram's horn with a silver cap.

Muller Freres: (glass) company that made lamps, vases, bowls, and other accessories from cameo glass and other types of glass in the first half of the 18th century. Pieces are marked "Muller," "Muller Croismare," or "Croismare Nancy."

mullet: (coins) a star with five or six points that usually has a hole in the middle; used to decorate coins.

multi-lens camera: (photography) a camera that could record many images on one plate. Invented in the 1870s.

multiple knobs: (glass) repeated knobs or other shapes on the stem of any glass object.

Muncie Pottery: (ceramics) a factory that operated in Muncie, Indiana, from 1922 until 1939, producing vases and planters for florists and articles such as bookends and candleholders for sale by gift shops. The ware is marked "MUNCIE."

muntins: (architecture, furniture) bars between panes or pieces of glass in windows, doors, or furniture.

mural: (fine art, decoration) a painting done directly on a wall. Murals often cover the entire wall and usually tell a story.

mural clock: a clock that hangs on a wall.

murano: (glass) glass with spiraling colors. Made in Italy.

mushroom knob: (furniture) a flat finial resembling a mushroom; used on the back posts of chairs.

mushroom paperweight: (glass) a paperweight with a mushroom-shaped bundle of millefiori rods and a base that is encircled with a twisted band of glass.

musical clock: a clock equipped with cylinders which have pins that hit bells and play a melody, usually on the hour, and sometimes on the half- or quarter-hour.

musical glasses: a felt-lined wooden frame outfitted with glasses sized so that when they are rubbed with wet fin-

gers, they emit musical notes. Popular in the 1600s and 1700s.

musical sleigh bells: (music) a set of bells attached to a leather strap and hung on a frame.

musical snuffbox: containers for snuff with musical movements. The oldest, some from the 1700s, are elaborately decorated, made of gold or silver, and the musical movements were small and lightweight. In the early 1800s, they were fashioned from painted tin, horn, and tortoise shell. As time went by, larger musical movements were used, and by the mid-1800s there was little room left in these boxes for snuff.

musical watch: a watch that, with the push of a button, would chime or ring the hour when it was dark. The earliest musical watches, invented before the luminous dial or the electric light, were born of necessity. With the invention of the steel comb, later musical watches could play a greater range of notes.

music cover: (paper) a cover from sheet music. Some have pictures of well-known people, others depict the theme of the song inside. Those from the 1800s, and later ones that portray certain movie stars, are collectible.

musket: (weapons) a matchlock or wheel-lock firearm first used by the military in the 1500s. The term has come to be used to describe any long-barreled firearm.

mustache cup: a gentleman's cup with a special mustache bar attached to the inside of the rim. During the Victorian era when large mustaches were in vogue, the bar kept a man's mustache dry when he drank his tea and coffee. Some of these cups are porcelain, some ironstone, some silver plate. A few were made for left-handed gents.

N

nail-head decoration: (furniture) a decoration in the form of a series of squares carved on furniture. Each square has a raised point that looks like a nail head in the center. From the Middle Ages until the 1600s.

nail plate: (weapons) a small ornamental plate on the stock of a gun or pistol opposite the lock. Also called *contreplatine* and *side plate*.

Nailsea glass: glass with white swirls on a clear or colored ground originally made in Nailsea, England, in the late 1700s. The first examples of this glass were strictly ornamental. As its popularity increased, more utilitarian items, such as flasks, vases, and lamps, were produced in this style in Nailsea and in other areas of England.

naive art: (folk art) paintings done in an unrefined manner, usually by nonprofessionals. Subjects may be landscapes, portraits, genre, or still life. Some of these works show a poor use of space and balance, but all are sought for their quaint charm and historical significance. See also *folk art* and *primitives*.

Nakara: (glass) opaque white glass vases, plates, boxes, and the like made by C.F. Monroe Company of Meriden, Connecticut, from 1900 until 1916. Articles were either hand painted or decorated with transfer designs; many had ormolu trimming. The company also made Wave Crest, but Nakara has deeper colors. See also *Wave Crest*.

namas: (textiles) small rugs for kneeling on during prayers.

namban: (orientalia) Oriental wares that have been decorated in a manner that reflects the European influence. For instance, Japanese pottery with European people often depicted in Oriental scenes.

Nanking: (ceramics) blue-and-white porcelain china made in Canton for export to England and the United States. Identifiable by its spear-and-post border. The popular Willow pattern depicts a person holding an umbrella and standing on a bridge; often trimmed with gold. Made from the 1800s until the early 1900s.

Nantgarw: (ceramics) translucent dinnerware made in Wales for a brief period of time in 1813 and again from 1817 until 1820. The factory-decorated pieces were simply painted. More elegant pieces were decorated in London. This ware is usually marked "Nantgarw," often with "CW" over it.

napkin rings: (tableware) figural or plain, circular holders for individual napkins; placed beside each plate setting. Popular from the mid-1800s until the early 1900s. Made of various materials including sterling, silver plate, wood, and porcelain.

nappery: 1. (textiles) table linens. **2.** (fashion accessories) collars or neckties.

nappy: 1. (kitchen, tableware) a round, shallow dish with a flat bottom and sloping sides; used for cooking or serving. **2.** (kitchen, tableware) a small bowl.

nasal: (armor) the nosepiece of a helmet.

Nash: (glass) fine art glass made by Arthur John Nash, who was employed by Thomas Webb and Son Glassworks in England prior to coming to the United States in 1889 and working for Tiffany Furnaces. He made iridescent glass at Tiffany. In 1928, his son, A. Douglas Nash, bought the company and renamed it A. Douglas Nash Corporation. Although they produced quality glass, the company went out of business in 1931.

nashiji: (decoration) a Japanese technique for applying lacquer. After lacquer is painted on an object it is sprinkled with gold dust. Then the object is polished.

Native American crafts: creative work done by the North American Indians. It can be divided into five major categories: basketry, beadwork, pottery, weaving, and wood carving. Most of what is collected today is from the 20th century.

natural wicker: (furniture) wicker that has not been painted or stained. This is more desirable to a collector than painted wicker. Natural wicker pieces may have been treated with a sealant for preservation, which does not alter the value.

Natzler, Gertrude and Otto: (ceramics) internationally famous ceramics workers who left Vienna and settled in Los Angeles about 1937. Gertrude designed pottery and Otto produced various original glazes. Their works are highly prized.

naval mirror: (furniture) a mirror with an upper panel on which has been painted a naval scene. Also called *tabernacle mirror*.

Nazi memorabilia: (collectibles) German military and political articles from the mid-1920s to 1945, when the National Socialist Party ruled Germany. Items dating from 1939 until the end of World War II in 1945 are the most collectible. These items include guns, daggers, swords, medals, and flags.

necessaire: (personal accessories) a small case used for toilet essentials such as combs and soap.

needlepoint: (needlework) small, even stitches done across counted threads, usually on canvas.

needlepoint lace: (textiles) lace stitched over a paper pattern.

needlework: (textiles) sewing, embroidery, or any other type of handwork done with a needle and thread on material.

nef: (clocks) a clock in the shape of a ship.

negative impression: (coins) an original design in reverse.

Negro nursemaid with white child: (black memorabilia, toys) composition and cloth dolls. The child has a bisque head. Made by Excelsior Toy Company *ca.* 1880.

neillo enamel: (jewelry) a decorating process. Designs are carved out of metal jewelry and filled in with a bluish black metallic substance. Dating to the Bronze Age and in use since then.

nested tables: (furniture) three or more tables of graduated sizes that store one beneath the other. May be separated and used individually.

nesting toy: a set of wooden or papier-maché figures of decreasing size that fit inside each other.

netsuke: (jewelry, fashion accessories) a small Japanese toggle used to attach a purse or other article to a kimono sash. Usually wood, ivory, or metal and decorated with inlays and/or carvings.

never hinged: (stamps) never mounted or pasted on anything. Usually abbreviated *N.H.* See also *hinge*.

Newcastle: (ceramics) An area of England renowned for its clay pipes during the 17th century. Famous pipemakers included Charles Riggs. Also a center for earthenware factories. Some fine, brown-glazed teapots were made in the area.

Newcomb Pottery: (ceramics) high-glaze art pottery decorated with southern (United States) motifs, such as dark Bayou scenes, made by students at Newcomb College in New Orleans, Louisiana (a woman's college that became part of Tulane). Produced from 1895 until 1950. Most pieces are marked "NC."

new die proof: (coins) the first coin from a working die. Not to be confused with the proofs that have a mirror finish and are struck for special purposes.

newel post: (architecture) a post supporting a handrail at the bottom or on the landing of a staircase.

New England armchair: (furniture) an armchair with a continuous half-hoop shape that includes both the back and arms.

New England Glass Company: a company founded in Cambridge, Massachusetts, in 1818. They made many types of glassware including pressed, blown-in-the-mold, three-mold, and art glass. In 1888 Edward D. Libbey moved the company to Toledo, Ohio, where it now operates as the Libbey Glass Company.

New Geneva: (ceramics) wares from a number of potters who worked in Greensboro, Pennsylvania, during the 1800s making utilitarian stoneware items.

New Hall: (ceramics) hardpaste and bone china made by the New Hall Porcelain Manufactory, established in the last part of the 1700s at Newhall in the Staffordshire section of England. Much of their hardpaste dinnerware is decorated with delicate floral sprays. In 1812 they started making bone china. Although most of the ware is unmarked, some of it bears the company name in a double circle.

New Martinsville: (glass) figurines, bookends, tableware, candlesticks, and vases made by the New Martinsville Glass Manufacturing Company, which opened in West Virginia in 1901. They were bought by the Viking Glass Company in 1944. Viking is still producing glass.

newspapers: collectible papers reporting historical events such as Lincoln's assassination, Pearl Harbor, Babe Ruth's death, or the sinking of the *Maine*. There are several considerations in determining value: Was it published directly after the event? Are there pictures? Is it on the front page? Are the headlines large? A yes to all these questions makes the paper desirable. Other papers that depict an era but not a notable happening, called *atmosphere newspapers,* are also collectible, but not as valuable.

nib: (desk accessories) the point of a quill or fountain pen.

nickel silver: (metal) a compound of nickel, copper, and zinc containing no silver. Formerly called *German silver.*

niddy-noddy: (textiles) a wooden reel shaped like an anchor at each end; used for winding yarns.

Niderviller Pottery: (ceramics) very fine quality hardpaste porcelain figurines and porcelain flowers in the Sevres style. Niderviller operated from 1754 to 1827 in France.

niello: a black metallic alloy of sulphur mixed with copper, silver, or lead; used between 1770 and the late 1800s. A powder from this mixture was pressed into engravings on silver boxes, creating a black decoration. Russian boxes were decorated with niello; also occasionally used in England and France.

night clock: an old, rare clock with a dial on which the numbers have been cut out. The dial revolves, and as the appropriate hour line lines up with the square that has been cut from the body of the clock, a lighted candle from within the clock reveals the time. Also called *candle clock.*

night crow: (domestic) slang for *chamber pot.*

night-watchman jug: (ceramics) a Toby jug in the form of a figure who is sitting down and holding a lantern and a hat. See also *Toby jug.*

Niloak Pottery: (ceramics) a pottery in Benton, Arkansas, that made art pottery from 1909 until 1946. Their best-known line is Mission Ware, a marblized, usually tan-and-brown, pottery. It is marked "Niloak," which is kaolin (a potter's clay) spelled backwards. In 1924 they added a novelty line.

Nippon: (ceramics) Japanese ware made for export to the United States from 1891 until 1921. In 1891 the McKinley Tariff Act dictated that all future goods imported to the United States must be marked with their country of origin. Japan chose to use *Nippon.* Items were backstamped with many marks, but the three most common are the rising sun, the wreath, and the maple leaf. The finest quality Nippon is marked in green; the middle grade in blue; and the lowest grade in magenta. The marks have been copied but they are not exact reproductions and usually appear on inferior pieces. In 1921 the United States ordered the names of the countries of origin to appear in English. From that time on, the word *Nippon* was replaced with *Japan.*

nipt diamond wais: (glass) ribs of glass joined together at specified points so they form a diamond pattern on an object.

nishiki-ye: (orientalia) Japanese pictures made of brocade, or prints of the brocade pictures.

Nock, Henry: (weapons) a leading London gunmaker in the late 1700s.

nocturnal: (clocks) a device resembling a slide rule by which an approximate time can be discerned through the use of the stars.

nodders: (figurines) novelty figurines of people and animals with heads that move freely. Bisque, celluloid, and porcelain were used to make these figures. They have heads, and often arms, attached with wires, allowing them to move, or nod, when the figure is touched or when a breeze disturbs them. Made during the 1700s and 1800s. Many reproductions exist.

noggin: 1. (tableware) small mug with handle. Usually made of pewter or wood. **2.** (tableware) any small drinking vessel.

noggin bottle: a small bottle for liquor. Usually holds a quarter of a pint.

nomad rug: (floor coverings) an asymmetrical, fringed rug made by a member of one of the nomadic tribes in central Asia.

nonadhesive: (stamps) a stamp printed directly on a postcard or envelope.

nonesuch chest: (furniture) a chest featuring architectural designs enhanced with inlay. So named because the first chests depicted the Palace of Nonesuch. Made in Germany during the 16th and 17th centuries.

Noritake: (ceramics) a Japanese company that began in 1904 as the Nippon Gomei Kaisha. Much of their hand-painted and transfer ware was made for export to the United States. The Morimura Brothers of New York were the distributors. The Larkin Soap Company gave away Noritake dinnerware with patterns made exclusively for them from 1916 to the 1930s. Best-known and most collectible among these is the Azalea pattern. Noritake has hundreds of marks, but the most common is "M" in a wreath used by the Morimura Brothers.

Norse: (ceramics) a black pottery made to resemble ancient bronze vessels from Scandinavia. Produced from 1903 to 1913 by the Norse Pottery Company in Wisconsin. The pieces were marked with a stylized *N* with the remaining letters of *Norse* worked into it.

North Celadon: (ceramics) beautiful vases and bowls from the Honan Province of China. These porcelaneous wares are glazed with an olive brown to greenish tone.

North Dakota School of Mines: (ceramics) ceramics with designs featuring cowboys and buffalo, by students from The North Dakota School of Mines from 1909 until 1949. The ceramics were fashioned from regional clays. Art deco and art nouveau also influenced the work. Very early examples are marked "UND," but most pieces are marked "University of North Dakota."

Northwood: (glass) custard glass, goofus glass, pattern glass, and opalescent glass made by the Northwood Company, which operated from 1896 to 1899, and the Harry Northwood Glass Company (1901 to 1923). Best known for their carnival glass. Most pieces are marked "N" with a line under it.

nosegay: (decoration) motif featuring a small bouquet of flowers (nosegay); used as an ornament.

novelty clock: a clock that tells time in a different manner or that has a novelty shape. These clocks were inexpensive and many of them were used as advertising giveaways or souvenirs. Shapes include ships, globes, animals, and flowers. Fashionable *ca.* 1850.

Nove Porcelain: (ceramics) a soft-paste porcelain made in Venice from about 1750 until around 1835. Pieces are marked with a red and gold eight-point star.

NS: (metal) abbreviation for *nickel silver*. Imprinted on the object.

Nu-Art: (glass) bookends, lamp shades, and other items made by the Imperial Glass Company in Ohio. They started making wares marked "NUART" in 1920.

numbered: (prints) method used with limited-edition prints to show what number each print is in the print run, and how many prints are in the edition. For example, 100/1000 means the 100th print in an edition of 1000. Early prints are generally clearer and therefore more desirable.

numismatics: (coins) the study of coins.

Nuremberg Egg: early small, drum-shaped watch made in South Germany.

nursing rocker: (furniture) a low rocking chair, usually without arms, in which mothers sat and nursed infants.

nutcracker: (household accessories) a device for cracking nuts. They have been made in a variety of shapes since the 1800s. Earlier nutcrackers were of simpler designs. All of them are collectible. A patent mark adds to the value.

nutmeg lamp: (lighting) a small night light made by Gausler, Hoffman and Company in the late 1800s.

nutmeg spoon: (kitchen) a silver spoon with a grater on the handle. Popular in the 1700s.

Nutting, Wallace: (photography, prints) a photographer from New England who took many pictures there and in Pennsylvania. Carefully tinted prints of his works are highly collectible. Look for Wallace Nutting's signature; unsigned examples are worth less.

Nymphenburg: (ceramics) a German porcelain factory that has been operating since 1753. Their figurines' marks include "CT."

Nyon Porcelain: (ceramics) a factory in Geneva that made porcelain with floral decorations from 1780 until 1813.

O

oak: (materials) a light yellow-ish wood that darkens as it ages. Popular for furniture in England up until the mid-1600s. American oak has been used extensively for furniture, especially in the Victorian era. Many of the 20th-century oak pieces are fashioned from Japanese oak.

oban: (coins) an Oriental coin.

obol: (coins) a small, silver Greek coin worth one-sixth the amount of a drachma.

obsidian ware: (ceramics) ware mimicking the appearance of obsidian, a dark-colored, green-flecked volcanic rock. Starting in 1850 many factories in the Staffordshire section of England were producing this statuary porcelain.

obverse: 1. (coins) the side of a coin or other double-sided object that bears the principal design or markings. **2.** (coins) on U.S. coins, the side with the date.

occasional table: (furniture) any small table, but primarily one used in the living room.

Occupied Japan: (orientalia) articles made from 1945 to 1951, when Japan was occupied after World War II. These wares are marked "Occupied Japan" and have become collectible.

octafoil table: (furniture) a round table with eight scallops around the edge. See also *scalloped*.

octant: (scientific instruments) a navigational instrument similar to the sextant. It uses a 45-degree angle with a double reflection to measure solar altitude.

odalisque: (fine art) female slaves in Eastern harems; depicted as reclining nudes by artists during the 19th century.

odor case: (personal accessories) a small, scented box in which handkerchiefs were kept.

oeil-de-perdrix: (decoration) enamel decoration on porcelain that resembles the eye of a partridge. It consists of small circles, usually done on a colored background.

off-paper: (stamps) stamps that have been canceled and then soaked and taken off the envelope or card on which they were used.

offprint: (books, paper) the reprint of a section of a publication. Done from the original typesetting.

ogee: (decoration) an elongated, S-shaped double curve.

oignon: (jewelry) a French onion-shaped watch. Popular during the 1700s.

oil-boiled calico: (textiles) chintz.

oil-gilding: (decoration) a method of gilding porcelain or glass; used in the 1700s, prior to the time gold was fired on.

oil stand: (lighting) an oil can, usually of japanned tin; used to fill oil lamps.

ojas: (ceramics) a water jug made of unglazed pottery that kept water cool.

old black Joe: (black memorabilia, toys) painted, composition-and-cloth, clockwork doll. Made by Ives *ca.* 1880.

old ivory: (ceramics) dinnerware with either a hand-painted or transfer design on ivory background made in Silesia, Germany, in the late 19th century. Many pieces are marked "Silesia."

ombre table: (furniture) a triangular card table designed for use in playing *Ombre,* a card game for three people.

on cover: (stamps) a stamp that has been canceled and is still stuck to the envelope or a part of it. Also called *on paper.*

O'Neale, Jeffrey Hamet: (design) book illustrator and artist who did miniatures and painted ceramics. He worked in the latter capacity for Chelsea, Worcester, and Wedgewood in the mid-1700s. His work incorporated illustrations from *Aesop's Fables,* landscapes, and animals. Many of his pieces are marked "O.N.P."

Oni: (orientalia) a sly-faced, impish looking figure with horns, often attired in a loin cloth; used in Oriental decorating.

onion foot: (furniture) a flat, onion-shaped foot; used mostly on cabinets and chests.

onionskin marble: a marble with solid spirals of multicolored bands throughout.

on paper: (stamps) a stamp that has been canceled and is still stuck to the envelope or a part of it. Also called *on cover.*

on your own knowledge: (auctions) a term used by auctioneers to indicate to the audience that the merchandise is not guaranteed to be what the auction house calls it, that any risk is on the part of the buyer, and he or she may not return an article because it isn't what an auctioneer said it was.

onyx: (materials) agate stone with bands of different colors.

onyx glass: several colors of glass mingled prior to forming an article. The result resembles onyx. Used especially in Venice and Germany.

onza: (coins) a gold Spanish coin.

O.P.: (books) an abbreviation used by booksellers that means *out of print.*

opalescent: (glass) glass with an iridescent look when placed in strong, direct light.

opaline: (glass) semi-opaque glass of white or light shades. Often decorated with enamel or gilt. Bristol glass is one type of opaline. See also *Bristol glass.*

opaque china: (ceramics) the generic name of an earthenware made by Swansea and other companies. It has a porcelaneous white finish.

open-back chair: (furniture) a chair with a slat or ladder back with space between the pieces that run from post to post. Any chair back that isn't solid.

open/closed-mouth doll: a doll with parted lips and teeth that come together so there is no opening into the head as there is in a molded-teeth doll. See also *molded-teeth doll.*

open handles: (decoration) handles with finger holes in them as opposed to closed handles, which are solid.

openwork: (decoration) an ornamental or structural area containing a pierced design; used on furniture and jewelry.

optical items: (collectibles) spectacles, microscopes, lorgnettes, binoculars and other old optical articles sought by collectors. Good condition and an unusual shape or quality add to the value.

Opus Anglicanum: (textiles) ecclesiastical embroideries woven of silk and metal threads. Created in England from the mid-13th century until the mid-14th century.

Orange-Jumper: (ceramics) earthenware depicting a horseman clothed in orange. Made at the Don Pottery, Yorkshire, England, in the early 1800s.

orb: (decoration) a circle or sphere.

orcel: (household accessories) a small vase.

orfrays: (textiles) cloth with gold embroidery.

Oriental coralene: (ceramics) Japanese china decorated with tiny beads of glass similar to coralene glass. Made in the early 1900s and marked with a date or "Patent Pending."

Oriental furniture: a general term applied to furniture imported from Eastern countries in the 19th century.

orientalia: goods from the Orient.

original gum: (stamps) The original adhesive. Abbreviated *O.G.*

original lithograph: (prints, fine art) a lithograph produced by drawing directly on a plate or stone by the artist. Twentieth-century American artists sign their original lithographs at the bottom. Foreign original lithographs are not always signed. Lithographs produced by photo-mechanical methods are not accepted as original. See also *lithography.*

original print: any print the artist has produced, supervised, or authorized. In any case, the artist is involved with the print run. Such prints are usually signed in pencil in the lower right-hand margin. See also *print.*

Orion Ware: (ceramics) a tinglazed, delftlike pottery made between 1525 and 1550. Rare.

ormolu: (metal) a metal alloy of various mixtures of copper and tin or zinc that resembles gold in appearance. Also called *mosaic gold.*

ornate: (decoration) elaborate decoration.

orrery: (scientific instruments) a mechanical model of the solar system.

osiers: (materials) small twigs from the willow tree; used for making wicker furniture because they are so pliable.

ossuary: an urn, vault, or other container for holding the bones of the dead.

ostrich egg cup: (household accessories) an ostrich egg made into a drinking cup. Seventeenth-century Germany.

ottoman: 1. (furniture) an upholstered seat or couch without arms or a back. **2.** (furniture) a foot stool.

oudenaarde: (textiles) a Belgian tapestry. Seventeeth and 18th centuries.

ovate: (decoration) egg-shaped or oval.

over-and-under: (weapons) a two-barreled gun with one barrel under the other one.

overdoor: (fine art) a painting on wood panel or canvas designed to be hung between the top of a door and the ceiling molding.

overglaze: 1. (ceramics) a second glaze applied over a primary glaze and then refired. **2.** (ceramics) a decoration applied over rather than under the glaze.

overlay: (decoration) the application of one layer over another — for example, when a thin layer of glass is applied over an existing object.

overmantel: 1. (decoration) a decorative mirror, often with a painted panel, for hanging over the mantelpiece. **2.** (folk art) a painted panel over a mantelpiece. Often done by itinerant artists.

overprint: (stamps) printing added on top of a stamp's original design.

ovolo molding: (furniture, architecture) a quarter-round convex molding.

oxbow front: (furniture) a Chippendale form — a curved front that is concave in the middle and convex at the ends.

oystering: (decoration) veneer made from the cross-sections of small tree branches that shows the cross-sectional grain in irregular concentric rings; used on furniture.

𝒫

padauk wood: (materials) an exotic reddish hardwood; used mostly for veneers during the 1700s.

Paden City Glass Company: (glass, ceramics) producers of pressed glass items in Paden City, West Virginia, from 1916 until 1951. Until the 1920s all their wares were clear, uncolored glass. Later they included colored, translucent, and opaque products in their line. Most work was done by hand until 1949, when they became automated. The quality suffered greatly and pieces made from 1949 to 1951 are vastly inferior. Colored pieces are the most desirable.

pad foot: (furniture) oval-shaped foot that is flat on the top; used on cabriole legs.

paduasoi: (textiles) heavy Italian silk.

paillons: (decoration) gold, silver, or colored spangles set in enameled pieces.

painted parsons: (advertising) signposts or signboards. Named for early American saying, "like parsons, they point the way but do not take it." They are collectible.

Pairpoint: (glass, metal) company that, from 1894, when they merged with Mt. Washington Glassworks, produced boxes, candlesticks, compotes, paperweights, urns, vases, lamps, and lampshades. Most well known for their lamps with one of three types of glass shades: a blown-out shade called *puffy Pairpoint* — reverse painted and often marked "Pat July 9, 1907"; a ribbed shade — reverse painted, often artist signed, and sometimes marked "Pairpoint Corp."; and a smooth reverse-painted shade, usually with a scenic design. The lamp bases are signed. In 1938 the company went out of business, but reopened later as The Gunderson-Pairpoint Glassworks, specializing in cup plates which are marked with a "P" in a diamond.

Pairpoint Limoges: (ceramics) white ware made by Limoges according to specifications given to them by Pairpoint. The blanks were then sent to the United States where Pairpoint decorated them. This ware is marked "Pairpoint" over a crown under which "Limoges" appears.

paktong: (metal) an alloy that looks like polished steel, but consists of copper, nickel, and zinc; used for fireplace utensils.

palache: (weapons) a Polish saber with a straight or slightly curved blade, hilt with short pommel, and short quillons, usually curved towards the blade. From the 17th century.

palampore: (textiles) a painted cotton wall hanging or bedspread.

pale: (metal) inferior soldering material or a bad soldering job.

palissy ware: (ceramics) a 16th-century French lead-glazed pottery. Usually adorned with fish, reptiles, and the like, or with figures of people.

Palladian: (furniture) heavily decorated, carved, often gilded furniture. Fruit, flowers, masks, and animals frequently figure in the design. Based on the 16th-century architecture of Palladio, an Italian; Palladian-style furniture was popular in the early 18th century.

palmer candles: (lighting) candles with both ends of the wick coming out the top and a loop in the bottom. These candles were burned in special holders. They gave more light than an ordinary candle.

pambe: (floor coverings) name for cotton used in Iranian rugs.

pamuk: (floor coverings) name for cotton used in Turkish rugs.

panache: (armor) a plume, or its holder, on a helmet.

panakin: (kitchen) a small saucepan with a wooden handle; used to warm brandy. Also called *pipkin*.

pan cupboard: (furniture) a low, wide cabinet with one door; used for storing pots and pans.

pandora: (music) an early pear-shaped guitar. Also called *cittern*.

panel-cut: (glass) glass decorated by cutting it with the flat edge of a grinding wheel.

paneled construction: (furniture) furniture made of panels held in a framework rather than just of heavy wood, resulting in lighter, more elegant pieces; used after the 15th century.

panharmonicon: (music) a device that could produce the sounds of a variety of instruments. Made by J. Maelzel in the late 1700s.

panoramas: (paper) scenes made out of paper and placed one behind the other to create a picture with depth.

pansiere: (armor) the lower section of a Gothic breastplate.

pantin: (paper) a paper doll with arms and legs strung together so that the doll appears to be animated when a string is pulled.

pantry boxes: (kitchen) food storage containers originally made of wood and often round; later made of tin plate.

pap boat: (domestic) a shallow, oval-shaped bowl with a long, tapered end; used for feeding infants and invalids. Made in silver and other materials from early 1700s. Also called *feeder* and *pap dish*.

pap dish: (domestic) a shallow, oval-shaped bowl with a long, tapered end; used for feeding infants and invalids. Made in silver and other materials from early 1700s. Also called *feeder* and *pap boat*.

paper dolls: (paper) paper images of adults and children that have been mass-produced since the 1700s. In the 1800s most of them depicted famous people of the era. Starting in the 1920s, paper dolls came on cardboard covers on books with cut-out clothes inside. The most desirable to the collector are those portraying movie stars, royal personages, or comic-strip characters. Uncut, mint paper-doll books bring at least twice as much as a book that has been cut.

paperweight: (desk accessories) a small, heavy object for placing on loose papers to secure them. Made of a variety of materials including wood, metal, and glass. Paperweights were first made in ancient Egypt, but they were rare until the mid-1800s, when England, Italy, Bohemia, France, and the United States all started producing glass paperweights. The finest are those made by the Baccarat, Clichy, and St. Louis glass factories in France. Fine, old glass paperweights in mint condition bring high prices from collectors.

paperweight eyes: (dolls) eyes that appear to move as a person moves around the doll. The eyes are made of glass and have detailed corneas and irises that are visible from the sides of the doll.

papier-maché: (materials) a mixture of starch, glue, and pulp paper molded into shapes, allowed to dry and harden, and then usually painted. Old papier-maché objects are collected.

papyrus: a document written on paper made from the papyrus plant, found in northern Africa and southern Europe; used by the Egyptians and other ancient people of that area.

parasol: (fashion accessories) a light umbrella used as a shield from the sun.

par avion: (stamps) French for *by air.* An accepted international standard.

parchment: 1. (materials) sheepskin or goatskin prepared for writing or painting upon. 2. (materials) paper made to imitate parchment.

parchment crest: (armor) a crest made of parchment; worn by 13th-century knights and their horses.

parfleche: 1. (Native American) rawhide cleaned of hair and dried on a stretcher. 2. (Native American) an article, such as a case or shield, made from parfleche.

parian doll: a doll made of unpainted stoneware or bisque.

parian ware: (ceramics) a white ceramic with a matte finish; used mostly for making small reproductions of statues. Also used with a glaze for tableware. Since the mid-1800s.

paris candle: (lighting) a large candle made of wax.

Parisienne doll: a doll with a bisque head and a leather body. Produced by many French dollmakers such as Jumeau and Rohmern during the late 1800s.

parison: (glass) the first of two molds used to make modern bottles. The parison forms the bottle, which is then transferred to the finishing mold. See also *finishing mold.*

Parison carpet: (floor coverings) a carpet made by the first carpet company in England. The Parison Carpet Company in Paddington, London, began producing floor carpets in 1747. By 1750 the carpets were being exported to America.

parquetry: (materials) strips of wood, sometimes of contrasting colors, pieced into a mosaic inlay. More common in floors than furniture.

Parrish, Maxfield: (fine art, prints) well-known artist and illustrator from the late 1800s until his death in 1966. After the 1940s his work lost its popularity, but in the early 1960s, his art was again in demand. The advertisements, books, magazines, and prints of his work increase in value each year.

partizan: (weapons) a broad-bladed pole weapon usually with short, curved branches at the base of the blade. From the 16th to 17th centuries.

parure: (jewelry) a set of matching pieces, usually earrings, necklace, brooch, and bracelet.

pas d'ane: (weapons) a sword guard formed of loops circling the blade. From the 14th century.

passementerie: (decoration) decorative edgings on garments and other items such as lace, beads, fringes, and frogs.

passglas: (glass) a drinking vessel with a notched glass thread encircling the top. The notches divide the glass, and as it is passed around a group, each member drinks from his or her own section. Of German origin.

paste jewelry: ornate jewelry designed like expensive pieces, but set with glass instead of precious gems. Popular in the 1700s.

pastel: 1. (fine art) pictures done with chalklike crayons. 2. (fine art) the crayons used for pastel drawings.

pastiche: 1. (fine art) a poor copy of a work of art. 2. (furniture) furniture rebuilt or modified to resemble a more valuable piece.

pastille burner: (domestic accessories) a burner in the form of a house, church, or other building. Similar to an incense burner. The roof of the building came off and a tiny cassoulette inside held perfumes that smoldered when lighted. Eighteenth and 19th centuries.

pata: (weapons) the gauntlet sword of India. The blade is long and straight, usually double-edged; the gauntlet almost reaches the elbow, and it has an iron strap hinged to the upper end that goes around the underside of the arm.

patch box: (personal accessories) a small box in which a lady kept her beauty spots. The boxes are dainty and composed of silver, gold, enamel, or pewter. **2.** (weapons) the cavity in the stock of a rifle in which bullets, wrapped in patches of oily cloth, were stored. **3.** (domestic) a box carried on the belt or slung from the shoulder; often used to carry cleaning rags and the like.

patch figure: (ceramics) a figurine with an unglazed patch left by the hunk of clay on which the figure stood during firing. Made at Chelsea and Derby, England.

patchwork: (textiles) small pieces of material sewn together either randomly or in a pattern, as in a patchwork quilt.

pâte de cristal: (glass) a glass paste mixture, similar to pâte de verre but with a higher lead content. See also *pâte de verre*.

pâte de verre: 1. (glass) a thick paste of powdered glass mixed with water and a volatile adhesive, which is applied in thin layers in a mold to the required thickness and then fired. **2.** (jewelry) a method of decorating jewelry with finely ground, colored glass that has been molded and fired. Popular with the makers of art nouveau jewelry during the late 1800s.

pate doll: doll with a hole in the top of its head through which a dollmaker can attach the doll's eyes and teeth. The hole is then plugged up and a wig glued on.

paten: (religious) a small, round, silver or gold plate used for communion. The oldest examples date to medieval times and have flat, broad rims. The centers are engraved with religious figures.

patent number: a number appearing on some items that identifies what year that particular item was patented.

patent rocker: (furniture) a rocking chair that operates via large coil springs attaching the chair to the base. Also called *platform rocker*.

patera: (furniture) a small, thin oval, round, or square plate; used as a base for ornamental detail.

paternoster blade: (weapons) a sword blade with pierced openings fashioned to allow the blade to be used as a rosary, enabling the user to count his prayers.

pate-sur-pate: (ceramics) white porcelain-paste low-relief appliqué; first used at Sevres.

patina: 1. (furniture) the surface sheen on wood resulting from wear, polishing, and age. **2.** (metal) the green or brown corrosion that appears on copper and bronze.

patination (furniture) a buildup of dirt, wax, polish, or any other foreign substance on wood furniture. The presence of patination indicates a piece is old. However, in some cases it has been faked.

pattern glass: pressed glass in a variety of colors and a seemingly endless number of patterns first made in volume in the 1840s. From that time until the American Civil War, it had a high lead content and was called *flint glass*. Later glass was nonflint. It was not until the 1890s that color was added. It fell from favor before World War I and is now one of the leading collectibles. See also *flint glass*.

Pauline Pottery: (ceramics) pottery in the Rockwood style made at Pauline Pottery from 1883 until 1905. The firm moved during that time from

Illinois to Wisconsin, where there was superior clay. Many of the wares were made for department stores and carry their names. Other pieces are marked "Pauline Pottery," "Edgerton Art Pottery," or "Trade Mark" with a crown. Much of this pottery is unmarked.

Paul Revere Pottery: (ceramics) a Boston, Massachusetts, firm that produced hand-decorated tiles, tea sets, children's ware, and other items from 1906 until it closed in the early 1940s. The company was started by a group of ladies who called themselves "the Saturday Evening Girls." The company used several marks including "P.R.P.," "S.E.G.," and "Boston, Paul Revere Pottery."

pave setting: (jewelry) a setting in which a cluster of stones is held together with small grains of metal. The stones are actually touching each other.

pavis: (armor) a very large shield used by two bowmen. It rested on the ground with the upper end supported by a prop. From the 15th century.

paw foot: (furniture) a carved furniture foot used from the 17th century through the 19th century.

peace pipe: (Native American) a ceremonial smoking pipe with a long stem and ornamentation; used by North American Indians. Also called *calumet.*

peachblow: (glass) distinctive glass with peachlike hues produced in the 1880s by several fine firms. Each has its special look: Hobbs, Brockunier and Company's peachblow has a glossy or acid finish shading from yellow to red; Mt. Washington's goes from blue-gray to rose; New England Glass Works' is either acid or glossy in rose shading to white. English firms were Thomas Webb & Sons, whose cased-glass peachblow is in

shades of yellow to red. Stevens and Williams' peachblow resembles Webb's. Gunderson Glass started making reproductions of New England Glass peachblow in the 1950s.

peak: (pewter) pewterers' term for *lead.*

pear-drop handle: (hardware) a brass backplate, often ornate, with a pull shaped like a pear; a common ornament on furniture drawers during the William and Mary period (1685 to 1720).

pear tankard: (tableware) a pewter tankard with a bulbous body. Also called *tulip tankard.*

pearwood: (materials) one of the hard fruitwoods used for furniture and picture frames. These woods are easy to work with and therefore lend themselves to turnings and carving. None of the fruitwoods has the beauty of mahogany or rosewood, so they are often painted or gilded for picture frames. Other close-grained fruitwoods used for furniture are applewood and cherry.

peat bucket: (domestic) container used for holding peat or turf blocks for fire building.

pebble jewelry: stones native to Scotland set in jewelry. Most of what is available is from the Victorian era.

peche mortel: (furniture) a stool and a chair combined to make a couch.

pedal car: (toys) a child-size vehicle, measuring 3 to 4 feet and powered by pedals or battery. These collectible toys were made in the form of cars, farm tractors, airplanes, trains, and trucks.

pedestal table: (furniture) a round-top table supported by a pedestal in the middle.

pediment: (furniture) the decorative part above the body of a cabinet or chest of drawers, with an outline low at the sides and a gable or arch in the middle.

peeking fan: (fashion accessories) a folding fan with holes covered with a transparent material. When the fan was open, a lady could demure behind it while she peeked through the holes observing what was going on. Popular in the mid-1700s. Also called *quizzing fan.*

peg foot: (furniture) a simple, tapered round- or square-shaped foot.

pegged furniture: a piece of furniture held together by wooden pegs that can be dismantled easily by removing the pegs. The most popular example is the trestle table.

pegging: (textiles) a very heavy type of crocheted work.

Peggy Plumper: (decoration) earthenware that features a man and a woman sparring and a humorous poem. The ware gets its name from the sparring woman who is known as *Peggy Plumper.*

peg tankard: (tableware) a 17th-century tankard with studs running from top to bottom on the inside. The studs were to measure the amount of ale drunk.

Peking glass: glass objects decorated to look like porcelain. Made in Peking as early as 1680. From the early 1700s, much of the glass was carved. Peking glass is still made and it is often difficult for a novice to distinguish old from new.

peloton: (glass) an art glass made by working colored threads of glass into glass gather. Wilhelm Kralik perfected this method in Bohemia in the 1880s. Occasionally enamel decoration was added.

Pembroke table: (furniture) a small drop-leaf table; used for breakfast. The leaves are supported on swinging wooden brackets.

pen-and-wash drawing: (fine art) a brush drawing on paper done with a dilution of India ink or monochrome watercolor. Also called *wash drawing.*

pen cancel: (stamps) a stamp canceled by hand with a pen. Usually done on revenue stamps, but in the last century, some countries canceled postage stamps by pen until their postmarks were in operation.

pencil: (heraldry) a small streamer bearing the knight's coat of arms attached to the end of his lance.

pencil-post bed: (furniture) a bed with four posts that are very thin and have eight sides each. Popular 1700 to *ca.* 1760.

pendant: 1. (lighting) a hanging lamp. **2.** (jewelry) a hanging ornament, usually on a necklace.

pendeloque: (jewelry) a faceted teardrop-shaped stone; used most often for pendants.

pennon: 1. (heraldry) a narrow banner or streamer attached to the head of a lance. **2.** (heraldry) a square flag ending with a triangular point. It identified a knight bachelor and bore his armorial design. The king, or high authority, converted the pennon into a banner by cutting off the point, signifying the knight had been raised in rank to a banneret.

Pennsbury: (ceramics) dinnerware, tiles, figurines, and other objects made in Morrisville, Pennsylvania, from 1950 to 1971. Pieces are marked "Pennsbury."

Pennsylvania Dutch: (folk art) the name given the Germans who settled in Pennsylvania. Their colorful peasantlike furniture and crafts suggest heritages from both Germany and England.

Pennsylvania slat-back chair: (furniture) a chair made between 1660 and 1800 with curved slats on the back and turned stretchers between the front legs.

penny black: (stamps) the world's first postage stamp, issued by Great Britain in May of 1840. It had a one-penny value and was printed in black. It was used for only one year because it had to be canceled with a colored postmark. See also *penny red*.

penny red: (stamps) a stamp issued in 1841 to replace the penny black because the colored postmark used to cancel the penny black could be washed off. The shades of red used for the new stamp allowed cancellation with indelible black ink. See also *penny black*.

penrhyn marble: (materials) slate painted to look like marble; used on table and dresser tops.

pentimento: (fine art) sign of correction made by the artist in an oil painting.

pepperbox: (weapons) a gun with several revolving barrels, usually moving around one central stationary one.

pepperette: (kitchen) early pepper shaker.

peppermint swirl marble: an opaque white marble with alternating bands of red and blue.

perambulator: (vehicles) a baby carriage or buggy. Also called *pram*.

percussion cap: (weapons) a copper cap filled with a fulminating mixture; used to ignite the powder in a gun.

perfins: (stamps) initials perforated in stamps; used by businesses and other groups that used large quantities of stamps to prevent theft by employees. Uncommon today because of the wide use of postage meters.

period: the era during which a piece was made.

perpetuana: (textiles) a woolen fabric that lasts a long time. Also called *everlasting cloth*.

Perry, Edward: (paper) a leading English manufacturer of paper goods. Best known for his papier-maché items. Dating to the early 1800s.

pesos: (coins) Spanish currency. Also called *piastres* and *Pieces of Eight*.

Peters and Reed: (ceramics) a company named for its founders that began producing tiles and flower pots in Zanesville, Ohio, in 1897. In the early 1900s they added several lines of art pottery including Moss Aztec, Chromal, Landsun, Montene, Pereco, and Persian. In 1922 the company's name was changed to Zane Pottery. Much of the ware made after that is marked "Zaneware." Peters and Reed is unmarked.

petit point: (needlework) a small embroidery stitch; used for covering chairs and settees.

petroglyph: a carving or drawing on a rock, such as those created by primitive peoples.

petuntse: (ceramics) Chinese name for *feldspathic rock*. This substance combined with kaolin (clay) is used to produce hard-paste porcelain.

Pewabic: (ceramics) a small art pottery company started in Detroit, Michigan, by Mary Chase, Perry Stratton, and Horace James Caulkins in 1907. Much of their early ware has a matte green glaze. Some later pieces are finished with a lustrous glaze. The ware is very hard. Many marks were used, including the company name with maple leaves and "Revelation Pottery."

pew group: (ceramics) a figural composition of a man and woman, or two men and a woman, seated on a settle or pew. First done in salt-glazed stoneware in the early 1700s in the Staffordshire section of England.

pewter: an alloy of antimony, lead, tin, or copper; used for tankards, underplates, and other tableware.

phaeton: 1. (vehicles) a light, four-wheeled carriage. **2.** (vehicles) a touring car.

philately: (stamps) the study and collection of postage stamps and other postal material.

philography: (paper) collecting autographs. The interest in autographs is growing, and as it does, the value of autographs grows with it. Supply dictates price and desirability. The signature of a dead celebrity generally brings more than that of a live celebrity. If someone did not sign many autographs, his or her signature brings more than that of a person of equal rank who gave autographs freely. A signature on a picture is worth less than one on a personal, handwritten letter, but more than one on a card.

phoenix bird porcelain: (ceramics) porcelain with a blue-and-white bird design produced by many potters in Japan since the early 20th century. There are many marks and many pieces are unmarked. Newer phoenix bird has a whiter background and the design, which is a harsher blue, is less intricate than on the older, most prized pieces.

Phoenix Glass: (glass) a company that specialized in glass for lighting fixtures when it first opened in Pennsylvania in 1880, but better known for the line of sculptured glass it produced from 1930 to about 1950. Their artware had a distinctive raised design. Consolidated Glass was almost identical, but Phoenix usually colored the background and left the raised design the color of the glass, while Consolidated usually left the background plain and colored the raised portions. See also *Consolidated*.

photographica: (collectibles) old cameras, albums, ambrotypes, daguerreotypes, tintypes, viewers, and other photography memorabilia.

Phyfe, Duncan (1768-1854): (furniture) the best-known American furniture maker. He created designs reflecting English Regency and French Empire styles. He worked in New York.

piano babies: (figurines) bisque babies, sized from 3 to 12 inches, created in dozens of poses by Heubach Brothers of Germany. Almost all of them were marked with an "H" in a rising sun over a "C." There are many reproductions.

piano-forte box: (music) a music box with two or more combs so the volume can be varied.

piano lamp: (lighting) a floor lamp that can be adjusted for reading music.

piastres: (coins) Spanish currency. Also called *pesos* and *Pieces of Eight*.

Picasso art pottery: (ceramics) art pottery made by Pablo Picasso and signed by him during the 1940s.

Pickard: (ceramics) a china company started in Chicago, Illinois, in 1897. At first they hand-decorated European blanks. Artists featured fruits, flowers, birds, and scenes in their work. In 1915 Pickard produced a line of gold wares. Since 1938 they have made their own blanks, and in 1976 they added an annual limited-edition Christmas plate. Most pieces are marked "Pickard."

picker: a slang term for one who searches out and buys items for antique dealers and auction houses.

pickle caster: (tableware) decorative pickle jar with a serving fork attached to its side. The metal frame that held the glass portion and the cover were of plate or sterling depending on the family's status. Popular from just after the Civil War until the late 1800s.

pickle dish: (tableware) oblong dish similar to a flat celery dish only smaller; used for serving pickles or olives.

pictorial: (stamps) any stamp with an illustration that is pictorial, but not a portrait, coat of arms, or geometric design.

picture sampler: (needlework) a sampler with a stitched picture instead of, or in addition to, a motto.

pie bird: (kitchen) a small device, usually in the shape of a bird, that is hollow inside, and has an open bottom and a smaller opening at the top (usually the bird's beak). The open bottom is placed in the middle of an unbaked pie crust, allowing the steam to rise and escape through the opening at the top while the pie is baking.

pieces of advantage: (armor) sections of plate worn over the regular armor during the joust.

Pieces of Eight: (coins) Spanish currency. Also called *pesos* and *piastres*.

piecrust table: (furniture) a table with the edge raised in a series of curves, like the crimped edge of a piecrust.

pier cabinet: (furniture) a high, narrow cabinet with shelves to display small collected items. Also called *curio cabinet*.

pierced: (decoration) decorative metal, woodwork, or paper in which areas of the background are cut, punched, or chiseled out to create an openwork design.

pierced carving: (decoration) a carved design that, in some spots, goes right through the wood; used to decorate furniture and frames.

Pierce, Howard: (ceramics) a designer of figurines, flower frogs, vases, and other decorative accessories with his wife and daughter in their studio in California since 1940. All decorating is done with an airbrush. He signed his early pieces with his name or initials.

pier glass: (furniture) a tall mirror originally designed to fit between two windows or over a chimneypiece.

pier table: (furniture) a table designed to be placed against the wall between two windows. Popular from 1700s on. Many of these tables were in the shape of a half circle.

pie safe: (furniture) a country-kitchen shelved cabinet with screened or perforated panels and door to allow air to circulate over fresh, cooling pastry.

pietra dura: 1. (furniture) a very fine quality of marble; often used for inlaying on furniture. **2.** (jewelry) literally *hard stone*. Jewelry featuring a Florentine mosaic pattern, utilizing flat pieces of hard stones such as agate or lapis lazuli.

pigeon blood: (glass) a dark red colored glass with an orange tint. Pigeon blood glass was fashionable during the late 1800s.

pigeonhole: (furniture) a small, open compartment in the cabinet of a desk or secretary for storing letters and the like.

pig iron: (metal) blocks of crude iron.

pike: (weapons) a spear with a small leaf- or diamond-shaped head mounted on a long shaft; used by the infantry from at least early Greece, primarily against opposing cavalry.

pilaster: (architecture, furniture) a rectangular column with a capital and base, set into a wall or protruding from a surface for ornamental purposes.

pile: (weapons) the head of an arrow.

Pilgrim furniture: the furniture made in New England by the Puritans during the 1600s. Also called *Puritan furniture*.

pillar doll: a doll with no moving parts; made of one solid piece of bisque or glazed porcelain. The dolls were supposedly named after a girl in an

1860s ballad who was so pleased with her new dress that she forgot to don her coat before rushing out into a blustering, freezing cold night to show off her new gown. Her body was found frozen stiff. Also called *frozen Charlotte*.

pillar rug: (floor coverings) a rug designed in China for use around a pillar.

pill lock: (weapons) a device for sparking the charge in a gun. Ignition was by percussion; however, the fulminate was either shaped like a pill or small ball, or contained in a tube or backed by paper. Introduced after the flintlock and before the percussion proper. Also called *detonator*.

pillow lace: (textiles) lace made by arranging pins in a pattern, then twisting threads from bobbins around the pins. Also called *bobbin lace* and *bolster lace*.

pillow sword: (weapons) a sword hung next to the pillow, ready for nocturnal defense. Early 17th century.

pin: (furniture) a small rod used to fasten separate articles together. Made of various materials.

pinchbeck: (jewelry) a metal resembling brass, but actually an alloy of copper and zinc, invented by London jeweler Christopher Pinchbeck in the early 1700s; used extensively for watch cases during that century.

pinch trailing: (decoration, glass) bands of glass pinched together into wavy lines and applied to glass objects as decoration. Also called *quilling*.

pineapple cup: (table accessories) a covered cup resembling a pineapple standing on a pedestal. Made in Germany in the 1500s and 1600s. Some examples are 30 inches high. Also called *ananaspokal*.

pink luster: (ceramics) a finish created by putting gold luster on a light background.

Produced by most potters in the Staffordshire area of England during the 1700s and 1800s. During the 1800s, Sunderland luster, a type of pink luster that has shadings of pink in circles, was made by Leeds and other companies. See also *Sunderland*.

pink pigs: (ceramics) figurines featuring pink ceramic pigs usually placed in bright green surroundings; popular souvenirs in the late 1800s and early 1900s. The more pigs and the more active they are, the more valuable the piece. These small collectibles are marked "Germany" or "Made in Germany." They have been widely reproduced.

pinnacle: (furniture) a tall, pointed, spirelike formation.

pinprick picture: (prints) a colored print perforated with many tiny holes. When held to a backlight the print appears to be illuminated. With the addition of a colored paper backing, the scene can be changed from day to night when held up to light. Popular in the Victorian era. See also *transparency*.

pin-up art: (paper) calendars, cards, magazine covers, playing cards, and other printed material depicting women in glamorous, provocative, often nude poses. The first pin-up girl was done by Charles Dana Gibson in the early 1900s. Other artists to look for are Joyce Ballantyne, Billy DeVorss, Gillete Elvgren, Cardwell Higgins, Earl Moran, George Petty, Charles Sheldon, and Alberto Varga.

pinx: (fine art) term that means *painted by;* often found after an artist's name.

pipe tongs: (domestic) small tongs for holding a hot coal to light the tobacco in a pipe.

pipkin: (kitchen) a small saucepan with a wooden handle; used to warm brandy. Also called *panakin*.

pique: (decoration) silver pieces embedded in a design

or randomly placed in such substances as ivory, horn, or tortoise shell. Popular on the Continent in the beginning of the 18th century. See also *pique point* and *pique posé*.

pique point: (decoration) tiny particles of silver embedded in tortoise shell, ivory, or horn articles. A type of pique. See also *pique*.

pique posé: (decoration) strips of metal, usually silver, embedded in various bases. A type of pique. See also *pique*.

Pisgah Forest: (ceramics) pottery founded by Walter Stephen in North Carolina in 1914. He produced pieces depicting pioneer life and also a line of turquoise crackle ware. His pieces are marked "Pisgah Forest." Walter Stephen died in 1961 but the business has continued.

pistol: (weapons) a firearm designed to be held and discharged with one hand. From the early 16th century.

pistol shield: (weapons) a shield with a pistol mounted at the center and the barrel protruding several inches; used in the 16th century.

pitcher: (kitchen) a cylinder-shaped container with a spout and loop handle.

pitside chair: (furniture) a chair made to be straddled by the sitter. It has high arms and a slanted back. Also called *cockfight chair*.

Pittsburgh glass: flint glass produced in Pittsburgh, Pennsylvania, by numerous glass companies during the 1800s.

placard: 1. (armor) the lower part of a Gothic breastplate. 2. (armor) an extra plate covering the lower part of the Gothic breastplate during tournaments.

plain-sawed: (furniture) wood sawed from a log in lengthwise, parallel cuts.

plain weave: (textiles) a weave in which the warp and filling threads are equally interlaced alternately. Also called *taffeta weave*.

planchet: (coins) a blank for a coin.

planish: (metal) to flatten or smooth a metal surface by hammering or rolling.

planter: (household accessories) a large, deep container for holding a plant. Also called *jardiniere*.

plaque: (household accessories) an ornamental plate designed for hanging.

plaquette: (decoration) rectangular or square veneer inlay within a contrasting veneer surface.

plate: 1. (armor) a piece of armor made of steel. 2. (metal) a layer of silver or gold applied over a metal of lesser value.

plate block: (stamps) a block of four or more unseparated stamps from a sheet margin that bears the plate number used in the printing.

plated: 1. (metal) a metal or alloy covered with another metal or alloy. Electroplating is the most common method of plating. See also *electroplate*. 2. (stamps) stamps that were separated from their original sheets and have been put back together in the order in which they were printed.

plate metal: (pewter) a fine quality of pewter.

plate pail: (kitchen) a round or square pail with a handle and a narrow strip cut from one side; used to transport plates to and from the kitchen in the 18th century.

plate signed: (prints) a term used to indicate that the artist has signed the plate rather than the print itself. Occasionally a plate-signed print will also be hand signed.

plate size: (prints) the actual size of the image of a print as opposed to the size of the paper on which it is printed.

plate warmer: (kitchen) a shallow, covered pan with a small opening to be filled with hot water. A plate is placed on top of the cover to keep the plate warm.

platform rocker: (furniture) a rocking chair that operates via large coil springs attaching the chair to a base. Also called *patent rocker*.

Platonite: (glass) a heat-resistant glass with fired-on color made by the Hazel Atlas Company.

plinth: 1. (architecture, fine art) the square slab or block upon which a statue, pedestal, or column is placed. **2.** (furniture) the base of a piece of cabinet work.

plique à jour: (enamel) a stained-glass effect created by filling the cells of a honeycomb structure with translucent enamel which allows the light to freely pass through.

plug bayonet: (weapons) a bayonet that can be quickly attached to the barrel of a rifle.

plush: (floor coverings, textiles) carpets and fabrics with thick, deep pile.

ply: (furniture) a single layer of veneer.

Plymouth earthenware: (ceramics) blue transfer-decorated earthenware made by the Plymouth Pottery Company in Plymouth, England, during the 1800s. Most pieces were marked with the Royal Arms and "P.P. Coy" or "L, Stone China."

plywood: (materials) multiple layers of wood veneer glued together, each layer at right angles to the adjacent strip.

poincon: (armor) the mark of an armorer, stamped or engraved on his work.

points d'esprit: (textiles) lace with small square dots on a small mesh background.

poissardes: (jewelry) long earrings.

pokal: (tableware) a large goblet with a cover, elaborately decorated in chasing or repoussé. Found in silver, pewter, and other metals.

Many of these goblets are engraved.

polder mitton: (armor) a guard worn on the elbow of the arm over regular armor in tournaments in the 15th century.

poleax: (weapons) a shafted weapon with an axe blade on one side of the head and a hammer or spike on the other. Middle Ages.

pole bed: (furniture) a bed with low posts; used from the late 1700s until the mid-1800s. Pole beds were made to fit lengthwise against the wall. They got their name from the separate pole that was suspended over the bed from the wall, mid-way between the head and foot, to hold a drape of material over the bed.

pole screen: a fire screen on a tripod base.

poleynes: (armor) knee caps of plate.

polychrome: (decoration) an object decorated with several colors.

polygons: (decoration) geometrical forms with any number of sides from five to twelve.

pomander ball: (household accessories) an uncut orange or lemon into which whole cloves have been stuck all over. The fruit is then rolled in powdered spices, usually cinnamon or orris root, then rolled in paper and set aside for up to a month. When the fruit has absorbed the fragrances of the spices, it acts as an a sachet or air freshener. See also *pomander case*.

pomander case: (metal) a perforated metal case made for storing pomander balls; often used by a lady to sweeten the fragrance of her clothes when they were packed in a trunk or suitcase while she was traveling.

pommel (or pummel): (weapons) the knob on the end of the hilt of a sword or knife, or on the butt of a pistol.

pomona: (glass) frosted lead glass often decorated with a metallic paint design; first made by the New England Glass Works in 1885. In 1888 the company was taken over by Libbey and moved to Toledo, Ohio. Pomona was produced until the early 1900s.

Pompadour fan: (fashion accessories) a fine quality fan, usually gilded, bejeweled, and painted. Popular from the early to mid-1700s.

Pompadour parasol: (fashion accessories) a parasol with a small shade on a long, jointed pole. The pole was jointed so that the shade could be adjusted for a lady's comfort; used in the late 1700s and early 1800s.

pond-lily pitcher: (ceramics) pitcher first produced by Bennington Pottery in Bennington, Vermont, during the mid-1800s. They are either blue-and-white or all white parian ware and feature a pond-lily design.

Pond rug: (floor coverings) a hooked burlap rug made from a stenciled pattern by D. Pond and Company in Maine.

poniard: (weapons) a small, thin dagger.

pontil mark: (glass) a mark or scar, often rough, left on a hand-blown glass object where the punty, or pontil, rod has been knocked off the piece. This mark is usually on the bottom of an object.

pontil rod: (glass) a long, metal rod attached to a glass object during the finishing process. It is used after the blow pipe has been removed. Also called *punty rod*.

pontipool ware: (metal) japanned tinware made in the 1700s.

pope and devil cup: (household accessories) a novelty cup that, when held one way, has an image of a pope and when reversed or held upside down, has the image of the devil. Made in the late 1700s.

porcelain: (ceramics) hard, very fine-grained white ceramic ware. True porcelain dinnerware is always translucent. It has a delicate look and feel not found in pottery or semiporcelain. Porcelain made before 1891 may be unmarked, or it may bear a company name and/or symbol; artist's symbol or number; the pattern name or number; or a registry mark.

porcelaneous: (ceramics) having the characteristics of porcelain, but not actually porcelain.

porphyry: (furniture) red or purple stone; sometimes used for tops on ornate tables.

porphyry ware: (ceramics) an earthenware of a red color resembling a type of red stone (porphyry).

porringer: (kitchen) a low metal bowl with a handle that is usually pierced; used to serve gruel or porridge.

Porter, Rufus: (decoration, folk art) an itinerant American decorator famous for his murals.

port-fire: (domestic) phosphoric matches that were packaged in small, sealed glass tubes. The matches ignited when the tubes were broken. Early 1800s.

port mantreau: (household accessories) a clothes tree.

portrait doll: a doll with the facial features and general appearance of a real person — anyone from a queen to a rock and roll star.

portrait medallion: (furniture) a large circular or oval medal with a face in relief.

portrait miniature: (fine art) a small portrait done on ivory or other material in oil or watercolor.

portrait plate: (ceramics) a plate decorated with the portrait of a famous person or a beautiful woman. Popular from about 1850 until the turn of the century. Many of these were hand painted; others were transfer decorated. KPM and Royal Vienna were leading producers. Look for the Royal Vienna beehive mark or "KPM."

posnet: (kitchen) a small skillet.

posset pan: (kitchen) a pan used to heat posset, a beverage of milk, wine, spices, and sugar thought to promote sleep in the 17th and early 18th centuries.

postage meter: (stamps) a mail-franking device. The machine can print the postage amount directly on an envelope or on tape for affixing to parcels. The amount of prepaid postage the meter is allowed to dispense is set by the post office prior to being sealed.

postal card: (stamps) a government-issue card bearing a printed stamp. See also *post card*.

postal stationery: (stamps) stationery bearing an imprinted postage stamp; sold at post offices.

post card: (paper) a card for mailing that does not require an envelope. Introduced in Austria in 1869; by 1880 post cards were popular in the United States. Early cards were published by Nister and Gabriel, and Raphael Tuck. Condition is important to the collector. See also *postal card*.

postmark: 1. (stamps) the part of a cancellation bearing the date and originating post office. **2.** (stamps) any significant postal marking.

posy ring: (jewelry) a ring engraved inside with a short motto or rhyme.

pot: (armor) a 17th-century term for any type of open helmet. Modern usage confines the term to a large, wide-brimmed helmet used by pikemen in the 17th century.

pot brush: (kitchen) a brush used for polishing metals.

pot button: (metal) a button made from a piece of brass taken from a brass pot.

pot dogs: (kitchen, hearth accessories) fire irons on which pots and pans rest while their contents cook over the coals.

potiche: (ceramics) a large, Chinese, covered jar made of porcelain.

potichomania: (glass) glass decorated with paper designs that have been fixed to the inside of the glass. This method of decorating was done in Oriental style and was popular about 1850.

pot lid: (ceramics) a pottery cover made for a commercial product. First made in England by F & R Pratt. Most have transfer designs under glaze. Made from the early 19th century until around 1890. Some of the best examples are signed "Jesse Austin" or "J. A."

pottery: (ceramics) an opaque clay earthenware fired at a low temperature.

pottle pot: (kitchen) a pot with a one-quart capacity.

pounce: (desk accessories) finely powdered pumice; used to prevent ink from spreading. It was sprinkled on the paper before or after writing.

pounce box: (desk accessories) a small vessel used to store and sprinkle pounce on writing paper. Also called *dredger*. See also *pounce*.

pouncing: (metal) embossing done on a thin layer of sheet metal by hammering it from the underside. This often produces a powdery appearance.

Poupard: (dolls) a doll with a head and upper body mounted on a stick, usually covered with a skirt, instead of a lower body.

poured wax doll's head: a doll's head made by pouring a small amount of wax into a mold, tipping it from side to side to make sure all areas are covered, allowing it to dry, and then pouring in more wax and repeating the process until the desired thickness is obtained. Many of these dolls have solid heads — the wax additions continued until the mold was full.

pourpoint: (armor) a close-fitting leather garment with padding and decorative needlework; worn as light armor under heavy armor in the 16th and 17th centuries.

pouty doll: a doll with a pouting look on her face.

powder bowl: (personal accessories) a bowl that holds a lady's face powder and often a powder puff. Styles may be plain or ornate, footed or flat; made of glass, metal, or porcelain. Also called *powder jar*.

powder flask: (weapons) a case for carrying gunpowder. Made of horn, leather, metal, wood, shell, or fabric.

powder horn: (weapons) one of the earliest and most widely used types of powder flasks; used to carry gunpowder. The horn is permanently capped at the wide end, and temporarily plugged at the small end.

powder jar: (personal accessories) bowl that holds a lady's face powder and often a powder puff. Styles may be plain or ornate, footed or flat; made of glass, metal, or porcelain. Also called *powder bowl*.

prairie school: (architecture) a style of architecture and design (furniture and accessories) developed by the American architect Frank Lloyd Wright, who designed the Guggenheim Museum in New York City and the Imperial Hotel in Tokyo. See *Wright, Frank Lloyd*.

pram: (vehicles) a baby carriage or buggy. Also called *perambulator*.

Pratt Fenton ware: (ceramics) a transfer-decorated ware produced in the 19th century in Fenton, England. Extensively reproduced.

Pratt ware: (ceramics) an 18th-century cream-colored ware made by Felix Pratt in the Staffordshire section of England.

prayer rug: (floor coverings) Oriental carpet, usually small, with a design that is plain on one end and comes to a peak or tower at the other, resembling the altar of the Mohammedan mosque.

precancel: (stamps) a type of stamp used since World War I that has the cancellation printed on it before it is sold; used for bulk mailings.

Precious Moments: (collectibles) a series of pastel-colored figurines with a religious overtone designed by Samuel Butcher and produced by Enesco since 1979. The most desirable are the first twenty-one, which are not marked. All others have a mark denoting the year they were made.

pre-Columbian artifact: an artifact from Central and South America that predates Columbus's arrival in 1492. Some date as far back as 4000 B.C.

Preiss, Ferdinand: (design, fine art) a German sculptor who produced art-deco-style dancers in ivory and bronze.

prene: (kitchen) an iron pan.

presale estimate: (auctions) the amount that authorities at an auction house think a particular item will bring; often published in the catalog at prestigious auctions. Presale estimates aren't available at all auctions.

presale exhibit: an exhibit prior to an auction of the merchandise to be offered at the sale. Also called *preview*.

presentation box: a gold or silver box, usually engraved, given in commemoration of an event or as a reward for some outstanding service. From the late 1700s to the early 1800s in England.

press: (furniture) an upright case or closet; used to store clothes or other articles. It may have drawers below.

press bed: (furniture) a folding bed that comes out of, and folds back into, a cabinet. Also called *close bed.*

press cupboard: (furniture) a tall cupboard in two sections with a recessed top. Both the top and bottom have drawers that are concealed by doors.

pressed back: (furniture) the back of a chair with a design pressed or stamped in, rather than carved.

pressed cane seat: (furniture) a prewoven cane seat set into grooves in a wooden frame.

pressed glass: patterned glass created by forcing molten glass into a patterned mold. A method developed in the United States during the 1820s as a substitute for cut glass. See also *cut glass.*

press-top highboy: (furniture) a highboy (tall chest of drawers on legs) with several drawers on the bottom and a cupboard on the top (where a classic highboy would have more drawers). Also called *Westchester highboy* and *cupboard-top highboy.*

prestamp cover: (stamps) postal stationery, such as an envelope; used before postage stamps were introduced.

preview: an exhibit prior to an auction of the merchandise to be offered at the sale. Also called *presale exhibit.*

pricket candlestick: (lighting) a candlestick with a spike (pricket) on which the candle is impaled. Made in many sizes from very small to 6-feet-tall examples, which were used in churches. Originated in China.

pricket plug: (lighting) a plug with a spike on one end of it. The plug fits into the end or socket of a conventional candlestick turning it into a pricket candlestick. See also *pricket candlestick.*

pricket socket: (lighting) a plug with a socket on the top and a deep, narrow hole in the bottom. The bottom hole fits over the spike on a pricket candlestick, making it into a conventional socket candlestick. See also *pricket candlestick.*

prickle: (domestic accessories) a basket made of willow or wicker.

prie-dieu: (furniture) a low chair with a high back; used for praying.

prig: (kitchen) a skillet made of brass.

priming flask: (weapons) a small flask used to carry the fine powder for priming matchlocks, wheel locks, and flintlocks. They are usually decorated.

primitives: paintings, crafts, and decorations on everything from furniture to tinware produced by people who had no formal training. Some of these works are remarkably good; others show a poor use of space and balance; but all are sought for their quaint charm and historical significance. Also called *folk art.* See also *naive art.*

Prince of Wales: (furniture) a chair made in the Adams or Hepplewhite style featuring a three-feather motif carved into the back.

print: (fine art) a duplicate of an original done by any of a number of printing methods. Original prints are very desirable. Some of the most sought are by: John J. Audubon, Currier and Ives, R. Atkinson Fox, Bessie Pease Gutman, Louis Icart, Kellog, Kurz and Allison, Wallace Nutting, and Louis Prang. See also *original print.*

print decoration: a transfer or decal decoration — not hand painted.

printed burlap: (textiles) Victorian-era burlap printed on both sides with the same designs used on costly carpets; used as rugs or wall hangings by people who could not afford quality carpeting.

Prior, William Matthew: (folk art) a folk artist from Boston who advertised he that painted portraits with "a flat likeness without a shade or shadow."

Priscilla sewing stand: (furniture) a portable sewing stand with a handle and two slant-top, covered storage spaces.

prison coverlet: (textiles) coverlet of linen, wool, cotton, or a combination of those materials woven by prisoners during the 1800s. They were made under the instructions of a master weaver and were marketed by county commissioners. None of these coverlets are signed or marked in the corner as was the custom of the day.

private treaty: (stamps) the agreed term for the private sale of stamps between two parties.

production cel: (motion picture memorabilia) an original drawing used to create animated films and cartoons. Also called *animation cel.*

profile perdu: (fine art, photography) a portrait in which the subject is neither full face nor profile but somewhere in between.

projection front: (furniture) a furniture unit with a protruding top drawer.

proof: 1. (coins) a coin with a mirror finish that has been made for display purposes rather than for circulation as currency. These coins often have a different metallic content from their counterparts that are struck for use. **2.** (stamps) print of a sheet of stamps used for checking the accuracy and register during various stages of stamp production. These include engraver's proofs and die proofs.

proof of armor: prior to firearms, armor that had been tested by having a bolt from a crossbow fired at it at short range. Later, armor tested by firing a musket at it. If the piece passed the test, it was stamped with the maker's mark.

provenance: the history and source of an item — where it was made or originated and who owned it.

prunt: (glass) a piece of molten glass applied to a glass object to decorate it. There often was a name or some advertising on the prunt.

pucella: (glass) an iron tool used in shaping blown glass.

puffed armor: (armor) stylish armor decorated with puffs and slashes in imitation of the civilian dress in vogue during the 17th century.

pulk: (furniture) a short, squat stool.

Pull, Georges (1810–1889): (ceramics) a 19th-century French potter who, with his teacher Charles Avisseau, produced earthenware figures and dishes from the molds of Bernard Palissy, a 16th-century potter.

pulsifer carpet: (floor coverings) a floor cloth with a painted design. Made from 1800 to about 1850 by N. Pulsifer in England. The rugs range in size from very small up to 18 by 36 feet.

punching: (metal) holes punched in metal to form a design. Floral patterns were particularly popular during the 17th century, when this process was used extensively to decorate silver.

punch kettle: (kitchen) a huge teapot used for making and serving hot punch. Popular in the 18th century.

punt mark: (glass) a manufacturer's mark on the bottom or base of a bottle; widely used after *ca.* 1850.

punty rod: (glass) a long, metal rod attached to a glass object during the finishing process. It is used after the blow pipe has been removed. Also called *pontil rod.*

pupitre desk: (furniture) a very large desk of the type used by scholars or in a counting house.

Purinton: (ceramics) a company that produced pieces decorated with fruit, flowers, and Pennsylvania Dutch designs done in a primitive style in bold colors. Although this company was started in Ohio in 1936, it was not until the firm moved to Shippenville, Pennsylvania, in 1941 that they started producing this country-style kitchenware for which they are known. The factory closed in 1959.

Puritan furniture: the furniture made in New England by the Puritans during the 1600s. Also called *Pilgrim furniture.*

pushti: (floor coverings) a small rug measuring approximately 2 by 3 feet.

putto: (fine art) a cherubic figure of a small male child — common in Renaissance art.

Putz: (religious) a display of religious figures such as the Nativity used at Christmas. Generally considered German, the Putz actually originated in Czechoslovakia.

puzzle: (collectibles) a picture or shape made up of small individual pieces. Jigsaw puzzles of wood, paper, or cardboard are collectible. The first puzzles were made by London mapmaker John Spilsbury in the 1760s. A missing piece greatly reduces the value of a puzzle. The box should be intact.

puzzle jug: (ceramics) a jug with a large, round body and a narrow, pierced neck. The challenge is to pour from it without spilling. Popular in England in the 1600s and 1700s.

pyralin: the earliest form of plastic. Invented by John Wesley Hyatt in the 1860s. Highly flammable. Also called *celluloid, French ivory,* and *pyroxylin.*

pyriform: (decoration) shaped like a pear.

pyrites lock: (weapons) a lock very much like the flintlock in principle and action but designed to use pyrites, a natural mineral sulfide, instead of flint.

pyrography: a method of producing designs on wood, leather, and other materials by the use of flames or heated irons.

pyroxylin: the earliest form of plastic. Invented by John Wesley Hyatt in the 1860s. Highly flammable. Also called *celluloid, French ivory,* and *pyralin.*

Q

quadran: (coins) a rare Roman coin featuring the head of Hercules.

quadrant: (scientific instruments) a measuring scale shaped in a quarter circle.

quadrigatus: (coins) common Roman Republican coin with Jupiter in a chariot on one side, a head on the other.

quaich: 1. (tableware) a mug with two handles. 2. (tableware) a Scottish drinking vessel made in the form of a barrel; used from 1600s on. First ones were made of wood, then silver trim was added. Later ones are of silver or pewter.

Quare, Daniel: (clocks) a London clockmaker in the late 1600s.

quarrel: 1. (furniture) a small square or diamond-shaped pane of glass in a latticed window. 2. (weapons) the arrow for a crossbow. It is shorter and heavier than arrows used with the long bow. Also called *bolt* and *carreau*.

quarrier: (lighting) a small, short, square wax candle.

quarter-bound: (books) a book that has a leather-covered spine. See also *half-bound* and *leather-bound*.

quarter-sawn (-sawed): planks or boards sawed from quartered logs so the seasonal rings are nearly at right angles to the wide face.

quarter-strike clock: a clock with a chime that sounds on the hour, half hour and quarter hour.

quartetto tables: (furniture) a set of four nesting tables, fitted together so that any one table can be pulled out without disturbing the others. Designed by Sheraton.

quatrecouleurs: (decoration) various shades of gold combined in a decoration.

quatrefoil: (decoration) an ornament with four lobes or leaves, or a flower with four petals.

quatrefoil table: (furniture) a round table with four scallops around the edges. See also *scalloped*.

Queen Anne doll: a carved, fixed-eyed, jointed doll; popular during the 1700s.

Queen Anne scale: a very fine balance scale; used to weigh spices during the 1800s. Most of them have copper or silver scoops.

Queen Anne style: (furniture) the simple, yet elegant, style of furniture produced from 1702 until the 1720s. Proportions were perfect, with gentle, curved lines. Figured veneers were used as adornment; carving was not used often.

queen's metal: (pewter) a fine pewter consisting of 9 parts tin to 1 part antimony, 1 part bismuth, and 1 part lead.

queen's pattern: (decoration) a pattern consisting of alternating spirals of red on a white background and white on a blue background embellished with gold; first used *ca.* 1770.

queen's ware: (ceramics) a yellow ware so named because of the queen's interest in it — experts disagree on which queen. It was either Queen Mary or Queen Charlotte.

quierboyle: (armor) leather boiled and molded into shape then allowed to dry and harden; used for armor throughout Europe and the East. Also called *cuir bouilli*.

quill case: a brass, pewter, silver, or tin cylinder with a top; used to carry a quill pen. Also called *quill holder*.

quill embroidery: (needlework, Native American) North American Indian embroidery that features dyed porcupine quills sewn onto leather.

quill holder: a brass, pewter, silver, or tin cylinder with a top; used to carry a quill pen. Also called *quill case*.

quilling: (decoration, glass) bands of glass pinched together into wavy lines and applied to glass objects as decoration. Also called *pinch trailing*.

quillon: (weapons) the cross piece on a sword that comes between the blade and the handle; designed to protect the hand from the blade.

quill pencils: (fine art) brushes of many sizes called, according to size, *crow, pigeon, duck, goose, extra small swan, little swan, middle swan,* and (the largest) *big swan.* Also called *hair pencils.*

quillwork: (decoration) thin strips of paper (about 1/8 inch wide) that are twisted, fluted, or rolled into tight scrolls and then arranged on a background surface into designs resembling mosaics.

quilt: (textiles) any double fabric sewn with padding in between layers. Often the layers are stitched in a design that goes through all the layers. Some quilts are made from pieces of scrap material sewn together. From the 17th century on.

quilted armor: armor made of several layers of material quilted or pourpointed together. Popular in Europe in the 14th century.

Quimper: (ceramics) a tin-glazed hand-painted earthenware pottery dating from the 1600s. Produced in Quimper, France, in three factories: the Grande Maison de HB established in the 1700s, with wares marked "HB" in some form — "HB" in a triangle is the most prized; Porquier ware, made from the late 1700s, marked "P" or "AP"; and Jule HenRiot beginning in 1886, marked "HR" or "HenRiot Quimper." In 1968 Jules HenRiot and the Grande Maison de HB merged.

quirk: (glass) a pane of glass that is an equilateral parallelogram with oblique angles.

quitesol: (fashion accessories) a parasol.

quiver: (weapons) a case for carrying arrows.

quizzing fan: (fashion accessories) a fan with holes covered with a transparent material. When the fan was open, a lady could demure behind it while she peeked through the holes observing what was going on. Popular in the mid-1700s. Also called *peeking fan.*

ℛ

rabbet: (furniture) a groove that runs the length of a piece of wood in which the edge of a second piece will fit. For example, the bottom of a drawer fits into the rabbets in the side pieces of the drawer.

rabbit's ear: (furniture) a Windsor-style chair with a back slat between two ends that stick up like rabbit ears.

rabbit stick: (weapons) a throwing stick; used by the Hopi and other tribes of the Southwest.

raden: (orientalia) an inlay of mother-of-pearl.

Radford: (ceramics) jasper ware in the manner of Wedgewood first made by Albert Radford in 1896 when he worked for Tiffany in Ohio. Also produced in Broadway, Virginia, and Zanesville, Ohio, until 1912. Other styles of Radford pottery are Redera, Ruko, Thera, and Velvety Art Ware.

radial markings: (coins) parallel grooves or markings around the rim of a coin.

radiating glory: (heraldry) a glory with lines indicating rays piercing the edges. See also *glory.*

radio bench: (furniture) a low, backless upholstered seat; placed near a radio before the age of television.

radio premium: (collectibles) an item given away, usually in exchange for a box top or other proof of purchase from a sponsor's products. Most of them feature the hero of the program. Amos and Andy, Buck Rogers, Charlie McCarthy, Dick Tracy, Fibber McGee and Molly, Jack Armstrong, the Lone Ranger, Orphan Annie, Superman, and Tom Mix are a few of the most popular characters.

ragboard: (fine art, prints) board made of 100 percent rag; the first choice for matting or mounting a print, since it contains nothing that will damage or change a picture over time.

rag doll: any cloth doll. Early examples were made from rags or sewing scraps.

rag rug: (floor coverings) a rug made from remnants of clothing or other cloth items, cut into long strips and woven.

rail: (furniture) a horizontal support for the frame of cabi-network or paneling.

railroad china: (railroad memorabilia) china specially designed for a railroad company and bearing their logo (either on the front or back-stamped). China from small lines, which were not operating long, are the most desirable to the collectors.

railroad menu: (railroad memorabilia) an ornamental menu to display the gustatory offerings of a dining car in the heyday of railroads. Early menus with decorative covers are the most popular. Often these menus are die-cut in the shape of a particular food and bear the name and logo of the railroad.

railroad playing cards: (railroad memorabilia) souvenir packs of playing cards distributed by railroads around the turn of the century. The earliest cards are in a two-piece slip case and the faces of these cards often have pictures on them. Later cards are in cardboard boxes with folding end closures. Early packs are the most desirable. Condition, both of cards and boxes, is very important to the collector.

raised: (design) that portion of a design protruding above the background surface.

raised work: (needlework) an ambitious type of embroidery that has a center decoration depicting a biblical scene and a border of fruits, flowers, leaves, birds, and animals. Popular in the 17th century. Also called *stump work.*

raising: (metal) the hand method of shaping a hollow vessel from a sheet of metal by hammering it on a block of wood to stretch and curve it.

rakan: (orientalia) depictions of the followers of Buddha; used in art and in decorating porcelain and other wares. Also called *lohan*.

rake: (furniture) the slant or angle of the back of a chair, sofa, or other piece of furniture.

raku ware: (ceramics) soft Japanese earthenware.

Ramsey, David: (clocks) a well-known clockmaker in Edinburgh and London from 1590 until 1655.

ram's foot: (furniture, silver) a cloven foot motif; used on spoon handles and furniture feet.

ram's head motif: (decoration) a motif representing the mask of a ram's head. Found on Adams furniture, as well as silverware, porcelain, and other items during the classical revival period of the 18th and 19th centuries. See also *Adams, Robert.*

Randolph, Benjamin (*ca.* **1762):** (furniture) an American furniture maker who produced fine, Chippendale-style pieces in Philadelphia from 1762 until 1792.

ranter: (tableware) a huge mug for drinking beer.

rapier: 1. (weapons) a long, straight, slender, two-edged sword with a cuplike guard; used in the 16th and 17th centuries. Replaced the broadsword when the use of armor was discontinued. **2.** (weapons) a light sword lacking a cutting edge; used in the 18th century only for thrusting.

rappen: (coins) a small, copper Swiss coin; issued from the late 18th century to the early 19th century.

rare: a term denoting the relative availability of a type of item. If an item is labeled *rare,* it means there are fewer examples available than if it were labeled *scarce*. A rare item usually, but not always, commands more money. See also *scarce*.

rasp: (tools) a grater.

ratafia glass: a cordial glass with a tall, narrow bowl. Dating from the late 1700s.

rat foot: (furniture) similar to a ball-and-claw foot, but instead of a ball, the foot is clutching a pad. See also *ball-and-claw foot.*

rattail spoon: (silver) a spoon distinguished by a tapered rib running down the back of the bowl; the most common type of spoon during the late 17th and early 18th centuries.

Raven, Samuel: (design) an English decorator who painted cigar cases, card cases, snuffboxes, and the like from 1818 until about 1843. He was extensively copied.

Ravenscroft Glass: (glass) the first flint glass. First made in England *ca.* 1675. Although examples are rare, those that have survived are usually marked with a raven's head.

rayed: (glass) a design resembling the spokes of a wheel that is incised on the bottoms of glass objects. It is usually visible from the top of the article as well as the bottom.

real: 1. (coins) a silver Spanish coin; issued from the 14th century. **2.** (coins) former monetary units of Spain, Brazil, and Portugal.

reamer: (tools) a cone-shaped kitchen utensil; used to extract citrus-fruit juice.

rebated sword: (weapons) a sword with a protected, blunt point; used for practice and modern fencing.

recamier sofa: (furniture) a sofa with high ends and a scrolled back. From the French Directoire period (1790 to 1805).

recased: (books) a book that has had the covers rebound.

recast: (metal) to use the original mold to cast an object after the original or first run has been completed. Unauthorized reproduction castings are from a new mold made from a cast object. During the casting there is some shrinking, therefore an object cast in a second mold will be smaller than the object recast in the original mold. There is also a loss of fine detail in objects remolded. For example, a reproduction of a Remington bronze will be smaller and lack the delicate details of the original.

recessed: an area set back from the main part. An indentation.

recessed carving: (furniture) carving in which the background is removed, leaving the design raised. The background is either punched or stippled to create an even surface and contrast to the design. Also called *sunk carving.*

rectilinear: (furniture) forming a straight line.

recto: (books) the right-hand page or front side of a leaf. See also *verso.*

red anchor mark: (ceramics) a famous mark used by Chelsea Porcelain.

red china: (ceramics) a fine red stoneware made at Staffordshire, England, in the 17th and 18th centuries.

redrawn: (stamps) artwork done on a stamp design that is already in circulation.

redware: (ceramics) earthenware of red clay made by American colonists. Starting in the 1600s and becoming very popular in the 1700s and 1800s, the country's red clay was used to fashion simple, practical items such as dinnerware, flowerpots, milk pans, and pie plates. Slip, a liquid clay, was often used to add decoration in the form of flowers, stars, or zigzag lines.

Red Wing: (ceramics) a pottery in Red Wing, Minnesota, that opened in 1878 and closed in 1967. They first produced crocks, flower pots, jugs, and other useful wares. A line of art pottery was added in the 1920s. In the 1930s vases and dinnerware were added. Early pieces are the most highly prized.

reeding: (furniture) parallel convex groovings resembling thin reeds.

reed top: (furniture) a cylinder-type desk lid constructed of a horizontal series of thin strips of wood glued at the back to canvas. It glides on curved runners at the front and is flexible enough to store in a perpendicular position at the back. Most often found on rolltop desks. Also called *tambour door.* See also *rolltop desk.*

reentry: (stamps) a correction made on an engraving that fails to cover or eliminate the original work. This usually results in a double image when the stamp is printed.

refectory porringer: (metal) a low metal bowl with solid handles, or ears, often with the insignia or symbol of an organization on it.

refectory table: (furniture) a long, narrow table with underleaves that pull out and up to extend the surface. (A refectory is a room where meals are served.) Also called *draw table.*

reflector telescope: (scientific instruments) a telescope that uses mirrors to gather light; used for celestial observations. Suggested by Newton in 1668, the method was not perfected until the 18th century.

reform flask: (ceramics) a spirit flask depicting prominent politicians and royal figures. These brown, stone-glazed flasks were made *ca.* 1832.

refractor telescope: (scientific instruments) the first and simplest telescope, in which lenses are used to gather light. Invented in 1608 by

Lippershey and used by Galileo in 1609.

Regal China: (ceramics) manufacturers of cookie jars, salt and pepper shakers, and Jim Beam Bottles. Regal China has been in business in Antioch, Illinois, since 1938.

regard ring: (jewelry) a ring set with a ruby, emerald, garnet, amethyst, another ruby, and a diamond — in that order. The first letter of the names of the stones combine to spell *regard.*

Regency: (furniture) the furniture period between Louis XIV and Louis XV, from 1715 to 1723. It reflected the beginning of an opulent style. Regency furniture has more curves, less bulk, and more added ornamentation than Louis XIV furniture. The cabriole leg was first used in this period — the years Philippe d'Orleans was Regent for the minority of Louis XV.

reggivaso: (furniture) an 18th-century sculptured vase stand, often in the form of chained black slaves, page boys, or mythological gods.

registry marks: (ceramics) letters and numbers given English earthenware by the Office of Registration and Design from 1842 until 1866 and then again from 1868 to 1883. These identifying marks appeared on the wares.

regular issue: (stamps) a stamp used for regular delivery mail as opposed to airmail or special delivery.

regulator clock: a sturdy 19th-century precision timepiece with a simple design; used for astronomical observations or as a standard for regulating other timepieces. They were designed with no striking mechanism in order to avoid undue vibration, and have three separated hands to reduce friction. They also have dead beat escapements and compensating pendulums for changes in temperature.

reistafel: (ceram dishes used to courses of an meal. Literally, *n*

relic box: a sn part of some relic built into it.

relief: (decoration) a form that projects out from or above a flat background.

relined: (fine art) an old canvas with another canvas bonded to the back of the original to cover a rip or a pin hole, or just to strengthen the canvas. Relined canvases are either glued or waxed. Waxed is better.

reliquary: (religious) a receptacle for sacred relics; used primarily in churches during the medieval era. Most feature fine carvings, enameling, gold, or precious gems. Some were made in the shape of a finger, arm, toe, or whatever relic they were meant to hold.

remargined: (books) the restoration of one or more of the outer margins of a page. If all four margins have been renewed the page is *inlaid;* if only the inner margin has been restored, the page is *extended.* See also *inlaid* and *extended.*

remarque: 1. (prints) a mark in the margin of an engraving plate indicating its state of development before completion. **2.** (prints) the proof or print carrying such a mark. **3.** (prints) a pencil sketch done outside a picture but on the same paper. Occasionally done in ink.

remboitage: (books) taking a book out of its original binding and placing it in another.

Remington, Frederic: (fine art) a painter and sculptor whose subjects were Indians, cowboys, and hunters of the American West. Late 18th and early 19th centuries.

Remington rolling block rifle: (weapons) a breechloader. Model 1870 is considered the most widely used breechloader in the world. It as the official military weapon of a number of countries and was also used as a sporting gun.

Renaissance: the European revival of classical ideals in art, literature, and learning. It began in Italy in the 14th century and spread to France, Spain, Germany, the Low Countries, England, and the rest of Europe. The term denotes the period of the 14th to 16th centuries, a time of transition from medieval to modern.

renaissance revival: (furniture) the 19th-century revival of designs copied from the 15th- to 17th-century European Renaissance.

repaired: objects restored to usefulness or beauty with glue, solder, screws, or other materials. Broken or missing parts are not replaced. See also *restored*.

repeater: (clocks) a clock or watch that will restrike, at the pull or push of a knob, the last hour and, in some, the last quarter hour or minute. The mechanism was invented in 1676 for telling time in the dark.

replica: 1. (design) a close copy or reproduction. **2.** (fine art) an exact copy of a work executed either by the original artist or with his supervision. **3.** (stamps) a reproduction of a stamp; usually used to fill out an empty spot in a collection. Because they are intentionally made with subtle differences from the original, they are not considered forgeries or fakes.

repoussé: 1. (decoration) a design hammered into metal on the reverse side. **2.** (decoration) the method for creating a repoussé design.

representational art: (fine art) art in which objects are portrayed realistically and are clearly recognizable.

reproduction: the duplication or copy of original objects. A true reproduction is an exact copy of an original; a poor or cheap reproduction lacks the details and quality of the original. See also *in the style of*.

rerebrace: (armor) armor plate for the upper arm. From the 14th century.

reseau: (textiles) the net foundation for lace.

reserve: (auctions) a minimum price set on an object to be auctioned. If no bid equals the reserve, the article is withdrawn.

resetting: (books) the regluing of the loose pages of a book.

Resht patchwork: (floor coverings) a mosaic patchwork for prayer rugs and covers. Produced at Resht, Persia, in the 18th and 19th centuries. The best examples have the designs inlaid in colored felts and the outlines and details stitched in colored silks.

resist printing: 1. (textiles) an ancient method of printing fabric by treating the area of design with a resist substance before applying dye. The finished cloth usually has a white design on a dyed background. **2.** (ceramics) method used to decorate pottery; similar to textile resist printing.

Restoration: (furniture) English furniture produced during the reigns of Charles II (1660 to 1685) and James I (1685 to 1689). Furniture is made of walnut, is less massive than early Jacobean, and is often gilded or inlaid. The style reflects a continental influence. Also called *Jacobean, late*. See also *Jacobean, early*.

restored: an object is repaired with broken or missing parts replaced and surface refinished if necessary.

restrike: a new impression made from an old plate or mold.

reticella work: (textiles) an Italian needlepoint fabric with elaborate cutwork; used extensively during the Renaissance period.

reticulated: (decoration) a design resembling a network, foliage, or a diamond cluster pierced through metal, glass, or porcelain.

reticule: a purse with a drawstring top.

revenue stamp: (stamps) a stamp issued for paying excise tax or other government fees for customs duty, stock transfer, document registration, and other legal transactions.

Revere, Paul (1735-1818): (silver) a Huguenot and American patriot who became a famous Boston silversmith after changing his name from Apollos Rivoire. Paul Revere bowls are still being made.

reverse painting: (decoration) painting on the underside or backside of glass objects, such as a glass lamp shade, mirror, or dish, with the obverse artwork showing through the glass.

revival piece: (furniture) a copy of an earlier American piece, usually of high quality. Made between the mid-1800s and the early 1930s.

rhodium: (metal) a white metal often used for plating.

ribband back: (furniture) a chair back with a ribbon-motif ornament.

ribbed: (furniture) grooves or furrows routed in wood. Also called *channeled.*

ribbon core swirl: (marbles) a glass marble with circling, ribbonlike swirls in the center.

ricasso: (weapons) the squared area of a rapier blade adjacent the hilt.

Richard glass: cameo art glass made during the 1920s in France. Richard's work depicts flowers and natural scenes in an acid-cut cameo glass, often with many layers. A one-time employee of Galle, Richard signed his pieces with his name.

Richmond bed warmer: (domestic) a copper bed warmer made in Boston, Massachusetts, around 1830 by H.D. Richmond. Pans held hot water, not coals.

Ridgeway case: (metal) a metal case for a pipe, matches, and tobacco; used by military men during the Civil War. Decorated with patriotic or military designs.

Ridgway: (ceramics) a good earthenware produced by Job and George Ridgway in their factory in Staffordshire, England. Starting in 1792, the Ridgway brothers made wares marked "Ridgway, Smith, & Ridgway." Later wares are marked "Job & George Ridgway." In the early 1800s each founded their own business — The Bell Works and Cauldon Pottery. Bell's stoneware and earthenware are largely blue transfer decorated. Pieces are marked "J. & W. Ridgway" or "J. & W. R." In 1848 the mark "William Ridgway" came into use. The Cauldon Pottery produced fine porcelain and other wares marked "J. R." in a crest. Ridgway Pottery is still being made.

Rie, Lucie: (ceramics) an Austrian-born potter who worked in London from 1938 until 1958. Her glazes, made with metallic oxides, and her modern-looking designs distinguish her pieces. Wares are marked with an impressed "R & L" in a rectangle.

rifling: (weapons) spiral grooves cut in the inside of the barrel of a firearm, causing the ball to rotate, providing greater accuracy.

right tinware: (metal) ware made of pure tin, not plate.

rim lock: (furniture) a lock mechanism completely within a rectangular case and attached to the inside surface of a door.

ring-and-ball turned: (furniture) a wood-turning design made up of alternate circular bands and balls.

ringed armor: armor made of metal rings fastened onto cloth or leather garments; used in Europe during the Middle Ages.

rising hood: (clocks) the original long-case clock with a hood that slides up in channels on the backboard and is held there with a latch while the dial is adjusted. As the heights of clocks increased, this type of hood proved impractical, and the hinged door came into use.

rising stretcher: (furniture) a stretcher that rises in a curve between the legs it supports.

rising sun ornament: (decoration) a carved, semi-circular form, similar in appearance to an open fan; used on American furniture in the late 18th century. The ornament suggests a rising sun with emitting rays. Also called *setting sun ornament.*

Riviera: (ceramics) a lightweight, inexpensive, unmarked dinnerware. Made by Homer Laughlin China Company from 1938 until about 1949. The plain colors include ivory, light green, mauve, red, and yellow.

rivière: (jewelry) a long necklace with diamonds or other gemstones set individually so the necklace is flexible. Worn in the early 1800s.

roan: (books) a thin, inferior leather; used as a substitute for Morocco on book covers. From late 18th century.

Robertson: (ceramics) a small pottery run by Fred H. Robertson and his son Fred, first in Los Angeles, California, in 1934 and by 1943, in Hollywood. Most pieces are hand-turned, but some are molded and have low-relief designs. The ware was known for fine crackle and crystalline glazes. The business closed in 1952. Robertson is marked "Robertson," "R," or "F.H.R."

Robj bottle: a figural bottle in earthenware, glass, or porcelain made from 1925 until 1931 for the Robj retail store in Paris. These art deco bottles were very popular in the United States.

Roblin: (ceramics) a San Francisco pottery established about 1890 and destroyed by the earthquake of 1906. Much of the ware was molded in relief. Linna Irelan, co-owner with Alexander Robertson, was responsible for the decorating and most pieces reflect her affinity for nature. Lizards and mushrooms adorn many Roblin pieces. This buff, red, or white clay ware is marked "Roblin" or with a bear.

rocailles: 1. (decoration) tiny seed beads made of glass; often sewn on garments. **2.** (decoration) designs using flowing lines.

Rockaway: (vehicles) a four-wheeled carriage with two seats, open sides, and a fixed top. First made in Rockaway, New Jersey.

Rockingham glaze: (ceramics) a well-known purplish brown manganese glaze; used in the 1800s by factories in Staffordshire and in the Rockingham factory in Swinton, England.

rocking ship clock: a clock with a ship that rocks with the swinging pendulum.

Rockwell, Norman: (fine art, collectibles) American artist whose distinctive illustrations graced the covers of many issues of the *Saturday Evening Post*. His artistic commentaries on life in middle America have been used on limited-edition plates, figurines, posters, calendars, and other items.

rococo: (furniture) an elaborate 18th-century style of ornamentation full of curves and images of rocks, shells, foliage, flowers and other natural motifs.

rococo revival: (furniture) a popular late-19th-century Victorian style of furniture patterned after the 18th-century French court furniture. See also *rococo.*

roemer: (glass) a pale green glass goblet with a spherical bowl and a conical foot. Dating back to medieval Germany, it became popular in England and Holland in the late 1800s.

Rogers, John: (fine art, figurines) statues made by John Rogers, a machinist in Manchester, New Hampshire, from 1859 until 1892. His groups, done in bronze or painted plaster, depict life during the period. The Civil War, horses, Shakespeare, and the theater were often his inspiration. He made eighty different designs.

rogin: (orientalia) a Japanese decorative technique of burnishing powdered silver on lacquer ware.

roiro: (orientalia) a Japanese black lacquer ware with a mirrorlike finish.

rolled: (books) a repetitive design or pattern applied to the cover of a book with an engraved wheel. The engraving wheel is called a roll.

rolled edge: (decoration) an edge curved into, or away from, the center of a glass, porcelain, silver, or other article.

rolling pin: (glass, kitchen) a roller for making pastry. Glass rolling pins were made at Bristol and Nailsea Glassworks in England in the 18th and early 19th centuries. They were made for sale in inexpensive markets. Many are painted or engraved with poetry or sayings. Most of them were hung as ornaments on kitchen walls.

rolltop desk: (furniture) a writing table or desk with the upper compartments covered with a curved panel of horizontal slats backed with canvas. The flexible lid slides up curved grooves to store against the backboard. See also *reed top*.

Romanesque: (fine art) religious art done prior to 1200 A.D.

romayne work: 1. (furniture) Renaissance carvings of heads within roundels, vases, scrollwork, and the like. 2. (furniture) portrait medallions copied from ancient Roman coins; used on the backs of Gothic chairs.

rondel dagger: (weapons) a dagger with a disc-shaped guard and pommel.

Rookwood Pottery: (ceramics) pottery made from ca. 1880 until 1967 in Cincinnati, Ohio. Pieces are marked with a flame around stylized "R" and "P" placed back-to-back. Wares made from 1900 until 1967 also have a Roman numeral indicating the year the piece was made. An artist's signature greatly adds to the value. Rookwood depicting animals, birds, or people command very high prices.

rope edge: (decoration) a ropelike design embedded around the edge of an article made of glass, silver, or other material.

Rorstrand: (ceramics) the oldest pottery works in Sweden, established in 1726. Their early soft-paste wares resemble delft. Informal decorations on hard-paste porcelain followed. They make annual Christmas plates.

rose cut: (jewelry) a diamond or other stone with twenty-four triangular facets, cut with a flat base rising to form a point at the top. Rose-cut diamonds are generally cut from macles (flat, triangular diamonds). From the mid-17th century.

rose-engine-turning: (ceramics) various basket-style patterns produced on ceramics.

Roselane: (ceramics) inexpensive novelties produced in California until 1973. Often marked "Roselane, Pasadena, Calif."

Rosemeade: (ceramics) pottery produced from 1940 until 1961 in North Dakota. Best known for their figures of animals and birds which were done either in high-gloss or matte finish. Often stamped "Rosemeade" or marked "Prairie Rose" on a sticker.

Rose Medallion: (orientalia) a popular pattern on Chinese porcelain from *ca*. 1840 until the early 1930s. Shadings of rose are dominant. The ware features panels decorated with birds, flowers, and Chinese figures. The earliest pieces are trimmed in fine gold and have no backmark. Late-1800s examples have an inferior gold trim. Starting in 1890, "China" was usually stamped on Rose Medallion. From 1918 on, "Made in China" was used.

rose-noble: (coins) a large, gold English coin, first issued by Edward IV in 1465. With variations, the coin continued to be struck for more than 200 years.

Rosenthal: (ceramics) a Bavarian pottery operating from 1879 until the present. Their early figurines and tableware are of a fine quality. Many pieces are hand decorated. The company now has a line of collector plates.

rose pompadour: (ceramics) a deep rose color used as a background on Sevres porcelain.

rose quartz marbles: usually pink, stone marbles that frequently have imperfections on them.

Roseville: (ceramics) a pottery founded in Roseville, Ohio, in 1890. The firm closed in 1954 after opening a branch in Zanesville, Ohio. Early wares had painted decorations. Later patterns included relief flowers, fruits, and other designs. most pieces are marked "Roseville, USA," and many have incised numbers. Since much Roseville was hand decorated, the value of a piece can be determined largely by the skill of the artist. The firm made ashtrays, baskets, bookends, ewers, jardinieres, lamps, pitchers, planters, tea sets, and vases.

rosewater ewer and dish: a ewer that held water and the dish into which water was poured at the table for finger washing. From the 16th century.

Rosso Antico: (ceramics) red stoneware produced by Josiah Wedgwood (1730-1795).

Rouen faience: (ceramics) tin-glazed earthenware made at Rouen, France. From the 14th century.

rouge de fer: (ceramics) the French term for a shade of iron red enamel used on Chinese porcelain during the Ming dynasty and later.

Rough-and-Ready Toby: (ceramics) a pitcher in the shape of General Zachary Taylor. Also called *Taylor Toby*.

roulette: 1. (stamps) the incisions made between stamps on a sheet for ease of separation. This form of perforating is desirable when an entire stamp sheet depicts a single design. When left intact, the slits are hardly noticeable and do not detract from the design. **2.** (paper) the small, toothed disk tool used to make dots, slits, or perforations on paper or engravings.

roundabout chair: (furniture) an armchair with the back extending around two sides, leaving two sides and a corner open in front. Also called *corner chair*.

roundel: 1. (furniture) a semicircular form, panel, or window. **2.** (decoration) a semicircular ornament used on woodwork from medieval times.

Round Glass House: (glass) an Irish glass works producing flint glass from the 1690s until *ca*. 1750. When the Round Glass House closed, no flint glass was made in Ireland until 1764.

router: (tools) a tool that furrows out or cuts away surface areas in wood and metal.

Rowland and Marcellus: (ceramics) an American firm that imported blue, transfer printed historical cups and saucers, pitchers, plates, and platters. They operated from 1890 until the 1920s. The imports are marked "Rowland and Marcellus" or "R & M."

Royal Bayreuth: (ceramics) a Bavarian firm founded in 1794 and still in operation. Originally producers of fine-quality dinnerware, the firm added other objects from ashtrays to wall pockets over the years. Their figural items, made from 1870 until about 1920, such as pitchers, and sugar and creamers in the forms of fruits, vegetables, lobsters, eagles, frogs, and the like are most sought after. Early pieces are marked "Royal Bayreuth" with "Bavaria" and a crest. Later, "U.S. Zone" or "Germany" replaced "Bavaria." Some Bayreuth is marked with a date.

royal binding: (books) a binding blocked with the royal arms of a monarch. It does not imply royal ownership.

Royal Bonn: (ceramics) a fine, exquisitely decorated porcelain made in Bonn, Germany, from the 1750s. Most pieces are marked "Bonn."

Royal Copenhagen: (ceramics) a pottery founded in Denmark in 1772 and still in operation. Although they have produced bowls, candlesticks, vases, and other useful items, they are best known for their high-quality figurines and the blue-and-white plates they release annually. Pieces are marked with a crown over three wavy lines.

Royal Copley: (ceramics) an inexpensive pottery made in Sebring, Ohio, by the Spaulding China Company from 1939 until about 1960. Many pieces show an art deco influence. The company made lamps,

pitchers, planters, vases, and other useful items, but it is the figurines that collectors seek. Gold trim adds to the value of a piece. Many items are marked "Royal Copley."

Royal Crown Derby: (ceramics) fine-quality porcelain made in Derby, England, by the Derby Crown Porcelain Company since 1890, when they were selected as manufacturers to Her Majesty. Several marks have been used. The earliest was "Derby" with a crown over it. "Royal Crown Derby, England" followed. In 1921 "Made in England" was used. Pieces marked "Bone China" are post-1945.

Royal Dux: (ceramics) porcelain and pottery figurines, vases, lamps, and the like made by The Duxer Porzellan Manufactur in Dux, Bohemia (now Duchcov, Czechoslovakia), since 1860. Old pieces are marked "E" in a pink triangle or oval and "Bohemia." After World War I, "Bohemia" was dropped and "Made in Czechoslovakia" was added. Older pieces have a matte finish. Later pieces have a glossy glaze.

Royal Flemish: (glass) a plain glass decorated with enamel designs. Made from 1889 by the Mt. Washington Glass Company. Characterized by raised lines that make pieces look like stained glass. Old pieces are quite valuable.

Royal Haeger: (ceramics) a line of dinnerware and accessories produced from 1938. Many pieces are marked "Royal Haeger" in script; others are unmarked.

Royal Rudolstadt: (ceramics) hard-paste porcelain first made in Germany in the 1700s. Marks include a pitchfork, "R," an anchor with "EB," and "RW" in a shield under a crown with "Crown Rudolstadt."

Royal Vienna: (ceramics) a hard-paste porcelain resembling Meissen. First made in

Vienna in 1719. Unmarked until the late 1700s, when a beehive mark under glaze was introduced.

Royal Worcester: (ceramics) porcelain made after 1862 by the Royal Worcester Porcelain Company, Ltd., of Worcester, England. The company name changed to Royal Worcester Spode after a 1976 merger with W.T. Copeland. Their figurines and plates are highly prized. Many marks have been used.

Roycroft: (design, books) an American company founded in 1895 by Elbert Hubbard. It began as a publishing company with the magazine *The Philistine* and went on to publish hundreds of illustrated gift books bound in chamois suede leather. The writings were inspirational, as was Hubbard's *A Message to Garcia* (1899) which sold more than forty million copies. Roycroft (King's Croft) expanded to include a school and factory for furniture, housewares, and art objects in the Arts and Crafts style. Hubbard went down on the *Lusitania* in 1915, but the company continued until 1938. The Roycroft trademark consists of an orb and cross.

Rozenburg: (ceramics) art nouveau ceramics made at The Hague, Netherlands, from 1885 until *ca.* 1915. The Rozenberg factory also made a thin, delicate porcelain called eggshell ware. See also *eggshell ware*.

rubbing: the transfer of a design or inscription by placing paper over a raised or indented surface and rubbing with charcoal or a like agent. Gravestone rubbing is an example of this art.

rubena: (glass) blown art glass that shades from red to clear. Made in the 19th century.

rubena verde: (glass) a transparent glass shading from reds to greens. Made in the late 19th century in West Virginia by Hobbs, Brockunier, and Company.

ruble: 1. (coins) large silver Russian coin. From the 17th century. 2. (coins) the basic monetary unit of the Soviet Union.

rudimentary: (furniture) simple; basic; imperfectly developed.

Rue bed stove: (ceramics) a pottery foot warmer made during the 1800s at the Rue Pottery in New Jersey.

Rumford case: (household accessories) small storage box made to look like a book. Invented by Count Rumford; used during the late 1700s and early 1800s to hide valuables in bookcases.

rummer: (tableware) a large cup or drinking glass with a short stem, oval bowl, and a small foot. Late 18th and early 19th century.

Rumrill: (ceramics) pottery designed by George Rumrill of Little Rock, Arkansas; manufactured by the Red Wing Union Stoneware Company in Minnesota in the 1930s, and later by the Shawnee Pottery Company in Zanesville, Ohio. Production ceased in the 1940s. Most pieces are marked "Rumrill."

runka: (weapons) a pole weapon with a long, narrow blade in the center and a short, lateral blade on each side; used in the 15th and 16th centuries.

runner: 1. (auctions) an aid or porter who transports articles during an auction. 2. (furniture) the supports on which a drawer slides. 3. (furniture) the curved base strips on a rocking chair. 4. (floor coverings) a long, narrow rug.

Ruolz: (metal) a process of gold or silver plating named for the man who invented it.

rupee: 1. (coins) a silver Indian coin issued from the 16th to 19th centuries. 2. (coins) the basic monetary unit of India and several other South Asian countries.

rush: (materials) stems from a group of grasslike marsh plants with pliable, hollow or pithy stems; used for woven chair seats, baskets, and the like.

rushlights: (lighting) candles made of rushes dipped in fat; used first in the 17th century.

Rush, William: (fine art, folk art) the first American sculptor. His mostly figural works have been classified as both folk and fine art.

rushwork: (furniture, decoration) baskets, chair seats and backs, mats, and other items made from rush. See also *rush.*

rustic wood: (furniture) furniture made from tree branches or animal horns.

Ryijy Rug: (floor coverings) a Finnish rug with a knotted pile and a floral, geometric, or plain pattern. Many of these rugs are dated and were made in the early 1800s.

S

Saarinen, Eero (1910-1961):
(furniture, design) Finnish architect who designed modern plastic chairs. He sometimes worked with Charles Eames. See also *Eames, Charles.*

Saarinen, Eliel (1873-1950):
(architecture) Finnish-American architect, father of Eero Saarinen.

sabatons: (armor) mid-16th-century foot armor. The tops are broad and cover only the upper part of the foot; straps run under the sole to keep sabatons in place.

sabeji: (orientalia) a finish on Japanese lacquer ware that resembles old iron.

saber: (weapons) a cavalry sword with a heavy, slightly curved, single-edged blade.

saber leg: (furniture) a slightly curved chair or settee leg. Popular in the late 18th and early 19th century. The front legs flare forward and the back legs curve out behind.

Sabino: (glass) art glass made in the 1920s and 1930s in France by Marius Ernest Sabino. The art deco styling was executed in colored, frosted, and opalescent glass. In 1960 Sabino again produced art glass. This newer glass is easy to distinguish because of its golden opalescence. Sabino died in 1971.

sabot: 1. (fashion accessories) a wooden shoe cut from a single piece of wood. **2.** (fashion accessories) a shoe or sandal with a strip of material across the instep.

sacristy chest: (furniture) a superbly made chest featuring hand carving and linenfold panels; used for storing a priest's vestments. Most of these chests are of Dutch, French, Italian, or Spanish origin.

sad: anything heavy. For example, sadiron. See also *sadiron.*

saddle bottle: a round-bottomed, gourd-shaped bottle made to carry in a sling.

saddle-cheek chair: (furniture) the term used for a wing chair in the 1700s.

saddle seat: (furniture) a chair seat that dips from the center to form a shallow depression on each side — like a saddle. Windsor chairs have this type of seat.

sadiron: (domestic) heavy iron that was heated on the top of the stove; used for ironing clothes. See also *sad.*

sadware: (pewter) heavy pewter chargers and plates. See also *sad.*

sagger: (ceramics) a thin, walled box made of fireclay; used to protect delicate articles being fired from direct contact with the flame in a kiln.

saif: (weapons) a slightly curved Arab saber with a hooked pommel.

sailor jug: (ceramics) a Toby jug depicting a sailor holding a pipe and glass, and sitting on a sea chest.

salade: (armor) a 15th-century steel helmet that covers the face. Some have a horizontal slit for the eyes; others have a moveable visor. A broad tail of various lengths extends backwards at the base of the helmet.

salamander: (kitchen) a wrought-iron bar with a circle or square on one end. This was heated over coals until it was red-hot and then placed very close to bread to brown it.

salamander marble: (furniture) cast iron painted to look like marble; used on furniture in the mid-1800s.

Salem rocker: (furniture) a rocking chair similar to the Boston rocker, but with a lower back. Made at Salem, Massachusetts, in the early 1800s.

Salem secretary: (furniture) a bureau with a china cabinet above and a double-door center section below with a drawer that pulls out to form a writing surface. The bottom also has a single-door storage compartment on each side of the double-door center.

Salem snowflake: (decoration) a six-point star decoration suggesting a snowflake; used as a background for carvings on furniture made at Salem, Massachusetts.

sales circuit: (stamps) the buying and selling of stamps within a closed group.

sallet: (armor) a light 15th-century helmet with a brim trailing at the back and a visor pivoted at the side; used by foot and mounted troops.

sallet stand: (furniture) a small stand with a bowl carved into the top; used in the 1600s and 1700s to serve salad at the dinner table.

saltcellar: (tableware) a small shaker or dish; used to hold and dispense salt.

salt glaze: (ceramics) a glaze formed by releasing salt into the kiln when the temperature is at its maximum. Sodium oxide and hydrochloric acid is formed from the decomposed salt. The sodium oxide combines with silica and alumina from the surface of the stoneware to form a thin layer of glaze.

salting: (auctions) including items that are new or that don't belong with the other articles offered for sale at an auction. Auctioneers frequently salt their auctions with merchandise that they have purchased.

saltire: (furniture) an X-shaped arrangement of stretchers on a chair, table, or other piece.

salute: (coins) a gold coin issued by French and English monarchs in the English possessions in France. Late 14th to mid-15th centuries.

salver: (household accessories) a tray or platter for serving food or drink.

Sambo: (black memorabilia) young black male figure.

samisen: (music) a Japanese three-stringed musical instrument with a long neck; resembles the banjo.

samite: (textiles) a high-quality silk material.

samovar: (household accessories) a metal urn or container with a spigot; used to boil water for tea or keep liquids warm. See also *urn*.

sampler: (needlework) fabric panel featuring "samples" of the stitches a young girl had recently learned. The panel usually has a cross-stitched alphabet, the name and birth date of the maker, and sometimes religious or inspirational sayings, along with decorative embroidered borders and images of trees, flowers, and houses. Popular since the 1600s.

samples-in-little: (collectibles) miniatures of wares carried by traveling salesmen.

Samson & Company: (ceramics) a porcelain factory in Paris, France, that specialized in reproducing old Chinese and European porcelain. The factory operated from 1845 until 1964. A range of marks — most copied from other manufacturers — were used. Some pieces are marked "S" in red on the underside of the base, but most Samson marks were placed over the glaze and many of them have been rubbed off.

sandbox: (desk accessories) a small vessel used to store and sprinkle sand on freshly written ink. Also called *sand dredger*.

sand casting: (metal) a technique for casting metal. A wooden mold is placed inside a two-part container packed with wet sand. The two-part container is divided and the wooden mold removed, leaving an impression. The two halves of the container are locked together again, and after the sand dries, molten metal is poured into the mold, creating a completed cast.

This method replaced the lost wax method in the mid-18th century and is still in use.

sand dredger: (desk accessories) a small vessel used to store and sprinkle sand on freshly written ink. Also called *sandbox.*

sand glass: two small globes of glass attached to each other. When one is filled with a specified amount of sand, time can be measured by how long it takes the sand to pass into the other. (Egg timers are made on this principle.) Old sand glasses were in sets of four and made of separate globes attached with an applied band.

sand toy: a toy with moving parts that are activated by trickling sand, like that in a sand glass. See also *sand glass.*

sandwich board: (advertising memorabilia) a hinged pair of large boards bearing advertising hung from the carrier's shoulders.

Sandwich glass: pressed glass pieces made from colored, cut, hobnail, opalescent, and other glass from 1820 until 1888 by the Boston and Sandwich Glass Company, one of the pioneers in pressed glass. They only made cruets, salts, and lamps when they first opened. Later bottles, bowls, candlesticks, compotes, goblets, pitchers, vases, and other accessories were added. The Sandwich styles have been copied extensively.

sanggram: (ceramics) a Korean technique of decorating pottery by filling the incised pattern with a contrasting-colored englobe or clay.

sans: French for without.

sarcanet: (textiles) a delicate, thin silk material.

sari: (fashion accessories) one-piece woman's outer garment with one end wrapped around the lower body to form a skirt and the other end draped over one shoulder, or over the head to create a hood.

Sarreguemines: (ceramics) a pottery founded in the mid-18th century in France. Majolica and transfer-decorated plates, pitchers, and urns usually bear the company name.

sashi-zoe: (weapons) the shorter of two swords carried by a Japanese samurai. Also called *wakizashi.*

satin glass: a colored or clear glass with a soft, dull, velvety-looking finish achieved by the use of a hydrofluoric acid. Satin glass was made by many companies. Some of it is painted or transfer decorated.

Satsuma ware: (ceramics) a cream-colored porcelain pottery decorated with gilding and enamel colors. Originally made in the Japanese province of Satsuma. Dates from the early 17th century; large quantities were exported in the 19th century.

saunders: (materials) a hardwood with a rose-musk aroma; used in furniture in the 1700s and 1800s.

sausage turning: (furniture) a wooden border design resembling sausage links.

sautoir: (jewelry) a long gold necklace extending below the waist and often terminating with a pendant or tassel.

Savery, William (1721-1788): (furniture) one of Philadelphia's finest furniture makers during the 1700s.

Savona maiolica: (ceramics) a tin-glazed earthenware made in Savona, Italy, during the 17th and 18th centuries.

sawbuck table: (furniture) a country table with an X-shaped frame. Produced in New England and Pennsylvania.

saya: (weapons) Japanese for *scabbard.* Usually made of wood. If made of metal, the liner is wood. See also *scabbard.*

scabbard: (weapons) a container for a knife, dagger, sword, or other bladed weapon. Also called *sheath*.

scagliola: (furniture) an Italian imitation marble and Florentine mosaic using gesso. The hard, durable finish takes a high polish. Sixteenth to 18th centuries.

scale case: a case containing rulers and measures; used by architects and designers during the 1700s.

scalloped: (decoration) having a series of curves inspired by mollusk (scallop) shells; found on the rims of wood furniture and molding, glass, and other objects.

scarab: (decoration, jewelry) the representation of a scarab beetle, an early Egyptian symbol of the soul.

scarce: a term denoting the relative availability of a type of item. When an object is scarce, its number is limited, but there are more examples available than if it were rare. See also *rare*.

scarf joint: (architecture) a joint made to hold the notched ends of two timbers together to form one continuous piece.

scarf pin: (jewelry) a straight pin with an ornamental, often jeweled head; used to keep a tie in place. Most examples are from 1880 to around 1920.

sceatta: (coins) a small English silver coin of the 7th and 8th century.

scepter: a staff representing royal or sovereign authority.

Schafer and Vater: (ceramics) a company that made novelty items from 1890 until 1920 in Volkstadt, Germany. Wares are marked "R" in a star.

scherenschnitte: (decoration) designs and silhouettes cut freehand from paper either in a single layer or folded once or many times. Also called *scissorwork*.

schiavona: (weapons) a straight, two-edged sword with a basket hilt; used by Dalmatian troops in the late 16th and early 17th centuries.

schischak: (armor) a helmet worn by Russians and Mongols from the 13th to 17th centuries. The helmet is round, rising to a sharp point, with small brims, a hinged guard for the ears and neck, and on some, a moveable nasal guard.

schmelzglas: (glass) glass that is the result of pouring several colors together and allowing them to mingle but not blend together as one; used for molded or blown-glass pieces. Enjoyed a high degree of popularity during the Renaissance in Venice and Germany. Also called *agate glass*.

Schneider: (glass) a glass company started in 1903 in Epinay-Sur-Seine, France, and still in business today. The wares that stimulate the most interest are those art glass pieces done before 1930. Some of this was art deco in style, some acid cut. Some pieces are signed "LeVerre Francais"; others are marked "Charder" or "Schneider."

Schoenhut: an enamel-painted wooden doll with joints patented by Albert Schoenhut on January 17, 1911. These dolls had stands. Later Schoenhut dolls have stuffed bodies and voices. The Bye-Lo Baby, made from 1924 until the firm closed in 1930, is probably Schoenhut's most popular.

school: (fine art) a group of artists who share a common style, idea, or artistic tendency. For example, the surrealist school.

school memorabilia: (collectibles) old school bells, books, clocks, and other school-related items.

school sheets: (paper) sheets of paper used in England from about 1780 until 1850 for students to practice handwriting. The edges were printed with educational information, quotes, or sayings. They are used as mats for mirrors today.

Schoop, Hedi: (ceramics) figurines, lamps, vases, and other objects done in ceramic by Hedi Schoop and the few people she employed from 1940 until 1958. She used gold and platinum trim extensively. Most pieces are marked with her name either stamped or incised.

Schwarzlot: (ceramics) German porcelain and earthenware pieces decorated with black or grey designs, sometimes highlighted with iron red or gold.

scimitar: (weapons) an Oriental sword with a convex blade.

scimitar blade: (tableware) a table knife blade with a curve that is similar to, but not as pronounced, as that of a scimitar sword blade. The knife and the fork that goes with it have pistol handles. From 18th century.

scissorwork: (decoration) designs and silhouettes cut freehand from paper either in a single layer or folded once or many times. Also called *scherenschnitte*.

sconce: (lighting) a decorative wall-mounted bracket for candles or lights.

scoop: (kitchen) a shovellike utensil with a deep, curved dish, usually with a short handle.

scoop pattern: (furniture) a fluted ornament dating to the Renaissance.

Scotch mull: (household accessories) a snuffbox made from the horn of a ram.

scotia molding: (furniture) a half-round concave molding.

Scottish dirk: (weapons) a 19th-century dagger with a broad blade and root wood handle.

Scott Publishing Company: (stamps) publishers of annual worldwide stamp catalogs.

The most prominent price authority in the United States and Canada.

scouting memorabilia: (collectibles) handbooks, badges, patches, pins, pocket knives, games, uniforms, and a host of other scouting paraphernalia representing the American scouting movement. Boy Scout items are more sought and generally bring higher prices than Girl Scout items.

scratchboard drawing: (fine art) a finished drawing that resembles a wood engraving. Scratchboard is a white coated cardboard that the artist coats with black ink. The drawing is then executed by scraping the lines, thereby exposing the white board. The result is a white drawing on black ground. First introduced in the 1800s.

scratch carving: (furniture) a type of incised carving. The pattern is scratched on the wood surface. Sixteenth and 17th centuries. See also *incised design*.

scratch ware: (ceramics) white salt-glazed stoneware with incised designs into which a mixture of clay and color has been rubbed before firing. Made in the 1700s; many pieces are dated.

scrimshaw: (folk art) the art of decorating whale ivory, bone, or shells with detailed carvings or designs. Practiced by sailors, particularly on whaling ships during long voyages to pass the time. Reproductions are made of polymer and fiberglass.

script hanging: (religious) fine pen-and-brush pictorial and script work done on paper; used for wall hangings in the 1600s in New England. Often erroneously called *Fraktur*, which was done by German immigrants a full century later. See also *Fraktur*.

scripture quilt: (textiles) a block quilt with Bible quotations stitched in the blocks.

scroll: 1. (coins) a banner on United States coins which usually displays a motto. **2.** (decoration) a spiral or convoluted form following the curves of a partially opened parchment scroll; used on furniture.

scrolled chair: (furniture) a chair with a solid high back that has a carved and scrolled top rail.

scroll foot: (furniture) a chair leg terminal or foot in the shape of a scroll. Popular in the mid-1700s. See also *scroll*.

scrubbed: (fine art) an oil painting which, during the cleaning process, has lost some of the paint — often right through to the canvas.

scrutoire: (furniture) a secretary-cabinet with a fall front for writing. The upper section has drawers and pigeonholes; the lower portion is a chest of drawers or a stand with legs. From the late 17th century. Also called *escritoire*.

scudo: (coins) large, silver Italian coin. From the 16th century.

sculpture d'appartement: a pair or group of ornate figures displayed in a salon or gallery. Mid-17th century to early 18th century in France.

scumbled: 1. (fine art) a style of art in which the edges of objects have been lightly rubbed to give a soft appearance. **2.** (fine art) the process of softening colors by adding a coat of semi-opaque paint.

scutcheon: 1. (armor) a shield on which armorial bearings or a coat of arms is carried. **2.** (armor) the shape of a shield.

scymiter: (weapons) an Oriental saber with a blade that has a considerable curve.

scythe: (tools) a long, bent-handled implement with a curved, single-edged blade; used for reaping or mowing.

sealed glass: a glass vessel with the seal of the glass house on it. A practice started by George Ravenscroft in 1676.

seal-top spoon: (tableware) an early spoon with a flat, seallike finial at the stem's end. Fifteenth to 17th centuries.

seatrails: (furniture) the chair or bench frame on which the seat is built.

seaweed marquetry: (decoration) an inlay design resembling the flowing sprays of seaweed; used on clock cases and furniture early in the 18th century.

Sebastians: (ceramics) miniatures produced from 1938 until the present. Old and discontinued examples in mint shape bring the most money. Most figures are marked "P.W. Baston." These figures are most prized in New England.

second rococo: (furniture) furniture made from 1830 to 1860 with a French influence. Also called *early Victorian*.

secretaire bookcase: (furniture) a drop-front desk with enclosed shelves above for books, and drawers or a cupboard below. The drop front is usually balanced by counterweights within the frame.

secretary: (furniture) a desk with a top that has shelves and compartments enclosed by doors.

sedan chair: (furniture) an upholstered legless chair with four bars extending from it. The chair was carried by four men, each one handling a bar.

sedan clock: a carriage clock that looks like a large watch. It has a 4- to 6-inch dial and a bow-shaped handle for hanging it in the carriage. These clocks have small movements behind the large dials.

seed beads: (decoration) tiny round beads; used for decorating fabrics.

seeds: (glass) the tiny bubbles in glass that occur when the furnace is not hot enough to eliminate all the trapped air bubbles.

segmented: distinguishable sections put together to form a whole.

sehna knot: (floor coverings) a knot found in carpets from Feraghan, Herat, Ispahan, Kerman, Sehna, Serebend, or Shiraz, Persia.

seicento: (fine art) Italian art and literature created in the 1600s.

sejant: (heraldry) heraldic term for *sitting.*

self bow: (weapons) a bow made from a single piece of wood that is not laminated or clad with other material.

selvage: (stamps) the margin that is separated from the stamps by perforation. Plate numbers and postal slogans are printed on the selvage.

semiporcelain: (ceramics) opaque pottery with the type of tough glaze used on porcelain.

semipostal: (stamps) a stamp that costs more than its postal value. The balance is a tax earmarked for a specific cause.

sen: (coins) a copper Japanese coin issued 8th to 10th century and again from the 16th century.

sena-ate: (armor) the backplate of Japanese armor.

Sephardic: anything made by a member of the occidental branch of European Jews settling in Spain, Portugal, and later in the Americas (primarily Rhode Island during the 1700s).

sequin: (coins) a Turkish coin.

Serass: (glass) crystal flint glass of the finest quality.

serif: (books, printing) lines that finish off the tops and bottoms of letters.

serigraph: (prints) a silk-screen print designed and printed by the artist. See also *silk screen.*

serpentine: (weapons) the match holder of a matchlock gun.

serpentine front: (furniture) a front shaped with a waving, or serpentine, curve. Popular during the second half of the 18th century.

serrated: having a toothlike, notched edge.

server: (furniture) a side table and storage unit; used in the dining room for the service of meals. Also called *serving table.*

serving table: (furniture) a side table and storage unit; used in the dining room for the service of meals. Also called *server.*

sesquicentennial: (stamps) a stamp commemorating the 150th anniversary of an event.

set: (stamps) one each of all the different stamps of a single issue. There must be more than three designs to make up a set.

settee: (furniture) a small upholstered sofa that seats two people.

setting sun ornament: a carved, semicircular form, similar in appearance to an open fan; used on American furniture since the late 18th century. The ornament suggests a sun with emitting rays. Also called *rising sun ornament.*

settle: (furniture) a long, high-backed wooden bench with side boards or arms, often with storage space below. The lines suggest an old-fashioned church pew.

setwork: (decoration) anything that is inlaid. See also *inlaid.*

Sevres ware: (ceramics) a delicate porcelain made in Sevres, France, from the mid-18th century to present. Considered the finest French porcelain.

sewing bird: (domestic) a metal bird with a clamp on the base for mounting on a table. The bird's beak opened to hold material.

sewing table: (furniture) a table, popular from the 1700s, with drawers and often a cloth bag for storage of sewing equipment.

sextafoil table: (furniture) a round table with six scallops around the edge. See also *scalloped*.

sextant: (scientific instrument) a navigational instrument used for measuring the altitude of celestial bodies. It is similar to the octant but uses a greater arc.

sgain dubh: (weapons) a small dagger with a straight blade and no guard; carried in the stocking by Scotsmen in the 18th century.

sgraffiato: (ceramics) a decoration that has been cut, incised, or scratched through the coat of slip to expose the color of the clay.

shade silhouette: a portrait in silhouette in which the face is black and without features. The clothes may have some detail, the hands may clutch a colored nosegay, but the face is always plain. See also *silhouette*.

shagreen: (materials) sharkskin, usually dyed green; used to cover tea caddies and cases for scientific instruments and domestic articles such as purses. From the 17th century.

Shaker box: oval or round, wood or tin box with a paper label; made and used by the Shakers to pack herbs and spices.

Shaker furniture: fruit wood, maple, pine, or walnut furniture of very simple design made by members of the Shaker religion in the 1800s. Highly prized.

shako: a stiff, military dress hat with a short visor, high crown, and plume.

shamshir: (weapons) curved Persian saber with a narrow, thick blade.

shank: (jewelry) the part of a ring that is worn around the finger and holds the head of the ring.

Sharps carbine, John Brown Model: (weapons) the rifle John Brown and his men carried when they seized the Federal Armory at Harpers Ferry in 1859. Although Sharps produced nine models, this model, made in 1852 and 1853, is the one most sought by collectors.

shaving mug: (ceramics) a mug first introduced in the 1830s by American manufacturers of shaving soap. The idea caught on, and most men had at least two mugs — one at home and one at the barber shop. Most of those found today date from 1850 to 1900.

Shawnee: (ceramics) a pottery producing corn-shaped dishes, novelties, and a line of cookie jars in Zanesville, Ohio, from 1937 until 1961. Items with gold trim are particularly prized by collectors. Most pieces are marked "Shawnee USA."

shearing sword: (weapons) a double-edged sword with a light, flexible blade; used in the 16th and 17th centuries.

Shearwater: (ceramics) figurines, vases, and other small items produced in Ocean Springs, Mississippi, from 1928 until the present. Many early figurines (which are the most highly prized) are marked "Shearwater" in a small circle.

sheath: (weapons) a container for a sword, dagger, knife, or other bladed weapon. Also called *scabbard*.

sheepshead clock: a lantern clock that has a chapter ring (ring of numbers) that extends considerably beyond the square frame of the dial plate.

sheet brass: (metal) thin sheets of brass made from molten metal. Originally made by manual hammering, then with water-powered hammers; from early 18th century, rolling machines were used.

Sheffield Plate: (silver) the first (and best) silver plate. Invented by Thomas Bolsover in the first half of the 18th century in Sheffield, England. The plate was formed by sandwiching rolled sheet silver to an inner layer of copper and fusing by heat. The technique was gradually replaced by electroplating, introduced in the 1830s. See also *silver plate.*

shelf clock: a clock, usually footed, made to stand on a shelf or mantel. Also called *mantel clock.*

shell box: a box covered with plaster and encrusted with small seashells. From the late Victorian era.

Shelley: (ceramics) a firm that has undergone many name changes since it was founded in 1872 as the Foley China Works in Stoke-on-Trent, England. The Shelley name is associated most closely with the dainty white porcelain that went into production in 1896. Most pieces are marked "Shelley, England." In 1971 the Doulton Group purchased the company.

shell ornament: (decoration) a motif resembling a seashell. Widely used from 1700 to 1775 on porcelain, silver, and furniture, particularly in rococo designs.

Shenandoah: (ceramics) pottery made in the Shenandoah Valley by many companies starting in the early 19th century. Bright colors were used. Much of the ware is marked by the individual company.

shepherd's crook arm: (furniture) chair and settee arm with a graceful curve, ending in the form of the shepherd's crook. Popular during the first quarter of the 18th century.

Sheraton, Thomas (1751-1806): (furniture) English furniture designer and Baptist preacher. His designs are characterized by straight lines and graceful proportions. He published *The Cabinet-Maker's and Upholsterer's Drawing Book* in four volumes.

shibuichi: (metal) a Japanese alloy composed of silver and three of the following metals: copper, lead, tin, and zinc. The value of the alloy depends on how much silver is used, and the color varies greatly according to the composition; used for ornamental work.

shield-back chair: (furniture) a chair design closely associated with Hepplewhite. The uprights and top rail form the shape of a shield.

shilling: (coins) a silver English coin first issued by Edward VI during his reign (1547 to 1553).

shing yao: (orientalia) the Chinese term for pure porcelain.

shiraz rug: (floor coverings) a Persian rug with diamond medallions or cone designs. Made by Kashkai nomads.

shishi: (orientalia) Chinese lion dogs.

shivering: (ceramics) a fault in the glaze caused by the raising or division of the glaze along cracks.

shofar: (music, religion) a trumpet made from a ram's horn; used to communicate signals, particularly warnings, in ancient times, and now sounded in synagogues at Rosh Hashanah and Yom Kippur.

shoji: (orientalia) a Japanese sliding door or partition comprised of translucent paper panels.

shovel spoon: (tableware) a small spoon in the form of a shovel; used for distributing salt held in an open saltcellar. Usually made of silver or plate.

shrinkage: (ceramics) reduction in size of porcelain caused by firing. Generally about 1/7 of original size.

shu: (coins) a silver, rectangular Japanese coin issued from 17th to early 19th century.

Shu Fu: (orientalia) Chinese porcelain with flying cranes, flower sprays, and figures in relief covered by a slightly opaque blue glaze.

Shute, S.A. and R.W.: (folk art) a husband-and-wife painting team in the early 1800s. Their works are very valuable.

sickle: (tools) a semicircular bladed implement with a short handle; used to cut grain or tall grass.

sideboard: (furniture) a dining room piece with compartments and shelves for storing dishes.

side boy: (furniture) a long table made to place against a wall.

side chair: (furniture) a chair with no arms.

side lantern: (lighting) a wall sconce enclosed in glass.

side plate: (weapons) a small ornamental plate on the stock of a gun or pistol opposite the lock. Also called *contreplatine* and *nail plate*.

side rails: (furniture) the two vertical uprights that form the back of a chair.

sifter sugar spoon: (metal) a spoon with a pierced bowl; used for sprinkling sugar evenly on food.

signed binding: (books) the binder's name on a label, stamped somewhere on the binding, or marked in ink at the edge of an end paper.

signet bangle: (jewelry) a tubular bangle bracelet with a hinge and a catch, and a space in the middle flattened for engraving. In vogue from 1890 until *ca.* 1912.

silhouette: (paper) a profile cut from paper. The profile is hand cut from dark paper and mounted on light paper, or hollow-cut from light paper and mounted on dark paper. Either way, the silhouette is dark. Popular from the early 1770s to about 1860 as inexpensive substitutes for artists' portraits. The daguerreotype, tin-type, and other photographic processes ended the vogue. See also *shade silhouette*.

silk screen: (prints) a method of color-stencil printing. The color medium is forced through a fine screen with a squeegee. Areas of the screen not to be printed are blocked out. A print produced in this method by the artist is called a serigraph. See also *serigraph*.

silver gilt: (silver) a gold wash on silver. The old method was to paint on a mixture of gold and mercury, then evaporate the mercury with heat, leaving the gold bonded to the silver. The modern method is electrogilding, the same technique used to plate silver on a base metal.

silver inlay: (decoration, furniture) silver or tin melted, mixed with mercury, and worked into a puttylike substance, then forced into designs previously cut into wood; used mostly in the 1700s.

silver leaf: (decoration) silver beaten into a thin leaf for gilding.

silver luster: (ceramics) earthenware with a metallic silver finish; produced by many companies from 1800 on. See also *copper luster, copper queensware, luster, pink luster,* and *Sunderland*.

silver overlay: (decoration, glass) a decoration cut from silver and applied to glass. *Ca.* 1800s.

silver plate: (silver) a thin coat of silver fused to a thicker sheet of copper or another base metal. The first method of plating was invented in Sheffield, England, in the 1740s. Rolled sheet silver was fused to copper by heat. At first only one side of the copper was plated, but by the early 1770s, the copper was sandwiched on both sides with silver. In the 1830s electroplating was invented and gradually it replaced the Sheffield type of plating. See also *Sheffield Plate*.

silver point: (fine art) a thin rod of silver used to draw lines on special paper coated with white pigment. This technique leaves minute particles of silver embedded in the surface. The lines are at first a light gray, then in time, darken as the silver tarnishes. Popular during the Renaissance, silver point is a standard technique today.

silver resist: (ceramics) a method of decorating pottery. A water-soluble solution was applied to areas of the vessel not to be silvered; the entire vessel was then coated with the silver luster and allowed to dry. Next, the entire surface was washed, removing the luster from the treated areas, leaving silver on the uncoated design. Then the vessel received a final firing. Early 1800s.

silver table: (furniture) a side table for storing and displaying fine silver.

simultaneous representation: (fine art) a multiple view of a person or object in a picture. The reflection of a mirror may be used for a second view, or, as done by the cubists, front and side views can be merged together.

Sinclaire: (glass) cut and engraved glass items usually depicting floral or natural motifs. Sinclaire and Company started in 1904 in Corning, New York, and in 1920 moved to Bath, New York, so they could make their own glass instead of buying blanks. Some pieces are marked "S" with a wreath and two shields.

singing bird box: a popular snuffbox topped with a small bird that sings when the box is wound up. Made in Geneva from 1790 until *ca.* 1830.

single-fired: (ceramics) ceramic wares that have been fired only after glaze has been applied.

single-twist stem: (glass) a goblet stem containing air, colored enamel, or colored thread spiraling within a clear glass center.

sinister: (heraldry) the left side of a shield.

sinking in: (fine art) dull spots on an oil painting that appear after it has dried. Commonly caused by uneven absorption of paint by the canvas or other ground material. A coat of picture varnish will correct the problem.

sitar: (music) an Indian lute made from a seasoned gourd with a long teak neck. Usually there are six or seven main playing strings above and thirteen resonating strings below.

Sitzendorf: (ceramics) fine porcelain figurines and table accessories produced in East Germany in the mid-19th century. Many pieces are marked "S" under a crown.

skeleton clock: a clock with the workings exposed, usually covered with a glass dome.

skeleton clock dial: a dial with the metal cut away from the chapter ring, leaving only the numbers and minute marks.

sketch: 1. (fine art) a preliminary drawing or painting, usually lacking detail. **2.** (fine art) an early stage of a work, such as a piece of stone, that has been roughly shaped in the image of the finished form of a sculpture.

skimmer: (kitchen) a flat utensil, usually perforated like a sieve and shaped similar to a ladle. Metal skimmers were usually used for removing fat from stews and soups; wooden skimmers had a handle at a 30-degree angle to the bowl and were usually used for skimming cream from milk.

skin: (fine art) to remove the surface varnish of an oil painting by cleaning the surface.

skirt: 1. (furniture) a fabric valance that conceals the legs of a chair or sofa. **2.** (furniture) a wooden strip, often decorative, placed low on a shelf, table or bed. See also *valance.*

skirt base: (metal, ceramics) a broad, spreading base; found on pewter flagons from the late 1600s.

skittle ball: any vase, decanter, bottle, or the like that looks as if it has been squashed on the top and bottom. Named after a ball with flat sides that was used in an old English game.

skull: 1. (armor) the fixed part of a closed helmet. **2.** (armor) a close-fitting helmet worn in the 15th and 16th centuries.

slab method: (ceramics) to form pottery by hand from a thick slice (slab) of clay.

slag glass: an opaque, marbleized glass made from the mid-1800s until about 1900 by many glass companies. Slag has been extensively reproduced.

slatback: (furniture) a chair back with plain horizontal pieces of wood across the back.

slave collar: (black memorabilia) a yoke used to harness a slave. Slaves were harnessed so they could pull tillers in the farm fields of their masters.

sleeper: (auctions) an item at an auction that doesn't get much attention and appears of little value, but suddenly takes off and is bid much higher than expected.

sleep eyes: (dolls) dolls with eyes that open when the doll is upright and close when the doll is laid down.

sleigh: (vehicles) a light, horse-drawn vehicle mounted on runners for traveling on snow and ice.

sleigh bed: (furniture) a 19th-century American bed that has high head- and footboards with upper rails that curve out in a scrolllike fashion to give the bed the appearance of a sleigh.

slice: (kitchen) a knife with a thin, broad blade; used for cutting and serving cheese and other food.

slider: (table accessories) a receptacle for moving food and drink on the dining table. It was fitted with a baize-covered base with small wheels, for ease of movement. *Ca.* 18th century. Also called *coaster.*

slingshot: (weapons) a Y-shaped stick with rubber straps and a piece of material to hold a small stone attached to the prongs. When the straps are pulled back and released, the stone is projected at the target.

slip: 1. (ceramics) potter's clay thinned for coating or decorating ceramics. **2.** (needlework) embroidery depicting combinations of fruits, flowers, and foliage; used extensively in the 16th and 17th centuries.

slip casting: (ceramics) a method of making ceramic ware by pouring slip, watery clay, into a mold, removing the water, and letting the clay dry. See also *slip.*

slipper chair: (furniture) a chair with a high back, short legs, and a low seat; used in the bedroom to sit on when putting on shoes.

slipper foot: (furniture) a furniture foot, usually on a chair, that curves outward to resemble a slipper.

slip seat: (furniture) a removable chair seat.

slip-top spoon: (tableware) a spoon with a hexagonal stem with the tip beveled or angled. In use from sometime in the Middle Ages to the 17th century.

slip trailing: (ceramics) thin, raised lines of slip; used to decorate pottery.

slipware: (ceramics) earthenware decorated with a coat of white or colored slip. See also *slip.*

slungshot: (weapons) a weapon used with a small, heavy weight attached to a thong.

slur bow: (weapons) a crossbow that has a barrel with a

slot to control the string as it slides forward and releases the arrow. From 16th century.

slush cast: (toys) a method of casting toys by pouring molten metal into a mold and moving it around so that the metal coats the mold. The result is a hollow figure or toy. Also called *hollow cast*.

small barrel organ: (music) a small, portable street organ with a hand crank. Capable of making special sounds like those of the piccolo, trumpet, and flute. Small barrel organs are scarce, collectible, and expensive. Made for about one hundred years, starting *ca.* 1800.

smalls: (auctions) items offered at an auction that are easily transported, like dishes, clocks, memorabilia, and other small pieces.

smallsword: (weapons) a light dueling sword, often richly decorated, with a slender blade for thrusting. In the mid-1600s it was double edged, but from about 1700 the blade was changed, and had a groove down the three sides.

smalt: (ceramics) a deep blue pigment produced from pulverized silica glass, potash, and cobalt oxide; used to decorate pottery and porcelain.

Smith and Wesson revolver, Model No. 1, second issue: (weapons) the first American revolver that fired metal-cased ammunition.

Smith Brothers: (glass) enamel-decorated opalescent or satin glass. Made by Alfred and Harry Smith in Massachusetts during the last quarter of the 19th century. A lion in a shield marks many pieces.

smock: (fashion accessories) a loose, coatlike outer garment; worn to protect the clothes while working or traveling.

smocking: (needlework) decorative needlework created by stitching small uniformly spaced gathers into a honeycomb pattern.

smoke bell: (lighting) a bell-shaped piece of glass hung over a lamp in the 1700s and 1800s to prevent the smoke from staining the ceiling.

smoker: (furniture) a stand that holds tobacco and smoking accessories.

smooch: (fine art) a technique for shading by smudging pencil, pastel, or crayon with the fingers or hand.

snaphaunce: (weapons) earliest type of flintlock that lacks the half-cock safety feature of the improved flintlock. From the mid-16th century.

snaplock: (weapons) a term referring to both flintlock and snaphaunce arms.

snow baby: (ceramics) a small bisque figurine in a white, grainy-finished snowsuit. Made from the early 1900s until World War II. Most are under 2 inches tall. The figures portray a variety of activities from riding a sled or sitting on a snow ball to flying an airplane or playing a musical instrument. They have been reproduced.

snow bird: (metal) a 19th-century cast- or wrought-iron bird shape attached to a metal pole. Snow birds were put on the roofs of buildings in cold climates to prevent the snow from sliding off the roofs onto passersby. Also called *snow robin*.

snow robin: (metal) a 19th-century cast- or wrought-iron bird shape attached to a metal pole. Snow birds were put on the roofs of buildings in cold climates to prevent the snow from sliding off the roofs onto passersby. Also called *snow bird*.

snow weights: (glass) paperweights containing a scene, a liquid, and white particles that give the illusion of snow when the paperweight is shaken.

snuffbox: small, usually decorated box with a hinged lid;

used for carrying snuff in the pocket or purse.

snuffer: 1. (lighting) a pair of shears with a box attached; used for cutting and collecting the charred wick (snuff) from a candle. **2.** (lighting) a long-handled device for extinguishing candles.

snuffer stand: (furniture) a small cabinet mounted on a stem and base; used to house candle snuffers in the late 1600s.

snuffer tray: (household accessories) an oval or oblong tray often with a ring or scroll side handle and small feet; used to hold snuffers in the 18th century.

soap box: (domestic) a brass, pewter, or silver receptacle with a spherical shape, a hinged cover, and a molded base; used for holding a ball of soap.

soap press: (kitchen) a bench press for pressing flakes of boiled soap into a huge bar from which smaller bars were cut.

soap rock: (ceramics) a steatite used as an ingredient in some soft-paste English porcelain. Also called *soapstone.*

soapstone: 1. (materials) soft rock with a high magnesium content and smooth to the touch; used to fashion figurines, vases, and the like. **2.** (ceramics) a steatite used as an ingredient in some soft-paste English porcelain. Also called *soap rock.*

socked on the nose: (stamps) a stamp that has been canceled dead center. This adds value.

socle: (furniture) usually plain, square base upon which a statue is rested.

sofa: (furniture) a long upholstered seat with arms and back. (From the Arabic *suffah.*) See also *davenport.*

sofa table: (furniture) a rectangular table, usually with two front drawers and hinged leaves at both ends, and one or two legs at each end mounted on graceful supports; originally placed behind a sofa or chair so the light of a candelabrum would provide illumination. Also used as a writing table. From late 1700s.

soft paste porcelain: (ceramics) porcelain that has a large quantity of bone ash. It is, as the name implies, a soft and not very durable product. Most old examples of soft paste porcelain have some damage. See also *hard paste porcelain.*

Soho lamp: (lighting) a candle lamp with a globe and shade made by the grocery firm of Crosse & Blackwell. The base was constructed so the candle could be raised or lowered by twisting a thumb screw. From the 1830s.

solar clock: a sundial.

solder: (metal) to affix metal pieces or parts together with heated metal, usually composed of tin and lead.

solerets: (armor) plate armor for the feet. Early solerets were made of metal strips riveted to leather; later the metal plates were attached to each other in a way that provided flexibility.

solid: (toys) a three-dimensional lead figure.

solid casting: (metal) a cast metal object without a hollow core.

solitaire: (household accessories) a tea set made to provide service for just one person.

Solomon's seal: (decoration) six-point star formed by two interlaced equilateral triangles. Also called *Star of David* and *Magen David.*

somber binding: (books) black leather binding, often with embossed black edges.

somnole: (furniture) a nightstand or bedside table.

Soqui: (decoration) a painter who decorated porcelain at the Sevres factory. Bird designs were his specialty.

soufflé dish: (tableware) a silver or plated bowl with two handles and a liner to hold a soufflé. From early 1800s.

Soumac rug: (floor coverings) a rug with mainly copper and blue colors in a tapestry weave and large star motifs on octagonal panels.

South American silver: usually heavy silver, often with a hammered finish. Often marked "925" or "Sterling." Considered inferior to American silver. See also *sterling silver*.

South Jersey Glass Company: a company that produced window glass and bottles until it closed in 1780. Founded by German emigrant Caspar Wistar in 1739 in Alloywaystown in South Jersey.

sovereign: (coins) a large, gold English coin issued by Henry VII and continued by other Tudor monarchs. Reintroduced in 1820.

soy frame: (tableware) silver or plated stand with a ring frame; used for holding a bottle of soy or sauce. From late 1700s.

spade foot: (furniture) a tapered four-sided foot; found on 18th-century furniture.

spadone: (weapons) a 16th-century two-handed sword.

spall: (stone, glass, ceramics) a chip or fragment from an object.

spandrel: 1. (furniture, architecture) a triangular space between the right or left exterior curve of an arch. **2.** (furniture, architecture) the space between two arches and the molding above them.

spangle glass: (glass) a cased (two-layered) art glass with metallic pieces embedded in it. Made by many glassworks both in Europe and the United States during the late 1800s. Fenton Art Glass Company reproduced this ware in

the 1960s. See also *cased glass*.

Spanish foot: (furniture) an angular, grooved foot with a scroll base; used as the terminal for late-17th-century chairs and settees.

Spanish work: (needlework) black silk thread embroidered in designs such as scrolls, leaves, and grapes on a black or white ground, usually linen. Also called *black work*.

sparking chair: (furniture) a chair built large enough to accommodate two. Also called *lover's chair*, *drunkard's chair*, and *sporting chair*.

spatter glass: a speckled glass of at least two, and sometimes many, colors. First made during the late 1800s and still in production. Similar to end-of-day glass, which glassmakers made by using leftover glass to create varicolored, often unusual pieces.

spatter ware: (ceramics) pottery made in Staffordshire, England, in the second quarter of the 19th century for export to America. Color was sponged on.

specialty auction: an auction offering examples of one specialty or collectible such as dolls, toys, ephemera, guns, or coins.

specific gravity: (metal) the density of a metal.

spelter: (metal) zinc; used as a casting metal in the 19th century for figures such as those that adorned the tops of mantle clocks.

spetum: (weapons) a 16th-century pole arm with a long, narrow blade and curved projections at the base of each side.

spice cupboard: (furniture) a small kitchen cabinet for storing spices; either mounted on the wall or placed on or near a work surface.

spice dredger: (kitchen) a receptacle, usually round, with a pierced top for sprinkling spices onto foods.

spice mill: (kitchen) a grinder for spices.

spider helmet: (armor) an open helmet with hinged vertical bars encircling it that can be rested against the crown or pulled down to protect the face and sides of the head.

spider-leg table: (furniture) a table with very thin gate legs.

Spinario: (ceramics) the figure of a boy removing a thorn from his foot. A widely copied statue in the Capitoline Museum in Rome.

spindle: (furniture) a thin, upright rod tapering from a central swelling; used as a support or backing for chairs, cradles, and other furniture.

spinet desk: (furniture) a desk copied after the 19th-century keyboard instrument with the same name. Popular in the 1930s.

spinning wheel: a wheel used for spinning yarn or thread. These early machines were operated either by hand or foot.

spiral turning: (furniture) a turning with a carved circular pattern.

spit: (hearth accessories) a metal bar that pierced through meat for roasting over a fire. The spit was hung on cobirons in front of the fire and was rotated by a grooved pulley to provide even heat on all sides of the meat. Rotation power was provided by hand early on, but by the 16th century large weights were used.

spit out: (ceramics) a blister on a ceramic glaze caused by an air or gas bubble.

spit stool: (furniture) a stool to sit on while turning a roasting spit.

splashboard stand: (furniture) a washstand that is built up on three sides of the top to prevent water from splashing on the wall and floor when in use.

splash luster: (decoration) a luster decoration that appears to have been splashed on a piece and has what resembles water marks in the luster.

splat: (furniture) the central upright member of a chair back.

splayed: (furniture) flared outward. The back legs of many chairs are splayed to improve stability.

splint seat: (furniture) a seat made of woven hickory or oak strips; found on early American chairs and stools.

split-turned ornament: (furniture) an ornament fashioned from a turned baluster that has been split in half.

Spode: (ceramics) a pottery founded by Josiah Spode (1733-1797) in 1770. The Spode factory began with earthenware and soon graduated to the manufacture of porcelain. Spode's recipe for bone china is still in use. The Spode factory was run by his son, Josiah Spode II, from 1797 to 1827, and by his grandson, Josiah Spode III, from 1827 to his death in 1829. In 1833 William Taylor Copeland, a partner of the Spodes, bought the firm from the executors and operated it under the name of Copeland & Garrett until 1847, when the name of Garrett was dropped. The company is now owned by Royal Worcester Ltd., and operates as Royal Worcester Spode Ltd.

spongeware: (ceramics) ware decorated by dabbing color on with a sponge.

spool salt: (tableware) a saltcellar shaped like a flattened hourglass.

spool-turned: (furniture) a repeated bulbous turning suggesting a row of spools.

spoon-back chair: (furniture) a Queen Anne chair with the back hollowed out like a spoon to fit the human back.

spooner: (kitchen) an early-18th-century receptacle for spoons. Also called *spoon tray*.

spooning: (furniture) the concave shaping of a chair back to fit the contour of the occupant.

spoon tray: (tableware) an early-18th-century receptacle for spoons. Also called *spooner*.

spoon warmer: (tableware) a shell-shaped receptacle for hot water; used in the 1800s for warming spoons.

sporting chair: (furniture) a chair just large enough for two people — made in Queen Anne and Chippendale styles. Also called *lover's chair*, *drunkard's chair,* and *sparking chair*.

sporting prints: prints depicting sporting events. Primarily from 1800 until 1850.

spout cup: (domestic) a cup used for feeding children and invalids during the 1700s. Most examples have a bulbous body, cover, handle, and spout.

Spr.: (books) abbreviation for *sprinkled;* used in bookseller's catalogs to indicate that the edges of the pages are sprinkled, or spattered, with color. See also *sprinkled*.

sprayed-leaf thumbpiece: a fan-shaped thumbpiece with gouged lines radiating from the foot in a leaflike pattern; used to raise a hinged cover on a tankard or other covered vessel.

sprigged ware: (ceramics) china with embossed floral sprays. Made by many manufacturers.

sprigging: (ceramics) a raised decoration formed in a press mold then applied to the surface of the object with slip.

Springfield doll: a fully jointed wooden doll made in Springfield, Vermont.

spring seat: (furniture) a chair seat with springs that are covered by padding and upholstery.

sprinkled: (books) color sprinkled, or spattered, on the edges of a book's pages to form a decorative pattern of small specks or spots. See also *Spr.*

spun brass: (metal) lightweight brass objects made with a die and rotating machine.

spunks: (kitchen) slivers of wood with sulphur tips; the first wooden matches.

spur: (metal, furniture) a pointed or spurlike attachment or projection.

spur marks: (ceramics) marks created by the spurs or stilts on which glazed wares are supported during firing.

squab: 1. (furniture) a soft cushion. **2.** (furniture) a squat couch or sofa.

squire jug: (ceramics) a Toby jug depicting a country squire sitting in a chair and wearing either a blue or green coat and brown pants and hat. See also *Toby jug*.

staffage: (fine art) the addition by a second artist of human or animal figures to a landscape or other scene to add interest.

Staffordshire: (ceramics) a district in England where many potteries operated in the early 1700s. Many of these manufacturers made figurines of people and animals. The Staffordshire dogs are particularly well known. In the early 1800s, factories also began to produce historical wares, usually with a blue-and-white transfer design, and often depicting American landmarks. Early examples are in a deep blue; later pieces are a lighter blue. By 1850 other colors were added. Much of the work is signed by the individual maker, but a great deal went unsigned. Some potters still remain in Staffordshire.

stained glass: glass colored by fusing metallic oxides into it or burning colored pigments onto the surface.

stake: (tools) an iron anvil or tongue on which to form silverware.

stamp condition: specific ratings for the quality or condition of a stamp. The ratings are, in order from most desirable to least desirable: superb, very fine, fine, very good, good, average, fair, and space filler (condition renders it worthless, but it can be used as a temporary substitute until a quality specimen is obtained).

stamped: 1. (metal) a metal object that has been stamped out with a die cutter. **2.** (metal) a design pressed onto a metal object with a stamp that has the design engraved on its surface.

stamped gold: (jewelry) thin sheets of gold stamped into forms of inexpensive jewelry mounts. Late 18th and 19th centuries.

standard: 1. (heraldry) a long, tapered flag bearing a heraldic device. **2.** (heraldry) a banner or ensign bearing the emblem of an official, city, state, or nation.

standard mark: (metal) the imprint on gold and silver objects that designates their quality — for example "sterling" for silver, or "22 karat" for gold. See also *sterling silver* and *karat*.

standfast candlestick: (lighting) a candlestick that is screwed to the surface on which it sits, making it a permanent fixture.

standing cup: a large, decorative cup with a long stem and foot; used for ceremonial purposes until the 18th century.

standing salt: (tableware) a large gold or silver, often footed bowl for salt; placed in the center of the medieval banquet table.

standish: (desk accessories) a footed, rectangular inkstand with space for inkwell, dredger, and quills.

Stanford: (ceramics) a line of dishes featuring an ear of corn as a motif. Very similar to Shawnee ware. Usually marked "Stanford."

Stangl: (ceramics) a line of pottery birds and dinnerware produced by Johann Martin Stangl for the Fulper Pottery Company in New Jersey. He changed the company name to Stangl when he took over Fulper in 1946. The factory closed in 1978. Stangl birds and dinnerware are sought by collectors. They are marked "Stangl."

stanza sampler: (textiles) a cross-stitched sampler with a romantic or religious verse.

Star of David: (decoration) six-point star formed by two interlaced equilateral triangles. Also called *Solomon's seal* and *Magen David*.

star setting: (jewelry) a metal star with a stone in the center. The stone or gem is held in place by small pieces of the metal at the base of each point of the star. Popular in the late 1800s.

state: (prints) the stage of a plate prior to its printing. For example, an artist's original plate might be corrected or altered one or more times before it is printed. The original plate would be state 1; state 2 would indicate a change, as would state 3, and so on. Proofs or impressions are made of each state to enable the artist to evaluate them.

statuette: (fine art) a carved or modeled figure that is half life-size or smaller.

stayrail: (furniture) horizontal cross piece that supports the frame.

steamboat kettle: (tools) a large brass or copper kettle with a firebox underneath; used by hatmakers to size felt for hats.

steamer: (kitchen) a deep, covered pot, often with an inside tray for holding food above the water.

steel engraving: (prints) a 19th-century method of engraving on steel plates rather than on plates of copper, a much softer metal that is capable of fewer impressions.

steelies: (marbles) hollow steel balls marked with a cross.

steeple turned: (furniture) a turning that is spiral shaped.

Steiff: (collectibles, toys) stuffed toys made in Germany. Teddy bears are particularly popular, although other animals such as cats, dogs, owls, birds, cows, donkeys, lions, and elephants are also sought by collectors. Steiff also made some wooden toys and dolls. A cloth tag sewn into a seam with the words "US Zone — Germany" dates a stuffed animal between 1948 and 1953. A small button in an ear was also used to mark the pieces: A button with "STEIFF" in raised block letters was used in the early 1940s; during the 1950s the raised letters were in script; during the late 1960s the script lettering was incised.

stele: an upright stone with an inscribed or sculptured surface; used alone as a monument or attached to the face of a building as a commemorative tablet.

stenciling: (decoration) the technique of applying lettering or designs by brushing paint, ink, or dye over openings cut in waterproof paper, celluloid or sheet metal; used to decorate walls and furnishings.

stepped lid: the term applies to the degree of elevation a lid can be raised on a vessel — for example, a double-stepped tankard.

stereoscope: (photography) a device with a wooden or metal frame and two cupped lenses for viewing the twin images on a stereoscopic card. The card is held in a sliding bracket at the end of an attached bridge on the device. The images merge to form a single three-dimensional scene. From about 1870. See also *stereoscopic view.*

stereoscopic view: (photography) a card with two nearly identical pictures of the same scene taken from two vantage points about two inches apart. When viewed through a special viewer the scene appears three-dimensional. From about 1870. See also *stereoscope.*

sterling silver: (silver, jewelry) an alloy of 925 parts silver and 75 parts copper. See also *coin silver, eight hundred (800) silver,* and *South American silver.*

Steuben glass: a glasswork started by famous glassmakers Frederick Carder and Thomas Hawkes in 1903 in Corning, New York. They made exquisite and expensive art glass. Since 1918 Steuben has been part of the Corning Glass Works.

Stevengraph: (fine art) a small picture woven of silk by Thomas Stevens, an Englishman, in the late 19th century. Most are matted and framed and carry his signature. He also wove bookmarks and postcards.

Stevens and Williams: glassmakers in Stourbridge, England, from about 1830 until the 1920s. The company produced alexandrite, engraved, and several other styles of glass, but they were best known for their cameo glass, which was less expensive than that of their competitors.

Stickley Furniture Company: furniture company where Gustav Stickley's younger brothers, L. and J. G. Stickley, produced quality Mission-style furniture from 1902 to 1923. They also produced hand-hammered copper metalware. More well known for their furniture. See also *Stickley, Gustav.*

Stickley, Gustav (1857-1942): (furniture) a well-known maker of Mission furniture, credited with its origin. His sturdy oak furniture was inspired by the Arts and Crafts movement in England, which, in turn, was influenced by Japanese design and medieval "honest" construction. His furniture, much of which is signed, is sought after by collectors.

Stiegel glass: a glassware made in Pennsylvania *ca.* the mid-1700s. Mostly, but not exclusively, enameled or etched. The style was very similar to that of many European glassmakers.

stile: (architecture) a vertical piece that frames the panel of a door or window.

stiletto: (weapons) a dagger with a straight, narrow blade designed for stabbing. From the 16th century.

still bank: a coin bank with no moving parts.

still life: (fine art) a painting of still or inanimate objects. Fruit, vegetables, flowers, and usually at least one man-made object such as a table or vase were popular subjects during the 1800s and 1900s.

stipple engraving: (decoration) a design on an engraving or etching that is made up of small graded dots; used on glass and wood.

stirrup cup: a handleless, footless sporting-trophy drinking cup in the form of a fox or greyhound head. From about 1750.

stirrup guard: (weapons) a knuckle-bow on a sword resembling half of a stirrup.

stock book: (stamps) a book with pages of shallow pockets in which a collector or dealer can store stamps before mounting them.

stomacher: (jewelry) a triangular piece of jewelry that was so large it went from the chest to below the waist. Worn during the 18th century; popular again briefly in the late 19th century. Early pieces are most valuable.

stone bow: (weapons) any type of bow used to shoot stones or other round projectiles.

stone china: (ceramics) a cheap, hard white earthenware that has been a substitute for porcelain; first used *ca.* 1805 in Staffordshire, England.

stones: (glass) specks of red and black in early flint glass — caused by a poor fusion between lead oxide and silica.

stoneware: (ceramics) a dense, hard-paste, nonporous pottery. See also *earthenware.*

stoning: (silver) to polish silver with an emery stone.

stork lamp: (lighting) a hanging lamp resembling a stork.

Storr, Paul (1771-1844): (silver) a top English silversmith during the early 1800s. Storr's pieces have his initials.

storyteller: (Native American) Pueblo clay figures of the storyteller surrounded by children.

stoup: (tableware) a drinking vessel such as a cup or tankard.

Stourbridge glass: a fine English glass made in the 1700s and 1800s in Stourbridge, England.

stovepipe hat: (collectibles) early fireman's dress hat, named for its shape.

straight saw marks: (furniture) marks that indicate a piece was made using a straight saw. The circular saw was not invented until 1815, so rounded or circular saw marks date a piece after that time.

straining bowl: (kitchen) a deep bowl with a platelike top that has one large hole in the middle and smaller pierced holes around it.

straining spoon: (tableware) a spoon with a pierced bowl. There are two sizes: The larger size is for serving vegetables and the like, and the smaller, for skimming tea leaves from tea cups.

strap hinge: (hardware) a long, band-shaped hinge.

strapwork ornament: (decoration) an ornamental strip of scrollwork, sometimes containing flowers and foliage. Popular on carved oak furniture and engraved silverware during the late 16th and early 17th centuries.

Strass diamond: (jewelry) a white paste stone with a high percentage of lead that resembles a diamond. Invented by Joseph Strass in the mid-18th century.

strawberry diamond cut: (glass) decoration used on Irish and English glass in the late 18th and early 19th century. A pattern of large diamonds is ground or cut in deep relief with the points flattened and cut with fine-relief diamonds.

strawberry dish: (tableware) a small, saucer-size silver dish for fruit. Early examples have a punched decoration; later pieces have fluted, scalloped borders. Seventeenth and early 18th centuries.

strawberry luster: (ceramics) ceramic ware decorated with strawberries and a pink luster trim. Made by many English companies in the 1800s. Seldom marked.

straw mark: (glass, ceramics) a flaw caused by waste material in the mold. The material burns up, leaving a scar.

straw work: (furniture) the use of tiny strips of colored and bleached straw to form landscapes, patterns, and designs on mirror frames and other small furniture pieces.

stretcher: 1. (fine art) the wooden frame on which an artist's canvas is stretched and secured. 2. (furniture) a bar or rod that runs between the legs of a chair or table.

stretch glass: glass made by spraying hot glass objects in such a manner that the finish resembles Tiffany glass. Popular with Fenton, Imperial, Northwood, and others from 1900 until the 1920s. See also *Tiffany glass.*

strike through: (fine art) a layer of paint that shows through the overpainting intended to conceal it.

striking plate: (hardware) a metal plate attached to a door frame into which the lock bolt is released by the key.

string holder: (domestic) a covered box or holder with a hole in it for pulling string through. Made of iron, pewter, silver, tin, wood, or other materials.

stringing: (decoration) lines of contrasting inlay; used for a border on furniture. Popular in the late 18th and early 19th centuries.

strip: 1. (fine art) to remove the varnish coat from an oil painting with solvents. 2. (furniture) to remove the original finish on a piece of furniture to bare wood.

striping: 1. (furniture) wood grain with long lines. 2. (decoration) any long, narrow band used to decorate.

struck: (coins) a coin produced from dies.

stuck shank: (glass) the stem of a glass object that is made separately and then put on with hot glass as the adhesive. Also called *applied stem.*

studio of: (fine art) a piece of art done under the instruction of, or in the studio of a specific artist, but not by the artist.

study: (fine art) a preliminary depiction of a projected drawing, painting, or sculpture. It is often a detail of that work.

stump leg: (furniture) a plain, turned leg resembling a tree stump; found on 18th-century chairs made in the North Country of England.

stump veneer: (decoration) a decorative veneer cut from the base of a tree where the roots join the trunk. Also called *butt veneer*.

stump work: (needlework) elaborate embroidery that has a center theme depicting a biblical scene, which is surrounded by a border of fruits, flowers, leaves, birds, and animals. Popular in the 17th century. Also called *raised work*.

style: the fashion in which a piece is designed. For instance, something may be Victorian style but not made in the Victorian era. It need not be an exact copy.

sucket fork: (tableware) a two-pronged fork with a spoon at the opposite end; used for eating fruit.

sugar basket: (tableware) a plain or pierced silver vessel for sugar. If pierced, they usually have a swing handle and glass liner. Often paired with a matching cream basket. From mid-18th century on.

sugar mold: (kitchen) a glazed-pottery mold for making maple sugar candy from maple syrup.

sugar shaker: (kitchen) a shaker resembling a large salt shaker; used during the Victorian era to shake sugar and cinnamon onto food.

sulphide: (glass) an early glass paperweight made by embedding an unglazed white china plaque with a design in relief, in glass. Also called *encrusted cameo*.

sulphide marble: a clear or colored glass marble with a figure inside. The colored marbles are quite rare.

sumi: (fine art, prints) Japanese for *ink* or *black watercolor*.

Sumida Gawa Ware: (orientalia, ceramics) wares with applied relief figures and heavy glazes produced at a porcelain factory started in 1890 in the Asakusa district of Tokyo. Early examples have black, green, or red backgrounds with a leatherlike texture. In 1924 the factory moved and at that time started using blue, brown, lavender, and orange. Some of the later pieces have a matte-finish background. Motifs include dragons, florals, the disciples of Buddha, and children.

sumi-ye (or sumi-e): (fine art, prints) Japanese pictures painted with ink, or printed in black only.

sumi zogan: (orientalia) the Japanese method of inlaying dark metal with a lighter one.

sumpter trunks: travel trunks or chests, often a pair, made to be carried on a pack horse.

Sunderland: (ceramics) ceramics with splashes of pink luster on them; often with transfer prints. Made by factories in Sunderland, England, in the 1700s and 1800s. See also *pink luster*.

sunflower pattern: (ceramics) a late and very popular pattern of gaudy Dutch. See also *gaudy Dutch*.

Sung dynasty: (orientalia) the period from A.D. 960 to 1279 in which the Sung emperors ruled China. Beautiful pottery was produced during these years.

sunk carving: (furniture) carving by removing the background and leaving the design raised. The background is either punched or stippled to create an even surface and contrast to the design. Also called *recessed carving*.

sunray clock: a clock with carved wooden sun's rays emanating from the circular dial. Originated from 1643 to 1715, during the reign of Louis XIV — the "sun king."

superstructure: (design, architecture) any structure built on top of something else.

supporting appointments: (decoration) symbols that surround the central device and add to the general motif.

surcoat: (armor) a loose outer coat or tunic; worn over armor in the 13th and 14th centuries.

surimono: (prints) Japanese prints used as greetings or to mark important occasions.

swag: 1. (decoration) a suspended decoration such as ribbons, garlands of fruits, or the like hanging at a window or doorway. **2.** (furniture) a motif featuring a garland of flowers, fruits, and leaves; used on furniture during the 17th and 18th centuries.

swagger stick: a short, slender cane decorated with cords and tassels. Popular in the 18th and early 19th centuries. A plain swagger stick is still carried by military officers in some countries.

swankyswig: (collectibles, glass) a glass container that was originally filled with cheese spread put out by the Kraft Food company.

swastika: 1. (decoration) ancient, universal cosmic symbol, formed by a cross with the ends bent at right angles. **2.** (militaria) the cross adopted by Germany under Hitler as the symbol of Nazism.

Swatow ware: (ceramics) porcelain ware heavily glazed with a rough finish, much of it boldly painted in bright enamels. Exported from Swatow, South China, in the late 16th and 17th centuries.

Swedes glass: (glass) an early glass made by Swedish immigrants in what is now Pennsylvania.

sweet grass: (Native American) a sweet-smelling grass used in basket making by the nations of the northeastern United States.

sweetmeat basket: (household accessories) a small, circular or oval silver basket. Early pieces are pierced with a cast floral border. Later examples are solid with engraved decoration. From the mid-18th century.

sweetmeat dish: (tableware) silver or ceramic dessert dish.

sweetmeat glass: glass vessel with shallow bowl, long stem, and foot; used for desserts in the 18th century.

swell front: (furniture) a front shaped in a convex curve.

swept-hilt rapier: (weapons) a sword with its hilt curved and embellished to form a guard.

swift: 1. (domestic) a cylinder on a carding machine. **2.** (domestic) a reel for winding yarn and thread.

switch key: (railroad memorabilia) a key stamped on the hilt with the name, initials, or logo of a railroad. Switch keys are usually made of bronze or brass, but there are some steel and iron keys. All are marked with an "S" and a serial number. Switch keys from short-lived, early railroads are the most sought.

switch lock: (railroad memorabilia) a lock with the railroad's insignia or initials; used to secure railroad switches. The earliest and most valuable are brass. Later examples are made of iron or steel. Heart-shaped locks are particularly sought.

switchman's hand lantern: (railroad memorabilia) a lantern, larger than the conductor's lantern, with the name of the railroad stamped on the metal and etched on the glass. The taller the globe the older the lantern. The most collectible are lanterns that were made to burn whale oil.

switch-stand lamp: (railroad memorabilia) an oil-burning lamp that was mounted on an iron switch stand during the era of steam engines. The lamps had four lenses — either two red and two yellow, two red and two green, or two yellow and two green.

sword cane: (weapons) a cane with a cavity to conceal a sword or dagger. Early 18th to late 19th centuries.

syllabub: (glass) a blown-glass bowl and underplate; used to make and serve the drink by the same name.

T

tabard: 1. (armor) a tunic or capelike garment worn over armor by knights, and by their heralds. The knight's coat of arms was emblazoned on it. 2. (heraldry) an embroidered pennant hung from a trumpet.

tabby: (textiles) a watered taffeta.

tabernacle mirror: (furniture) a mirror with a painted naval scene in an upper panel. Also called *naval mirror.*

tabla: (music) one or a pair of small hand drums of India.

table-chair: (furniture) a convertible chair with a back that pivots to form a tabletop. From the 16th century. Also called *chair-table.*

table clock: a clock designed with a horizontal dial facing upward so that it can be viewed from above a table.

table Suzie: (tableware) a lazy Susan with compartments for condiments and sauces; used at the table from 1800 until about 1850.

tablet: (stamps) a square or rectangle within a stamp's design that carries an inscription or the denomination figure.

tableware: all the silverware, dishes, glassware, and vessels used at the table for a meal.

taboret: 1. (furniture) a low stool without arms or back. 2. (furniture) a low cabinet or stand; often used for plants, especially ferns.

Tabriz carpet: (floor coverings) a carpet woven in Tabriz, Persia. Patterns are often of hunting scenes, animals, and court scenes. Silk is often woven in with the wool.

taffeta weave: (textiles) a weave in which the warp and filling threads are equally interlaced alternately. Also called *plain weave.*

tag sale: an estate sale where, rather than auctioning off the items, they are marked with a sale price. Buyers, usually a few at a time, are allowed to view the items and place their buyer's number tag on those items they want to purchase. This type of sale is often held when there are very large collections involved.

tailor's goose: (tools) an iron with a gooseneck handle; used by tailors.

takamakiye: (orientalia) a Japanese lacquer ware with a molded composition design in high relief.

Talavera maiolica: (ceramics) a tin-glazed earthenware in blue, white, and polychrome colors. Made in Talavera, Spain, in the late 16th century.

talc: (fine art) a miniature portrait, usually of a lady, done on copper or silver with several sheets of mica. Parts of a costume were painted on the sheets of mica. The artist "dressed" the lady by placing the mica sheets over the portrait. Also called *costume miniatures.*

tallboy: (furniture) a two-section chest of drawers supported on high legs. Also called *highboy* and *chest-on-chest.*

tall-case clock: a tall floor clock with hanging weights and pendulum. Also called *long-case clock* and *grandfather's clock.*

tallow cut: (jewelry) a method of cutting gemstones to produce a round stone with a flat top.

tambour door: (furniture) a door composed of wooden slats attached to a canvas backing or liner, as used on a rolltop desk. Also called *reedtop.* See also *rolltop desk.*

tambour work: (needlework) chain-stitch embroidery worked with a steel hook on material stretched over a round frame. Late 18th and early 19th centuries.

tang: (weapons) the upper portion of the sword blade onto which the hilt is fitted.

T'ang dynasty: (orientalia) the period from A.D. 618 to 907; considered the golden age of China, when the empire reached its greatest expansion and was the most powerful and civilized country in the world. Literature, paintings, and pottery were superb, and during this period translucent white porcelain was invented.

tangent screw: (scientific instruments) a device used in the alignment of an alidade or index. See also *alidade*.

tankard: (tableware) a large, metal or ceramic drinking mug with a single handle and often a hinged cover.

tantalus: (household accessories) a device to hold a decanter. There is a top piece that locks, preventing anyone from using the contents without a key.

tan-ye: (orientalia) Japanese prints hand colored with *tan*, a red lead pigment.

tanzaku: (orientalia) narrow, vertical Japanese prints inscribed with verses.

taper: 1. (lighting) a very slender candle. **2.** (lighting) a long wax-coated wick; used to light candles or oil and gas lamps.

taper box: (lighting) a small, round container with handle and a hole in the lid to remove wax taper, which is coiled inside the box.

taperstick: (lighting) a holder similar to candlestick but smaller; used to hold a wax taper. From the late 17th century.

tapestry: (textiles) heavy, woven reversible cloth; used for decorative wall hangings, upholstery, and drapes.

target balls: (glass) blown-glass balls, about 3 inches in diameter; used as targets from 1840 until *ca.* 1920, although their allure diminished with the invention of the clay pigeon in 1880. Many target balls are marked with a name and a date.

tari: (coins) a silver coin issued by Knights of St. John in Malta.

tarnish: (metal) the discoloration of a metal object and its loss of luster due to oxidation, as with silver and brass items.

tarsia: (furniture) an Italian form of intricate inlay or marquetry using wood, bone, metal and mother-of-pearl. From the 15th century.

tatting: (textiles) a delicate, looped and knotted lace created with a shuttle and a single strand of thread.

taufschein: (paper) a decorated baptismal certificate, usually done entirely by hand but occasionally partly printed; used mostly by German immigrants. See also *Fraktur*.

Taylor Toby: (ceramics) a pitcher in the shape of General Zachary Taylor. Also called *Rough-and-Ready Toby*.

tazza: 1. (tableware) a metal or ceramic wine cup with a shallow, circular bowl. Sixteenth and 17th centuries. **2.** (tableware) a flat dish or salver with a central foot.

teabowl: (ceramics) a teacup without a handle.

tea caddy: (kitchen) a metal, porcelain, or wooden box for storing tea leaves and keeping them fresh. In the 18th century, tea was very expensive, so many 18th-century tea caddies have locks and keys. Boxes from the 19th century, when tea was less expensive, are larger and unlocked. Some boxes have two compartments for different types of tea.

tea canister: (kitchen) a glass, metal, or pottery container for tea. Bottle-shaped prior to mid-18th century; vase-shaped after. Tea-filled canisters were stored in a caddy. See also *tea caddy*.

tea cart: (furniture) a small table with wheels; used for serving food and beverages. Also called *hostess cart, hostess wagon,* and *tea wagon*.

tea-leaf ironstone: (ceramics) ironstone dinnerware decorated with a copper-luster leaf design. Popular, and made by many firms, from 1880 until *ca.* 1900.

tea poise: (furniture) a covered table or stand supported by a pedestal. Made to hold several tea caddies.

tea-poy: (furniture) a pedestal table with lifting tray top; used to hold a tea service.

tears: (glass) air bubbles trapped within the stem of drinking vessels for decorative purposes. Popular in the first half of the 18th century.

tea wagon: (furniture) a small table with wheels; used for serving food and beverages. Also called *hostess cart, hostess wagon,* and *tea cart.*

Teco: (ceramics) a line of art pottery produced by the American Terra Cotta and Ceramic Company from 1901 until 1922. The company was known for its green ware which had a grayish tint to it, but the blue, brown, rose, and yellow ware that they added later bring higher prices on today's market. Most pieces have a matte finish. Wares are generally marked with the company name.

T. E. G.: (books) abbreviation for *top edge gilt.*

tektite: (materials) generally small, rounded glass objects, brown to green in color, believed to be from meteorites; used to make jewelry and artifacts.

telegraph fan: (fashion accessories) a fan with the letters of the alphabet on it. These fans came with small pointers so a lady could send a silent message by pointing to the letters on the fan. Popular in the 1700s.

telephone bid: (auctions) a bid taken by telephone during the auction. The telephone bidder competes against the floor just as if he or she were there. In order to do this, the bidder must make a prior arrangement with the auction house to be called when the item in question comes up for bid.

telephone set: (furniture) a small table with space for the telephone, a directory, and a seat or bench that may be attached. Also called *gossip bench.*

temmoku: (ceramics) a Japanese slip-glazed pottery in black or brown.

tempera: (fine art) a medium in which color pigments are mixed with a glutinous substance such as egg yolk. The principal method for easel painting until the 15th century, when oil painting was developed.

tenon: (furniture) a projection of wood or other material that is formed to fit into a corresponding hole or groove (mortise) to form a joint. See also *mortise.*

Teplitz: (ceramics) pottery made in Teplitz, Bohemia, in the late 1800s and early 1900s. Much of the ware is marked "Teplitz" or "Turn." The art nouveau style was favored by the many manufacturers in this area.

teroma: (glass) glass decorated with a pebbly paint.

terra alba: (fine art) gypsum; used to make plaster of paris and fillers.

terrace: (fine art) a flaw in marble that can be successfully filled in with cement.

terra cotta: (ceramics) a hard, fired, glazed or unglazed ceramic clay; used especially for statuettes, pottery, and roof tiles. Colors range from gray to purple-red, depending on the firing, but brownish red is most common.

terrarium: (household accessories) a small container or enclosure, usually of glass, to house small plants or animals.

tessera: (ceramics, fine art) a small square of glass, stone, or other hard material used in making a mosaic.

tester: 1. (furniture) a horizontal cloth covering used for protection or ornamentation. **2.** (furniture) the rooflike wooden covering over a four-poster bed. Also called *canopy*.

tête-a-tête: (furniture) a settee or small, two-seat sofa with the seats facing in opposite directions. The back forms an S curve.

tête-beche: (stamps) French term used in philately to identify a stamp erroneously printed upside down in a pair. As proof of its inverted position, the pair must be attached to at least one other upright stamp.

textilograph: (textiles) a ribbon picture made into a bookmark, postcard, or the like. Late 1800s.

theorem painting: (folk art) a still life done with stencils. Many are done on velvet, wool, or silk, but some are on paper.

thousand-eye sconce: (lighting) a metal sconce with a reflector made up of small pieces of mirror. When the candle is lit, the light bounces off the mirror particles in many directions.

thread circuit: (glass) a very thin band of applied glass encircling a bowl rim or the neck of a glass vessel.

threading: (silver) a border on any silver object composed of one or two engraved lines.

thread setting: (jewelry) a gemstone setting surrounded by a thin strip of gold.

three-piece glass: a metal three-piece drinking vessel, with the bowl, stem, and foot soldered together.

thumbpiece: a small lever above the hinge on a covered vessel that allows the lid to be raised by the thumb. Common to flagons and tankards. Also called *billet*.

thurible: a vessel, open or perforated, to hold burning incense. Also called *censer*.

tiara: (jewelry) a crownlike ornamental headpiece.

tic-tac-toe frame: a frame with corner pieces that cross and extend beyond the frame instead of being mitered. Popular during the mid-1800s.

tidal clock dial: a dial that indicates daily the time of high tide. It can be set for any location.

tidbit: (tableware) a tier of from two to four plates of graduated sizes with the largest on the bottom and the smallest on the top, connected in the centers by a (usually) metal pole. Most are 12 to 15 inches tall; used for serving finger foods.

tied: (stamps) a stamp on cover with the cancellation running across both.

Tiffany, Charles L. (1812-1902): (design) founder of Tiffany and Company, New York City. His jewelry, gold, and silver products were of the finest quality, and his name is synonymous with excellence. His son, Louis, founded Tiffany Studios. See also *Tiffany, Louis Comfort*.

Tiffany Glass: handmade iridescent glass called favrile glass. Patented by Louis Comfort Tiffany in 1880. Tiffany designed and made large-scale works like stained-glass windows and small decorative objects like glasses, goblets, and lamp shades in the art nouveau style. See also *favrile*.

Tiffany, Louis Comfort (1848-1933): (design) the leading and most gifted designer of art nouveau lamps in America. His father, Charles, was founder of Tiffany and Company. Although Louis designed the lamp as a total unit, it is his shades made of favrile, his own iridescent glass, for which he is best known. The shades have either floral or geometric designs. Tiffany lamps command very high prices. See also *Tiffany,*

Charles L., Tiffany Glass, and *favrile.*

Tiffin Glass: a subsidiary of the U.S. Glass Company; best known for the black satin glass they made during the 1920s.

tiger eye marble: a golden quartz stone marble with dark brown spots that have golden highlights.

tiger jug: (ceramics) a pottery drinking jug with a wide belly and a finish that resembles tiger skin.

tilting chair: (furniture) a chair with back legs that terminate in a ball and socket, which allowed the sitter to tilt without tipping. An invention of the Shakers, made from 1820 to 1850.

tilt-top table: (furniture) a table hinged at the top of its center post, allowing the table-top to be tilted to a vertical position. Also called *tip-up table.*

tin: 1. (metal) a malleable, silver-colored metallic element. **2.** (metal) to plate or coat with a thin layer of tin.

tinder box: 1. (hearth accessories) a metal or wooden container; used to store flint, steel, and cloth for starting a fire. **2.** (hearth accessories) a box for storing kindling wood.

ting: (orientalia) a metal or ceramic Chinese cauldron with three feet and two loop, or ring, handles.

tin glaze: (ceramics) a glaze made of lead and tin ashes.

tinsel picture: (fine art) a picture made by cutting tinsel paper into shapes and mounting the shapes on paper or board.

tint: 1. (decoration, prints, fine art) a pale or delicate coloring or hue. **2.** (prints, fine art) to dilute a color with white. **3.** (prints) to add colors to a print by hand.

tinted lithograph: (prints) a lithograph print that has had two impressions — the first in black, the second in a tint.

tintype: (photography) a positive image made directly on a thin, iron (or other material) plate covered with a sensitized film. From the 1850s. Also called *ferrotype.*

tinware: (household accessories) boxes, trays, dishes, and other domestic wares made of tin and usually painted. Popular in the 18th and 19th centuries.

tipped in: (books) a loose page, picture, document, or the like that has been inserted into a book with glue.

tip-up table: (furniture) a table hinged at the top of its center post, allowing the table-top to be tilted to a vertical position. Also called *tilt-top table.*

tired: material or a structure that shows signs of wear.

toasting fork: (kitchen) a long-handled device with either two tines or a wire cage on the end to hold bread for toasting.

tobacco stopper: a stopper with a decorative top and flat bottom; used to pack tobacco into the bowl of a pipe. Popular during the 18th and 19th centuries. Although most of them are brass or bronze, there are some examples in pewter, lead, and silver.

Toby jug: (ceramics) a drinking mug in the form of a person — often a famous person.

togidashi: (orientalia) rubbing down painted designs on lacquer work to obtain an even surface and make the design look like a watercolor; a Japanese technique.

Tokko: (orientalia) the Japanese name for a Buddhist thunderbolt symbol.

toleware: (household accessories) kitchenware and accessories made of tin, hand painted or stenciled, and often gilded.

tomahawk: (Native American) a lightweight ax; used as a weapon or tool by North American Indians.

tomback: (metal) an alloy of 1 part tin, 1 part zinc, and 16 parts copper; mostly used for making snuffboxes during the 1700s.

tom-tom: (music) any of various hand drums with small heads and long, narrow bodies.

tondo: (fine art) a painting, plaque, or relief in the shape of a circle.

tongue-and-groove: (furniture) a joint made by fitting a protruding tongue on the edge of one board into a matching groove in a second board.

tooling: (decoration) a decoration made by carving or stamping the surface of leather.

Tootsietoy: (collectibles) a toy made by Tootsie, a company known chiefly for their model cars and the Cracker Jack prizes they manufactured, starting in 1911. Examples marked with the Tootsie name were made after 1930. From 1914 until about 1936, the cars were made as exact replicas. Post-World-War-II cars aren't made to scale.

topical stamp: a stamp depicting one particular subject or theme. Many collectors seek stamps on only one subject, such as animals, aviation, royalty, or presidents.

topographic landscape: (fine art) a landscape painting that accurately depicts the terrain and features of a specific scene.

top rail: (furniture) the top crosspiece on a chair back.

topsy-turvy: (dolls, black memorabilia) a doll with a head at each end of its body and a skirt that can be turned inside out and pulled over either of the heads, concealing it. Many of these dolls were made with one black head and one white head.

torchere: (lighting) a candle stand large enough to be placed on the floor. Usually 4 to 6 feet tall.

toreutics: (decoration) the technique of working a design in relief on various materials.

torquay motto ware: (ceramics) pottery with verses, sayings, or quotations on it. Made in South Devon, England, by scratching the lettering through the slip decoration, leaving the lettering exposed in the red clay. First made in the mid-19th century.

torque: (jewelry) a necklace, collar, or arm band made of a strip of twisted metal; worn by the ancient Gauls, Germans, and Britons.

tortoise shell: (materials) the mottled, translucent, brownish covering of the dorsal plates of sea turtles; used to make jewelry, combs, and other articles before the advent of modern plastics.

tortoise shell glass: an art glass that looks like tortoise shell. Achieved by combining clear brown and yellow glass. Boston and Sandwich Glass Works produced some outstanding examples. See also *tortoise shell*.

tortoise shell ware: (ceramics) a lead-glazed earthenware mottled with blue, brown, and green.

totem: (Native American) a carved and usually painted image of an animal, plant, or other object that serves as an emblem of the family.

totem pole: (Native American) a colorful, carved pole, representing family emblems and mythical characters; widely used by Indian nations in the northwestern United States.

touchmark: (metal) the maker's imprint on a metal object.

touring car: (vehicles) a large automobile with a convertible top, seating five or more persons. Popular in the 1920s and early 1930s.

tourmaline: (jewelry) a transparent gemstone of variable color.

tracery: 1. (architecture) the curved or foliated ornamentation found on Gothic windows and arches. **2.** (decoration) any design patterned after tracery.

track walker's lamp: (railroad memorabilia) a lantern with a large front lens and a small red lens on the back; used by workers who walked along railroad tracks.

traction fissures: (fine art) cracks in the surface paint or varnish that have expanded to form wide gaps revealing an underlying paint layer or ground; common in old oil paintings.

trade card: (paper) a small, colorfully illustrated cardboard card circulated during the 19th century by a merchant. Each one bears the name and address of an establishment and the merits of a particular product, as well as an attractive picture. Also called *advertising card.*

trade figure: (advertising memorabilia) a figure that was placed in front of a business to identify the establishment's product or service. The cigar store Indian is an example. See also *trade sign.*

trade sign: (advertising) a pictorial sign that easily identified a business. They were made in such shapes as a boot, a tooth, a fountain pen, a gun, or eye glasses. Popular during the 19th century. See also *trade figure.*

trailed ornament: (glass) a glass-decorating technique. The glassblower attaches looped threads of glass to the surface of a glass vessel, allowing the threads to melt in.

trailed slip: (ceramics) a method of decorating pottery by trailing clay slip over the object from a spouted container. See also *slip.*

trail ornament: (decoration) a border pattern of leaves in a formal spray or running design.

trammel: (hearth accessories) a hook, usually adjustable by links or a rod, for hanging pots over a fire.

tramp art: (household accessories) hand-carved items — usually by chip carving — made by itinerants from about 1860 to the early 1940s. Wood from cigar boxes, as well as from fruit and vegetable boxes, were made into picture frames, small chests, and the like. Because the wood of cigar boxes is quite thin, it was glued or nailed together in layers. See also *chip carving.*

transfer: (fine art) the removal of a painting from its ground — canvas, linen, wood, or plaster — in order to remount it on a new support.

transfer design: (decoration) a design that has been transferred onto a porcelain or earthenware object from a copper plate or wooden block. Some are applied overglaze, some underglaze. Generally, transfer decorated pieces are not as highly prized as hand-painted pieces.

transfer printing: (decoration) the application of engraved designs onto pottery, porcelain, metal, or enamel — by gelatin prior to the 18th century, and by paper tissues after. A transfer process called decalcomania was developed in the 19th century and has replaced the earlier methods. See also *decalcomania.*

transformation playing cards: (games) playing cards that have the suit symbols — heart, diamond, club, and spade — embellished to create faces, figures, furniture, and other objects. From early 19th century.

transitional: (design) any furniture, porcelain, or other accessory in a style that represents the transitional stage between one period and another.

transparency: (prints) two prints attached, one covering the other. When held up to a

217

strong backlight, the bottom print bleeds through to alter the top scene — figures from the bottom scene appear to be in the surface print. Popular in mid-19th century. Pinprick pictures were a simple form of transparency. See also *pinprick picture*.

trapunto: (textiles) a quilting design worked in high relief through layers of cloth.

treasury inkstand: (desk accessories) an inkstand with four feet, a double lid with a hinge in the center, and four compartments.

tree of life: (decoration) a large tree symbolizing the life cycle; used as a motif through the ages in various forms on everything from porcelain to needlework to painting. Popular with American folk artists.

treenware: (kitchen) any food-preparation utensil carved of wood, including spoons, molds, and bowls. Also called *woodenware*.

trefoil: (decoration) an ornament made up of three lobes.

trefoil table: (furniture) a round table with three scallops around the edge. See also *scalloped*.

trencher: (kitchen) a wooden platter. Originally trenchers were dinner plates of wood; used before the common use of china and pewter plates.

trencher salt: (tableware) a small individual saltcellar lacking a foot.

trestle: (furniture) a braced frame used to support a table-top or other structure.

trestle table: (furniture) a long table supported by trestles. From the Middle Ages on. See also *trestle*.

tricoteuse: (furniture) a pedestal table with either a round or rectangular top and a yarn basket built into it.

tric-trac table: (furniture) a gaming table with a recessed top for a game board.

trilateral: (furniture) three sided.

trilingual: (stamps) a stamp with a motto or message printed in three languages.

triple reed dish: (ceramics) a dish with multiple moldings around the rim.

triptych: 1. (fine art) a three-panel painting. **2.** (books) an ancient hinged writing tablet with three waxed leaves. **3.** (religious) a three-panel altar painting. The middle panel is larger than the side panels.

triskelion: (decoration) a figure made with three curved lines, branches, or legs radiating from the center.

trivet: 1. (hearth accessories) a three-legged metal stand; used to support cooking vessels in a fireplace. **2.** (kitchen) a small stand with three feet; used to hold hot dishes on a table or counter.

trompe l'oeil: (fine art) French for *trick the eye*. A painting that is so realistic that it looks like a photograph.

trowel: 1. (tools) a hand tool with a flat blade for spreading and leveling mortar and cement. **2.** (tools) a small garden scoop.

Troxel Pottery: (ceramics) slip-decorated redware made by Samuel Troxel in Pennsylvania from about 1825 until 1840.

trucage: (fine art) French for *forgery*.

trumpet: (collectibles) a device used by firefighters to call out directions at a fire. Working models are of painted tin; dress models are more elaborate, some are of silver.

trundle bed: (furniture) a low bed on casters stored under another bed.

tschinke: (weapons) a light German wheel lock gun, usually rifled; used for bird shooting in the 17th century.

tsuikoku: (orientalia) a design carved into a thick layer of black lacquer. A Japanese technique.

tsuishu: (orientalia) a design carved into several built-up layers of red lacquer. A Japanese technique.

Tucker porcelain: (ceramics) a French-style porcelain made by Tucker and Hemphill in Philadelphia during the early 1800s.

Tudor style: (furniture) a style developed during the Tudor dynasty in England (1485 to 1603), which began with Henry VII and ended with Elizabeth I. During these years architecture and furnishings were essentially Gothic, although there was a Renaissance influence both in particular structures, such as the tomb of Henry VII in Westminster Abbey, and in the introduction of Italian ornaments and motifs. See also *Gothic style* and *Renaissance*.

Tula work: (silver) decoration with niello and gold; used on silver. Named for Tula, Russia. See also *niello*.

tulip chest: (furniture) a chest decorated with either painted or carved tulips. Made in New England or elsewhere from *ca.* 1650 until 1750.

tulip tankard: (tableware) a pewter tankard with a bulbous-shaped body. Also called *pear tankard*.

tumbler: 1. (tableware) a plain, small drinking glass with a round base and straight sides. From mid-1600s. **2.** (clocks) the part in a lock mechanism that releases the bolt when moved by a key.

tumble up: (household accessories) a glass bottle with a long neck. A small tumbler seated upside down over the bottle neck serves as the bottle top; usually used on a nightstand by the bed to quench night-time thirst.

Tunbridge ware: (household accessories) inlaid wood objects made in the Tunbridge Wells district of London. From the late 17th century.

tune card: (music) a card affixed to the inside lid of a cylinder music box listing the songs the cylinder plays.

turkey sofa: (furniture) low sofa first made by Sheraton.

Turk's head: (kitchen) a deep, metal or ceramic baking mold with a swirled design; used for cakes and breads. The products baked in them resemble turbans. Popular from *ca.* 1820 until 1900.

turn: to shape on a revolving wheel or lathe.

turning: (furniture) any decorative form on a furniture part shaped on a lathe.

turquoise: (materials) a stone frequently used by Native Americans to decorate jewelry or hammered-silver articles.

twill: (textiles) fabric with diagonal parallel ribs.

twill canvas: (fine art) diagonally woven canvas, as distinguished from canvas with a square weave; widely used in 18th and 19th centuries.

twisted-wire furniture: furniture with ornate shapes and designs.

two-faced doll: a doll head on a stick that turns to bring two to five faces to the front of the doll.

two-piece glass: (tableware) a drinking glass with a stem drawn from the bowl and a separate foot attached.

tyg: a beaker or drinking vessel with several handles.

type: 1. (coins) the image stamped or impressed upon either side of a coin. **2.** (stamps) a version or variety of a stamp issue. Usually a slight change in the stamp's design.

typography: (collectibles) the composition of printed material from movable type. Type cases, copper and zinc plates, and other items that predate modern offset printing are now collectible.

U

u.: (stamps) abbreviation for *used* in catalog listings.

uchiwa-ye: (orientalia) fan-shaped Japanese pictures.

Uhl Pottery: (ceramics) a pottery founded in Evansville, Indiana, by German immigrants that made stoneware jugs, crocks, urns, pitchers, vases, and the like from 1854 until the 1940s. Pieces are marked with an acorn logo and the company name.

ukelin: (music) a stringed instrument of the ukulele family. Popular in the 1920s.

un.: (stamps) abbreviation for *unused* in catalog listings.

Uncle Tom: (black memorabilia) black male figure who is cheerfully subservient to whites.

uncut: (books) a book with page edges that are neither trimmed nor slit.

underdish: a plate made to go under another dish or bowl; usually glass but some are ceramic. Most baptismal bowls have underdishes.

underglaze: 1. (ceramics) a first glaze that is covered by another glaze. **2.** (ceramics) a design painted under a glaze.

underpainting: (fine art, ceramics) one or more preliminary underlayers of paint beneath the final coat or glaze.

undertint: (fine art) a thin, transparent first coating of pale color over a white ground. Also called *veil*.

undertone: (fine art) the color effect of a pigment when it is diluted with white, or seen with transmitted light.

Unger Brothers: (metal) a company in Newark, New Jersey, that produced brushes, mirrors, hair receivers, and other grooming accessories in sterling and silver plate. Starting in the 1880s, they adopted the art nouveau style. Their wares were marked "UB." In 1909 they closed.

uniber: (armor) the face guard of a helmet.

uniface: (decoration) an article that is flat on one side and molded with a face or design on the other.

Union porcelain: (ceramics) quality wares made by the Union Porcelain Works from the mid-1800s until it closed in the early 1900s. Many pieces are brightly painted; most are marked "Union Porcelain Works Greenpoint N.Y."

Universal Post Union (UPU): (stamps) the international organization that represents member nations. It acts as the authority in setting standards and mail-handling procedures between countries.

Universal Potteries: (ceramics) a pottery that made semiporcelain and earthenware dinnerware and kitchen items in Cambridge, Ohio, from 1934 to 1956, when they stopped producing the wares and started producing tiles. They closed in 1976. The early wares have become inexpensive collectibles.

unopened: (books) the leaves or pages of a book are untrimmed, leaving the top and outer edges of the sections still intact.

unreserved: (auctions) items will be sold at auction for whatever price is bid on them no matter how low it may be. There is no minimum bid required.

upholstered furniture: furniture covered with fabric, and later, padding. Early upholstery consisted only of material stretched across a frame. Next, padding was placed under the material, and later, cushions over the material. Springs were added in the 18th century, and by the 19th century overstuffed chairs and sofas were commonplace.

upright: (furniture) the two outer vertical rails that extend from the seat of the chair to support the chair back. These are braced and connected by the top rail. Some chair styles have legs that extend beyond the seat to form the uprights.

Urbino: (ceramics) a leading manufacturer of maiolica in the 16th and 17th centuries.

urn: 1. (household accessories) a large, covered, metal or ceramic container with a spout and heating feature for serving hot liquids. Older urns have spirit lamps for heat; newer ones use canned heat or electricity. See also *samovar*.

2. (metal, ceramics) a covered vase for storing ashes of the cremated.

urn stand: (furniture) a high, generally four-footed stand designed to display urns. Some have cabinets built into them.

urushi-ye: (orientalia) Japanese lacquer prints treated with metallic dust.

usu-niku-bori: (orientalia) Japanese carving in low relief.

𝒱

Vajra: (decoration) Sanskrit name for the Buddhist thunderbolt symbol.

valance: (furniture) a fabric skirt or board hung across the top of a window, bed, or shelf to conceal the structural details. See also *skirt*.

valentines: (paper) expressions of admiration dating from the mid-19th century. Those collected may be postcards, have mechanical parts, feature Kewpies, utilize Kate Greenaway characters, or be humorous. Some are block printed, some lithographed.

Vallerysthal: (glass) art glass, cameo glass, opaline glass, and other glass products produced by the Klenglin et Cie Company in Lorraine, France, starting in 1872. At the end of the 1800s they began making pressed-glass covered animal dishes. Most of their wares are marked "Vallerysthal," often in a leaf. They are still in business.

Val Saint-Lambert: (glass) a company operating in Belgium since the early 1800s that produces quality cameo glass, etched glass, engraved glass, and molded glass. They export table glass, vases, candlesticks, and other accessories.

value: 1. (fine art) degree of lightness. The darker the color, the lower the value. **2.** (stamps) the stamp's face value. **3.** (stamps) the catalog-listed market price of a stamp.

vambrace: (armor) armor protecting the forearms.

Van Briggle Pottery: (ceramics) a pottery started in Colorado Springs, Colorado, in 1901 by Artus Van Briggle. He perfected a matte finish which he used on the heavy, distinctive lamps, vases, and other pieces that he and his wife Anne produced. Pieces often have molded relief designs and soft rose, yellow, green, blue, gray, or white glazes. "AA," "Van Briggle," and a date are incised on all wares made before 1907. Some of the pieces were marked this way until 1920, when the date was dropped and "Colorado Springs, Colorado" was added. Pieces marked "899" were made before 1912.

vanity table: (furniture) a table with one or more mirrors at which a woman can sit to apply cosmetics. Also called *dressing table*.

vargueno: (furniture) Spanish cabinet with a fall front or doors; used in America in 1600s and 1700s.

vasa murrhina: (glass) a transparent glass in which small flecks of colored glass have been embedded. Made in Sandwich, Massachusetts, in the late 1800s. This glass is difficult to distinguish from aventurine and spatter glass.

vase-and-ring: (furniture) a turning that combines a horizontal vase form with a circular band.

vase carpet: (floor coverings) an Oriental rug with a design featuring stylized vases of flowers. The design is interlocking and develops from one central motif.

vaseline: (glass) a yellow glass with a slightly glowing look. Named after Vaseline Petroleum Jelly.

vaseline marble: a yellowish green glass marble with tiny bubbles. Made of vaseline glass.

Vauxhall mirror: (furniture) a plate-glass mirror with a small bevel. Made in the 17th and 18th centuries at Vauxhall Works, the first company to make mirrors in England.

veduta: (fine art) a scene depicting the whole or major portion of a town or city.

veil: (fine art) a thin, transparent coat of oil color applied over a white ground. Also called *undertint*.

veilleuse: (ceramics) a small, novelty pottery candle holder in the form of a stove; used on bedside tables in the 1700s and 1800s.

vellum: 1. (books) a quality parchment of calf-, lamb-, or kidskin; used for pages and bindings of fine books. **2.** (paper) a heavy, quality paper resembling vellum.

velocipede: (vehicles) an early bicycle with no pedals or with pedals attached to the front wheel.

velour: (textiles) any of various materials with a short, soft pile resembling velvet; used for upholstery and drapes.

velvet: (textiles) a soft, rich fabric made in a range of weights of wool, silk, cotton, rayon, or silk; used for upholstery and drapes.

veneer: (furniture) a thin sheet of wood with rich grain overlaid on a body of plain wood.

Venetian glass: glass made during the 13th century, when glassmaking began at Venice. These glassmakers were considered the best until the late 1600s. Venetian glass is thin, and due to the use of manganese, clear.

Venetian grounded point lace: (textiles) an elaborate needlepoint meshed lace with flower motifs. Made in Venice in the 18th century.

Venetian pillow lace: (textiles) an early pillow lace that resembles early needlepoint lace.

venisons: (kitchen) nesting bowls ranging from a pint to a peck. Made in England in the 1800s.

ventail: (armor) the lower part of the face guard on a 16th-century helmet. If the face guard has three sections, the middle one is the ventail.

verdigris: (metal) a greenish blue pigmented deposit that forms on copper, brass, or bronze surfaces. Caused by the action of acetic acid on copper.

verdun: (weapons) a 16th-century long-bladed dueling rapier.

verdure: (textiles) a tapestry with plant and floral designs. In the 1500s, verdures were free-flowing with scrolls. Later they became more formal.

Verlys: (glass) clear and frosted bowls, vases, and figurines bearing a resemblance to Lalique. First made in France in 1931 and in the United States from 1935 until 1950. French pieces are of a superior quality. Pieces are marked "Verlys." On French pieces the mark is molded; on American examples it is etched.

vermeil: (metal) gilded silver. The 19th-century process involved applying red or orange transparent lacquer over a silver-plated base metal to provide a golden finish; used on jewelry, and flatware.

vermicelli collar: (glass) a wavy string of glass around the stem or neck of a glass object. Also called *vermicular collar*.

vermicelli ground: (ceramics) decorative background on porcelain done in one continuous, wavy line, usually in gold.

vermicular collar: (glass) a wavy string of glass around the stem or neck of a glass object. Also called *vermicelli collar*.

vernier: (scientific instruments) a small fractional scale attached to a larger scale, such as an index.

Vernis Martin: 1. (decoration) a lacquer perfected by Vernis Martin in the 1730s. It was made in many colors but green was the most prevalent. **2.** (decoration) any lacquer used during the 1700s in France.

Vernon Kilns: (ceramics) a pottery established in Vernon, California, as Vernon Pottery Ltd., in 1931. The name was changed to Vernon Kilns in 1948. The company made dinnerware in bright colors, as well as figurines and other pieces designed by Don Blandings, Walt Disney, and Rockwell Kent. It closed in 1958.

verre de fougere: (glass) glass made in inland districts of France by burning bracken and using the resulting potash as an ingredient. Also made in Germany where it is called waldglas. See also *waldglas*.

verre de Nevers: (glass) small glass figures and articles done in the Venetian style. Made in the small town of Nevers, France, from the 16th to the 18th centuries.

verre de soie: (glass) a white or soft green iridescent art glass with a silky finish. First made by Frederick Carder for the Steuben Glass Works from 1905 to 1930. It has been copied since.

verre eglomise: (glass) clear glass with colored foil cut into designs or painted decorations on the back. The foil or paint was then covered with a layer of varnish or glass to protect it. Named after J.B. Glomy, an 18th-century glazier and art collector.

verso: 1. (books) the left-hand page or the reverse side of a leaf. See also *recto*. **2.** (coins) the back side of a coin or medal.

vert antique: (fine art) finish applied to casts of plaster and other materials to simulate the green patina that naturally forms on old bronze or copper.

vesta case: (metal) small, decorative, cases made of metal, usually silver; used to carry matches safely before the advent of safety matches. From the mid-1800s.

vetro di trina: (glass) clear glass with embedded strands of white glass forming involved patterns in the object. Also called *lace glass*.

Vicar and Moses: (ceramics) a figure of a vicar sleeping in his pulpit while a clerk conducts services. Produced extensively by manufacturers in the Staffordshire section of England. First made by Ralph Wood; his pieces are so marked.

Victoria: 1. (vehicles) a light, four-wheeled carriage for two passengers with a folding top and an exposed, elevated driver's seat in the front. **2.** (vehicles) an early auto with a folding top over the rear seat.

Victorian: (design) furniture and accessories in a style strongly influenced by the English styles of Queen Victoria's reign, 1840-1901. Very popular in America.

Victorian beading: (needlework) decorative beadwork by Victorian women. The most noteworthy is Berlin work using beads, instead of the usual wool, to create brightly colored patterns on canvas. See also *Berlin work*.

Victoriate: (coins) silver coin from the Roman Republic with Victory crowning a trophy on one side and Jupiter on the other.

Vienna art plate: (household accessories) a metal tray featuring a portrait of a woman and a wide, decorative border; used by several companies for advertising during the late 1800s and early 1900s. The designs are copies of those used on Royal Vienna plates. See also *Royal Vienna*.

vignette: 1. (books) an open decorative design in a book. **2.** (fine art, prints) a portrait without a border; the edges fade, or blend, into the surrounding page. **3.** (stamps) the portion of a stamp that has a picture; distinguished from areas with lettering and a border.

Villeroy and Boch: (ceramics) a company created when three potteries in Mettlach, Germany, merged in 1841. They later established factories in other locations. Mettlach steins are one of their best-known and most collectible products. They also made plates, tureens, vases, and the like. Most of the wares are incised with a coded date. Hard-paste porcelain items are still made at the factory.

vina: (music) a slender, stringed musical instrument of India with a long, fretted finger board and resonating gourds at both ends.

vinaigrette: (personal accessories) a small, decorated box or bottle with a perforated top; used for holding smelling salts, perfume, or the like.

vinous: the color of wine, or related to the consumption of wine.

Vinova porcelain: (ceramics) soft-paste porcelain made between 1776 and 1820 in Turin, Italy. Wares are marked "V" with a cross.

vintage: 1. old, but still in use, as in *vintage clothing*. **2.** (vehicles) antique, or a model from a specific year, when referring to automobiles.

viol: (music) musical instrument with six or seven strings, a low-arched bridge, and a fretted fingerboard. Invented a few years before the violin. Used in the 1500s and 1600s.

virginal: (music) a small, legless harpsichord usually played by young girls, hence the name; 16th and 17th centuries.

visor: (armor) a face guard attached to a helmet. From the 12th century.

Vistosa: (ceramics) wares similar to Fiesta ware, but with finials and handles with molded-flower decorations. Made for a few years starting in 1938. Although it was not successful in its time, it is now being collected.

vitreous: (glass) to be of glass or have glasslike qualities, such as gloss or hardness.

vitric panel: (glass) a sheet of glass.

vitrine étagére: (furniture) a cabinet with a glassed-in base and open shelves on top.

vitruvian scroll: (decoration) a border with a scroll design repeated in such a manner that the result resembles waves; used on carpets, ceramics, metal objects, buildings, and the like.

voice box: (dolls) a small cylinder or box inside a doll that enables it to cry or make noise. Usually activated when the doll is tilted or laid down.

voider: (kitchen) basket of wood, wicker, or metal used to hold and transport dirty serving dishes, crumbs scraped from the table, and the like. Dates to 1600 in the United States and to medieval Europe. Often made of silver.

volant: (decoration) depicted with wings extended in flight.

Volkmar, Charles: (ceramics) a ceramic artist who was associated with several firms in the United States from 1879 until 1912. His painting on ceramics was underglaze and marked "Crown Point Ware" or "Volkmar," or in a variety of other ways utilizing his name or initials.

Volkstadt: (ceramics) company that originally produced soft-paste porcelain in Thuringia, Germany, when they began in 1760. They are still in business making hard-paste pieces. Most of their wares, old and new, are marked with crossed pitchforks.

volute: (decoration) twisted, spiral, or scroll shape or design.

volvelle: (scientific instruments) a device of calibrated discs and graduated circles used for computation.

Vulliamy: (clocks) a family considered to be part of the last of the old school of English clockmakers. Justin Vulliamy started making clocks and watches in London in 1730. His son and grandson continued in the business until 1854.

W

waddy: (weapons) a heavy club or stick thrown by Australian aborigines.

Wade: (ceramics) any of several companies that operated in England under the Wade name or direction since 1867. In 1947 Wade opened a pottery in Ireland. In 1959 all of the companies joined together to form the Wade Group of Potteries. They still make inexpensive figurines, dresser items, teapots, and other accessories. Many pieces are dated.

wafer: (desk accessories) a round piece of dry paste, often with color added, that was moistened and used to seal letters.

wafer irons: (desk accessories) scissorlike tongs with molds on the ends; used to emboss and press wax seals into documents.

wager cup: (household accessories) a drinking vessel in the form of a woman holding a cup over her head. The cup is hinged and the woman's skirt turns over to form a larger cup. Originals date from 16th century, but many copies were made in the 18th and 19th centuries. Often made of silver. Also called *wedding cup.*

wagonette: (vehicles) a light horse-drawn wagon with two seats behind the driver's seat that face each other and run the length of the wagon.

wagon-spring clock: an American thirty-day clock with a large coil, or wagon, spring instead of a weight. Also called *cart-spring clock.*

wag-on-the-wall: (clocks) a weight-driven clock with the movement in a case. The pendulum, and often the weights, hang below the case.

wainscot: 1. (materials) boards used for paneling the lower section of an interior wall that is finished differently from the remainder of the wall. **2.** (materials) quarter-cut oak.

wainscot chair: (furniture) an early chair with the seat and back formed of solid panels.

waiter: (household accessories) a small tray; often used by servants for presenting mail, calling cards, or a glass of wine. Many 18th-century examples are made of silver.

Wakefield, Cyrus: (furniture) a popular wicker maker of the 1850s.

wakizashi: (weapons) the shorter of two swords carried by a Japanese samurai. Also called *sashi-zoe.*

waldglas: glass made in Germany and inland districts of France by burning bracken and using the resulting potash as an ingredient. Called *verre de fougere* in France. See also *verre de fougere.*

Wallis furniture: furniture made from 1835 to 1850 in Salem, Massachusetts, by Joseph Wallis.

wallpaper: (stamps) slang expression for stamps of questionable value and not in catalog listings.

wall pocket: (ceramics) a vase made for hanging on the wall. Many are shaped like fish, cornucopias, masks, or other novelties. They originated in 18th-century England.

wall vitrine: (furniture) a hanging cupboard or showcase made of glass.

Walrath, Frederick: (ceramics) maker of high-quality pottery from the early 1900s until 1920 when he died. He worked in his own studio in New York and then for Newcomb Pottery in New Orleans. Pieces from his New York studio are marked "Walrath Pottery" and many are dated.

Walter, Almaric: (glass) a noted glassmaker who worked in Nancy, France, from 1904 until the 1930s creating superior glass paperweights, vases, and other objects in pate-de-verre glass. He signed his work "A. Walter, Nancy H. Berge Sc."

Walton, John: (ceramics) figurine designer from 1810 until 1835 in Staffordshire, England. He made figurines with bright colors and background trees. He usually used black in his decorating and incorporated a blue scroll in the base. Some of his figures are marked "Walton."

wampum: (Native American) small cylinder-shaped beads made from shells; used as currency and jewelry by North American Indians.

wampumpeag: (Native American) white shell beads; used as wampum by North American Indians. See also *wampum.*

war bonnet: (Native American) a ceremonial and fighting headpiece with a feathered band or cap and a feathered tail extending below the shoulders and often below the waist; used by various Plains tribes.

war club: (Native American) a weapon with an iron or stone head and a short handle.

ward: (hardware) the part of a lock that prevents the wrong key from opening the lock.

ward iron: (weapons) the finger guard on a knife or sword.

war hammer: (weapons) a weapon used for smashing armor. Details vary, but a long, sharp point on the back, and a set of claws or a blunt peen on the front, were common.

warm colors: (fine art) colors dominated by red and yellow.

war memorabilia: (collectibles) civil defense helmets, ration books, propaganda posters, and anything else related to civilian wartime activity. See also *militaria.*

warming pan: (metal) a covered pan, with or without perforation in the cover, and a long handle; used to hold hot coals to prewarm the bed. Also called *bed warmer.*

warp: (textiles, floor coverings) the basic threads that run lengthwise from one end of a piece of fabric or a rug to the other. See also *woof* and *weft.*

Warwick China Company: (ceramics) a company that opened in Wheeling, West Virginia, in 1887. They continued producing glazed vases, mugs, pitchers, jardinieres, creamers, and other articles until they closed in 1951. Background colors are usually browns or beiges; some pieces have cream and pink. Wares are decorated either with a hand-painted or transfer design. Pieces are marked "Warwick" and sometimes "IOGA" with the factory mark.

wash: (fine art) the application of a diluted watercolor on paper.

wash boiler: (domestic) an oval tub for boiling water, washing clothes, and sometimes bathing.

wash drawing: (fine art) a brush drawing on paper done with a dilution of India ink or monochrome watercolor. Also called *pen-and-wash drawing.*

wash set: (domestic) standard equipment for washing and grooming found in bedrooms before running water. A set usually included a large basin for washing, a pitcher for the water, a toothbrush holder, a shaving dish, a shaving mug, and a covered commode. Few sets remain intact with all the original pieces.

wash stand: (furniture) three-legged or four-legged stand with a bowl for washing. A three-legged stand has a washbowl, a shelf, and a container for soap. The four-legged style usually has a chest of drawers with a basin sunk into the top. A board folded over the bowl when it was not in use.

wassail bowl: (household accessories) a large, deep, two-handled vessel that is traditionally passed counterclockwise around a group of revelers who share a celebratory drink.

waster: (ceramics) a piece that is flawed when it's removed from the kiln.

watch clock: a 17th-century alarm clock. Also called *alarum.*

watch fob: (jewelry) a short ribbon of fabric, leather, or chain attached to a pocket watch and worn hanging from the vest or waist pocket (also called a fob), allowing the user to easily slide the watch in and out. Examples from the late 1800s and early 1900s are being collected. Those with advertising, political slogans, or souvenirs are the most sought-after.

watch papers: paper put between two watch cases to ensure that they fit snugly together. Between 1700 and the mid-1800s, most watches had two cases: the first, which housed the movement, fit inside a second, ornate gold or silver outer case. The paper between the two cases was decorated and embellished with paintings and messages of love or words to commemorate the event for which the watch was given. These papers are collectible.

watch stand: a small stand for hanging a watch on at night. Either free-standing or mounted on a wall.

water: 1. (textiles) a wavy pattern woven into a textile. **2.** (jewelry) the limpidity and luster in diamonds and other precious stones.

water clock: a clock powered by drops of water from a reservoir. A more recent model is powered by a spring, has a basin-shaped face filled with water, and a floating object that indicates the time.

watered steel: (weapons) bars of hard and soft steel doubled and welded several times, then etched; used to make swords, knives, and gun barrels. Experts claim that the finest steel ever produced was made this way by early Japanese swordsmiths. Also called *Damascus steel.*

Waterford: (glass) a fine flint glass made in Waterford, Ireland. The first glassworks opened there in 1729 and continued until 1851. Their pieces are not marked but can be identified by those who know quality glass. In 1951 the factory reopened; their cut-glass pieces are signed "Waterford."

water gilding: 1. (decoration) a method of applying precious metal leaf to decorative work. The ground surface is moistened with water just before the leaf is laid. It can be burnished to a mirror finish. **2.** (decoration) gold leaf put on with a soft brush over a sizing made of several ingredients, including wax.

water leaf: (decoration) an ornament in the form of a large leaf with no veins; used on silver and silver plate during the late 1700s and early 1800s.

watermark: 1. (paper) a mark impressed in paper when it is being made. It can be seen when paper is held up to light. Watermarks often identify the manufacturer. **2.** (stamps) a design or letters that have been pressed into a paper sheet of stamps during its manufacture.

watermelon bell: (black memorabilia, toys) a cast-metal pull toy with two black male children slicing watermelon. By N. H. Hill, *ca.* 1903.

water whistle: (folk art) a pottery whistle shaped like a bird. The body held water, and the whistle was operated by blowing through the bird's beak.

Watt Pottery: (ceramics) makers of kitchen pottery wares from 1922, when they bought Globe Pottery in Ohio. They are best known for their hand-decorated line, made from 1935 until they closed in 1965. Popular patterns are Autumn Foliage, Apple, Red and Blue Tulips, Rooster and

Starflower. Pieces are marked.

Wave Crest: (glass) boxes, vases, tableware, and other accessories made of a creamy white glassware by the Pairpoint Manufacturing Company of New Bedford, Massachusetts, and decorated by the C. F. Monroe Company of Meriden, Connecticut, from 1898 until 1916. The glass has swirls and blown designs and is adorned with transfer or hand-painted decorations. Much of the ware is marked "Wave Crest."

waxed doll: a papier-maché doll or a wooden doll that has a finishing coat of wax.

waxjack: (desk accessories) a stand for holding a coil of sealing wax; first used in mid-1700s.

wax portrait: (fine art) a three-dimensional portrait molded in wax, mounted, and framed.

waxy plaster: the finish on a plaster of paris piece that has been soaked in warm linseed oil then rubbed dry.

weathercock: (domestic) a weather vane in the shape of a rooster. See also *weather vane.*

weathering: (glass) the chemical reaction between the composition of an old glass bottle and the elements in the soil in which it has been buried. One bottle may show a great deal of weathering while another bottle right next to it may have no signs of weathering at all.

weather vane: (domestic) a thin, light structure of wood or metal, usually shaped like a rooster, horse, or arrow, that is mounted on an elevated spindle and pivots by the direction of the wind. See also *weathercock.*

weaver's chair: (furniture) a chair with long legs resembling a large high chair; used by weavers for sitting at a loom.

Webb: (glass) fine art glass made by Thomas Webb and Sons of Stourbridge, England, from 1837 until the present. They are well known for the use of butterfly motifs in their designs, as well as for their Webb Burmese and Webb peachblow patterns. Most pieces are signed.

wedding cup: (metal) a drinking vessel in the form of a woman in a long, full skirt holding a cup over her head. The cup is hinged and the skirt turns over to form a much larger cup. Tradition has it that the bride drank from the small cup and the groom toasted her from the large one. Originals date from the 16th century, but many copies were made during the 18th and 19th centuries. Often made of silver. Also called *wager cup.*

wedding mirror: (furniture) a box-framed mirror with a painting on the top part of it and a painted border. Painted doors fold over the mirror.

wedge thumbpiece: a thumbpiece that is part of the lid on a tankard or other vessel.

Wedgewood, Josiah (1730-1795): an English potter, celebrated for transforming pottery making into a major industry. He developed jasper ware, classical figures in white cameo relief on an unglazed blue (sometimes black) background. Wedgewood also made queen's ware, a cream-colored earthenware; Egyptian ware, vases of black composition; veined ware in imitation granite; and an unglazed semiporcelain.

Wednesbury: enameled ware done in the South Staffordshire area of England from 1776 to 1840 by the Yardley family.

Weesp Porcelain: (ceramics) a hard-paste Dutch porcelain made during the 1700s. It has three marks: early ware bears a crossed swords mark with four dots; later pieces are marked "ML"; and the latest are marked "Amstel."

weft: (textiles, floor coverings) the basic or foundation threads interlaced through the warp in fabric or a rug. See also *warp* and *woof.*

Weil Ware: (ceramics) pottery by Max Weil, who used American clay and hand decoration to produce cookie jars, dinnerware, and figurines. His company started in the 1940s in California and closed in 1956. Most pieces are marked with a burro and "Weil Ware."

well: (ceramics) the hollow part of a utensil or bowl.

well desk: (furniture) a slant-front desk with a sliding panel inside that makes it easy to get to the top drawer when the desk front is open.

Weller Pottery: (ceramics) a company that made pottery from 1873 until they closed in 1948, first in Fultonham, Ohio, and then in Zanesville, Ohio. In 1893 they started producing the line of artware for which they are best known. Most pieces are signed "Weller" and have an incised mold number.

Wellington chest: (furniture) a tall chest of drawers with a wooden piece hinged on one side. This piece swings over the drawers and locks so that the contents of the chest is protected from burglars.

Welsh dresser: (furniture) a cabinet with an enclosed section on the bottom, topped with a drawer (or drawers) and shelves on which to display plates.

Welshman Toby jug: (ceramics) a Toby jug depicting a figure in a chair with a goat between his knees. Rare.

Wemyss ware: (ceramics) a lead-glazed Scottish ware adorned with flowers and animals in underglaze. First produced in the late 1800s.

Westchester highboy: (furniture) a highboy (tall chest of drawers on legs) with several drawers on the bottom and a cupboard on the top (where a classic highboy would have more drawers). Also called *press-top highboy* and *cupboard-top highboy.*

west country measure: (metal) an English tavern measure with a bulbous body and a narrow neck. Usually made of copper, but sometimes of pewter.

Western Americana: (collectibles) everything from saddles and bridles to lanterns and books, prints, sheet-music covers, and other collectibles that depict life in the early Western United States.

Westmoreland: (glass) a company founded in the mid-1800s in Ohio that first made milk glass and crystal tableware. In 1890 the factory moved to Pennsylvania and started producing covered animal dishes, lamps, vases, and other accessories. They made carnival glass until about 1920. Their fine milk glass is what they are best known for. Paper labels were used on early wares; "W.G." was a later mark; "W" in a circle with "Westmoreland" was in use when the firm closed in 1985.

whalebone: (materials) the hornlike material that forms plates in the upper jaws of whales. The plate filters plankton. Scrimshaw pieces are often made of whalebone. Also called *baleen.*

whale oil lamp: (lighting) a lamp that burned whale oil. Made of glass, china, or metal.

whatnot: (furniture) a portable stand; used for books and other small objects in the 1800s and 1900s.

wheat-ear ornament: (decoration) an ornament carved in the shape of a wheat top (wheat ear); used on chair backs in the late 18th century.

wheel engraving: (decoration) engraving done with a lapidary's wheel on glass, rock crystal, and semiprecious stones.

wheel lock: (weapons) a firing mechanism in which a piece of pyrite is pressed against a rotating wheel, causing sparks that ignite the gun powder; used extensively on hunting guns from 1520 until the 1700s, but rarely used on military guns.

Whieldon: 1. (ceramics) fine marbled and Egyptian wares produced in the Staffordshire region of England in the mid-18th century by Thomas Whieldon. The mottled ware was done in the shapes of fruits and vegetables. Whieldon's work is not marked. **2.** (ceramics) any ware that resembles the work of Thomas Whieldon. His work was copied so extensively by other potters that *Whieldon* has come to refer to all pieces of this type.

whimsies: (glass) small glass objects made by glassmakers in their spare time. These are not marked and may be in a variety of shapes from shoes to witch balls to candy-striped canes and paperweights.

whirligig: (folk art, toys) a toy with parts that whirl when the wind blows.

whiskey decanter: (collectibles) ornate or figural whiskey bottles first produced by James Beam Distilling Company. Since Beam introduced these collectibles in 1955, many other companies have made them, but Beam bottles are still the most in demand. Condition is important, but whether a bottle is full or empty has no effect on the price.

white armor: bright or polished armor, as distinguished from armor that has been blackened or russeted.

white earth: (ceramics) a pure white clay.

white gold: (jewelry) an alloy of nickel, zinc, and gold; made to mimic the more expensive platinum.

white iron pyrites: (jewelry) a mineral of iron disulfide, a man-made material fashioned into stones, beads, and the like; extensively used during the Victorian era. Also called *marcasite*.

white metal: any of various alloys containing a high percentage of tin or lead, such as pewter. A common base metal for figure castings in the 19th century.

white work: (needlework) white thread embroidered on a white background.

Whitney, Eli (1765-1825): (weapons) in addition to inventing the cotton gin, the manufacturer of the first muskets to have standardized, interchangeable parts.

whorl foot: (furniture) a foot with an upturned scroll.

wicker furniture: furniture woven in basketwork fashion of various natural or synthetic materials. Popular during the late 1800s.

Wiener Werstatte: (design) the Vienna workshops founded by Kolomann Moser and Josef Hoffmann in 1901. They designed furniture, ceramics, glass, and metal objects, most in the art nouveau style, until the firm closed in 1932.

wig stand: (personal accessories) a stand topped with a head-size oval; used for storing or dressing a wig.

Willard, Simon: (clocks) inventor of the banjo clock (patented 1802) and leading Massachusetts clockmaker from 1774 until 1839.

Willets: (ceramics) company in Trenton, New Jersey, best known for the American Belleek they made in the 1880s and 1890s. This look-alike of Irish Belleek is marked with the company name, often with a snake and "Belleek."

Williamite glass: a glass drinking vessel engraved with an orange tree and a picture of William III.

Willow pattern: (ceramics) a popular pattern of porcelain featuring willow trees, usually a pagoda, and a bridge. Most often seen in blue-and-white. Produced by Mintons, Spode, Davenport, and Adams, and other manufacturers.

Wincanton pottery: (ceramics) a tin-glazed earthenware made in England from 1737 until 1748. Most pieces are decorated with motifs within panels on a speckled background.

Winchester Model 1873: (weapons) gun known as "the gun that won the West." It had fifteen shots, came in a variety of calibers, barrel lengths and shapes, sights, and stocks. Produced from 1873 to 1919.

Windmills, Joseph: (clocks) a prominent London clockmaker from 1670 until 1725.

windmill weights: (metal) weights used to hold down the rods on windmills and slow the blades during a storm.

window harp: (music) a box about 4 or 5 inches high and the same depth made wide enough to just fit inside a window casing. Musical strings held taut inside the box play notes resembling the sounds of a harp when the window is open and the breezes flow over them.

Windsor chair: (furniture) a wooden chair usually with a high, spoked back and legs that slant outward connected by a crossbar. Popular in America and England in the 18th century.

Windsor tray: (household accessories) an oval tin tray; first used in the 1820s.

wind toys: any toy that relies on the wind to operate it. Made since the late 1800s.

wine fountain: (household accessories) a large silver vessel with a tap on the side; used to keep wine. Popular in the last half of the 1600s and the early 1700s. Most examples are English.

wine funnel: (kitchen) a funnel that tapers down to a detachable strainer; used to decant wine.

wine glass cooler: (household accessories) a shallow glass receptacle with either one or two lips on the rim.

wine label: a silver, copper, or enameled label with the name of the owner or family initials imprinted on it; placed around the necks of decanters since about 1750.

wine table: (furniture) a small table, about 18 inches high, with a three-legged base leading to a pedestal that holds a galleried or dish top; used for serving wine.

wine taster: (household accessories) a small, shallow silver vessel for sampling wine. Some have two handles, some one handle, and others no handles. They often have a coin in the bottom. *Ca.* 1650.

wine warmer: (household accessories) a stand with a metal back that was placed by the fireplace with a bottle of wine in it; designed to heat the wine or quickly bring it to room temperature.

wing chair: (furniture) a high-backed chair with side pieces, or wings, that protected the sitter from drafts. Also called *grandfather chair.*

wing lantern clock: a clock with an anchor-shaped pendulum. The case has projections on either side that cover the flukes (ends) of the anchor. Popular from *ca.* 1675 until 1700.

Winslow, Edward: (silver) a Boston silversmith in the 1700s; best known for his sugar boxes.

wire armor: mail armor made of wire rings. Fourteenth and 15th centuries.

wire work: (metal) table baskets, toast racks, epergnes, and other household accessories woven of Sheffield-plate wires between 1785 and 1815. This process was copied later by other firms.

Wistar, Caspar: founder of the South Jersey Glass Company, producers of window glass and bottles.

witch balls: (glass) glass globes ranging in size from 2 inches to about 18 inches in diameter. Either of clear, colored, or painted (usually on the inside) glass. During the Victorian era, it was rumored that these balls would keep a house free of evil spirits and bad luck.

witch bottle: a bottle filled with pins, human hair, fingernails, bones, and the like. They have been found often in ditches, river beds, or under hearths in English homes. So named because these strange relics would supposedly ward off evil spirits.

Wolverhampton paper ware: papier-maché objects made in Wolverhampton, England, from 1770 until 1825.

woodcut: 1. (decoration) a relief design accomplished by cutting a board or plank with a knife or similar tool. **2.** (prints) an original print made from a relief design cut into the parallel grain surface of a piece of wood. See also *wood engraving*.

wooden clock: a weight-driven, twenty-four-hour clock with works made of wood. Made in the 1700s and early 1800s.

wood engraving: (prints) a printing method utilizing carved wood blocks; used extensively during the Victorian era, especially to illustrate books. The blocks used in wood engraving are cut on the end grain, which is a harder, more durable surface than the parallel grain surface used for woodcuts. See also *woodcut*.

wooden Indian: (folk art, advertising memorabilia) a carved, life-size effigy of an Indian first used, along with other similar figures, by the Dutch in 1600 to promote the sale of tobacco. The English followed suit, and from 1610 until 1750 they employed these figures. By the 19th century they were a common sight in front of American tobacco shops.

wooden peg doll: carved wooden, often jointed dolls with painted faces and shoes. The larger dolls have ball joints and the smaller ones have peg joints.

woodenware: (kitchen) any food-preparation utensil carved of wood, including spoons, molds, and bowls. Also called *treenware*.

wood latch: (hardware) a door latch made of wood; used frequently on early New England homes. They are sought by collectors of primitives.

woodworking tools: (collectibles) hand tools, particularly older, handmade examples. Most carpentry tools were handmade before the Civil War, and in rural areas, craftsmen continued to make their own tools well into the 20th century. There are five categories of hand tools: planes, saws, boring tools, edging tools, and measuring devices. Within each category, there are an endless number of specialty tools, such as rabbet plane, cornice plane, jointer plane, and jack plane.

woof: 1. (textiles) the threads that run crosswise or at right angles to the warp threads. See also *warp* and *weft*. **2.** (textiles) the texture of a material.

Worcester: (ceramics) a fine grade of china or porcelain made in Worcester, England, since 1751.

working die: (coins) the die used to strike coins that are to be circulated.

work table: (furniture) modern term for late-18th-century tables for storing a lady's needlework. Some have four tapered legs, some trestle feet. Features include drawers, pouches for materials, and writing boards.

wreathing: (ceramics) spiral marks that appear on porcelain; a defect.

wrigglework: (decoration) zigzag lines engraved on silver, pewter, and other metals.

Wright, Frank Lloyd (1869-1959): (architecture, design) developer of the "prairie" architectural style of houses. These buildings had low horizontal lines and projected eaves. Each house was meant to harmonize with the environment. Wright also designed a limited number of machine-made furniture pieces for the individual houses. These pieces reflect the influence of the Arts and Crafts movement. See also *prairie school* and *Arts and Crafts.*

wrinkles: (fine art) the irregular ridges and furrows that form in paint, varnish, and lacquer finishes with age; caused by faulty application.

writing box: a storage box for writing quills, quill cutters, and sealing wax (or wafers). Each box has an inkwell, and most are hinged in the middle, opening from each end. Usually made of sterling, silver plate, or pewter, although some are wood.

wrything: (glass) a decorative swirling rib or flute on a glass object.

wyvern: (decoration) heraldic winged beast; usually a two-legged dragon.

X

X-frame: (furniture) an X-shaped frame; used on chairs and stools from the Middle Ages until the 17th century.

xylography: (fine art, prints) an old term applied to woodcuts and wood engravings.

Y

yag: (weapons) a small, light, very powerful Turkish bow.

yard-of-ale: (glass) a tall (3 feet or more) glass drinking vessel with a fluted top and a long, narrow body leading to a hollow ball at the bottom. When the glass is filled with ale it cannot be put down because of the round bottom, so the drinker must finish it all. Made by glass houses in Bristol and Nailsea as well as others, from 1685 on.

yashnak: (textiles) a veil worn by a Moslem woman in public to hide her features.

yastik: (floor coverings) a small rug that measures about 18 inches by 30 inches.

yataghan: (weapons) a Turkish short saber or long knife with no cross guard. Also used in North Africa.

year clock: a clock that only needs to be wound once a year.

year set: (stamps) all regular stamps issued by any one country during any one year.

yehon: (books) a Japanese picture book.

yellowbacks: (books) a series of cheap reprints of novels that were bound in yellow cardboard with pictures on the bindings. Many fine authors, including Thomas Hardy, Jane Austen, and Anthony Trollope, had novels included in the series.

yellowing: (fine art) the discoloration of a painting; usually caused by grime that has become embedded in the varnish.

yellow ware: (ceramics) earthenware kitchen bowls, cookie jars, molds, mugs, and the like with a clear glaze; named for the buff to dark yellow clay used to make the wares during the 1800s and 1900s.

yi-hsing stoneware: (orientalia) unglazed red and brown Chinese teapots that were shipped to Europe along with tea from the late 17th to the 19th centuries. The earlier ones have a more perfect enamel decoration than later specimens. Many feature naturalistic trees and fruits.

yoko-ye: (prints) horizontal Japanese prints.

Yorkshire clock: a poorly proportioned, wide, long-case clock. Made *ca.* late 1700s.

yumi: (weapons) Japanese for *bow*.

Z

Zanesville glass: (glass) whiskey bottles with round bodies and a vertical swirl pattern produced in Zanesville, Ohio, from 1815 until 1851. Some of the bottle necks are collared; others have a ringed rim. Colors vary.

Zanesville Pottery: (ceramics) a pottery in Zanesville, Ohio, from 1900 until 1962. The company made large earthenware articles like jardinieres, pedestals and umbrella stands. Most pieces are marked "LA MORO." Not to be confused with Zane Ware.

Zane Ware: (ceramics) vases, jardinieres, and art pottery made by the Peters and Reed Pottery of Zanesville, Ohio, from 1921 until 1941, when the company was sold. Many of the pieces are artist-signed. The art lines include

Crystalline, Drip, Powder Blue, and Sheen.

zar: (floor coverings) a small carpet that measures over 3 feet and under 4 feet.

zoetrope: (photography) motion picture machine from the early 1800s. A series of pictures positioned on a wheel gave the illusion of motion when the wheel was spun. Edison took the idea, put it on celluloid, and the motion picture industry began.

zones of recession: (fine art) the three areas of a painting or other composition that create the illusion of spatial depth — foreground, middle distance, and background.

Zsolnay: (ceramics) a pottery that has operated at Pecs, Hungary, from *ca.* 1862 until the present. Vases, ewers, pitchers, and figurines with Hungarian, Japanese, Turkish, or Renaissance designs done in thick glazes are the distinguishing features of this pottery. Today's figurines have a green-gold finish. Newer wares are marked "TTM." There are several earlier marks. Most of them include "Zsolnay, Pecs."

Zurich porcelain: (ceramics) both hard-paste and soft-paste porcelain produced at the Zurich Pottery and Porcelain Factory from 1763 to 1800. The figurines marked with a blue "Z" are highly prized.

United States Patent Numbers and Dates

Through 1964

United States patent numbers date from 1836, when the patent office came into being. Many 19th- and 20th-century antiques and collectibles are marked with a patent number indicating the year that the object was patented. Patent numbers are helpful in determining that an item was manufactured in, or more likely, *after* the year of the patent. The list below gives the first and last numbers issued each year. For instance, if you see Pat. No. 2,492,988 on a piece that you are examining, you know that it was made in or after 1950, since it falls between the lowest and highest numbers issued that year. Always keep in mind that a patent number does not necessarily indicate the year that the article you are investigating was made.

Year	Patent Numbers		Year	Patent Numbers	
1836	1-	109	1870	98,460-	110,616
1837	110-	545	1871	110,617-	122,303
1838	546-	1,105	1872	122,304-	134,503
1839	1,106-	1,464	1873	134,504-	146,119
1840	1,465-	1,922	1874	146,120-	158,349
1841	1,923-	2,412	1875	158,350-	171,640
1842	2,413-	2,900	1876	171,641-	185,812
1843	2,901-	3,394	1877	185,813-	198,732
1844	3,395-	3,872	1878	198,733-	211,077
1845	3,873-	4,347	1879	211,078-	223,210
1846	4,348-	4,913	1880	223,211-	236,136
1847	4,914-	5,408	1881	236,137-	251,684
1848	5,409-	5,992	1882	251,685-	269,819
1849	5,993-	6,980	1883	269,820-	291,015
1850	6,981-	7,864	1884	291,016-	310,162
1851	7,865-	8,621	1885	310,163-	333,493
1852	8,622-	9,511	1886	333,494-	355,290
1853	9,512-	10,357	1887	355,291-	375,719
1854	10,358-	12,116	1888	375,720-	395,304
1855	12,117-	14,008	1889	395,305-	418,664
1856	14,009-	16,323	1890	418,665-	443,986
1857	16,324-	19,009	1891	443,987-	466,314
1858	19,010-	22,476	1892	466,315-	488,975
1859	22,477-	26,641	1893	488,976-	511,743
1860	26,642-	31,004	1894	511,744-	531,618
1861	31,005-	34,044	1895	531,619-	552,501
1862	34,045-	37,265	1896	552,502-	574,368
1863	37,266-	41,046	1897	574,369-	596,466
1864	41,047-	45,684	1898	596,467-	616,870
1865	45,685-	51,783	1899	616,871-	640,166
1866	51,784-	60,657	1900	640,167-	664,826
1867	60,658-	72,958	1901	664,827-	690,384
1868	72,959-	85,502	1902	690,385-	717,520
1869	85,503-	98,459	1903	717,521-	748,566

Year	Patent Numbers		Year	Patent Numbers	
1904	748,567-	778,833	1935	1,985,878-	2,026,515
1905	778,834-	808,617	1936	2,026,516-	2,066,308
1906	808,618-	839,798	1937	2,066,309-	2,104,003
1907	839,799-	875,678	1938	2,104,004-	2,142,079
1908	875,679-	908,435	1939	2,142,080-	2,185,169
1909	908,436-	945,009	1940	2,185,170-	2,227,417
1910	945,010-	980,177	1941	2,227,418-	2,268,539
1911	980,178-	1,013,094	1942	2,268,540-	2,307,006
1912	1,013,095-	1,049,325	1943	2,307,007-	2,338,080
1913	1,049,326-	1,083,266	1944	2,338,081-	2,366,153
1914	1,083,267-	1,123,211	1945	2,366,154-	2,391,855
1915	1,123,212-	1,166,418	1946	2,391,856-	2,413,674
1916	1,166,419-	1,210,388	1947	2,413,675-	2,433,823
1917	1,210,389-	1,251,457	1948	2,433,824-	2,457,796
1918	1,251,458-	1,290,026	1949	2,457,797-	2,492,943
1919	1,290,027-	1,326,898	1950	2,492,944-	2,536,015
1920	1,326,899-	1,364,062	1951	2,536,016-	2,580,378
1921	1,364,063-	1,401,947	1952	2,580,379-	2,624,045
1922	1,401,948-	1,440,361	1953	2,624,046-	2,664,561
1923	1,440,362-	1,478,995	1954	2,664,562-	2,698,433
1924	1,478,996-	1,521,589	1955	2,698,434-	2,728,912
1925	1,521,590-	1,568,039	1956	2,728,913-	2,775,761
1926	1,568,040-	1,612,699	1957	2,775,762-	2,818,566
1927	1,612,700-	1,654,520	1958	2,818,567-	2,866,972
1928	1,654,521-	1,696,896	1959	2,866,973-	2,919,442
1929	1,696,897-	1,742,180	1960	2,919,443-	2,966,680
1930	1,742,181-	1,787,423	1961	2,966,681-	3,015,102
1931	1,787,424-	1,839,189	1962	3,015,103-	3,070,800
1932	1,839,190-	1,892,662	1963	3,070,801-	3,116,486
1933	1,892,663-	1,941,448	1964	3,116,487-	3,163,864
1934	1,941,449-	1,985,877			

BIBLIOGRAPHY

Andacht, Sandra. *Oriental Antiques and Art.* Radnor, Pennsylvania: Wallace-Homestead Book Company, 1987.

Bagdade, Susan and Al. *Warman's English and Continental Pottery and Porcelain.* Willow Grove, Pennsylvania: Warman Publishing, 1987.

Baker, Stanley L. *Railroad Collectibles.* Paducah, Kentucky: Collector Books, 1985.

Bell, Jeanenne. *Old Jewelry.* Florence, Alabama: Books of Americana, 1985.

Boger, Louise Ade. *Furniture Past and Present.* Garden City, New York: Doubleday, 1966.

Bredehoft, Neila. *The Collector's Encyclopedia of Heisey Glass, 1925-1938.* Paducah, Kentucky: Collector Books, 1989.

Breed, Robert F. *Collecting Transistor Novelty Radios.* Gas City, Indiana: L-W Book Sales, 1990.

Butler, Joseph T. *American Antiques 1800-1900, A Collector's History and Guide.* New York: Odyssey Press, 1965.

The Compact Edition of the Oxford English Dictionary. Oxford, England: Clarendon Press, 1971.

Comstock, Helen, ed. *The Concise Encyclopedia of American Antiques.* New York: Hawthorn Books, 1965.

Conder, Lyle, *Collector's Guide to Heisey's Glassware for Your Table.* Gas City, Indiana: L-W Book Sales, 1991.

Currier, William T. *Currier's Price Guide to American Artists 1645-1945 at Auction.* Brockton, Massachusetts: Currier Publications, 1989.

Davidson, Marshall B. *The American Heritage History of Colonial Antiques.* New York: American Heritage Publishing, 1967.

Dean, Patricia. *Early American Furniture.* Orlando, Florida: The House of Collectibles, 1984.

D'Imperio, Dan. *Flea Market Treasure.* Blue Ridge Summit, Pennsylvania: Tab Books, 1984.

Drepperd, Carl W. *Primer of American Antiques.* Garden City, New York: Doubleday, Doran, 1945.

Duncan, Alastair. *Art Nouveau and Art Deco Lighting.* New York: Simon and Schuster, 1978.

Editors of Collector Books. *The Fine Art Value Guide.* Paducah, Kentucky: Collector Books, 1989.

Editors of House of Collectibles. *Offical Price Guide to Music Collectibles, 6th Edition.* New York: House of Collectibles, 1986.

Editors of McCalls Needlework and Crafts Magazine. *McCalls Needlework Treasury.* New York: Random House, 1964.

Ehlert, Gene. *Official Price Guide to Collector Plates, 5th Edition.* New York: House of Collectibles, 1988.

Florence, Gene. *Pocket Guide to Depression Glass.* Paducah, Kentucky: Collector Books, 1985.

Franklin, Linda Campbell. *Identification and Value Guide, 300 Years of Kitchen Collectibles.* Florence, Alabama: Books of Americana, 1984.

Friz, Richard. *Official Price Guide to Collecting Toys, 4th Edition.* New York: House of Collectibles, 1987.

— . *Official Price Guide to Political Memorabilia.* New York: House of Collectibles, 1987.

Gaston, Mary Frank. *The Collector's Encyclopedia of Flow Blue.* Paducah, Kentucky: Collector Books, 1983.

— . *Antique Brass.* Paducah, Kentucky: Collector Books, 1985.

— . *Antique Copper.* Paducah, Kentucky: Collector Books, 1985.

— . *Collector's Guide to Art Deco.* Paducah, Kentucky: Collector Books, 1989.

— . *Blue Willow Revised 2nd Edition.* Paducah, Kentucky: Collector Books, 1990.

Gibbs, P.J. *Black Collectibles Sold in America.* Paducah, Kentucky: Collector Books, 1987.

Gilbert, Anne. *Antique Hunting.* New York: Grosset and Dunlap, 1975.

Griaulle, Marcel. *Folk Art of Black Africa.* New York: Tudor Publishing, 1950.

Hayward, Helena. *The Connoisseur's Handbook of Antique Collecting.* New York: Hawthorne Books, 1960.

Hegenberger, John. *Collector's Guide to Treasures from the Silver Screen.* Radnor, Pennsylvania: Wallace-Homestead Book Company, 1991.

Huxford, Sharon and Bob. *The Collectors Encyclopedia of Roseville Pottery.* Paducah, Kentucky: Collector Books, 1976.

Huxford, Sharon and Bob, eds. *Schroeder's Antiques Price Guide.* Paducah, Kentucky: Collector Books, 1989.

Ivankovich, Michael. *The Price Guide to Wallace Nutting Pictures, 3rd Edition.* Doylestown, Pennsylvania: Diamond Press, 1989.

Jacobs, Mark and Ken Kokrda. *Photography in Focus.* Skokie, Illinois: National Textbook Company, 1981.

Jenkins, Emyl. *Emyl Jenkins Appraisal Book.* New York: Crown, 1989.

Jordan, Charles and Donna. *The Official 1988 Price Guide to Antiques and Collectibles, 8th Edition.* New York: The House of Collectibles, 1987.

Kauffman, Henry J. *Pennsylvania Dutch American Folk Art.* New York: Dover, 1964.

Ketchum, William, Jr. *The Catalog of American Collectibles.* New York: Mayflower Books, 1979.

— . *Chests, Cupboards, Desks & Other Pieces.* New York: Alfred A. Knopf, 1982.

Khin, Yvonne M. *The Collector's Dictionary of Quilt Names and Patterns.* Washington, D.C.: Acropolis Books, 1980.

Klug, Ray. *Encyclopedia of Antique Advertising.* Gas City, Indiana: L-W Promotions, 1978.

Kovel, Ralph and Terry. *Kovels' Antiques and Collectibles Price List 1990.* New York: Crown Publishers, 1989.

Litchfield, Frederick. *Pottery and Porcelain.* New York: M. Barrows, 1950.

Luckey, Carl F. *Luckey's Hummel Figurines and Plates, 7th Edition.* Florence, Alabama: Books Americana, 1987.

Mallerich III, Dallas J. *Greenberg's American Toy Trains.* Radnor, Pennsylvania: Wallace-Homestead Book Company, 1990.

Marks, Mariann K. *Majolica Pottery.* Paducah, Kentucky: Collector Books, 1983.

Mayer, Ralph. *A Dictionary of Art Terms and Techniques.* New York: Thomas Y. Crowell Company, 1981.

McKearin, George S. and Helen. *American Glass.* New York: Crown Publishers, 1941.

McQuary, Jim and Cathy. *Collector's Guide to Advertising Cards.* Gas City, Indiana: L-W Promotions, 1975.

Miller, Judith and Martin. *Miller's Pocket Antiques Fact File*. New York: Viking Penguin, 1988.

Miller, Judith and Martin, eds. *Miller's International Antiques Price Guide*. New York: Viking Penguin, 1988.

Morris, William, ed. *The American Heritage Dictionary of the English Language*. New York: American Heritage Publishing Company, 1969, 1970.

Murphy, Catherine and Kyle Husfloen. *The Antique Trader Antiques and Collectibles Price Guide*. Dubuque, Iowa: Babka Publishing Company, 1987.

Nickerson, David. *English Furniture*. London: Octopus Books, 1973.

Overstreet, Robert M. *The Official Overstreet Comic Book Price Guide*. New York: The House of Collectibles, 1991.

Panyella, August, ed. *Folk Art of the Americas*. New York: Harry N. Abrams, 1981.

Peterson, Harold L. *How Do You Know It's Old?* New York: Charles Scribner's Sons, 1975.

Phillips, Phoebe, ed. *The Collector's Encyclopedia of Antiques*. New York: Crown Publishers, 1973.

Pollard, Ruth M. *Official Price Guide to Collector Prints, 7th Edition*. New York: House of Collectibles, 1986.

Reed, Morton. *Cowles Complete Encyclopedia of U.S. Coins*. New York: Cowles Book Company, 1969.

Revi, Albert Christina, ed. *The Spinning Wheel's Complete Book of Antiques*. New York: Grosset & Dunlap, 1949.

Rinker, Harry L., ed. *Warman's Americana and Collectibles, 2nd Edition*. Elkins Park, Pennsylvania: Warman Publishing, 1986.

— . *Warman's Antiques and Their Prices, 23rd Edition*. Willow Grove, Pennsyslvania: Warman Publishing, 1989.

Robertson, R.A. *Chats on Glass*. New York: Dover, 1969.

Rush, Richard H. *Antiques as an Investment*. New York: Bonanza Books, 1968.

Sroufe, Ted. *Midway Mania*. Gas City, Indiana: L-W, Inc., 1985.

Stone, George Cameron. *A Glossary of the Construction, Decoration, and Use of Arms and Armor.* New York: Jack Brussel, 1961.

Supnick, Mark E. *Collecting Shawnee Pottery.* Gas City, Indiana: L-W Book Sales, 1989.

Swedberg, Robert and Harriett. *Wicker Furniture Styles and Prices.* Radnor, Pennsylvania: Wallace-Homestead Book Company, 1988.

— . *American Clocks and Clockmakers.* Radnor, Pennsylvania: Wallace-Homestead Book Company, 1989.

Van Patten, Joan. *The Collector's Encyclopedia of Nippon Porcelain.* Paducah, Kentucky: Collector Books, 1986.

Van Tassel, Valentine. *American Glass.* New York: Gramercy Publishing Company, copyright 1950 by M. Barrows and Company, Inc.

Warren, Geoffrey. *All Color Book of Art Nouveau.* New York: Bounty Books, 1974.

Webster's Ninth New Collegiate Dictionary. Springfield, Massachusetts: Merriam Webster, 1986.

Williams, Anne D. *Jigsaw Puzzles.* Radnor, Pennsylvania: Wallace-Homestead Book Company, 1990.

Young, Walter G. *Stamp Collecting A to Z.* San Diego and New York: A.S. Barnes and Company, 1981.